OXFORD LEGAL PHILOSOPHY

Series Editors: TIMOTHY ENDICOTT, JOHN GARDNER,
and LESLIE GREEN

Corrective Justice

OXFORD LEGAL PHILOSOPHY

Series Editors
Timothy Endicott, John Gardner, and Leslie Green

Oxford Legal Philosophy publishes the best new work in philosophically-oriented legal theory. It commissions and solicits monographs in all branches of the subject, including works on philosophical issues in all areas of public and private law, and in the national, transnational, and international realms; studies of the nature of law, legal institutions, and legal reasoning; treatments of problems in political morality as they bear on law; and explorations in the nature and development of legal philosophy itself. The series represents diverse traditions of thought but always with an emphasis on rigour and originality. It sets the standard in contemporary jurisprudence.

Corrective Justice

Ernest J. Weinrib

OXFORD
UNIVERSITY PRESS

OXFORD
UNIVERSITY PRESS

Great Clarendon Street, Oxford, OX2 6DP,
United Kingdom

Oxford University Press is a department of the University of Oxford.
It furthers the University's objective of excellence in research, scholarship,
and education by publishing worldwide. Oxford is a registered trade mark of
Oxford University Press in the UK and in certain other countries

© E. Weinrib, 2012

The moral rights of the author have been asserted

First Edition published in 2012

Impression: 1

Crown copyright material is reproduced under Class Licence
Number C01P0000148 with the permission of OPSI
and the Queen's Printer for Scotland

British Library Cataloguing in Publication Data
Data available

Library of Congress Cataloging in Publication Data
Library of Congress Control Number: 2012942995

ISBN 978-0-19-966064-3

Printed in Great Britain by
Clays Ltd, St Ives plc

To Lorraine

Series Editors' Preface

Ernest Weinrib is best-known for his 1995 monograph *The Idea of Private Law*. Nobody who works in the theory of private law could fail to be gripped by it or to be influenced by it. Although the main ideas set out in that book had been explored by Weinrib in a series of earlier articles, it was their synoptic presentation in book form that had the greatest impact on the subject. For those who disagree with its approach as much as for those who agree, *The Idea of Private Law* inaugurated a new era in private law theory, marked by a new philosophical energy amongst private law scholars and a revitalized interest in private law categories amongst legal theorists.

In this new book, Weinrib collects important writings from the period since *The Idea of Private Law* (with significant revisions and additions). As well as nuancing and reinforcing his original claims, Weinrib demonstrates their extensive reach. While the emphasis in *The Idea of Private Law* was primarily upon the law of torts, and the law relating to reparative damages for negligence in particular, this new book gives extensive attention to other remedies (injunctions, gain-based awards, etc.) and to other causes of action (breach of contract, unjust enrichment). Nor do its horizons end with the private law of municipal legal systems; in the last third of this book, Weinrib shows us how fertile his distinctive patterns of thought can be in other settings, such as in Jewish law, in the political theory of the welfare state, and in the theory and practice of legal education. Weinrib is one of the leading legal theorists of our era. His ideas, for all their declared classical and Enlightenment origins, are breathtakingly original and far-reaching in their implications. We are proud to include this important new work in *Oxford Legal Philosophy*.

Timothy Endicott
John Gardner
Leslie Green

June 2012

Acknowledgments

Much of this book reworks, sometimes substantially, material that has appeared in a variety of journals and edited volumes: "Correctively Unjust Enrichment," in *Philosophical Foundations of the Law of Unjust Enrichment*, ed. Rob Chambers, Charles Mitchell, and James Penner (Oxford University Press, 2009), 31–53; "Two Conceptions of Remedies," in *Justifying Private Law Remedies*, ed. Charles Rickett (Hart Publishing, 2008), 3–32; "Can Law Survive Legal Education?" (2007) 60 Vanderbilt Law Review 401–38; "The Disintegration of Duty," in *Exploring Tort Law*, ed. Stuart Madden (Cambridge University Press, 2005), 143–86; "Planting Another's Field: Unrequested Improvements under Jewish Law," in *Understanding Unjust Enrichment*, ed. Jason W. Neyers, Mitchell McInnes, and Stephen G. A. Pitel (Hart Publishing, 2004), 221–46: "Punishment and Disgorgement as Contract Remedies," (2003) 78 Chicago-Kent Law Review 55–103; "Poverty and Property in Kant's System of Rights," (2003) 78 Notre Dame Law Review 795–828; "Correlativity, Personality and the Emerging Consensus on Corrective Justice" (2001) 2 Theoretical Inquiries in Law 107–59; "Restitutionary Damages as Corrective Justice," (2000) 1 Theoretical Inquiries in Law 3–37. I am grateful to the publishers of these articles for permission to make use of them for this volume.

I have been very fortunate in working for the last four decades at the Faculty of Law, University of Toronto, which has become a major centre for the theory of private law. There I have enjoyed the constant benefit of thoughtful and stimulating colleagues, enthusiastic but skeptical students, and a series of supportive deans. A draft of this book was the subject of the weekly discussions of the Faculty's Law and

Philosophy Discussion Group during the 2010–11 school year. The book has been much improved by the scrutiny its ideas received from the participants in the group's discussions and from other colleagues: Peter Benson, Alan Brudner, Simone Chambers, Bruce Chapman, Abraham Drassinower, Harry Fox, Louis-Philippe Hodgson, Amnon Lehavi, Mark Migotti, Benny Porat, Arthur Ripstein, Hamish Stewart, and Jacob Weinrib.

My elaboration of the Kantian themes in this book benefited from the fact that at the same time my colleague Arthur Ripstein was working on *Force and Freedom*, his path-breaking study of Kant's legal and political philosophy. I was the happy beneficiary of numerous protracted conversations with Arthur about the details and implications of a Kantian approach to legal philosophy. Similarly, I owe particular thanks to Jacob Weinrib, whose acuity as an interpreter of Kant's legal philosophy compelled me to greater accuracy in presenting Kantian ideas.

My greatest debt is to my wife Lorraine, to whom this book is dedicated. Her least important contribution to my life, but the one most relevant to this book, is that, initially as a constitutional lawyer appearing before appellate courts and subsequently as a law professor, she made me aware, and constantly reminded me by her example, of the adamantine necessity for coherence in legal thinking.

Contents

Introduction

It has been said of Martin Buber that the fundamental insight underlying all of his thought is that "primary reality lies neither in the subject nor the object, ie, in the poles of the relation, but in the relation
itself."[1] A similar distinction between the poles of a relation and the
relation itself—and a similar claim that the poles can be understood
only through the relation between them—is the theme of this book.
For Buber, the relation in question was the dialogic I–Thou relation,
in which the related entities realize themselves by confronting each
other as ends in themselves. The relationship with which this book
deals is that of parties linked through the norms of private law, and
thus through the possibility that one may be found liable to the
other.

The theme of this book may seem very distant from Buber's concerns. Unlike the warm self-realization of the I–Thou relation and the
encounter with God as the eternal Thou, private law is a domain of
contested claims and institutional coercion. Insistence on one's rights
under private law is often, as Hegel put it, "a fitting accompaniment of
a cold heart and restricted sympathies."[2] Yet, though private law gives
rise to a different kind of relationship than those that Buber postulated, its relational character is nonetheless crucial to its operation and
intelligibility. A finding of liability always relates a particular plaintiff
to a particular defendant. Moreover, in sophisticated legal systems
liability is supported by reasons that attempt to set out (not always

---

[1] Manfred Vogel, "The Concept of Responsibility in the Thought of Martin Buber,"
(1970) 63 Harv. Theological Rev. 159.
[2] Hegel's *Philosophy of Right*, tr. T. M. Knox (1952), s. 37R.

felicitously, of course) why the norm being applied is fair to both parties and how it participates in an ensemble of norms that treats their relationship as a coherent normative unit. Given the relational nature of liability, these reasons must themselves be relational. And given the aspiration to fairness and coherence, the reasons must treat the parties as equal persons whom the law does not subject to normatively arbitrary demands. Accordingly, private law gives rise to a question that parallels the issues that animated Buber: what does it mean for private law to be expressive of a relationship in which plaintiff and defendant each stand to the other as ends in themselves?

Corrective justice is the term given to the relational structure of reasoning in private law. This term has a venerable history, having first been formulated by Aristotle and then continuously discussed and refined in the two and a half millennia since.[3] It conceptualizes the parties as the active and passive poles of the same injustice (as the doer and the sufferer of injury in Aristotle's account). It directs us, accordingly, to normative considerations that pertain not to either (or even to each) of the poles taken on its own, but to the relationship as such.

The material in this book presents what these relationally normative considerations are and how they work across various bases of liability. Over the last few decades corrective justice has become well entrenched in the theory of tort law. In this book, however, the theoretical issues raised by tort law, though present, are not dominant. The book includes treatment of the areas of contract law, unjust enrichment, restitution, and the law of remedies. It also explores the significance of corrective justice for the comparative study of law (using a specific set of issues from Jewish law), for legal education, and for considering the connection between property and the state's obligation to the poor. It thus presents corrective justice as crucial to understanding both the normative character and the intellectual significance of the phenomenon of liability in its many forms.

The key to the structure of reasoning denoted by corrective justice is, as I shall argue in the opening chapter, the idea of correlativity. Under this idea the reasons for liability treat the parties' relationship as a bipolar unit in which each party's normative position is intelligible only in the light of the other's. The significance of correlatively structured reasoning is that the justification for regarding something as an injustice, and consequently for holding the defendant liable to the

---

[3] Izhak Englard, *Corrective and Distributive Justice: From Aristotle to Modern Times* (2009).

plaintiff, is the same from both sides. Because such reasoning deals with the relationship as such and not with its poles considered independently, it simultaneously explains both why the plaintiff wins and why the defendant loses.

The advantages of viewing private law as actualizing this structure of reasoning are many. First, because the structure focuses on the relationship between the parties rather than on the parties taken separately, it is fair to both of them. Considerations unilaterally favorable or unfavorable to either of the parties play no role. Neither party can, accordingly, rightly complain of being sacrificed to forward the interests of the other. Indeed, reasoning within this structure does not refer to their individual interests as such, but rather to the relational implications of their interaction. Second, the reasoning is not composed of a hodgepodge of considerations applying to the parties individually and then somehow traded off against one another. Rather it is directed toward treating the relationship as a unified whole, thereby producing reasons that coherently interlock with one another. Third, these virtues of fairness and coherence provide a standpoint for criticism that is internal to the relationship and can therefore not be dismissed as irrelevant to the controversy between the parties or beyond the institutional competence of the court. Fourth, because any sophisticated legal system aspires to the fair and coherent treatment of the disputes before it, this standpoint for criticism is internal to the law, in the sense of being fully consonant with the law's own aspirations and with the doctrinal and institutional arrangements that reflect those aspirations.

The goal of this book, then, is to exhibit how this reasoning works with reference to the common law, to criticize examples of legal doctrine that fail to adhere to the corrective justice structure, and to draw out the implications of this structure for such activities as legal education and comparative law. Thematic is the idea that reasoning within private law features a distinctive mode of legal thinking and discourse that reflects the relational nature of liability.

Corrective justice illuminates the structure of legal reasoning by working back to the content of private law from the adjudicative and remedial features of liability. Adjudication involves a claim by a particular plaintiff against a particular defendant. If the plaintiff succeeds, the remedy awarded requires the defendant to pay damages or give specific relief to the plaintiff. Both the adjudicative and the remedial stages of the parties' controversy thus link them in a bipolar relationship. Corrective justice is the theoretical notion through which the implications of this adjudicative and remedial bipolarity are discerned in the structure of the norms. The underlying contention is that unless the norms that define the injustice themselves have a bipolar structure, the practice of correcting this injustice through bipolar adjudicative and remedial processes would make no sense. Properly understood, therefore, corrective justice is not exclusively about the remedy's role in rectifying what the plaintiff has suffered at the defendant's hands. Rather, it is also about the structure of norms that such bipolar rectification presupposes.

The structure of corrective justice bears on the content of the reasoning in private law through two mutually complementary movements of thought. The first is the negative idea that corrective justice disqualifies any reasoning inconsistent with its relational structure. Excluded on this ground are considerations, such as a party's deep pocket or insurability against loss, that refer to the position of only one of the parties. Similarly excluded are instrumental considerations such as the promotion of economic efficiency, for although these may refer to both of the parties, they relate the two parties not to each other but to the goal that both parties serve.

The positive idea complementary to this is that reasoning about liability operates through concepts that are themselves correlative. At the point of liability, the relevant correlative concepts are those of right and correlative duty. In private law every right implies that others are under a duty not to infringe it, and no duty stands free of its corresponding right. As I argue in the opening chapter, what is presupposed in the rights and duties of private law is the conception of the person as a free being who has the capacity of setting his or her own purposes. In the light of this conception of the person, rights and their correlative duties function as the juridical markers of the freedom of the parties in relation to each other.

Much of the book is devoted to explicating the way in which rights so conceived figure in various legal contexts. This involves relating the highly abstract conceptual apparatus of corrective justice to the detailed exposition of legal doctrine. The point of blending theory and doctrine in this manner is to show that corrective justice, far from being an empty formal category as some have asserted, provides a distinctive approach to controversial issues across the whole range of liability.

The book's exploration of corrective justice proceeds largely by illustration rather than by the methodical unfolding of corrective justice's nature and implications. Except for the theoretical handling of the concepts of correlativity and personality in chapter 1, the book describes a series of particular problems and issues, and then brings corrective justice to bear on them.[4] Because the aim of the present book is to display the resources that a theory of corrective justice brings to the treatment of specific issues, it seemed appropriate simply to move from issue to issue, and then to draw some of the themes together in the Conclusion. Almost all the issues discussed here have been matters of legal or academic debate over the last decades. To that extent, the book attempts to formulate the contribution that an ancient idea may make to reflection about current controversies.

By connecting rights and their correlative duties to the freedom of self-determining activity, the book presents an unmistakably Kantian picture of private law. It should, accordingly, occasion no surprise that the book makes reference to Kant's ideas. However, because Kant is so formidable a figure and his vocabulary so forbidding, it might be helpful to specify the limited purpose for which Kant is invoked.

Despite reference to Kant's ideas of private law in these pages, the book pays no attention to Kant's own paramount philosophical ambition of expounding the metaphysics of legal obligation. Kant's treatment of the basic categories of private law comes in his work *The Doctrine of Right*, which is the first part of his *Metaphysics of Morals*. Metaphysics for Kant comprehends "all that can be known a priori,"— that is, independently of experience; the metaphysics of morals "con tains the principles which in an a priori fashion determine and make necessary all our actions."[5] *The Doctrine of Right*, accordingly, is an exposition of the principles of interaction between free beings that hold a priori. However important Kant's metaphysical claim about law might be to students of his philosophy, it is of no interest to lawyers and plays no role in the exposition of corrective justice in this book.

The use to which this book puts Kant's ideas is juridical, not metaphysical. Kant is of interest because of the light he casts on the basic concepts of contemporary private law. Kant's writing powerfully elucidates what it means to think of private law systematically in terms of rights. These rights are not merely conclusions attached to the operations of positive law, but features of interaction that, by virtue of their

---

[4] A methodical exposition of the theory of corrective justice can be found in my previous book, *The Idea of Private Law* (1995).

[5] Immanuel Kant, *Critique of Pure Reason*, tr. Norman Kemp Smith (1929), A841, B869.

content, impose obligations on others that are both normatively justified as markers of reciprocal freedom and legitimately enforceable by
legal institutions. In developing his account of these rights, Kant also
erects a barrier against widespread but questionable assumptions that
are still current today. Among these are the still oft-repeated dogmas
that, because rights (especially property rights) presuppose a distribution, corrective justice ultimately rests on a distributive foundation, or
that promisees of contractual performance do not have a juridical
entitlement to expectation damages. Of particular importance for this
book's treatment of contract law and unjust enrichment is Kant's
explanation of the legally well-entrenched distinction between *in rem*
and *in personam* rights. The most explicitly Kantian chapter is the
interpretive effort in chapter 8 to unravel Kant's conceptions of property and public support for the poor. The chapter attempts to explain
as clearly as possible the non-distributive foundation of property in
Kant's thought and the connection between property and redistribution. It fits into the overall theme of this book by presenting an
account of property that conforms to corrective justice and by situating corrective justice within the legal order as a whole. This interpretive chapter aside, the book makes use of Kantian material only to the
extent that it casts light on particular problems in understanding private law and can be formulated without reliance on Kant's metaphysical conceptions.

At the end of the day, one might ask: understood as the actualization of corrective justice, what purpose or purposes does private law
serve? The answer to this question depends, of course, on what the
question means.

One possibility is that the question seeks to determine whether
private law (or not insignificant parts of it) should be replaced by distributive schemes like worker's compensation or no-fault automobile
insurance. In other words, can private law be justified against alternative legal arrangements? When the question is understood in this way,
two broad points should be noted. First, the corrective justice approach
to private law, taken on its own, implies nothing about this issue one
way or the other, because the acceptance of corrective justice does not
entail rejection of distributive justice. These two forms of justice are
different ways of ordering legal relations. Accordingly, a given slice of
social life, such as workplace injuries or automobile accidents can be
coherently treated under either form of justice. One can consistently
affirm that, so long as a given class of injuries falls under private law, it

should be dealt with in accordance with the coherent conception of private law that corrective justice provides, and yet believe that those injuries would be better dealt with through a distributive scheme. Second, the choice between the two forms of justice for dealing with particular injuries involves consideration of the role of both corrective justice and distributive justice within a contextually rich account of the legal character of the state. The issue between corrective and distributive justice cannot be determined on the basis of corrective justice alone, for no comparison is possible if only one of the comparanda is in view. All that a corrective justice approach to private law can do on its own is to show the infirmity of the argument that private law should be replaced because it is inevitably incoherent.[6] That is something, but is not dispositive of the question as a whole. Revealing the inadequacy of one argument does not preclude the existence of other and perhaps better ones. And yet no progress on this issue from a theoretical perspective can be made at all unless the relational nature of private law is properly appreciated.

A second possibility is that the question about the purpose of private law is directed to private law in itself, rather than to the choice between private law and what might replace it. Then the answer from the corrective justice perspective is straightforward. The point of private law is to subject the interactions between one person and another to a system of coherent norms that is fair to both. It does this by viewing the parties as free beings who interact with each other as holders of rights (to physical integrity, to property, to contractual performance, and so on) that are the juridical manifestations of their freedom. These rights are secured through the adjudicative and remedial processes of coercive legal institutions operating in accordance with corrective justice's relational conception of public reason.

Conceived in this way, private law is an inherently normative phenomenon. The corrective justice approach seeks to work out (or to understand how the law works out) the principles, concepts, and rules suitable to the relationship between the parties that the adjudicative and remedial processes presuppose. In exhibiting the structure for this enterprise, corrective justice indicates the distinct kind of practical reasoning that supports fair and coherent determinations of liability. Because the law itself strives to treat the relationship between the

---

[6] Marc A. Franklin, "Replacing the Negligence Lottery: Compensation and Selective Reimbursement," (1967) 53 Va. L. Rev. 774.

parties fairly and coherently, it is worth taking the reasoning present in the legal material seriously on its own terms. As will be apparent from this book, this is not to say that every reason that courts offer actually conforms to corrective justice. Rather, it indicates the structure that legal reasoning has to have if that reasoning is to work out the implications of the private law's own institutional character and normative aspirations. That is why, as I put it years ago in words that scandalized some readers, "the purpose of private law is to be private law."[7]

---

[7] Ernest J. Weinrib, *The Idea of Private Law* (1995), 5.

1

Correlativity and Personality

1. Introduction

The point of liability is to undo the injustice that the plaintiff suffers at the defendant's hand. Over the last several decades the importance of this simple and obvious idea—what Aristotle termed "corrective justice"—has been increasingly recognized. This chapter articulates its structure and content.

Among English-speaking scholars, the recent history of corrective justice has been one of eclipse and rediscovery. Formulated by Aristotle in antiquity, nurtured by the scholastic tradition in the Middle Ages, and then reworked by modern philosophers of natural right, corrective justice had long been a staple of legal theory. However, by the second half of the twentieth century, instrumental conceptions of law had largely supplanted it. Having been displaced by policy analysis and its concomitant intellectual disciplines, the characteristic concepts and underlying assumptions of corrective justice were no longer part of the common intellectual inheritance of academic lawyers. In the late twentieth century interest in corrective justice revived, primarily through the emergence of tort theory out of the clash between economic analysis and its opponents.[1] Because corrective justice focuses on the normative relationship between the parties, it readily appealed to theorists who viewed tort law as a repository of moral reasoning about responsibility for injury rather than as a device for promoting economic goals.

---

[1] Izhak Englard, "The System Builders: A Critical Appraisal of Modern American Tort Theory," (1980) 9 J. Legal Stud. 27.

The organizing idea of corrective justice is that of correlativity. Under this idea, liability reflects the conclusion that the defendant and the plaintiff have respectively done and suffered the same injustice. Correlativity structures this injustice: the elements of liability can be explicated only in terms of concepts whose normative force applies simultaneously to both parties. Liability thus involves a conception of fairness that recognizes the equal normative status of the two parties and treats their normative positions as mirror images of each other.

Corrective justice is exposed to two potential misconceptions. The first misconception is that corrective justice is a substantive rather than a structural principle. A substantive principle directly presents a proposed content for legal doctrine. This content may have a limited scope that comprehends certain bases of liability but not others. Viewed as a substantive principle, corrective justice might be thought, for instance, to illuminate only particular doctrines of tort law but neither tort liability generally nor other bases of liability such as contract law or unjust enrichment. In contrast, a structural principle refers to a pattern of argument to which the content (whatever it is) of private law should conform. Viewed as structural principle, corrective justice applies throughout the whole law of obligations, on the grounds that correlativity is built into the very structure of liability as a normative phenomenon directly linking plaintiff and defendant. The second misconception is that corrective justice is so abstract an idea that it contributes little to the specification of the content of private law, or that it is concerned only with the remedial mechanism through which wrongs, whatever they are, are corrected. This ignores the close connection between corrective justice and a robust conception of rights. These rights and the duties correlative to them constitute the content of private law across the various bases of liability.

In this chapter I address both of these potential misconceptions. In response to the first, I examine the normative significance of correlativity as a pervasive feature of liability. In response to the second, I trace the conceptual relationship between the correlativity of corrective justice and liability as a regime of rights. In particular, I focus on the idea of personality as the abstraction through which the nature of these rights is understood.

I thereby present a juridical conception of corrective justice. The conception is juridical in the sense that it reflects, though at an abstract level, the justifications internal to liability in private law, treating them as normative in their own terms rather than as the disguised surrogates for extrinsically justifiable social goals. The juridical conception views the determination of liability as a distinctive domain of practical reason that subjects the interaction between the plaintiff and the defendant to a coherent ordering that is fair to both of them. Because legal argument attests to the law's self-reflective engagement with its own fairness and coherence, the principles and concepts already present to private law can provisionally be regarded as constituents of that ordering. Thus, in its endeavor to exhibit the normative ideas interior to a fair and coherent regime of liability, the juridical conception of corrective justice draws on the law's own efforts.

Fundamental though it is, correlativity is not the only component of the juridical conception of corrective justice. That conception also features a distinct notion of the person that philosophers in the natural right tradition have termed "personality." Personality in this context is not a psychological but a normative idea: it refers not to the pattern of an individual's behavioral characteristics, but to a presupposition about imputability and entitlement that is implicit in the rights and duties of private law. This presupposition is that, as participants in a regime of liability, the parties are viewed as purposive beings who are not under duties to act for any purposes in particular, no matter how meritorious. This capacity for purposive action underlies the rights and duties that are its juridical manifestations. In not requiring action for any particular purpose, personality reflects the structure of the law of obligations as a system of negative duties of non-interference with the rights of others. This does not mean that so circumscribed a notion of duty is exhaustive of one's obligations in all moral contexts. Rather, personality encapsulates a normative standpoint that is indigenous to private law.

In the juridical conception of corrective justice, correlativity and personality are complementary ideas. They are the mutually entailed parts of a single conception but they highlight different aspects of it. Just as correlativity is the most abstract representation of the terms on which the parties interact in private law, so personality is the most abstract representation of the parties themselves as interacting beings. And just as correlativity exhibits the structure of the justifications that pertain to private law, so personality articulates the presupposition that informs the content of those justifications. Correlativity and personality pass over the same theoretical ground from different directions.

Accordingly, one would have expected that the increasing academic recognition of correlativity would be accompanied by a similar recognition of personality. That, however, has not occurred. This is because of the apprehension that personality, with its roots in the natural rights philosophies of Kant and Hegel, implies both a philosophical claim about the truth of Kant's or Hegel's conception of rational agency[2] and a methodological claim that the theory of private law is derived from a more comprehensive philosophical program. They reject personality because they reject what they take to be these further implications.

In this chapter I point out that these further implications do not follow from the presence of personality within the juridical conception of corrective justice. Personality articulates at the high level of abstraction what is implicit in private law as a regime of rights and their correlative negative duties. Personality's status within the juridical conception is no different from that of correlativity. With respect to both personality and correlativity, the juridical conception operates by working back from the principles and concepts of private law to the most general ideas latent within them. Thus the juridical conception regards corrective justice neither as deriving from nor as implying the philosophical truth of Kant's or Hegel's conception of rational agency. Of course, this does not exclude reference to Kantian and Hegelian texts and ideas as a source of insight about the nature of private law when understood as corrective justice. Nor does it exclude the possibilities of deriving corrective justice from, or establishing the truth of, rational agency; consideration of those possibilities, however, would require philosophical argument that lies beyond the bounds of the theory of private law and does not affect it. What the juridical conception of corrective justice asserts is merely that correlativity and personality are implicit in private law as complementary ideas, so that accepting one of them is inconsistent with rejecting the other.

2. The complementary abstractions

The juridical conception of corrective justice is the centerpiece of a theory of liability. The object of the theory is to understand liability as a distinct and familiar normative practice, in which the law assesses

---

[2] The term rational agency in this connection refers to Kant's notion that the will rationally generates rules for its own conduct or Hegel's notion that the will realizes itself by willing, through the various stages of normative experience, a content that is appropriate to its own rational form.

and responds to the claim that a plaintiff makes against a defendant. Considered as a normative practice, liability includes both the legal consequences that a court might impose and the grounds that justify those legal consequences.

Within this practice justification has a pervasive role. The rules, concepts, and principles that figure in the assessment of the plaintiff's claim are the ingredients and the products of a justificatory process. Moreover, the institutions of liability are designed for the presentation of these justifications and for giving effect to the conclusions that may be drawn from them. Consequently, the normative significance of a finding of liability depends on the cogency of the justifications that support it.

The juridical conception of corrective justice takes the justificatory ambitions of this practice seriously by focusing on its internal normative dimension. The juridical conception repudiates the idea that the justifications that figure in private law derive from goals that are desirable independently of the role that they can coherently play in a liability regime. Instead, its eye remains fixed on the practice itself, on the institutional structure through which it unfolds, and on the reasoning through which it expresses its distinctive mode of justification. The juridical conception of corrective justice thus honors the law's reasoning as a good faith attempt—sometimes successful and sometimes not—to make the exercise of official power the product of an internally coherent ensemble of justificatory considerations.

The aim of the juridical conception is to disclose the structure and the normative presuppositions of the law's internal processes of justification. It takes the doctrinal and institutional features that are characteristic of a regime of liability, and asks what must be presupposed about them and about their interconnection if the law is to be (as it claims) a coherent justificatory enterprise. The answer lies in identifying the most abstract unifying conceptions implicit in the doctrinal and institutional arrangements of private law. Thus the juridical conception of corrective justice purports to bring to the surface ideas that are latent in liability as a normative practice.

Within the juridical conception the movement of thought is from the particulars of liability to its most abstract characterization, thus carrying to its extreme the tendency to abstract that marks legal thinking. Although the events that give rise to a legal relationship are particular, the law treats these events in terms of categories. The particularities of the events are legally relevant only inasmuch as they instantiate a category applicable to the legal relationship to which they give rise. Just as legal thinking views particulars in the light of these categories, so the juridical conception of corrective justice abstracts further from these categories to the barest and most general ideas underlying the law's construction of the parties' relationship.

The juridical conception of corrective justice gives voice to the internal structure of a liability regime by presenting its doctrinal and institutional features as the specifications of its most pervasive and general characteristics. If these characteristics can be understood as expressing a set of unifying and complementary ideas, the liability regime will be seen as coherent to the extent of its participation in those ideas. When presented abstractly, these ideas afford an uncluttered view of the nature of liability, because they pertain to liability as such without being confined to any particular doctrine. Their very abstractness brings into view the systematic connections that might obtain among the considerations adduced to support the manifold features of liability. Moreover, they provide a critical perspective internal to the law, because justifications that do not fit within these unifying ideas are problematic from the standpoint of liability itself.

These ideas emerge from the notion that liability is justified when a certain kind of connection obtains between the parties. This description of liability indicates that a theory of liability must comprehend two general features. The first is the nature of the connection between the parties: what is it that allows the law to single out two specific parties from all the people in the world and link them as plaintiff and defendant? The second is the nature of the parties: in view of the diversity of human interests and characteristics, what conception of the parties is normatively capable of serving as the basis of the defendant's liability to the plaintiff? The unifying ideas implicit in liability are the answers, formulated in the most abstract terms, to these two questions.

The conceptions of the parties and of the connection between them are mutually complementary. In dealing with liability, we are interested in the parties only because of the normative connection between them; and we are interested in that connection only because the parties are normatively capable of association in terms of liability. Accordingly, the parties must be conceptualized in a way that makes liability the necessary mode of connecting them; and the connection between the parties must be conceptualized in a way that makes necessary a certain construal of what, from the standpoint of liability, is normatively significant about them. These two unifying ideas are thus the same idea presented under different aspects. Indeed, if they were not the same idea, the legal phenomenon to which they apply would have to be understood not as a unity but as a pluralism of at least two independent ideas. This conclusion would defeat the aspirations of the juridical conception by indicating that liability—and the justificatory considerations that underlie it—was incapable of being understood as an internally coherent whole.

In the juridical conception of corrective justice, the two complementary ideas are correlativity and personality. Correlativity, which was first highlighted in Aristotle's account of corrective justice,[3] is the abstract formulation of the connection that exists between the parties in a regime of liability. Personality, which was most fully articulated in the philosophical tradition of natural right that culminated in Kant and Hegel,[4] presents in similarly abstract terms what is normatively significant about the interacting parties for purposes of liability. Although the two ideas are ultimately congruent, they start from different aspects of liability. Correlativity abstracts from the institutional framework of the plaintiff–defendant lawsuit and inquires into the structure of the justifications that coherently fit into this institutional framework. Personality abstracts from the doctrinal framework of rights and duties in order to exhibit the content of private law justification in its most general form; it then extends its attention to the institutions that give coherent effect to that doctrinal framework. Together, correlativity and personality are the interlocking foundation stones of a theory of liability.

3. Correlativity

Aristotle presents corrective and distributive justice as two contrasting forms of justice. Corrective justice, which deals with voluntary and involuntary transactions (today's contracts and torts), focuses on whether one party has done and the other has suffered a transactional

---

[3] Aristotle, *Nicomachean Ethics*, V, 4.

[4] Immanuel Kant, *The Metaphysics of Morals*, tr. Mary Gregor, in *The Cambridge Edition of the Works of Immanuel Kant: Practical Philosophy* (1996), [6:242]. Numbers in square brackets refer to the pagination found in the standard German edition of this work and reproduced in the margins of *The Cambridge Edition*. G. W. F. Hegel, *Philosophy of Right*, tr. T. M. Knox (1952), ss. 34–40.

injustice. Distributive justice deals with the distribution of whatever is divisible (Aristotle mentions honors and goods) among the participants in a political community. For Aristotle, justice in both these forms relates one person to another according to a conception of equality or fairness (the Greek *to ison* connotes both). Injustice arises in the absence of equality, when one person has too much or too little relative to another.

The two forms differ, however, in the way they construe equality. Distributive justice divides a benefit or burden in accordance with some criterion that compares the participants' merit relative to one another. Distributive justice therefore embodies a proportional equality, in which all participants in the distribution receive their shares according to their respective merits under the criterion in question.

Corrective justice, in contrast, features the maintenance and restoration of the notional equality with which the parties enter the transaction. This equality consists in persons having what lawfully belongs to them. Injustice occurs when, relative to this baseline, one party realizes a gain and the other a corresponding loss. The law corrects this injustice when it re-establishes the initial equality by depriving one party of the gain and restoring it to the other party. Aristotle likens the parties' initial positions to two equal lines.[5] The injustice upsets that equality by adding to one line a segment detached from the other. The correction removes that segment from the lengthened line and returns it to the shortened one. The result is a restoration of the original equality of the two lines.

As its name indicates, corrective justice has a rectificatory function. By correcting the injustice that the defendant has inflicted on the plaintiff, corrective justice asserts a connection between the remedy and the wrong. From the perspective of corrective justice, a court does not treat the situation being adjudicated as a morally neutral given and then ask what is the best course for the future, all things considered. Rather, because the court aims to correct the injustice done by one party to the other, the remedy responds to the injustice and endeavors, so far as possible, to undo it.

Aristotle's account makes it clear that this rectification operates correlatively on both parties. A remedy directed to only one of the parties does not conform to corrective justice. For the court merely to take away the defendant's wrongful gain does not suffice, because then the

---

[5] Aristotle, above n. 3, at 1132b6.

plaintiff is still left suffering a wrongful loss. Nor does it suffice for the court merely to replenish the plaintiff's loss, for then the defendant will be left holding his or her wrongful gain. The remedy consists in simultaneously removing the defendant's excess and making good the plaintiff's deficiency. Justice is thereby achieved for both parties through a single operation in which the plaintiff recovers precisely what the defendant is made to surrender.

From these two features of the corrective justice remedy—that it responds to the injustice and is correlatively structured—a third follows. A correlatively structured remedy responds to and undoes an injustice only if that injustice is itself correlatively structured. In bringing an action against the defendant the plaintiff is asserting that they are connected as doer and sufferer of the same injustice. As is evidenced by the judgment's simultaneous correction of both sides of the injustice, what the defendant has done and what the defendant has suffered are not independent items. Rather, they are the active and passive poles of the same injustice, so that what the defendant has done counts as an injustice only because of what the plaintiff has suffered, and vice versa. The law then rectifies this injustice by reversing its active and passive poles, so that the doer of injustice becomes the sufferer of the law's remedy. Only because the injustice is the same from both sides does the remedy treat the parties as correlatively situated. Thus throughout the transaction, from the occurrence of the injustice to its rectification, each party's position is normatively significant only through the position of the other, which is the mirror image of it.

The idea that correlativity informs the injustice, as well as its rectification, is a central insight of the juridical conception of corrective justice. This insight points to the kind of justifications that are appropriate for determinations of liability. To think of something as an injustice is not to refer to a brute event but to make a normative ascription. The correlativity of the injustice is, therefore, the correlativity of the normative considerations that underlie that ascription. Because the defendant, if liable, has committed the same injustice that the plaintiff has suffered, the reason the plaintiff wins ought to be the same as the reason the defendant loses. Thus in specifying the nature of the injustice, the only normative factors to be considered significant are those that apply equally to both parties. A factor that applies to only one of the parties—for example, the defendant's having a deep pocket or being in a position to distribute losses broadly—is an inappropriate justification for liability because it is inconsistent with the correlative nature of the liability. Accordingly corrective justice not only rectifies injustice in transactions; by structuring the justificatory considerations relevant to transactions, it is also regulative of the notion of injustice that is applicable to them.

Thus, correlativity is the structural idea that underlies the most obvious and general feature of liability, that the liability of the defendant is always a liability to the plaintiff. Liability consists in a legal relationship between two parties each of whose position is intelligible only in the light of the other's. In holding the defendant liable to the plaintiff, the court is making not two separate judgments (one that awards something to the plaintiff and the other that coincidentally takes the same from the defendant), but a single judgment that embraces both parties in their interrelationship. The defendant cannot be thought of as liable without reference to a plaintiff in whose favor such liability runs. Similarly, the plaintiff's entitlement exists only in and through the defendant's correlative obligation. The court's finding of liability is the response to an injustice that, accordingly, has the same correlative shape as liability itself.

Justifications for holding someone liable that exhibit the parties as the doer and sufferer of the same injustice render the law both coherent and fair. Legal reasoning composed of such justifications treat the parties' relationship as a normative unity that embraces them both rather than as a hodgepodge of factors separately relevant only to one or the other of them. With this justificatory coherence comes fairness as between the parties. A justification that fails to match the correlative structure of the parties' relationship necessarily favors one of the parties at the expense of the other, thereby failing to be fair from the standpoint of both. In contrast, by insisting that the normative considerations applicable to liability reflect the parties' correlative situation, corrective justice construes private law as setting terms for the parties' interaction that take account of their mutual relationship and are therefore fair to both of them.

Aristotle's original account contrasts the correlativity of corrective justice with the categorically different structure of distributive justice. Corrective justice links the doer and sufferer of an injustice in terms of their correlative positions. Distributive justice, on the other hand, deals with the sharing of a benefit or burden; it involves comparing the potential parties to the distribution in terms of a distributive criterion. Instead of linking one party to another as doer and sufferer, distributive justice links all parties to the benefit or burden they all share.

The categorical distinction between correlativity and comparison is certified by the difference between the numbers of parties that each admits. Corrective justice links two parties and no more, because a relationship of correlativity is necessarily bipolar. Distributive justice admits any number of parties, because in principle no limit exists for the number of persons who can be compared and among whom something can be divided.

The consequence of Aristotle's contrast between corrective and distributive justice is that no distributive consideration can serve as a justification for holding one person liable to another. The correlative structure of liability entails the irrelevance of any factor that is normatively significant only because of its possible role in a distributive comparison. For purposes of justifying a determination of liability, corrective justice is independent of distributive justice.

Accordingly, the idea of correlativity brings out the interior structure of justification within the connection that liability forges between a particular plaintiff to a particular defendant. In considering liability we might wonder: why is the plaintiff entitled to recover from this defendant rather than from someone more evil, or why is the defendant held liable to this particular plaintiff rather than to someone more needy? The correlative nature of liability shows that such questions are misplaced. Evil and need are moral categories that may well figure in other normative contexts, but they are not pertinent to liability. It may make sense as a matter of distributive justice, for instance, to divide benefits or burdens on the basis of a comparison of relative virtue or need. Virtue and need, however, do not connect any two particular persons as correlatively situated.

The irrelevance of virtue and need as justificatory considerations for liability exemplifies a wider principle that applies to anything whose normative significance is not correlatively structured. In insisting that correlativity is the general organizing feature for justifications of liability, corrective justice requires practical reason to adopt and maintain a special posture, or to be shifted, as it were, into a special normative gear,[6] to which every aspect of liability must conform.

For the law of obligations, the overarching justificatory categories expressive of correlativity are those of the plaintiff's right and the

---

[6] The metaphors of posture and gear are adopted from the illuminating discussion of correlativity by Michael Thompson, "What Is It to Wrong Someone? A Puzzle about Justice," in *Reason and Value*, ed. R. J. Wallace et al. (2004), 333, 346.

defendant's corresponding duty not to interfere with that right. Unlike need and virtue, a right is an intrinsically relational idea that immediately signifies the existence of a duty correlative to it. Right and duty are correlated when the plaintiff's right is the basis of the defendant's duty and, conversely, when the scope of the duty includes the abstention from the kind of right-infringement that the plaintiff suffered. Under those circumstances the reasons that justify the protection of the plaintiff's right are the same as the reasons that justify the existence of the defendant's duty.

Negligence law provides a paradigmatic example of the operation of this correlativity in the common law. For the defendant to be held liable, it is not enough that the defendant's negligent act resulted in harm to the plaintiff. The harm has to be to an interest that has the status of a right, and the defendant's action has to be wrongful with respect to that right.[7] In Justice Cardozo's words, "What the plaintiff must show is 'a wrong' to herself; i.e., a violation of her right, and not merely a wrong to someone else, nor conduct 'wrongful' because unsocial but not 'a wrong' to any one."[8] Under the condition stated by Cardozo, freedom from the injury of which the plaintiff is complaining is both the content of the plaintiff's right and the object of the defendant's duty. Then correlativity obtains, because the parties are the doer and sufferer of the same injustice, and the reason for the plaintiff's entitlement to win the lawsuit would be the same as the reason for the defendant's liability to lose it.

The identity of the content of the right and the object of the duty informs what it means to do and suffer the same injustice. One suffers an injustice when one's right is infringed. One does an injustice when one breaches one's duty not to infringe another's right. This doing and suffering come together in the same injustice when the duty breached is correlative to the very right that was infringed. Given the correlative positions of the parties, imputing the breach of such a duty to the defendant justifies his or her liability to the plaintiff. For the juridical conception of corrective justice, then, an injustice is an inconsistency with the plaintiff's right that is imputable to the defendant.

The various branches of civil liability work out the circumstances for such imputability. As Cardozo's statement illustrates, the concepts and principles of tort liability set out the conditions under which the

---

[7] See below, chapter 2.
[8] Palsgraf v. Long Island Railroad Co., 162 N.E. 99 (N.Y.C.A., 1928), at 100.

defendant's conduct counts as a wrongful infringement of the plaintiff's right. Similarly, the central doctrines of the law of contract (offer and acceptance, consideration, unconscionability, and expectation damages) allow the parties, through the mutuality of their conduct, to establish in the plaintiff a right to the defendant's performance of the promised act.[9] And the law dealing with unjust enrichment at another's expense gives legal specificity to the plaintiff's right to the defendant's restitution of a gratuitous benefit that was neither given nor accepted donatively.[10]

4. Personality

The juridical conception of corrective justice abstracts to the most pervasive organizing ideas of private law. Correlativity is one such organizing idea. It is the abstraction that presents the many particular relationships between parties in private law—and the justifications applicable to those relationships—in terms that match the bipolar nature of liability. By attending to correlativity, the juridical conception of corrective justice concludes that, first, to the extent that private law is fair and coherent, the justifications underlying liability evince a correlative structure and, second, right and duty are the normative categories that conform to this structure. The question that then arises is whether the rights and duties of private law in turn fall under a parallel abstraction. In other words, can the normative content of the parties' positions, as well as the correlative structure of their relationship, be illuminated through some abstraction that coherently organizes the manifold of liability?

It goes without saying that this abstraction must be fully consistent with the conception of liability as correlative, because the content of the rights and duties has to fit the correlative structure that they instantiate. This desideratum means that rights cannot be conceived merely as shorthand references to components of the plaintiff's welfare, for then rights will ultimately be as unexpressive of correlativity as welfare itself. From the standpoint of corrective justice, the advance

---

[9] On the nature of contractual right, see below chapter 5. On the relationship among the central doctrines of contract law, see Peter Benson, "The Unity of Contract Law," in *The Theory of Contract Law: New Essays*, ed. Benson (2001), 118.

[10] Below, chapter 6.

achieved by introducing the notion of right and correlative duty would be undone by the non-correlative conception of the content of those rights as being based on welfare.

Thus, under the juridical conception of corrective justice, rights are not normatively significant for private law simply by virtue of the fact that they enhance the plaintiff's welfare. Of course, having a right contributes to a person's welfare by protecting some interest from wrongful interference. And it is also true, of course, that private law responds to the infringing a right by measuring diminutions of the right-holder's welfare under the legally recognized heads of damages. That, however, does not mean that rights are synonymous with aspects of welfare or that their normative significance is to be understood in terms of it. In the law's contemplation, the increase in welfare through having a right and the decrease through the infringement of a right are the consequences rather than the grounds of the right. That is why (as in cases of negligently caused economic loss)[11] a decrease in welfare that does not violate the plaintiff's rights is not actionable, and conversely (as in cases of nominal damages) a violation of a right that does not decrease the plaintiff's welfare is. Welfare serves only the secondary function, only injustice has occurred and a remedy is being considered, of quantifying the injury done to the object of the right. The reason that rights matter for private law lies elsewhere.

The insignificance of welfare as such is also evident on the duty side. Tort law, for instance, is a regime of negative duties that mandate non-interference with the rights to which they are correlative. If the rights themselves represented aspects of welfare, one would expect that at least certain aspects (human life itself, for instance) would be so important that, at least in an extreme circumstance, persons would be under a positive duty to promote or preserve them. As the law's distinction between misfeasance and nonfeasance indicates, this is not the case. The promotion of another's welfare, even the saving of another's life in an emergency, counts merely as the bestowal of a benefit and therefore not obligatory. The fact that private law deems no aspect of welfare important enough to ground a positive obligation to forward it indicates that welfare as such is not what is significant about the rights that the law recognizes.

[11] Peter Benson, "The Basis for Excluding Liability for Economic Loss in Tort Law," in *Philosophical Foundations of Tort Law*, ed. David Owen (1995), 427 (analyzing tort law's reluctance to recognize economic loss as a basis of liability in the absence of an infringement of a right).

The upshot of these considerations is that welfare does not lie at the heart of the abstraction that might capture the organizing idea implicit in the rights and duties of private law. What does?

Correlativity can serve as a model for what an answer to this question involves. As an abstraction aimed at illuminating the nature of liability, correlativity presents no novel claims. Nor does it reflect some obscure or hitherto unnoticed consequence of private law that, through virtuoso analysis, is worked up to disclose a mysterious but supposedly comprehensive truth.[12] The significance of correlativity is not in the heavens but before our very noses, inescapably present whenever we consider liability. In its reference to correlativity corrective justice merely takes the most manifest aspect of private law—that liability links plaintiff and defendant—and works out its theoretical implications. This it does by extrapolating from the plethora of private law causes of action to the feature that is pervasive in and presupposed by all of them. Similarly, in articulating the abstraction pertinent to the content of rights and duties, corrective justice merely looks for what is pervasively present in particular rights and duties.

What is present is the parties' capacity for purposiveness, which assumes legal significance when externalized. On the duty side, this is evident in the trite doctrine of tort law that the defendant cannot be liable in the absence of an "act," defined as an external manifestation of the volition.[13] Mere physical movement is irrelevant to liability; there must be the outward expression of an inwardly determined purpose. However, although tort law insists that the wrong originates in an exercise of purposiveness, it does not condition liability on the failure to act for a particular purpose, however meritorious. As the nonfeasance doctrine attests, tort law makes obligatory no particular purposes, not even purposes that would preserve another's most fundamental interests. Thus the indispensable presupposition of the defendant's having breached a duty is the sheer purposiveness of the defendant's action, rather than a conception of some set of particular purposes that should have guided the defendant's conduct.

The same picture appears in connection with rights. The acquisition or transfer of a right involves the exercise, in a legally cognizable manner, of the acquirer's or the transferor's purposiveness toward the subject matter of the right. As in the case of acts that violate rights, an

[12] In this respect, contrast the economic analysis of law.
[13] *Restatement (Second) of Torts*, s. 2 (1965).

external manifestation of the volition is necessary if the law is to ascribe consequences to what one has done. Moreover, the legal basis for the thing's being used in the exercise of the owner's purposive capacity is what acquisition creates (and transfer terminates). Accordingly, the law regards a right as the power to treat something as subject to one's will as a consequence of an antecedent connection that one's will has established with the thing in question. Yet the law regards as irrelevant the specific purpose that motivates the acquisition, transfer, or use. Nor does it require that the right, once acquired, be used for any particular (and arguably laudable) purposes, such as to increase the utility of all or to maximize wealth or to produce an equality of resources. Of course, the acquisition, transfer, and use of one's entitlements is fueled by one's particular needs, interests, and desires, but the law pays these no heed when determining the entitlements' validity. The law responds merely to the external indicia of an exercise of purposiveness, rather than to a schedule of required or desirable purposes.

Thus, in the acquisition, transfer, use, and violation of a right, private law presupposes the exercise of one's capacity for purposive activity without specifying any set of necessary purposes. In this respect, a liability regime differs from other normative domains. While morality, for example, also presupposes purposiveness in the moral actor, it aspires to specify particular purposes essential to living a moral life. Similarly, distributive justice requires the identification, at least at some level of generality, of the particular purposes at which a distribution ought to aim. In contrast, the presupposition of purposiveness without regard to particular purposes is specific to a regime of liability.

As the basis of the private law's attention to the parties, purposiveness without regard to particular purposes defines the conception of the person that underlies liability. This conception is what the natural right tradition called "personality."[14] Just as the ancient Roman legal texts use "person" when discussing the indicia of one's legal standing, so personality refers to the capacity for purposive agency that forms the basis for the capacity for rights and duties in private law. Personality encapsulates the normative standpoint from which private law has to view the parties if it is to regard them as having its rights and being subject to its duties.

---

[14] See especially Hegel, above n. 4.

The rights and duties in a coherent liability regime specify the manifestations of personality in the parties' legal relationship. Because personality signifies the capacity for purposiveness without regard to particular purposes, no obligation exists to exercise this capacity toward any particular end. Any duties that reflect personality are therefore the negative correlates of rights. These rights arise insofar as the capacity for purposive agency is not merely an inward attribute but achieves external existence in social interactions through its exercise by or embodiment in an agent. Among these rights are the right to the integrity of one's body's as the organ of purposive activity, the right to property in things appropriately connected to an external manifestation of the proprietor's volition, and the right to contractual performance in accordance with the mutually consensual exercises of the parties' purposiveness. The existence of these rights gives rise to correlative duties of non-interference whose content and application depend on the nature of the right. Moreover, these rights and duties are actualized through a set of judicial institutions that endows them with a determinate shape, makes public the mode of reasoning that accords with what is presupposed in them, and undoes the consequences of conduct inconsistent with them.

Personality is the abstraction that captures the conception of the person presupposed in the justifications appropriate to the doer–sufferer relationship. The correlativity of doing and suffering means that welfare as such, because it is not correlatively structured, does not serve as the basis of liability; accordingly, the agency of the parties cannot be conceived in terms of the importance to them of their welfare. Instead, the parties' interaction presupposes a conception of the person in which doing and suffering are each normatively significant because of their relationship to the other. Personality offers such a conception. From the standpoint of the doer of injustice, personality as the capacity for purposiveness contains the indispensable conditions for the ascription of responsibility for the effects of one's action. From the standpoint of the sufferer, personality is the basis of the rights that mark out a sphere that others must treat as inviolate. Injustice occurs when this purposiveness is actualized on both sides of this relationship, through the right infringed and the correlative duty breached. Within the parties' interaction personality thus operates in a correlative mode.

Personality illuminates the injustice done and suffered as the infringement of a right. Not every harm or disadvantage counts as an

injustice for purposes of corrective justice. The mere doing and suffering of something that adversely affects the sufferer is not in itself significant. What is done and suffered must be an injustice, with the
specific kind of injustice being the infringement of a right. Personality
models this kind of injustice by presenting a conception of the parties
for whose normative status welfare does not matter except insofar as it
forms the content of a right. For persons conceived in this way, being
better or worse off does not in itself constitute an injustice. In this
respect, the idea of personality replicates at an abstract level the law's
own distinction between *damnum* and *iniuria*.

Thus, personality is the conception of the parties formulated at a
high degree of abstraction. This conception organizes and unifies the
justificatory considerations that pertain to liability. It organizes them
by exhibiting the content of rights and duties as expressive of the
capacity for purposiveness that they presuppose. It unifies them by
exhibiting the single abstraction implicit in private law's multiplicity
of rights and duties. Personality can then function as a conception to
which the legal reasoning that underlies the various rights and duties
must conform if they are to fulfill the possibilities for coherence that
are latent within them.

Its attention to personality brings the juridical conception of corrective justice into contact with the natural right philosophies of Kant
and Hegel. These philosophies locate personality in private law and
then, in their different ways, reconstruct the entire normative realm
on the basis of conceptions of rational agency for which personality is
the indispensable first stage. The juridical conception draws on the
notion of personality articulated in these philosophies. One might
conclude that the juridical conception of corrective justice thereby
purports to derive the theory of private law from a supposedly correct
philosophical account of rational agency. That conclusion would be a
mistake for two reasons.

First, the juridical conception of corrective justice does not proceed by postulating a conception of agency and then deriving the
theory of private law from it. Rather, the juridical conception always
works backward from the doctrines and institutions of private law to
the most pervasive abstractions implicit in it. These abstractions (correlativity and personality) then serve to illuminate the justifications
that figure in a fair and coherent private law. The argument moves
from private law as a normative practice to its presuppositions, which
then serve as vehicles of criticism and intelligibility that are internal

to the practice. Personality matters to the theory of private law not because personality is the source from which that theory is derived, but because personality is latent in the normative practice that the theory aims to comprehend.[15]

Second, the juridical conception does not depend on the correctness of any philosophical account of rational agency. The juridical conception of corrective justice is concerned only with the normative perspective specific to private law, not with rational agency as such. To be sure, in their accounts of rational agency Kant and Hegel formulated the notion of personality and analyzed its significance for private law. Their expositions of the rights and duties of corrective justice are exemplary in their systematic elaboration of the relationship among various of the concepts that figure in a regime of liability. Because Kant and Hegel articulate their differing accounts under the most rigorous constraints of coherence, they provide a repository of insights, often ignored by English-speaking scholars, about the nature of coherence within legal relationships and about the role of specific doctrines in achieving that coherence. However, their treatments of personality as an aspect of rational agency would have been nugatory even for their own purposes unless personality was indeed immanent in the conceptual structure of private law. It is this immanence that the juridical conception highlights. The Kantian and Hegelian accounts of private law are available to the juridical conception not because they reflect the correct view of rational agency (though one or the other of them may do so), but because they bring out the internal connections integral to a coherent understanding of liability.

Of particular interest to the judicial conception of corrective justice are the ways in which Kant and Hegel connect personality to the various kinds of rights in private law. Contemporary scholars often assume that the rights presupposed by corrective justice are themselves a product of distributive justice. On this view, corrective justice is alleged to rest on a distributive basis, so that the normative autonomy that corrective justice claims for private law is undermined right from the beginning.[16] Each in his own way, the two great thinkers of the

---

[15] For an example of the mistaken view that the juridical conception works by derivation, see Jules Coleman, *Risks and Wrongs* (1992), 478, n. 1. For a description of the movement of thought in the juridical conception as a process of working back from the juristic experience of private law, see Ernest J. Weinrib, *The Idea of Private Law* (1995), 19.

[16] For example, Hanoch Dagan, "The Distributive Foundations of Corrective Justice," (1999) 98 Mich. L. Rev. 138.

natural right tradition provide an antidote to this assumption. The fundamental rights of private law, including property and contract, get entrenched in their accounts not through an exercise of distributive justice but through an exploration of the normative implications of personality within a regime of corrective justice. Their presentations are closely tied to philosophical premises that, as such, are not part of the juridical conception of corrective justice. Nonetheless, their accounts of these rights are available to the juridical conception to the extent that they reflect fundamental features of the private law.[17] Within the juridical conception these accounts can then be used not only to disabuse scholars of the notion that the rights of private law are inescapably distributive, but also to assist in drawing out what, from the standpoint of corrective justice, are the theoretical implications of the features in question. In this respect, too, the Kantian and Hegelian accounts matter to the juridical conception of corrective justice not because it is derived from them but because they are serviceable to its theoretical purposes.

Thus, although the presence of personality within the juridical conception takes its inspiration from the Kantian and Hegelian elucidations of rational agency, the juridical conception itself has no stake in rational agency. Rational agency is constitutive of the entire normative order of values. The juridical conception of corrective justice, in contrast, concerns itself only with values that reflect the distinctive nature of justification in private law. It therefore views the capacity for purposiveness simply as the moral power that is implicit in the rights and duties of private law. No more ambitious claim is necessary for its purposes. It may well be (as Kant and Hegel thought) that personality so conceived is after all an aspect of rational agency and that rational agency is indeed constitutive of the entire order of normative values. Those conclusions, however, require a further philosophical argument, which, even if successful, would not itself be part of the juridical conception. In other words, the cogency or truth of rational agency is a matter for philosophy and not a matter for the theory of private law.[18]

---

[17] For instance, Kant purports to show that contractual obligation arises as a synthetic a priori judgment under the concept of causality. This account of contract is of interest for the juridical conception of corrective justice not because it contains a correct philosophical argument—an issue irrelevant to that conception—but because it makes intelligible the deep-seated legal distinction between *in rem* and *in personam* rights. See below chapter 5.

[18] On the distinction between theory and philosophy, see John Rawls, "The Independence of Moral Theory," in *Collected Papers* (1999), 286–302.

In sum, then, the juridical conception of corrective justice offers the following picture of liability. Liability is the normative practice through which the law responds to the doing and suffering of an injustice. Implicit in this practice are two ideas that are the most abstract representations of the practical reasoning specific to justification within private law. The juridical conception arrives at these ideas by working back to them from the most general features of liability, including the bipolarity of litigation, the distinction between nonfeasance and misfeasance, and the role of rights and correlative duties. The first idea, correlativity, represents the connection between the parties as doer and sufferer of an injustice. Correlativity structures the fair and coherent terms on which the parties interact and to which the justifications that pertain to their interaction ought to conform. When regarded correlatively, doing and suffering form a single normative unit in which the injustice imputed to the doer is the same as the injustice done to the sufferer. The second idea, personality, represents the parties who interact on the basis of correlativity. Personality signifies the capacity for purposive action without regard for particular purposes. This capacity is implicit in the rights and duties of private law.

These two ideas are complementary, each implied by the other. Correlativity is the most abstract conception of the structure that connects rights to duties in private law; personality is the most abstract conception of the content of those rights and duties. Correlativity represents the interrelation of the parties; personality represents the parties in their interrelation. For each of them liability is the response to the doing and suffering of an injustice, but they highlight a different aspect of it: correlativity highlights the connection of doing to suffering, and personality highlights the nature of the injustice as an inconsistency, imputable to the defendant, with a right of the plaintiff. Together they exhibit the doing and suffering of injustice as an internally unified and normatively coherent phenomenon.

5. Stone on external validation

Among contemporary tort theorists, no one has articulated the disquiet occasioned by the idea of personality with greater clarity than Martin Stone. Stone combines a familiarity with the classic expositions of natural right, a reflectiveness about the nature of tort theory,

and an underlying sympathy with the juridical conception of corrective justice. Taking over the idea of correlativity, Stone sees the doing
and suffering of the same wrong as the defining theme of corrective
justice. However, he rejects personality on the ground that the place
that the juridical conception assigns to it rests on a mistake about
the theoretical significance of corrective justice.

Stone understands corrective justice as describing "an abstract
framework for arguments concerning the terms on which one person
is responsible for the harmful effects of her actions on another."[19] The
theoretical significance of corrective justice is that it makes us aware
of the contours of a practice in which a distinctive sort of reason is in
play; by grasping this sort of reason one understands the contours of
the practice.[20] Corrective justice exhibits "a characteristic sort of reason *already* captured in the ongoing activity of argument and judgment directed towards the situation to which modern liability rules
are a judicially evolved response."[21] The idea of correlativity constitutes "the abstract framework" for the sort of reason in question, by
showing that requisite kind of reason is present when the grounds for
saying that the defendant has done wrong are the same as the grounds
for saying that the plaintiff has suffered wrong.

So far, Stone and the juridical conception of corrective justice are
ad idem. For the juridical conception, tort law is an ongoing normative practice characterized by a distinctive exercise of practical reason.
The task that the juridical conception sets for itself is to exhibit at an
abstract level the organizing ideas internal to that exercise of practical
reason. Correlativity, formulated in precisely the terms that Stone uses,
is one of those ideas.

Stone, however, thinks that by introducing personality the juridical
conception goes off the rails. Personality is an idea formulated by Kant
and Hegel as an aspect of rational agency. The purpose of invoking it
within the juridical conception, Stone claims, is to provide a grounding from which corrective justice can be derived. Personality functions to satisfy a demand for the external validation of corrective
justice by pointing to a ground—rational agency—that is available in
advance of the legal practice that is derived from it. This demand is

---

[19] Martin Stone, "On the Idea of Private Law," (1996) 9 Canadian J. of L. and Juris. 235,
at 253.
[20] Ibid., 258.
[21] Ibid., 259.

misplaced, Stone points out, because no external validation of corrective justice is called for. One's interest in corrective justice arises only when one has accepted the notion that tort law expresses genuine reasons; corrective justice then brings one to a better understanding of what it is that one has accepted. Corrective justice does this by being the abstract framework that exhibits, in the words quoted above, "a characteristic sort of reason *already* captured in the ongoing activity." In this way the relationship between corrective justice and tort law "traces a circle."[22] However, this very circularity might engender the baseless but unnerving suspicion that one has failed to make contact with genuine matters of reason. In the effort to remedy this non-existent deficiency, someone within this circle might suppose that "there might be some set of considerations to which one could appeal that would rationally compel *anyone* to enter the circle."[23] The introduction of personality, Stone suggests, is the unnecessary response to this unnecessary thought.

Stone allows that personality, although in his view external, is not reductive.[24] The paradigmatic instance of a reductive validation is economic analysis. This is because economic analysis reduces the kind of reasons that figure in determinations of liability to something else. Instead of seeing tort law through a characterization of what it is, economic analysis sees it in terms of goals (wealth maximization, market deterrence, and so on) that are desirable independently of it. Economic analysis thus deflects attention from practical reason as operative within tort law to some other exercise of practical reason. The juridical conception of corrective justice does not do this. The account it produces matches the kind of reasoning that figures within the normative practice that it is an account of.

What makes personality external, in Stone's view, is that it validates corrective justice through derivation. His thought seems to be that arguments purporting to validate corrective justice in this way go beyond what is necessary to understand liability as the kind of normative practice that it is. Such arguments are external even if they are non-reductive, because they invoke considerations that are not themselves part of the self-contained intelligibility of tort law. Corrective justice "goes beyond" the distinctive sort of reason found in tort law

---

[22] Ibid., 263.
[23] Ibid.
[24] Ibid., 264.

"only in being more general and reflective."[25] Validation, however, goes beyond tort law in a different way. It locates the outside source of the normativity that feeds into corrective justice and from which corrective justice can be "derived" in a subsequent intellectual operation.

Stone concludes that once one overcomes the longing to derive corrective justice from rational agency, personality ceases to matter. The sole reason he sees for introducing personality into the juridical conception is to satisfy a mistaken feeling that only by breaking out of the circularity of corrective justice can one establish its rational credentials.

This reconstruction of the motivation for including personality within the juridical conception of corrective justice is suspect for a number of reasons. First, the juridical conception of corrective justice has no embarrassment about circularity. The juridical conception can be summed up in the brazenly circular proposition that the only purpose of private law is to be private law.[26] The juridical conception treats liability as a self-contained normative practice that it seeks to understand in terms of its internal unity. Circularity it regards as a virtue. To step outside the circle in search of a source from which to derive what is inside it risks leaving unintelligible the starting point on which the rest depends.[27]

Second, the juridical conception of corrective justice already has a means of validation and does not need the one that Stone ascribes to it. What validates the juridical conception is its success in representing at an abstract level the coherence of practical reason as it operates to determine liability. This in turn requires that the complementary ideas of correlativity and personality cohere with each other and that together they make explicit how the injustice connects the doer and the sufferer as parties to a coherent normative relationship. Coherence implies a self-contained circle of mutual reference and support among the elements of what coheres. It validates what is within this circle by pointing not outward to some transcendent ideal but inward to the harmonious interrelationship of its constituents. In contrast to the notion of validation that Stone criticizes, this notion of validation does not go beyond what is necessary for understanding liability as the kind of normative practice it is.

---

[25] Ibid., 265.

[26] Weinrib, *The Idea of Private Law*, 5.

[27] Ernest J. Weinrib, "Legal Formalism: On the Immanent Rationality of Law," (1988) 97 Yale L.J. 949, at 974.

Contrary to what Stone suggests, personality does not function as the means of externally validating the juridical conception of corrective justice. Its status is no different from that of correlativity, which Stone himself accepts as central. Personality only articulates the conception of agency presupposed in a regime of liability. It is merely private law's own notion of entitlement and obligation distilled to its most abstract formulation, just as correlativity is private law's own notion of the nexus between the parties similarly distilled to its most abstract formulation. As it does with correlativity, the juridical conception reaches personality by working backward from the features of liability through reflection on juristic experience, not by working forward to private law from a validating notion of rational agency. The significance of personality within the juridical conception is that it exhibits the conception of the person appropriate to liability as a specific mode of association. Personality is as much inside the circle traced by corrective justice as is correlativity.

By in effect arguing for the elimination of personality from the juridical conception of corrective justice, Stone may also be making a further point. Perhaps he is also suggesting that personality has no necessary place even within the circle. From his detailed account of negligence law solely in terms of doing and suffering,[28] one might infer that Stone thinks that correlativity alone is sufficient to exhibit the distinctive sort of reason that animates tort law. This might explain his preoccupation with the supposed link between personality and external validation. Being unable to discern a role for personality on the inside, he assigns it the spurious task of validating corrective justice from the outside. Conversely, because he views personality solely as an aspect of rational agency, he does not see its significance as the moral power presupposed in a regime of liability.

On this reading of Stone, his criticism of the juridical conception is that one of its two complementary ideas is superfluous. All the work can be done by correlativity. By not mentioning personality in his treatment of tort doctrine, he might be taken as challenging the juridical conception to tell him what he is missing.

I have already noted that, within the juridical conception of corrective justice, correlativity exhibits the structure that justifications must have if they are fairly and coherently to connect the plaintiff to

---

[28] Stone, "The Significance of Doing and Suffering," in *Philosophy and the Law of Torts*, ed. Gerald J. Postema (2001), 131.

the defendant. Accordingly, it disqualifies considerations (such as welfare) that do not have the requisite structure, and insists on considerations (such as rights and their correlative duties) that do. Indeed, unless rights were available, corrective justice could not be actualized in practice, because private law would be unable to comply with its structural standard. But while correlativity needs rights, it gives no positive indication of their nature and content. Personality performs this function. Drawing on the law's doctrines concerning the role of purposiveness in the acquisition and transfer of rights, the juridical conception of corrective justice postulates personality as the abstraction that brings out the connection between the content of any person's right and the external manifestation of that person's volition.

The significance of personality for representing the nature and content of rights provides the answer to the supposed inquiry as to what Stone is missing by his single-minded focus on correlativity. Stone, in common with the juridical conception, sees corrective justice as providing a "more general and reflective"[29] understanding of the distinctive kind of reason found in tort law. Hence his interest in correlativity. However, tort law's distinctive kind of reason also presupposes the existence of rights. The idea of correlativity shows, negatively, that the rights of private law cannot coherently be based on non-correlative notions, but it does not positively indicate the nature and content of these rights. Unless Stone, contrary to his theoretical aims, is willing to forgo a more general and reflective understanding of these rights, he will have to appeal to some such idea as personality. This is because personality (to use Stone's language about correlativity) "supports—by continuing in a more abstract way—the sort of practical thinking instinct in the law's everyday elaboration."[30] The idea of personality, in other words, represents precisely the kind of explanation that Stone seeks.

Perhaps the reason that contemporary scholars miss the significance of personality is that they come to corrective justice through tort theory. A tort theorist naturally focuses on the correction of the wrong rather than on the nature of the right. It then becomes comparatively easy to see that the structure of the correction must mirror the structure of the wrong, and that consequently, because the former involves correlativity, the latter must also. Just as tort law assumes the existence

---

[29] Above n. 19.
[30] Stone, "The Significance of Doing and Suffering," above n. 28, 168.

of rights but concentrates on specifying what constitutes an infringement of those rights, so tort theorists preoccupy themselves with the role of wrongdoing while ignoring the significance of rights or taking them for granted. Then the abstraction that reflects the nature of the wrongdoing assumes greater salience than the abstraction that reflects the nature of the infringed right.

This observation suggests a wider issue. It is the case that contemporary tort theory has been crucial to the renewed interest in corrective justice. However, that form of justice is not exemplified solely by tortious wrongdoing. Correlativity and personality are abstractions drawn from the normative relationship of plaintiff and defendant within a liability regime. Accordingly, all grounds of obligation in private law, including the law of contract and the law of unjust enrichment, actualize a correlatively structured and rights-based form of justice. Corrective justice thus opens the door to a more comprehensive understanding of the normative character of private law. Only when we aim at that more comprehensive understanding will contemporary scholarship have paid adequate attention to the insight that Aristotle first formulated.

6. Corrective justice as theoretical framework

A corrective justice approach to the understanding of private law attempts to discern the normative character of liability as a familiar practice within which justification has a pervasive role. Corrective justice takes the justificatory ambitions of this practice seriously by focusing on the law's internal normative dimension. With its eye fixed on the institutions through which the practice unfolds and on the mode of justification that is distinctive to a liability regime, it focuses on the structure of the relationship between the two parties. Because the liability of the defendant is always a liability to the plaintiff, correlativity ranks as the most abstract formulation of that relationship. And because the rights and duties through which this correlativity operates express the purposiveness of the plaintiff and the defendant without mandating particular purposes, personality ranks as the most abstract formulation of the parties to that relationship. Correlativity and personality are thus the complementary ideas that constitute the juridical conception of corrective justice.

These complementary ideas then become the key to understanding and assessing private law's concepts, principles, and doctrines. The only considerations that conform to corrective justice are those that apply (or figure within a larger ensemble of considerations that applies) correlatively to both parties. Thus, in its regulative function corrective justice holds the practice of liability to the normative implications of liability's own correlative structure.

Understood in this way corrective justice is a normative structure that is fair to both parties. Fairness in this context refers not to the determination of one's appropriate share as a matter of distributive justice, but to reasons for liability that, by treating the parties as correlatively situated, favor neither of them at the expense of the other. Because the fair terms of a bilateral interaction cannot be set on a unilateral basis, considerations whose justificatory force extends only to one party are inadmissible. Corrective justice therefore requires justifications for liability that pertain to the relationship between the parties rather than to one or the other of the parties in isolation.

Furthermore, corrective justice so conceived is an integrating idea that discloses the nature of coherence within a system of liability. One aspect of its integrating power is that, because the injustice—and therefore the justification for holding the defendant liable—is identical from the standpoint of both parties, corrective justice presents the finding of liability not as the consequence of a miscellany of disconnected factors applicable to one party or the other, but as the outcome of reasoning coherently applicable to the relationship as a whole. Being correlative to each other, the doing and the suffering of injustice form a single juridical sequence in which each party participates only through the presence of the other. Accordingly, all the elements of liability must themselves constitute a coherent ensemble that expresses the unity of the parties' legal relationship. A second integrating aspect is that corrective justice connects the injustice and its rectification. Under corrective justice, the setting of the remedy is not an opportunity for the court to do what is best for the future, all things considered. Rather, because the rectification consists simply in undoing, to the extent possible, the very injustice that has been committed, the remedy is a response only to the factors that make up the injustice. The nature of the right infringed determines the nature of the remedy to be awarded. A third integrating feature is that, since all the relationships of private law are subject to the demands of correlativity, the coherence of legal justification can operate not only within any given relationship, but also systemically across relationships, encompassing all the grounds of liability in their interconnection.

Any sophisticated system of liability aspires to realize the values of fairness and coherence. Corrective justice provides the most abstract representation of the meaning of fairness and coherence with respect to liability. Even when legal doctrine is unfair or incoherent and therefore ought to be changed, corrective justice constitutes the immanent critical standpoint informing the law's effort to work itself pure. Thus, corrective justice as a theoretical construct and liability as a familiar normative practice are reciprocally illuminating. Corrective justice is the structure of justification implicit in the practice; and to the extent that it is fair and coherent, the practice, through its doctrines, institutions, and modes of discourse, is the specific realization of corrective justice in a functioning system of liability.

By attending to the normativeness implicit in liability as a familiar practice, corrective justice directs us away from contemporary consequentialist and reductionist understandings of law. Corrective justice repudiates the idea that the justifications that figure in private law derive from goals that are desirable independently of the role that they can coherently play in a liability regime that is fair to both parties. Instead, corrective justice attempts to bring to the surface the structure of normative thought latent in the institutions and concepts of a fair and coherent regime of liability. Corrective justice thus allows one to discern in private law the possibility of vindicating the notion that law is, in Aquinas' striking phrase, "a certain ordering of reason."[31]

---

[31] Thomas Aquinas, *Summa Theologica*, I–II, Q. 90, A. 4 ("quaedam rationis ordinatio").

2

The Disintegration of Duty

1. The general conception of duty

In his great judgment in *Donoghue v. Stevenson*[1] Lord Atkin, before articulating the neighbor principle, noted a deficiency in the judicial treatment of duties of care in negligence. Only rarely had the common law formulated "statements of general application defining the relations between the parties giving rise to a duty of care."[2] Instead, proceeding on a case-by-case basis, the courts had concerned themselves with the particular kind of relationship before them on any occasion and had therefore focused on the specific status of one or other of the parties, "whether manufacturer, salesman or landlord, customer, tenant, stranger, and so on."[3] Thus, the only way to determine whether a duty of care existed was to see whether the case could be referred to some "particular species"[4] that the law had already recognized. He continued:

And yet the duty which is common to all cases where liability is established must logically be based upon some element common to all the cases in which it is found to exist.... [T]here must be, and is, some general conception of relations giving rise to a duty of care, of which the particular cases found in the books are but instances.[5]

---

[1] [1932] A.C. 562 (H.L.).
[2] Ibid., at 579.
[3] Ibid.
[4] Ibid., at 580.
[5] Ibid.

The neighbor principle[6] was Lord Atkin's attempt to set out this general conception.

The general conception of the duty of care—its theoretical basis, its structural constituents, its more recent disintegration back into particular duties, and the need to recapture what a general conception of duty implies—is the subject of the present chapter.

Lord Atkin regarded the existence of a general conception as a necessity ("there must be, and is, some general conception"). Although he said little about the nature of this necessity, he presumably had in mind something like this: the common law, by its own internal logic and dynamism, cannot treat the particular instances of duty as a chaotic miscellany of disparate and independent norms.[7] Duties of care are constituents of a normative system. The coherence of such a system requires that all duties of care should be thematically unified through the same underlying principle. The general conception of duty reflects the common aspect that each particular duty must have if it is to be systematically related to every other particular duty. The necessity to which Lord Atkin refers is a juridical one: the general conception of duty is an implication of the internal coherence required by the law's systematic nature.

In recent years the sense of juridical necessity apparent in Lord Atkin's judgment has waned. Lord Atkin's own formulation of the general conception in terms of a duty to avoid foreseeable harm to a neighbor, path-breaking as it was, has been recognized not to provide a practical test. Moreover, the very idea of a general conception is sometimes thought to be superfluous given the casuistic nature of common law reasoning.[8] Even in courts that accept the need for an overarching framework for the duty of care, the general conception takes the form of multi-staged formulae that are verbally comprehensive without necessarily being juridically coherent.[9] The widely

---

[6] "The rule that you are to love your neighbour becomes in law, you must not injure your neighbour; and the lawyer's question, Who is my neighbour? receives a restricted reply. You must take reasonable care to avoid acts or omissions that you can reasonably foresee are likely to injure your neighbour. Who, then, in law is my neighbour? The answer seems to be persons who are so closely and directly affected by my act that I ought to have them in contemplation as being so affected when I am directing my mind to the acts or omissions which are called into question." Ibid.

[7] This point was made by Deane J. in Stevens v. Brodribb Sawmilling, [1986] 160 C.L.R. 16, at 51 (H.C. Aust.).

[8] For an example, see Dawson J. in Hill v. Van Erp [1997] 188 C.L.R. 159, 177 (H.C. Aust.).

[9] Below, section 4.

accepted idea that duty is a matter of "policy" (whatever that might mean) has led to a distaste for the abstract practical reasoning that undergirds a general conception of duty.

The result has been a disintegration of duty in two related senses. First, because each kind of duty reflects the particular set of policies deemed appropriate to it or the particular constellation of casuistic considerations from which it emerges, the preoccupation with particular species of duties, which Lord Atkin decried, has returned. Duties are differentiated, usually according to the kinds of harms with which they deal (physical injury, economic loss, psychiatric injury, and so on), without attention to (in Lord Atkin's words) "the element common to all cases in which [a duty] is found to exist" and therefore without awareness of the strands that weave all duties of care into a coherent system in which each duty illuminates, and is illuminated by, all the others. Second, not only has the whole ensemble of duties disintegrated into a collection of particular kinds of duties, but the very idea of a duty has disintegrated. Instead of the duty of care being an internally coherent normative category, it has been fragmented into the separate factors that determine the duty's ground and limits. Hence, the reasoning in support of a duty is marked by ad hoc compromises among these separate factors rather than by an elucidation, in the context of a particular case, of the conception under which the defendant's act and the plaintiff's injury form a unified normative sequence. These two senses of disintegration go together, because the absence of coherence within the notion of duty renders otiose the necessity for coherence that Lord Atkin postulated among particular duties.

This disintegration of duty has undermined the most notable achievement of negligence law in the twentieth century. However indeterminate Lord Atkin's own formulation of the general conception of duty, other leading negligence cases also took up and advanced the striving for coherence to which he gave voice. In contrast, the more recent disintegration of duty manifests a failure to develop tort law in a normatively coherent way. If I am right about this, a principal task for negligence law in its ongoing evolution is to grope its way back to the conception of coherence that was implicit in Lord Atkin's celebrated judgment.

In this chapter, I want to discuss these developments from the standpoint of corrective justice. This standpoint is especially germane, because corrective justice is the theoretical notion that accounts for whatever coherence private law might have. Corrective justice ties coherence to the justifications that inform private law's characteristic concepts. Legal doctrine is viewed as coherent only to the extent that its underlying justifications are coherent. These justifications, in turn, are coherent only if their force as reasons is congruent with—rather than artificially truncated by—the structure of the relationship between the parties. Because liability relates the defendant as doer of the injustice to the plaintiff as sufferer of the same injustice, a finding of liability is coherent when the reasons for considering the defendant to have done an injustice are the same as the reasons for considering the plaintiff to have suffered that injustice. As was argued in chapter 1, the normative basis of such coherence is a right of the plaintiff that imposes a correlative duty on the defendant.

Seen in the light of corrective justice, Lord Atkin's comments can be understood as follows. The notion that the law of negligence is a coherent system of justification precludes particular duties of care from being regarded as isolated norms. Rather, the particular duties are systemically related to one another because they participate in a shared general conception of duty. To play its role as a necessary determinant of coherence across particular duties, the general conception of duty must itself be an expression of the very coherence that it imparts. For "the relation between the parties" (as Lord Atkin calls it)[10] to be coherent, that relation has to be regarded as correlatively structured through the defendant's doing and the plaintiff's suffering of the same wrong. This in turn has two complementary aspects. On the one hand, the general conception of duty must be part of an integrated ensemble of concepts that allows the sequence from the defendant's doing of the negligent act to the plaintiff's suffering of the injury to be understood as a normatively coherent unit in which the injustice done and the injustice suffered are the same. On the other hand, the general conception of duty considered in itself must be formed from normative elements that reflect the correlativity of the defendant's duty to the plaintiff's right. When these two aspects are present, the general conception of duty then embodies the correlative structure of justification that renders any particular duty coherent both with the other members of the ensemble of negligence concepts and with other particular duties. There "must be" such a general conception (as Lord Atkin insists) because otherwise

---

[10] Above, n. 2.

the law of negligence would be incoherent—a possibility that he assumes the law cannot acknowledge.

Taking corrective justice as the theoretical notion underlying Lord Atkin's insistence on a general conception of duty, this chapter discusses the disintegration of duty in the following steps. Section 2 is concerned with the first of the aspects of coherence mentioned above—that is, with how duty fits with other negligence concepts (failure to exercise reasonable care, factual causation, and proximate cause) to connect the defendant's act to the plaintiff's injury in a normatively coherent way. Accordingly, the section outlines the role of the landmark cases of the twentieth century in treating the injustice done by the defendant as identical to the injustice suffered by the plaintiff. Section 3 deals with the second aspect of coherence; it sets out the internal structure of the duty of care—that is, what its constituents must be if it is to reflect a coherent conception of the doing and suffering of a wrong. In so doing, the section sets out the general conception of the duty of care that juridical coherence requires. The duty of care will thereby be exhibited as having a definite structure toward which the legal reasoning of any particular case ought to be oriented. The presence of such a structure suggests that it is mere dogmatism to maintain, as tort scholars often do, that duty is nothing but "a shorthand statement of a conclusion, rather than an aid to analysis."[11] Section 4 examines the two-stage test for negligence that has been used in Canada and elsewhere. My argument is that this internally fractured test, as applied by the Supreme Court of Canada, provides a conspicuous example of the disintegration of duty and, accordingly, is inadequate for the development of a coherent jurisprudence of negligence. Finally, section 5 discusses the meaning and relevance of the much-invoked "policy" for the determination of the duty of care. The disintegration of duty is the consequence of thinking that duty is a matter of policy, and that policy, in turn, refers to the various independent goals that liability might serve. On this view each particular kind of duty represents the balance of goals, in themselves diverse and competing, that is peculiar to it. However, another notion of policy refers to the exercise of practical judgment in elucidating what the general conception of duty might mean in particular circumstances. The general conception provides not (as has often been

---

[11] W. Page Keeton et al., *Prosser and Keeton on the Law of Torts*, 5th ed. (1984), 358.

assumed) a test of duty, but a structure of thinking that is actualized in legal reasoning through the casuistic assessment of facts or comparison of cases or through the elucidation of its particular normative features in the overall context of a legal system that values coherence. This second notion of policy is, I suggest, not only compatible with but indeed required by the general conception of duty.

2. The place of duty among the negligence concepts

How, then, does negligence doctrine treat the defendant and the plaintiff as the correlatively situated sufferer and doer of the same wrong? Negligence concerns the plaintiff's being wrongfully injured through the defendant's creation of an unreasonable risk. If negligence liability is to be a coherent normative phenomenon, the injury and the risk-creation have to be understood as the constituents of a single wrong that is elucidated through an integrated ensemble of legal concepts. In this way, the differing experiences of the parties as doer and sufferer and the temporal gap between the doing and the suffering are subsumed under a unified set of normative categories that render the wrong done identical to the wrong suffered.

Coherence requires that the injustice relate act to injury and vice versa. Precluded are definitions of the injustice between the parties in terms that pertain to one of them alone. As negligence law recognizes, the injustice does not consist merely in the unreasonably created risk considered in itself; that would one-sidedly focus on the defendant's wrongful action and entail liability for unreasonable risk-creation even without damage. Nor does it consist in the harmful effect considered in itself; that would one-sidedly focus on the plaintiff's injury and entail strict liability, rather than negligence.[12] Nor, again, does the injustice consist in the combination of wrongful action and injury each considered one-sidedly; that would mean that, although the defendant has committed a wrong and the plaintiff has suffered one, these are two different wrongs, each resting on its own foundation.

---

[12] For a recent analysis of negligence either in terms of risk caused or harm suffered without attending to the possible unity of the sequence as a whole, see Heidi M. Hurd and Michael S. Moore, "Negligence in the Air," (2002) 3 Theoretical Inquiries in Law 333, at 348.

Rather, the injustice embraces the entire span from the act to injury: the defendant's act is viewed as a wrong because of its potential to cause this kind of injury, and the plaintiff's injury is viewed as a wrong because its potential occurrence is a reason for considering the defendant's act wrongful. Then the sequence from act to injury forms the single wrong that the defendant can be said to have done and the plaintiff to have suffered.

To be coherent, tort doctrine elaborates legal concepts that treat the defendant's act and its effect on the plaintiff as an integrated sequence in which there is a single injustice that is the same for both parties. In legal terms, this sequence begins with the defendant's breach of the standard of reasonable care and ends in the factual causation of injury. However, the sequence can be regarded as integrated only if its two termini operate not as atomistic elements that the law simply adds together, but as constituents of liability that, for purposes of tort law, each derive their significance from the other. Hence, the unreasonableness of the risk created by the defendant must lie in the possible occurrence of the kind of injury that the plaintiff suffered. This way of relating the negligent act to the injury makes the injustice of unreasonable risk-creation the same for both parties.

The signal achievement of negligence law in the twentieth century was to develop the concepts of negligence analysis in a way that coherently links the unreasonable risk to the harm suffered. Duty and proximate cause are crucial components in this linkage. These concepts connect wrongdoing and injury by describing the wrongful risk in terms of the range of the potential victims and consequences through which the risk is to be understood as wrongful. Duty connects the defendant as a wrongdoer to the plaintiff as a member of the class of persons wrongfully put at risk. Similarly, proximate cause connects the defendant's negligence to the plaintiff's suffering of the kind of injury or accident the risk of which rendered the defendant's act wrongful. Because both duty and proximate cause are requirements of liability, the defendant is not held legally responsible for the materialization of a harm that is not within the set of possibilities that supply a reason for exercising due care. When, however, the injury suffered by the plaintiff is to a member of the class of persons that the defendant wrongfully put at risk and is the kind of injury or accident that due care is supposed to avoid, then the wrongfulness of both the defendant's action and the plaintiff's injury is referable to the same sort of risk. Under those circumstances, the sequence from the defendant's creation of an unreasonable risk to the materialization of that risk in injury to the plaintiff constitutes the same injustice for both parties.

The leading twentieth-century cases on duty and proximate cause gave legal expression to this conception of negligence liability. Three developments were particularly noteworthy. The first, of course, was *Donoghue v. Stevenson*[13] (and its American predecessor *MacPherson v. Buick Motor Co.*).[14] In place of a fragmented collection of duties that varied according to the particular social and contractual relationships between the parties, *Donoghue* established that the duty of care flowed from the defendant's risk-creating action as such and from its reasonably foreseeable effect on those who ought to have been within the defendant's contemplation. The general conception of the duty of care formulated in this case thereby connected the defendant as the creator of an unreasonable risk and the plaintiff as a person whose endangerment made the risk unreasonable.

A more explicit and complete development of the same idea appeared in Cardozo's judgment in *Palsgraf v. Long Island Railroad Co.*[15] Cardozo held that there could be no liability unless the defendant's breach of duty was a wrong in relation to the plaintiff. Because in that case the defendant's conduct was not wrongful toward the plaintiff (although it was arguably wrongful toward someone else), the defendant was held not to be under a duty with respect to the plaintiff's loss.

Cardozo's explicit purpose was to construe the wrongfulness of negligence in a way that was specifically appropriate to tort law. He noted "the shifting meanings of such words as 'wrong' and 'wrongful.'"[16] What the plaintiff had to show was a wrong that was "a violation of her own right, and not merely a wrong to some one else, nor conduct 'wrongful' because unsocial but not 'a wrong' to any one."[17] To detach the notion of wrong from a beach of duty owing to the plaintiff "is to ignore the fundamental difference between tort and crime."[18] For Cardozo, tort liability—in contrast to other kinds of societal judgments about culpability—featured a wrong done by the defendant in relation to the plaintiff. Accordingly, the very reason for thinking that the defendant acted wrongfully also had to be the reason

---

[13] Above n. 1.
[14] 111 N.E. 1050 (N.Y.C.A, 1916).
[15] 162 N.E. 99 (N.Y.C.A, 1928).
[16] Ibid., at 100.
[17] Ibid.
[18] Ibid., at 101.

for thinking that the injury suffered by the plaintiff was wrongful. The duty of care in negligence law was to be understood as rendering the normative significance of the wrong identical for both parties. "Negligence . . . is thus a term of relation."[19]

Cardozo's outstanding contribution was to align the relational nature of tortious wrongdoing with the relational significance of unreasonable risk. In the words of the opinion, "The risk reasonably to be perceived defines the duty to be obeyed, and risk imports relation."[20] As a way of referring to the harmful potentialities inherent in a given act, risk is not intelligible in abstraction from a set of perils and a set of persons imperiled. A negligent act releases a set of harmful possibilities that due care should have avoided. The plaintiff cannot recover unless the injury she suffered actualizes a possibility within this set. The imperiling of the foreseeably affected class of persons is the reason for considering the defendant's act negligent; it also must be the reason for thinking that the plaintiff has been wronged. Only if the plaintiff is among that class does the reason for thinking of the defendant's action as wrongful pertain to the plaintiff. Because in *Palsgraf* the prospect of the plaintiff's injury was not a reason for considering the defendant's action negligent, the defendant was not under a duty toward her.

Cardozo's treatment of duty forges a normative connection between the defendant's action and the plaintiff's injury. The connection is normative, because it is based on the reason for considering an act to be wrongful. Given that the structure of the relationship between the parties is one of correlativity, that reason must simultaneously provide a ground both for holding the defendant liable and for holding the plaintiff entitled to recover. Under Cardozo's analysis of the relational quality of unreasonable risk, the duty of care makes the same reason pertain to both parties.

In contrast, Andrews's dissenting judgment in *Palsgraf* connects the parties in a historical but not a normative way. The connection is merely historical, because the element of fault required for the defendant's liability to the plaintiff is satisfied by the fact that the defendant's negligence is the historical antecedent of the plaintiff's injury. In Andrews's view, the injury suffered can be the basis of the plaintiff's recovery even though the wrong was relative to a third party rather than the defendant. Unanswered is the question of why the merely

[19] Ibid.
[20] Ibid., at 101.

historical connection between the defendant's negligent act and the plaintiff's injury should justify liability on the basis of fault. It is no answer to say that this negligence caused the injury; that answer, by transforming cause into the determinant of the plaintiff's recovery, should also apply to causally effective action that is innocent (and thus as nonculpable relative to the victim as the defendant's conduct in *Palsgraf*). Negligence liability would then collapse into strict liability.

Another difficulty flows from Andrews's postion. Ever since the devastating critique of strict liability by Oliver Wendell Holmes, no one has been able to sustain the position that liability should be based on causation.[21] The particular problem that Holmes identified is that causation is unable to generate its own limits, so as to preclude a regression to causes however distant. Andrews is not insensitive to this problem. He insists that for the defendant to be liable, the negligence must be not merely a cause, but the proximate cause of the damage. However, having rejected the notion that the parties are normatively connected (and thus liability is limited) through the idea of unreasonable risk, he has no coherent conceptual framework within which judgments about the proximateness of causation can be situated. In Andrews's own account the determination of proximate cause turns out to be an arbitrary exercise in practical politics, intelligible more through rhetoric and metaphor than through legal analysis.[22]

A more coherent conception of proximate cause than the one Andrews put forward emerged from yet another major development of tort jurisprudence in the twentieth century, the Privy Council's decision in the *Wagon Mound* case.[23] The case held the requirement of proximate cause unsatisfied when the defendant negligently exposed the plaintiff to the risk of one kind of injury, but the plaintiff suffered an injury of a different kind. This decision made proximate cause run parallel to Cardozo's conception of duty.[24] Just as *Palsgraf* required that

---

[21] O. W. Holmes, *The Common Law* (1881), Lecture III. For a criticism of Richard Epstein's more recent attempt to vindicate strict liability, see Ernest J. Weinrib, *The Idea of Private Law* (1995), 172–77.

[22] Above n. 15, at 103.

[23] Overseas Tankship (UK) v. Morts Dock and Engineering (Wagon Mound No. 1) [1961] A.C. 388 (P.C.).

[24] The connection of *Wagon Mound* and *Palsgraf* is sharply put in a leading text on tort law in the United States: "The decision is the logical aftermath of Cardozo's decision in the *Palsgraf* case, since there is an obvious absurdity in holding that one who can foresee some harm to A is liable to consequences to A which he cannot foresee, but is not liable for similar consequences to B." Page Keeton et al., *Prosser and Keaton on the Law of Torts*, 296. A similar point was made in the *Wagon Mound* opinion; see above n. 23, at 425.

the plaintiff be within the class of persons unreasonably imperiled, so *Wagon Mound* required that the injury or accident be of the sort that renders the defendant's risk-creation unreasonable. Thus, with respect both to the person injured and to the injury or accident, the harm that occurred actualized the possibilities for danger that it was negligent for the defendant to have created. Duty and proximate cause both functioned to make the wrongfulness of what the defendant did the same as the wrongfulness of what the plaintiff suffered.

When this complex of leading cases is considered as a whole, the main categories of negligence liability—duty, breach of duty, proximate cause, and factual cause—form a coherent set that traces the sequence from the defendant's negligent act to the plaintiff's injury. Breach of duty and factual causation are the termini of this sequence, with the former referring to the defendant's creation of unreasonable risk and the latter to the materialization of risk in injury to the plaintiff. Duty and proximate cause integrate these termini into a normatively coherent unit by characterizing in terms of the same unreasonable risk the wrongfulness of what the defendant did and of what the plaintiff suffered. The result is that the duty of care is a member of an interconnected ensemble of concepts through which the parties to a finding of negligence can be understood as doer and sufferer of the same injustice.

3. Right and correlative duty

Having situated the duty of care within the ensemble of concepts that allows negligence liability to be understood as a normatively coherent phenomenon, I want in this section to focus more specifically on the duty itself. What are its constituents and how do they give expression, in accordance with corrective justice, to the correlativity of right and duty? The answer to this question indicates the internal structure of the duty of care, thus revealing (in Lord Atkin's words) "the general conception of relations giving rise to a duty of care, of which the particular cases found in the books are but instances."[25]

Cardozo's judgment denying liability in *Palsgraf* provides the most explicit judicial elucidation of the correlativity of right and duty in the negligence context. Cardozo observes that liability requires that

---

[25] Above, n. 1.

"the plaintiff sues in her own right for a wrong personal to her, and not as the vicarious beneficiary of a breach of duty to another. A different conclusion would involve us, and swiftly too, in a maze of contradictions."[26] In *Palsgraf* the defendant arguably created an unreasonable risk to the third party's package but was being sued for a wrongful infringement of the plaintiff's right to bodily integrity. The right that the defendant unreasonably put at risk was therefore different from the right whose wrongful infringement was the basis of the plaintiff's complaint. The duty to the person carrying the package was thus not correlative to the plaintiff's right in her bodily integrity. Liability to the plaintiff would mean that the defendant was being held liable for the infringement of a right that its employee did not wrongfully imperil, so that the award of damages would then not represent the wrong that the defendant did. The contradiction is that under these circumstances liability to the plaintiff would be inconsistent with the nature of tort law as a mechanism for obligating defendants to make reparation for the rights that they have wrongfully injured.

As Cardozo points out, *Palsgraf* featured a particularly striking example of "the maze of contradictions." *Palsgraf* was a case in which the defendant's breach of duty and the plaintiff's complaint involved a diversity both in the nature of the rights (property and personal integrity) and in the holders of the rights (the passenger carrying the package and the injured plaintiff). Cardozo correctly observes that the same contradiction would obtain even if the rights were of the same order but the person foreseeably endangered was different from the person actually injured.[27] He also suggests, as *Wagon Mound (No.1)* later decided, that the contradiction would also be present if the discrepancy between the defendant's breach and the plaintiff's injury were to rights of different orders.[28] In all these instances there would be no liability because the plaintiff would have been injured with respect to a right that was not the basis of the duty that the defendant breached.

When negligence law is conceived in terms of the correlativity of right and duty, the issue of the duty of care is composed of two constituents. First, the interest of the plaintiff that is protected against the defendant's conduct must have the status of a right as against the

---

[26] Palsgraf v. Long Island Railroad Co., above n. 15, at 100.
[27] Ibid.
[28] Ibid., at 101.

defendant. Second, the duty breached must be correlative to that right. These two constituents are the complementary aspects of a unified conception of the duty of care, because a right both implies and is required by the correlative structure of liability. A right *implies* correlativity because a right always entails the existence of a corresponding duty. A right *is required by* correlativity, because (along with its corresponding duty) it is the only normative concept that has the correlative structure inherent in a regime of liability. Thus, the notions of right and correlative duty together form a unified general conception of the duty of care.

Cardozo's treatment of duty in the *Palsgraf* case gives paradigmatic legal expression to this conception of the duty of care. For Cardozo, the principal issue presented by the case was that of correlativity. Because in that case the defendant's conduct was not wrongful toward the plaintiff (although it was arguably wrongful toward someone else), the defendant was held not to be under a duty with respect to the plaintiff's loss. Although Cardozo's focus was on the absence of correlativity between the duty breached and the injury, Cardozo also insists that the duty breached has to be correlative to a right: "Negligence is not actionable unless it involves the invasion of a legally protected interest, the violation of a right."[29] Because "the commission of a wrong imports the violation of a right,"[30] the plaintiff is precluded from recovering unless the defendant's conduct is a wrong in relation to that right. Hence, "[w]hat the plaintiff must show is a wrong to herself, i.e., a violation of her own right."[31] That the plaintiff had a right to her bodily security was not disputed in the case, but the defendant's action was not wrongful relative to that right. Thus, Cardozo affirms that the existence of a right in the plaintiff is presupposed in the requirement that the duty breached by the defendant be a wrong relative to her.

Accordingly, Cardozo's opinion presents the two interrelated functions of the inquiry into the defendant's duty. The first function is to establish whether the plaintiff's damaged interest has the status of a right, because it is only to a right that the defendant's duty can be correlative. The second function is to establish whether correlativity obtains in the case at hand—that is, whether the defendant breached a

[29] Ibid., at 99.
[30] Ibid., at 101.
[31] Ibid., at 100.

duty correlative to that right by creating an unreasonable risk to persons such as the plaintiff. When these two functions are brought together, the question of duty produces a structure of inquiry geared to ascertaining whether the parties can plausibly be regarded as the doer and sufferer of the same injustice. Action by the defendant that is incompatible with the plaintiff's right marks the injustice of the defendant's conduct, and that injustice is the same for both parties.

Injury to a right differs from the suffering of harm or loss. A right immediately signifies the existence of a correlative duty; harm or loss does not. Neither the harm as something suffered by the plaintiff nor the process of suffering it at the defendant's hand establishes a link between the parties that is at once correlative and juridically normative. Being harmed is merely a fact—that the harmed person is now less advantageously situated than before—that in itself has no correlative normative significance. And the plaintiff's suffering of harm at the defendant's hand links the parties historically through the link between consequence and cause or grammatically as object and subject of the same verb, rather than normatively as the doer and sufferer of an injustice. Because one can be harmed without being wronged, harm considered in itself is not a notion from which one can, within the correlative structure of negligence law, impute a wrong. Harm matters only inasmuch as it stands under a right, for only when the duty breached by the defendant is correlative to the plaintiff's right do the parties occupy correlative normative positions. Accordingly, if the loss of which the plaintiff is complaining is not the subject matter of a right or if the defendant's conduct is not wrongful with respect to that right, then the defendant is not under a duty of care to the plaintiff.

The supposed absence of a right accounts for some of the situations where the common law does not recognize (or earlier had been reluctant to recognize) the existence of a duty. In situations of nonfeasance, for example, the entitlement claimed is not merely to one's own physical integrity—which *ex hypothesi* the defendant has not endangered— but to the defendant's positive assistance. Under the common law, however, one has no general right to be benefited by another. Similarly, the perceived absence of a right in the plaintiff also may explain, at least in part, the law's slowness to recognize negligence liability for psychiatric and prenatal injury. In the case of psychiatric injury, the psychological interest was perhaps regarded as too speculative or insubstantial to count as part of one's right to physical integrity. Over the past century a stronger appreciation of the psychological aspect of physical integrity has rightly led to a steady broadening of liability and to a growing dissatisfaction with arbitrary restrictions.[32] In the case of prenatal injuries, the common law position that legal personality begins at birth allowed them not to be viewed as violations of the child's rights. This fallacious view has now been repudiated: even if the plaintiff was not in existence at the time of the negligent act, that act can subsequently materialize in a wrongful infringement of the plaintiff's right to physical integrity.

The role of rights has also been crucial for the traditional approach to liability for economic loss.[33] Traditionally the common law restricted liability to situations in which the economic loss represented the quantified value of a right belonging to the plaintiff and negligently injured by the defendant. On this basis the plaintiff could recover for "financial damage...consequential on foreseeable physical injury or damage to property"[34]—that is, for lost earnings because of physical injury or for the lost economic value of property negligently damaged by the defendant. In such cases the basis of liability was the plaintiff's right to physical integrity or to the exclusive use of the property. Concomitant to these rights—indeed, part of their meaning—was a correlative obligation on others (including the defendant) not to wrongfully interfere. The economic loss was merely the monetary measure of the right's infringement. Conversely, if the economic loss was independent of a right that ran between the parties, the plaintiff could not recover for it. The law thereby recognized that a set of economic advantages enjoyed or anticipated by the plaintiff was not in itself the subject matter of a right. Although such economic advantages make the plaintiff better off than he or she would be without them, they have no inherently correlative significance for anyone else; the defendant, therefore, was not liable for them. Negligence law expressed this conclusion about these free-standing economic losses by saying either that no duty of care existed toward someone whose

---

[32] The treatment of psychiatric injury in England, where "control mechanisms" function "as more or less arbitrary conditions" to restrict liability (White v. Chief Constable of South Yorkshire Police [1999] 2 A.C. 455, at 502 (H.L.)) has been particularly unfortunate; see the criticism of the English approach in Tame v. New South Wales; Annetts v. Australian Stations Pty [2002] 191 A.L.R. 449 (H.C. Aust.).

[33] On economic loss, see the important article by Peter Benson, "The Basis for Excluding Liability for Economic Loss in Tort," in *Philosophical Foundations of Tort Law*, ed. David Owen (1995), 427.

[34] Spartan Steel & Alloys v. Martin [1972] 3 All E.R. 557, at 571 (C.A., per Lawton L.J.).

proprietary right was not injured or that such losses, being the result of an injury to someone else's rights, were too remote.[35] The traditionally restrictive approach to economic loss, then, excludes liability except as compensation for wrongful injury to the plaintiff's right. In the standard instances of lost income or diminished value, the right in question is, respectively, a right to bodily integrity and a right to property or possession, where the entitlement against the defendant is merely an aspect of the plaintiff's exclusive entitlement against the whole world. These rights precede the plaintiff's interaction with any specific defendant. With respect to them the defendant is under a duty to act with reasonable care because the whole world is.[36] During the twentieth century another kind of right gained recognition in the context of economic losses resulting from negligent misrepresentation.[37] This was a right based on justified detrimental

---

[35] The former formulation is exemplified by Weller v. Foot and Mouth Disease Research Institute [1966] 1 Q.B. 569 (Q.B.D.), the latter by Connecticut Mutual Life Insurance v. New York and New Hampshire Railroad [1856] Conn. 265 (S.C.). The paradigmatic situation, of which these cases are examples, is that of the plaintiff who operates a business that depends on some facility (e.g., a bridge, pipeline, electrical cable) that the plaintiff does not own but that is negligently damaged by the defendant, causing the plaintiff economic loss because business operations cannot proceed as normal. One cannot plausibly argue that, within the systemic logic of the law, the plaintiff has a right to the free-standing economic gain that he or she was prevented from realizing. Because the parties are strangers, there is no possibility of an *in personam* right. Nor can the plaintiff have an *in rem* right to the prospective economic gain. First, the intentional diversion of the gain by a competitor is permissible; but it would be a very odd *in rem* right if someone could rightfully interfere with it intentionally but not negligently. Second, the plaintiff can have a right to an external thing only if the plaintiff has acquired that thing; but there is no mode of acquisition for the prospective economic gain from the existence of another's facility. Indeed, the classic case of acquisition, Pierson v. Post, 3 Caines (N.Y.) 175 (1805) repudiates the notion that the prospect of a gain in itself creates a right. (I am indebted to Abraham Drassinower for discussion of these points.) And so the plaintiff's argument must be based on the suffering of the economic loss even though the plaintiff had no right to what was lost. This is the argument that the common law traditionally rejected using the language of duty or remoteness.

[36] The question of whether in any particular case the plaintiff had a right as against the defendant is of course subject to legal argument, even in the case of the proprietary and possessory rights that are paradigmatic in this context; see, for example, Courtenay v. Knutson [1957] 26 D.L.R. (2d) 768 (B.C.S.C.) (liability to the bailee of a barge). An interesting variant is Perre v. Apand [1999] 164 A.L.R. 606 (H.C. Aust.), where the defendant, by supplying diseased seed to one potato grower, caused potatoes of the plaintiff, a neighboring potato grower, to be embargoed even though the plaintiff's crops were not infected. The defendant was held liable for the plaintiff's economic loss; although the defendant's land was not contaminated, the defendant's negligence caused it to be treated as if it were.

[37] Glanzer v. Shepard, 135 N.E. 275 (N.Y.C.A., 1921); Hedley Byrne v. Heller [1964] A.C. 465 (H.L.). See the exemplary treatment by Benson, above n. 33, at 450–54.

reliance, created through the interaction of the parties and giving the plaintiff an entitlement as against the defendant specifically, to recover the economic loss flowing from the defendant's reliance-inviting conduct. Although the plaintiff has no right against the world for economic loss as such, in situations of justified detrimental reliance the plaintiff recovers for economic loss because of the special relationship that arose between the parties. The relationship is special in that, given the circumstances in which the misrepresentation took place, the defendant can reasonably be regarded as having invited the plaintiff to rely on it for a particular transaction or kind of transaction, and thus as having voluntarily assumed responsibility for the loss that results from that transaction.[38] After leading the plaintiff reasonably to rely on the representation or on other reliance-inviting conduct for the kind of transaction in question, the defendant cannot fairly disclaim responsibility for the consequences. What places the loss within the scope of the defendant's duty is the imputation to the defendant, based on his or her knowledge of the purpose to be served by the representation, of an express or implied invitation to the plaintiff (or to the class of persons that includes the plaintiff) to rely on the representation for that kind of purpose.[39] This purpose, known by the defendant and detrimentally acted upon by the plaintiff, links the defendant's act to the plaintiff's loss by making the prospect of the loss the reason for considering the act to have been negligent. Using the analogy of contract,[40] one might say that by making the representation the defendant has offered the plaintiff information that purports to be reliable for the purpose of a particular kind of transaction, and that the plaintiff, by detrimentally acting on this information, has accepted it as reliable for the purpose for which it was offered. Therefore, to the extent of the plaintiff's detrimental reliance, tort law views the plaintiff's pre-existing economic situation as an entitlement that runs against the defendant. The basis of the entitlement—the invitation to rely for a particular (kind of) purpose—also defines the scope of the duty

---

[38] The fact that the entitlement is created through the interaction of the parties and is thus personal to them rather than good against the whole world puts the parties into what Lord Devlin called "a relationship equivalent to contract"; Hedley Byrne v. Heller, above n. 37, at 530.

[39] For example, in Haig v. Bamford [1976] 72 D.L.R. (3d) 68 (S.C.C.), the defendant knew the purpose for which it was asked to prepare an audited financial statement. Similarly, in Hedley Byrne v. Heller, above n. 37, the defendant knew the purpose of the plaintiff's inquiry about its client's credit-worthiness.

[40] See above n. 38.

correlative to it. Accordingly, detrimental reliance that falls outside the purpose for which the representation was made does not lead to liability even if the reliance that the representation in fact occasions is reasonably foreseeable.[41] Because it is created by justified detrimental reliance, the entitlement in question applies only as between the parties; it does not count as a right held by the plaintiff against the world as a whole. Recognition of such an entitlement thereby leaves intact the traditional restrictions on recovery for economic loss, which reflect the idea that economic advantage (and the prospect of impairing it) does not as such generate duties in everyone else to avoid causing loss.

In the traditional treatment of liability for economic loss, no difficulty arises about what some of the more recent cases regard as crucial, the avoidance (in Cardozo's famous words) of "liability in an indeterminate amount for an indeterminate time to an indeterminate class."[42] It is of course true that, given the interdependence of economic activity within society, economic losses to some will foreseeably lead to further economic losses to others, which in turn will foreseeably lead to still further economic losses, and so on. But the indeterminacy of losses is problematic only if liability is a response to the suffering of a loss. Implicit within the traditional treatment of economic loss, however, is the notion that tort law concerns itself not with losses as such but with injuries to rights, so that economic losses matter only as quantifications of those injuries. The plaintiff's right, therefore, both grounds and limits the defendant's liability.

One should, therefore, appreciate the significance of references, such as Cardozo's, to indeterminate liability in the traditional treatment of economic loss. The point is not that liability for economic loss as such exists but has to be cut off to avoid indeterminacy. Rather, the prospect of indeterminacy is adduced to indicate the implausibility of supposing that such liability exists to begin with. As Cardozo himself said, the indeterminate nature of the supposed liability "enkindle[s] doubt whether a flaw may not exist in the implication of a duty that exposes to these consequences."[43]

In recent years some jurisdictions (Australia and Canada among them)[44] have abandoned the traditional framework of liability for eco-

---

[41] Caparo Industries v. Dickman [1990] 1 All E.R. 568 (H.L.).
[42] Ultramares v. Touche, 174 N.E. 441 (N.Y.C.A., 1931), at 444.
[43] Ibid.; see also Weller v. Foot and Mouth Disease Research Institute, above n. 35.
[44] Caltex Oil (Australia) v. The Dredge "Willemstad" [1976] 11 Aust. L.R. 227 (H.C.); Canadian National Railway v. North Pacific Steamship [1992] 91 D.L.R. (4th) 289 (S.C.C.).

nomic loss. The basis of the defendant's liability has shifted from injuring a right to inflicting a loss. Loss differs from right in that it lacks both the distinct legal content and the correlative significance that together impose coherent limits on liability. Yet, as is universally acknowledged, some limit must be formulated because the interdependence of economic interests makes it intolerable for liability to follow merely from the foreseeability of creating an economic loss. Accordingly, the duty of care imposed on the defendant by the foreseeability of the plaintiff's loss is made subject to the limitation of a policy-based notion of "proximity."

This development has been accompanied by a transformation of the role of Cardozo's famous phrase about indeterminate liability. Almost invariably invoked in the judgments on economic loss, it is no longer taken as an indication that the basis of negligence liability must be sought elsewhere than in the foreseeable loss. Instead, it has become the prelude to attempts to mark the border to which liability based on foreseeable loss is to expand. The prospect of indeterminate liability prompts the court to assess whether, in the circumstances of the particular case, the plaintiff's loss was (despite its foreseeability) insufficiently proximate to the defendant's negligence. That foreseeability of loss is the basis of liability is taken for granted; the focus is on the criterion for limiting liability.[45]

However, formulating the limiting conditions that satisfy the requirement of proximity in a principled way has turned out to be troublesome. This is hardly surprising. Unlike the notions of right and correlative duty, loss and proximity do not form a unified juridical conception. Proximity limits foreseeability by considerations that are not intrinsic to it. On the one hand, foreseeable losses are initially regarded as possibly worthy of attracting liability simply by reason of their being foreseeable losses. On the other hand, such losses are not ultimately regarded as worthy of attracting liability except through the additional presence of proximity factors that artificially limit the reach of liability. Because the same normative considerations do not both ground and limit liability, a constant tension arises between the unrelated normative impulses that respectively support and confine the defendant's duty. Having abandoned the inner coherence of having restrictions on liability that are conceptually indigenous to the

---

[45] Bruce P. Feldthusen, "Liability for Pure Economic Loss: Yes, But Why?" (1999) 28 West. Aust. L. Rev. 84.

correlativity of right and duty, the courts struggle to formulate new and artificial restrictions on the excessively broad liability that would be engendered by the mere foreseeability of loss.[46] In this respect, the new approach to liability for economic loss represents a jurisprudential decline.

How, finally, does correlativity illuminate Lord Atkin's general conception of the duty of care? Adapting the biblical precept that one is to love one's neighbor, Lord Atkin famously characterized the "neighbor" to whom the duty of care is owed as "persons so closely and directly affected by my act that I ought to have them in mind as being so affected."[47] In the correlative conception of liability, the obligation on the defendant to have these persons in mind arises from their possession of a right that runs against the defendant and thus places the defendant under an obligation not injure it. An act "closely and directly" affects this right when the act's tendency to endanger the right is a reason for considering the act negligent. The duty that results is one that draws its justification from its correlativity with the plaintiff's right. Such a duty defines the "relationship between the parties" in terms that are at once legal and general. The legal dimension lies in demanding not the beneficence of neighborly love, which Lord Atkin considered excessively broad for a legal system, but the more restricted avoidance of injury. The general dimension lies in construing this legal notion of injury as expressing the most general normative categories applicable to the relationship between the parties in private law, that of right and correlative duty. Because correlativity requires that the content of the right be the same as the object of the duty, the plaintiff's suffering is unjust for the same reason that the defendant's action

---

[46] Among the markers of proximity that have been suggested are: knowledge that the defendant has or ought to have of the specific individual(s) likely to suffer economic loss (Stevenson J. in *Canadian National Railway*, above n. 44); Mason J. in *Caltex Oil*, above n. 44; knowledge that the defendant has or ought to have of the class of first line victims (McHugh J. in *Perre*, above n. 36); salient features about the defendant's actual or constructive knowledge of the prospective injury, about the nature of the detriment and about the nature of the damages claimed (Stephen J. in *Caltex Oil*, above n. 44); the relationship between the parties, physical propinquity, assumed or imposed obligations and close causal connection (McLachlin J. in *Canadian National Railway*, above n. 44); the pre-existence of contractual arrangements between the parties (Martel Building v. Canada [2002] S.C.R. 860). Acknowledging that their treatments of the problem of indeterminate recovery are themselves quite indeterminate, Stephen J. and McLachlin J. expect that over time the judicial decisions will crystallize the characteristic features of various situations for future guidance. One can be skeptical, however, that the positive law will provide legal certainty if it lacks conceptual coherence.

[47] Above, n. 1.

is. This conception of the duty of care thus captures the coherence presupposed in Lord Atkin's insistence that, aside from particular duties, there must be a general conception of duty that all particular duties instantiate.

4. The two-stage test for the duty of care

As the previous sections indicate, one can discern two broad strategies for elucidating the duty of care. One strategy, represented pre-eminently by the landmark cases of the twentieth century, coherently integrates the duty of care both into the entire ensemble of negligence concepts and into the correlativity of right and duty. Under this strategy the plaintiff's right both grounds and limits the defendant's liability. An alternative strategy, evident in Andrews's dissenting opinion in *Palsgraf* and in the more recent economic loss cases, allows the foreseeability of loss initially to expand the scope of liability, which is then limited by some other mechanism. In Andrews's opinion the danger to anyone creates a duty to whoever is in fact injured, but proximate cause excludes certain consequences from the expanded liability that would otherwise ensue. In the more recent economic loss cases, the foreseeability of loss triggers a duty subject to considerations of proximity that address the problem of indeterminacy. Under this strategy the limit emerges from a factor independent of the one that creates the initial possibility of liability.

In the last decades of the twentieth century several common law jurisdictions developed a comprehensive version of this latter strategy. Starting from the idea that Lord Atkin's neighbor principle "ought to apply unless there is some justification or valid explanation for its exclusion,"[48] the House of Lords worked out a two-stage test for the duty of care.[49] This test was adopted elsewhere and, although subsequently abandoned in England and Australia, continues to be used in a number of jurisdictions.[50] The two-stage test required the courts to consider, first, whether the parties had a relationship as neighbors that was sufficient to give rise to a prima facie duty and, then, whether

---

[48] Home Office v. Dorset Yacht [1970] A.C. 1004, at 1027 (H.L., per Lord Reid).

[49] Anns v. Merton London Borough Council [1978] A.C. 728 (H.L.).

[50] Daniel More, "The Boundaries of Negligence," (2003) 4 Theoretical Inquiries in Law 339, 343−45.

there were any considerations that ought to negative or limit the duty. Foreseeability of loss was a significant component of the first stage, opening the road to a broad liability that the second stage could narrow.

Perhaps the most steadfast champion of the two-stage test has been the Supreme Court of Canada, which has continued to apply it even after its repudiation by the House of Lords. In its current Canadian formulation the two-stage test goes as follows:

In order to decide whether or not a private law duty of care existed, two questions must be asked:
    1. is there a sufficiently close relationship between the parties...so that in the reasonable contemplation of the [defendant], carelessness on its part might cause damage to [the plaintiff]? If so,
    2. are there any considerations that ought to negative or limit (a) the scope of the duty (b) the class of persons to whom it is owed or (c) the damages to which the breach of it may give rise?[51]

The first stage of this formulation incorporates the traditional notion of reasonable foreseeability to establish a prima facie duty. At this stage the judge attempts to discern "whether, as a matter of simple justice, the defendant may be said to have had an obligation to be mindful of the plaintiff's interests."[52] The second stage allows that prima facie duty to be circumscribed or cancelled because of the presence of "policy concerns that are extrinsic to simple justice but that are nevertheless fundamentally important."[53]

The two-stage test has radically altered negligence law in Canada. Negligence analysis no longer consists in scrutinizing the parties' relationship in the light of a coherent series of concepts. The mode of argument that underpinned the great doctrinal achievements of the twentieth century has been abandoned. Instead of examining whether the materialization of the risk created by the defendant is an injustice to the plaintiff, the test directs the court to a mélange of justice and policy considerations. This momentous change has had several questionable features. In this section I outline these features, then illustrate the operation of some of them by comparing a Canadian case with its

[51] Kamloops v. Nielsen [1984] 10 D.L.R. (4th) 641, at 662 (S.C.C.).
[52] Hercules Managements v. Ernst & Young [1997] 146 D.L.R. (4th) 577, at 591 (S.C.C.).
[53] Ibid.

English counterpart, and finally discuss a recent Canadian case that, although reaffirming and supposedly clarifying the two-stage test, may mark the court's initial step back to a more coherent jurisprudence.

Application of the two-stage test has the following characteristics. First, policy considerations relevant to the second stage have the power to override the conclusions about justice reached in the first stage. These policy considerations are uncontrolled by the relationship between the parties and indeed may be beyond the court's institutional competence to judge. A plaintiff can therefore be denied compensation on the basis of policy considerations that, while one-sidedly pertinent to the defendant or to persons carrying on a similar activity, have no normative bearing on the position of the plaintiff as the sufferer of an injustice. From the plaintiff's point of view, the denial of recovery, operating (as the court says) extrinsically to simple justice, amounts to the judicial confiscation of what was rightly due to the plaintiff in order to subsidize policy objectives unilaterally favorable to the defendant and those similarly situated.

Second, even as policy analysis the second stage is one-sided. It refers only to policy considerations that negative liability, not to those that might confirm liability. Under the court's formulation, the plaintiff's claim for compensation is entirely constituted by the first stage; the second stage is devoted to factors favorable to defendants. Although the court occasionally gestures in the direction of a policy adverse to the defendant, it rarely engages either in an extended examination of that policy or in a rigorous comparison of the competing policy considerations.[54] Indeed, to do so would expose a further difficulty: that,

---

[54] In defense of the court on this point, Justice Major said that:

> this criticism is too narrow in view of what was said in *Hercules* [above, n. 52]. In that case LaForest J. considered not only indeterminate liability, which is a policy consideration that negates liability, but also deterrence, which is a policy consideration that favours liability. Although the concern for indeterminate liability won the day, it is clear that the policy analysis was not completely one-sided.

Major, "Anns and the Law of Negligence," in The Continuing Legal Education Society of British Columbia, Torts—2001, posted 12 April 2001 at <http://www.cle.bc.ca/CLE/Analysis/Collection/01-5123601-anns>. In *Hercules* the court's entire treatment of deterrence was as follows:

> Certain authors have argued that imposing broad duties of care on auditors would give rise to significant social and economic benefits so far as the spectre of tort liability would act as an incentive to auditors to produce accurate (i.e., non-negligent) reports. [References]. I would agree that deterrence of negligent conduct is an important policy consideration with respect to auditors' liability. Nonetheless I am of the view that, in the final analysis, it is outweighed by the socially undesirable consequences to which the imposition of indeterminate liability on auditors might lead.

Hercules, above n. 52, 593. It seems extravagant to characterize this desultory mention of deterrence as showing that deterrence was "considered" in the "policy analysis."

given the heterogeneity of possible policy considerations, a rigorous comparison would require the elaboration and application of some metric of social gains and losses—a task beyond judicial competence. How, for instance, is a court to know whether, in a case of negligent misrepresentation by auditors, the benefits of deterring carelessness are outweighed by the disadvantages of indeterminate liability?[55] It is therefore hardly surprising that the policy considerations that interest the court are those that, as the wording of the test indicates, "ought to negative or limit" the duty.[56]

Third, the relationship between plaintiff and defendant is fragmented not only by the very presence at the second stage of policy concerns extrinsic to that relationship, but also by the disjunction between the justice and policy considerations of the two stages. This disjunction, in turn, requires judges to balance categorically different considerations, in order to determine whether in a given case the policy considerations are more important than the justice considerations that they can displace. How is this balancing of incommensurables to be done? In effect, the two-stage test puts into circulation two different normative currencies between which no rate of exchange exists.

Fourth, the two-stage test transfigures the notion of foreseeability itself. When considered within the framework of injustice done and suffered, foreseeability is an intrinsically correlative notion through which the law constructs the identical nature of the injustice on both sides by linking the plaintiff's injury to the reason for characterizing the defendant's action as wrongful. Accordingly, foreseeability is internally limited by the scope of the wrongfulness to which it refers. In contrast, under the two-stage test, foreseeability constitutes a "relatively low threshold"[57] for recognizing a prima facie duty, which is

---

[55] *Hercules*, above n. 52, at 593.

[56] For example, in Dobson v. Dobson [1999] 174 D.L.R. 1, at 31 (S.C.C.) the court held that a mother was not liable for the prenatal injuries that she caused her own child by her negligent driving. Although injury was foreseeable under the first stage, the court negatived liability on policy grounds in order to safeguard the pregnant woman's autonomy and privacy. However, the court also rejected the suggestion that the existence of a mandatory automobile insurance regime justified liability on policy grounds. Thus, a judicially enunciated policy prevented the victim of negligent driving from gaining access to insurance proceeds whose availability had been legislated. Elsewhere, in Canadian National Railway v. Norsk Pacific Steamship, above n. 44, the court had given extensive attention to insurance factors in determining whether to deny liability, but insurance is apparently not available as a policy factor that can support liability at the second stage of the two-stage test.

[57] Ingles v. City of Toronto [2000] 183 D.L.R. (4th) 193, at 202 (S.C.C.); Ryan v. City of Victoria [1999] 168 D.L.R. (4th) 513, at 525 (S.C.C.). In these cases the court treats proximity

then extrinsically limited by policy considerations. Any reasonably prospective damage counts as being foreseeable under the first stage of the test, without inquiry into why the defendant's action should be characterized as a wrongful infringement of the plaintiff's right.[58]

Fifth, even taken on its own the first stage is internally fractured. Although the formulation of the first stage refers to the existence of "a sufficiently close connection between the parties," that connection is analyzed not (as coherence would require) in terms of a reason for characterizing the defendant's action as a wrong relative to the plaintiff's right, but as a combination of two factors, foreseeability (with its low threshold) and proximity. Thus, in its first stage the two-stage test takes over the tensions, noted in the discussion of economic loss in the previous section of this essay, that result from ascribing to proximity a policy-based limiting function; the second stage then piles on top of proximity yet another layer of policy considerations that also have a limiting function. Within this complex structure, "proximity" is merely a conclusory label that, as the court frankly observed, states a result without itself providing a principled basis for liability.[59] It stands for a variety of case-specific factors that go to the determination of whether it is fair and just, having regard to the relationship between the parties, to impose a prima facie duty of care.[60] Where the duty of care has already been recognized by law, proximity is the term under which

---

as yielding a low threshold that is synonymous with reasonable foreseeability, not as imposing an additional restriction. *Ryan* formulates the first stage as follows:

> In order to establish a *prima facie* duty of care, it must be shown that a relationship of proximity existed between the parties such that it was reasonably foreseeable that a careless act by the [defendant] could result in injury to the [plaintiff].
>
> In *Ingles* the formulation is substantially the same, except that "would" replaces "could."

[58] As Robert Keeton observed:

> [P]utting the crucial question in terms of whether the injuries were foreseeable…carries the misleading implication that the scope of legal responsibility extends to every consequence that is foreseeable as a possibility in any degree…The crucial standard is better expressed as the question whether all her injuries were within those risks by reason of which the defendant's conduct was characterized as negligence.

Robert Keeton, *Legal Cause in the Law of Torts* (1963), 55. A graphic expression of how low the threshold of foreseeability can be appears in Modbury Triangle Shopping Centre v. Anzil [2000] 176 A.L.R. 411, at 436 (H.C. Aust., per Hayne J.):

> In almost every case in which a plaintiff suffers damage it is foreseeable that, if reasonable care is not taken, harm may follow. As Dixon CJ said in argument in Chapman v. Hearse, 'I cannot understand why any event that does happen is not foreseeable by a person of sufficient imagination and intelligence.' Foresight of harm is not sufficient to show that a duty of care exists.

[59] *Hercules*, above n. 52, at 588.
[60] Cooper v. Hobart [2001] 206 D.L.R. (4th) 193, at 204 (S.C.C.).

one subsumes the various factors that differentiate the different categories of liability, such as physical and proprietary harms, negligent misrepresentation, certain cases of economic loss, the municipality's obligation to prospective purchasers to inspect new housing developments, the duty of public authorities who have undertaken a policy of road maintenance to execute the maintenance with due care, and so on.[61] In this way proximity thematizes not the unifying principle underlying the general conception of duty, but the disparateness of particular kinds of duty.

In short, the introduction of the two-stage test has transformed Canadian negligence law into an enquiry into one-sided policy considerations at the ultimate stage that are extrinsic to justice between the parties and that are mysteriously balanced against a first stage that combines an excessively expansive notion of foreseeability with the invocation, under the term "proximity," of a miscellany of limiting case-specific factors. This ramshackle enquiry, composed of mutually alien parts that labor to contain the specter of unlimited liability that it itself lets loose, is hardly conducive to the elaboration of coherent and principled justifications for liability. The test represents a high point for the disintegration of duty. It conceives of the notion of duty as internally fragmented between and within its stages. It also conceives of the duties themselves as particular species each of which represents its own specific considerations of policy and proximity. All that remains of Lord Atkin's notion of a general conception is the comprehensive verbal umbrella that applies to, but does not coherently unify, these different duties.

A contrasting pair of cases illustrates some of these themes. In the past few years the highest courts in England and then in Canada have dealt with the liability of auditors for negligently preparing the annual report of a corporation's accounts. As is well known, investors in the stock market buy and sell on the basis of the information in these reports. Previously, accountants had been held liable for the reliance losses caused by negligence in a report they knew was prepared for the guidance of a specific class of investors with respect to a specific class of transactions.[62] The question that now arose was whether investors generally could recover for their admittedly foreseeable reliance on statements in a report prepared for the corporation's annual meeting. Both

<hr>

[61] Ibid., at 205.
[62] Haig v. Bamford [1976] 72 D.L.R. 68 (S.C.C.).

the English and the Canadian courts answered in the negative, but they used different modes of reasoning.

For the House of Lords,[63] the crucial issue was whether the requisite normative link existed between the defendant's negligence and the plaintiff's loss. Foreseeability of the loss could not ground liability, because the duty of care could not be considered in abstraction from the kind of damage which the defendant must avoid causing. In this case the audit was presented to fulfill a statutory obligation aimed at the informed exercise by the corporation's stakeholders of their powers of corporate governance. Because the plaintiff's loss was not connected to the purpose of the audit, the defendant owed no duty of care with respect to that loss.

The Canadian case[64] followed the English decision in result but transformed the structure of its thought. Applying the two-stage test, the Supreme Court of Canada determined that a prima facie duty of care arose because investor reliance on the audit was both reasonable and foreseeable. This duty, however, was negatived by the undesirable social consequences of the indeterminate liability generated by so broad a conception of foreseeability. Among these consequences were the increased insurance premiums, the higher costs faced by accountants, the opportunity costs in time spent on litigation rather than on generating accounting revenue, reduction in the availability in accounting services as marginal firms are driven to the wall, and increased costs for consumers. Looking to the purpose of the auditor's report, as was done in the English case, was, "in reality, nothing more that a means by which to circumscribe—for reasons of policy—the scope of the representor's potentially unlimited liability."[65]

The contrast between these two cases is stark. The English judgment straightforwardly applied the mode of reasoning that had been set out in the classic twentieth-century cases adapted to negligent representation. The House of Lords examined whether the investor suffered the kind of loss that lies within the scope of the auditor's duty, which, in turn, was defined and limited by the purpose for which the audit was required. Given that such audits are not prepared for the guidance of decisions to buy or sell shares, the defendant could not be viewed as having assumed responsibility for the plaintiff's losses. Because these investment transactions fell outside the range of the defendant's duty,

---

[63] *Caparo*, above n. 41.
[64] *Hercules*, above n. 52.
[65] Ibid., at 590.

the plaintiff's loss, despite being the foreseeable outcome of a negligently prepared report, did not count as the suffering of a wrong at the defendant's hands. In this judgment the purpose of the audit functions as the normative idea through which the court considers the connection between parties. The reasoning is relational throughout, and liability is denied because the plaintiff's loss is not normatively correlated to the defendant's negligence.[66]

The Canadian case transforms this relational reasoning into a policy-based restriction on liability. The two-stage test, so the court claims, allows us to recognize the relational criteria "for what they really are— policy-based means by which to curtail liability."[67] Reliance that is reasonable and foreseeable, now no longer situated within the framework of doing and suffering the same injustice, creates a prima facie duty that is "potentially infinite."[68] To solve this problem of its own creation, the court curtails the scope of the duty by reference to policy factors. Hence, what the court calls the simple justice of the plaintiff's claim yields to the need to preserve the availability of accounting services in Canada. The court does not explain why justice is to be sacrificed to the need for accounting services, or why the policy to maintain accounting services outweighs the policy of deterrence, or how the court knows that the current level and pricing of accounting services in Canada is optimal. Instead of offering reasons for thinking that the defendant did not wrong the plaintiff, the court indulges in speculations beyond its competence about the undesirable consequences of liability for the providers and consumers of accounting services.[69]

These particular differences in the two judgments reflect a wider contrast between the nature of the justifications that they employ. The

---

[66] The following passage from the English case is a striking judicial formulation of the notion that the sequence from negligence to injury forms a single normative unit:

> [A] postulated duty of care must be stated with reference to the kind of damage that the plaintiff has suffered and in reference to the plaintiff or the class of which the plaintiff is a member...His duty of care is a thing written on the wind unless damage is caused by the breach of that duty; there is no actionable negligence unless duty, breach and consequential damage coincide...; for the purpose of determining liability in a given case, each element can be defined only in terms of the others.

Caparo, above n. 41, at 599 per Lord Oliver, quoting Brennan J. in Council of the Shire of Sutherland v. Heyman [1985] 60 Aust. L. Rep. 1, at 48 (H.C. Aust.).

[67] *Hercules*, above n. 52, at 592.

[68] Ibid., at 591.

[69] For similar speculations as to whether auditor liability for foreseeable loss is in the public interest, see Esanda Finance Corporation v. Peat Marwick Hungerfords (Reg) [1997] 142 A.L.R. 750, at 782 (H.C. Aust., per McHugh J.).

English judgment assumes that the justifications relevant to liability embrace both parties as the doer and the sufferer of the same injustice. Because of liability's correlative significance for both parties, such justifications are required if a judgment is to provide coherent reasons for considering whether one party is liable to the other. Conversely, a court that decided issues of liability without reference to such justifications would fail to treat the parties fairly in relation to each other. The reasoning in the Canadian judgment provides an example of this failure. Its expansive conception of foreseeability at the first stage focuses on the prospective damage that might result from the defendant's action without articulating the reason for regarding that damage as a wrongful injury to the plaintiff's right. Similarly, its restrictive elucidation of policy at the second stage deals only with the effect of liability on accountants and is thus unrelated to the plaintiff's claim to have suffered a wrong. As a result the judgment contains a series of unintegrated considerations that are divorced from the articulation of the wrong that might link the parties to the action. Such considerations are inherently incapable of fairly and coherently determining whether the defendant should be held liable to the plaintiff.

More recently the Supreme Court of Canada has reaffirmed the two-stage test, but in terms that might open a path back to a more coherent approach to the duty issue. In *Cooper v. Hobart*[70] the plaintiff was an investor who was suing for money lost by advancing funds to a registered mortgage broker who had used the funds for unauthorized purposes. The investor sued the statutory regulator, the Registrar of Mortgage Brokers, claiming that her losses would have been avoided or diminished had the Registrar acted more promptly in suspending the broker or notifying investors that the broker was under investigation. The court held that under the two-stage test the Registrar did not owe the investor a duty of care even though the investor might well have been able to show that her losses were the reasonably foreseeable consequence of the defendant's alleged negligence.

The crucial determination was that the proximity required by the first stage was lacking. The Registrar's powers and duties were entirely the creation of statute, and an analysis of the statute showed that the Registrar's duties were owed to the public rather than to individual investors. The point of the regulatory scheme was to ensure efficiency

---

[70] Cooper v. Hobart, above n. 60; see also the companion case Edwards v. The Law Society of Upper Canada [2001] 206 D.L.R. (4th) 211 (S.C.C.).

in the mortgage marketplace. This required the Registrar to consider not only the private interests of individual investors but also the public interests in access to capital through mortgage financing and in public confidence in the system as a whole. Consequently, the statute could not be construed to impose on the Registrar a tort duty of care that is specific to individual investors. Such a duty would be inconsistent with the overall regulatory purposes evident in the powers granted under the statute. The statutory purpose thus defined the notion of proximity applicable to the relationship of the parties. The court's conclusion was that even if foreseeability was present, proximity was not. Therefore, the search for a duty of care did not survive the first stage. However, for the sake of completeness, the court proceeded to the second stage, where it found that even if a prima facie duty had been established, it would have been negated for overriding policy reasons.

Even as the court reaffirms the two-stage test, a significant feature of this decision is the comparative effacement of the second stage in the overall architecture of the court's thought. The second stage remains as the point at which one examines "residual policy considerations" that concern not the relationship between the parties but the effect of postulating a duty on the legal system and society more generally.[71] However, in contrast to the court's previous jurisprudence, which had often treated the second stage as decisive, the second stage has now become less prominent.

There are three indications of this. First, the court explicitly says that the second stage will never arise if the duty of care has fallen within a recognized category of liability. Moreover, in this case (where the court indicated that overriding policy reasons would have negated a prima facie duty, even had one been found at the first stage) the considerations mentioned as relevant did little independent work. Most of the "residual policy considerations" centered on the Registrar's exercise of a public function entailing discretionary decisions that balance public and private interest. The policy considerations of the second stage were therefore not different in kind from the considerations that went to proximity at the first stage. Third, the court treated the purpose of the statutory provisions as relevant to the elucidation of proximity in the first stage, in striking contrast to its earlier treatment of the statutory requirement of an audit in the negligent mis-

---

[71] Cooper v. Hobart, above n. 60, at 206.

representation case mentioned earlier. The effect of using the statute to inform proximity is to bring the analysis close to the parallel English case, in which the duty was defined and limited by the purpose for which the statute mandated an audit. The court's application of the two-stage test in *Cooper v. Hobart* can, accordingly, perhaps be regarded as implicitly repudiating its earlier reduction of relational criteria to policy factors that are extrinsic to the parties' relationship.

Accordingly, the following picture emerges from *Cooper v. Hobart* about the second stage. The second stage is now to have only a restricted application; considerations that appear at the second stage may replicate the contents of proximity at the first stage; and factors previously considered at the second stage as extrinsic to the relationship are now to be analyzed as relational at the first stage. Perhaps, as its previous content is poured out of the second stage into the first and what remains is seen as redundant, Canadian courts will pay less and less attention to the second stage. Presumably, a duty found at the first stage will rarely be negated at the second stage.[72] If so, the new case will be seen as the first step in the atrophy of the two-stage test.

What about the first stage? *Cooper v. Hobart* contains a welcome emphasis on the relational nature of the considerations that govern the first stage.[73] Perhaps this attention to the relational aspect of the duty issue will be further strengthened if the second stage does indeed atrophy, and the reasoning about duty is effectively confined to the examination of what is foreseeable and proximate. For the moment, however, the court has not yet developed a fully adequate view of what it means for considerations to be relational. Instead of being understood as a coherent and integrated whole, the first stage is seen as an amalgam of foreseeability plus proximity, with proximity itself embodying a collection of specific indicia that vary with the particular relationship in question. Perhaps its newly announced sensitivity to the relational quality of the first stage will eventually lead the court to two salutary realizations. The first is that proximity cannot capture what is normatively significant about the relationship between the parties so long as it is regarded simply as something that is added to an expansive notion of foreseeability from the outside in order to restrict

---

[72] An example of this rare occurrence is R. v. Imperial Tobacco Canada [2011] 3 S.C.R. 45, in which the court held that policy reasons at the second stage negated a duty of care regarding negligent misrepresentations on which the plaintiffs' reliance was invited.

[73] "The proximity analysis involved in the first stage of the *Anns* test focuses on factors arising from the relationship between the plaintiff and the defendant." *Cooper*, above n. 60, at 203.

it. Rather (if these terms are to be used) proximity should be understood to reveal the restricted meaning that forseeability itself has in the negligence context—that is, that foreseeability is a way of inquiring into the risks by reference to which the defendant's action is characterized as negligent. The second is that the relational quality that the court now highlights has to be expressed in normative categories that are themselves relational. Accordingly, behind the particular duties must stand a general conception of duty governed by the correlativity of right and duty—that is, by a normative framework whose elements are intrinsically related to each other. Then the duty issue will again take its place in the coherent ensemble of concepts that treats the defendant's creation of the unreasonable risk and the plaintiff's suffering from the risk's materialization as falling under the same correlatively structured wrong.

5. Two notions of policy

This final section will focus on the connection between duty and policy. Throughout the common law world the notion that the formulation of the duty of care involves a determination of policy is accepted almost as a truism. In his tort judgments Lord Denning often gave voice to this supposed truism. For instance, whether correction officers owe a duty to persons whose property might be damaged by the escape of borstal trainees is, he said, "at bottom a matter of public policy that we as judges must resolve."[74] Similarly, in dealing with liability for economic loss he observed that "whenever the courts draw a line to mark out the bounds of duty, they do so as a matter of policy."[75] The argument in this section is that the link with policy, at least as it is commonly understood, has played a major role in the disintegration of duty and yet rests on a misconception.[76] The misconception involves running together two distinct notions of what policy means.

---

[74] Dorset Yacht v. Home Office [1969] 2 All E.R. 564, at 567 (C.A.).

[75] Spartan Steel & Alloys Ltd. v. Martin [1972] 3 All E.R. 557, at 561 (C.A.); see also Lamb v. London Borough of Camden [1981] Q.B. 625, at 636 (C.A.).

[76] The difficulties in the invocation of policy have been illuminatingly discussed in essays by Martin Stone; see Stone, "Focusing the Law: What Legal Interpretation is Not," in *Law and Interpretation: Essays in Legal Philosophy*, ed. Andrei Marmor (1995), 31, 72–84; Stone, "Formalism," in *The Oxford Handbook of Jurisprudence and Philosophy of Law*, ed. Jules Coleman and Scott Shapiro (2002), 166, 187–204.

The first notion is the common view that policy involves articulating some independently desirable goal(s) and then dealing with a particular tort case in a way that forwards these goals or, if they are in tension, balances some against others to produce a result that is desirable overall. The goals are independent both in the sense that they rest on justifications that are independent of tort law, to which they are then applied, and that they are independent of one another, so that they may represent incompatible normative impulses that need to be balanced. For instance, a favorite policy of Lord Denning was that losses should be widely distributed, because it is easier for many to bear comparatively small losses than for a single person to bear a comparatively heavy one.[77] The justification for this policy is independent of tort law, in that the policy states a normatively appealing way to deal with any sort of loss, not with a loss merely caused by tortious wrongdoing. Indeed, tort law imposes an artificial limit on its operation by restricting the distribution of losses to the insurance pool brought into play by tort law's initial allocation of the loss.[78] Moreover, when this policy favors the defendant, it may come into conflict with other policies, such as deterrence, that would be forwarded by liability. Hence, a determination that takes account of all the heterogeneous policies can be regarded as involving a process of balancing those that favor the plaintiff against those that favor the defendant.

The invocation of such independent policies entails the disintegration of duty as a systematic and coherent concept. Given the heterogeneity of the available policies and their different weightings in the balancing process, a systematically unified conception of duty based on (in Lord Atkin's words) "the element common to all cases in which [a duty] is found to exist"[79] is out of the question. The variety of policies and the shifting balance among them leaves no place for a common element on which the various duties (again in Lord Atkin's words) "must logically be based."[80] In these circumstances there can only be different specific kinds of duty, with each kind representing the particular policies or the particular balance among policies that are recognized as decisive in situations of that sort. Moreover, the conception of duty is inwardly fragmented into the various policies that

---

[77] Spartan Steel & Alloys v. Martin, above n. 75, at 564; Lamb v. London Borough of Camden, above n. 75, at 637 (C.A.).

[78] Weinrib, *The Idea of Private Law*, 36–38.

[79] Above n. 1.

[80] Ibid.

favor one party or the other. The duty issue is therefore seen as the locus not for defining the wrong identically from the standpoint of both parties, but for forwarding or balancing policies that rest on considerations that apply differently to each of them.

Were the duty issue necessarily to involve policies of this sort, the general conception of duty as coherently linking the parties as doer and sufferer of the same wrong would be a chimera. That such policies are crucial to determining the duty of care is often taken for granted. In *Cooper v. Hobart*, for instance, the Supreme Court of Canada approved the proposition that a decision about duty "is in fact a conclusion embracing within it, and yet concealing the identity of, the several considerations of policy, and the balancing of interests which have led the court to decide that a duty is owed."[81] Thus, the court regards it as self-evident that the duty issue requires the consideration of a multiplicity of policies that represent interests to be balanced.

But is this really self-evident? It is notable that in *Cooper v. Hobart* itself the court, after proclaiming the necessity of balancing, seemed at the first stage to resolve the proximity issue (which it declares to be an issue of policy) without doing any balancing whatsoever. The judgment did not compare the interests of the investors with the interests of the Registrar of Mortgage Brokers, putting each set of interests into notional pans whose contents were calibrated to some notional measurement of weight, and seeing which pan notionally sank.[82] Rather, it analyzed the statute under which the Registrar of Mortgage Brokers operated to show that the Registrar's duty was of a public nature and thus not owed to specific individuals. The court merely drew out what it thought, rightly or wrongly, was implicit in the statutory scheme within which the Registrar functioned. The exercise in question was not one of balancing policies or interests but of specifying the nature of the Registrar's duty through analysis of the institutional framework created by the statute.

The comment about policy in *Cooper v. Hobart* exemplifies a peculiar inversion. The comment posits the existence of a familiar practice about which unsophisticated observers might make certain assumptions, and then treats those assumptions as an illusion that can be dispelled by

---

[81] Cooper v. Hobart, above n. 60, at 202.

[82] The procedure envisaged would perhaps be reminiscent of the timeless spoof on balancing in Aristophanes' *Frogs*, where Dionysus in the underworld judges between Aeschylus and Euripides by employing a set of scales that balances the ponderous verse of the former against the fluffy verse of the latter.

pointing to what is "in fact" the case. The practice in question is the giving of reasons for holding that a duty of care exists, and the illusory assumption is that this practice does not involve attention to "the several considerations of policy and the balancing of interests." The comment then purports to dispel this illusion by insisting that determinations of duty "in fact" do require the embracing of multiple policies and the balancing of interests. But at the point of application this effort at enlightenment is immediately undermined by reasoning that exemplifies the very illusion that was supposed to have been dispelled. The court's consideration of the actual duty at stake suggests that the comment about policy has gotten it backward. It turns out that the illusory assumption, rendered familiar over the years by constant scholarly and judicial repetition in the aftermath of legal realism, is that the duty issue necessarily involves the balancing of the interests represented by different policies. The illusion can be dispelled by attention to what "in fact" happens in cases that ignore this supposed necessity.

There is, however, a second notion of policy that is both required by and consistent with the conception of tort liability as a response to the doing and suffering of a wrong. Consider Lord Diplock's judgment in *Home Office v. Dorset Yacht*,[83] where the issue was whether correction officers were under a duty of care to a yacht owner whose vessel was damaged when borstal boys under their supervision were negligently given an opportunity to escape from an island on which they were working. In terms of the framework for duty suggested above in section 3, this called for a determination of whether the officers' negligent behavior breached a duty that was correlative to the plaintiff's undisputed right in the boat. Lord Diplock began by signaling his agreement with Lord Denning's view that issue was "at bottom a matter of public policy that we, as judges, must resolve."[84] However, the significance that Lord Diplock attached to public policy was different from the one that appears in many of Lord Denning's judgments. Whereas Lord Denning often equated policy with independent goals such as loss-spreading, Lord Diplock understood the reference to the judges' role in resolving matters of policy to be an invitation to explore the specifically judicial function of casuistically developing the law. The task for Lord Diplock was not to identify and balance independent goals, but to elucidate the meaning of Lord

---

[83] [1970] A.C. 1004, at 1057 (H.L.).
[84] Ibid., at 1658.

Atkin's general conception of duty in the circumstances of the present case. This required a number of steps: first, an identification of the relevant characteristics, as informed by the general conception, of the kinds of conduct and relationships that have been held to give rise to a duty; second, a comparison, again influenced by the general conception, of the characteristics of the situation he was considering with the characteristics of other situations where a duty had been found; and, third, in a novel case in which these sets of characteristics from different situations were not congruent, an evaluation, still under the guidance of the general conception, of the significance of the differences and of the substitutability of a present characteristic for a missing one. The general conception of the duty of care thereby constituted the standpoint from which the characteristics of various situations were selected, compared, and evaluated.

In *Dorset Yacht*, this reference to policy—that is, to the process of casuistic judgment under the general conception of duty—worked as follows. Previous cases had held the correction authority liable for negligence that resulted in one detainee's injuring another.[85] Lord Diplock considered it a "rational extension"[86] of the principle in those cases to substitute for the custodian's right to control the physical proximity between detainees the knowledge that the custodian had or ought to have had of the particular risk to which, because of the physical proximity of its property, the plaintiff would be exposed by the defendant's negligence. The general conception of the duty of care, which Lord Atkin formulated as owed to persons so closely and directly affected by the act that the actor ought to have them in contemplation, led Lord Diplock to differentiate between the particular risk of damage consequent on escape, which affected only those in the vicinity, and the general risk of suffering from criminal activity, to which all members of the public are exposed. It was the former that constituted the unreasonable risk created by the defendant's conduct, and that therefore rendered the plaintiff a person so closely and directly affected that the prospect of this damage ought to have been in the defendant's contemplation. Because the escape was from an island and could not be attempted without watercraft, the owners of boats moored in the vicinity were within the class to whom a duty of care

---

[85] Ellis v. Home Office [1953] 2 All E.R. 149 (C.A.); D'Arcy v. Prison Commissioners, The Times, 17 November 1955.

[86] *Dorset Yacht*, above n. 83, at 1071.

was owed. The damage to the plaintiff's yacht was, therefore, the materialization of a risk that was unreasonable because of the prospect of this
kind of damage. Thus, the parties were the doer and sufferer of the
same wrong.

This second notion of policy reflects the existence of scope for
judgment in the determination of a duty of care. The duty of care
does not operate in a mechanistic or syllogistic fashion. This is especially the case when particular kinds of duties or duties in particular
cases are regarded as instantiations of a general conception of duty.
The general conception is, after all, a conception and not a recipe or
even a "test." The general conception does not state a specific formula
from which one can immediately discern whether a duty is present in
any and every particular case; rather, it brings out what the idea of
duty must be if the law of negligence is coherently to link the defendant's negligent act and the plaintiff's injury. The very generality of the
conception means both that it is not defined by reference to any particular situation in which a duty is found and that it informs all such
particular situations. It therefore requires to be related to its instantiations through an exercise of judgment, the point of which is to exhibit what, in the view of the person making the judgment, the duty of
care means in the circumstances of a particular case. Accordingly, the
general conception of duty does not render superfluous this exercise
of judgment but guides it, indicating that the judgment is to be directed toward the existence of a right and of negligence with respect to
that right. In this way the exercise of judgment is an operation of
practical reason that plays itself out within the ensemble of concepts
that the law constructs for considering whether the defendant has
done and the plaintiff has suffered the same injustice.

Lord Diplock's opinion is outstanding for providing an account by a
great judge of how this process of judgment might be described. He
does not regard the general conception of the duty as a "test" that is
applied externally to the facts, like a touchstone to gold; that would "mis-
use as a universal"[87] what Lord Diplock regards instead as a useful guide
to the relevant characteristics. Rather, because the process of judgment is
supposed to bring together the general conception of duty and the
determination of a particular duty, it operates simultaneously from both
ends. On the one hand, it attends to the fact situation at hand and to the
history of judicial determinations in analogous fact situations. On the

[87]   Ibid., at 1060.

other hand, it elucidates the relevance of particular facts and similarities by reference to the general conception of duty that Lord Atkin articulated. As Lord Diplock says, the judge starts by identifying "the relevant characteristics common to the kinds of conduct and relationships between the parties which are involved in the case for decision and to the kinds of conduct and relationships which have been held in previous decisions of the courts to give rise to a duty of care,"[88] but the judge must "know what he is looking for; and this involves his approaching his analysis with some general conception of conduct and relationships which ought to give rise to a duty of care."[89] The result is the fusion of general and particular in a judgment about whether the defendant in the case at hand breached a duty owed to the plaintiff.

Under the second notion of policy the scope for judgment need not involve, as it did in *Dorset Yacht*, a casuistic comparison of the characteristics that give or have given rise to a duty of care. It can also involve the elucidation through legal argument of the issues of law that pertain to the relationship of the parties as doer and sufferer of the same wrong. Among the legal issues that may require elaboration in any given case are the nature of the plaintiff's right (for example, under what circumstances, if at all, does the plaintiff have a right to security from psychiatric injury?),[90] the nature of correlative wrongdoing by the defendant (for example, is the distributor of a product under a duty of care with respect to its safety?),[91] and the relevance of the connection between the supposed duty of care and other juridical considerations affecting the parties. Thus, problems in determining the duty of care "may concern the need to preserve the coherence of other legal principles, or of a statutory scheme which governs certain conduct and relationships."[92] An example is the long-standing controversy, now exemplified in the

---

[88] Ibid., at 1058.
[89] Ibid. One can contrast Lord Diplock's view that casuistic analysis proceeds under a general conception with that of Dawson J. in Hill v. Van Erp, above n. 8, at 177:

> Reasoning by analogy from decided cases by processes of induction and deduction, informed by rather than divorced from policy considerations, is not, in my view, dependent for its validity on those cases sharing an underlying conceptual consistency. It is really only dependent on the fact that something more than reasonable foreseeability is required to establish a duty of care and that what is sufficient or necessary in one case is a guide to what is sufficient or necessary in another.

However, it is hard to see how one case can serve as a guide to another unless there is implicit some common standpoint that informs the comparison between them.
[90] Above n. 32. See also above n. 36.
[91] Watson v. Buckley and Osborne, Garrett and Co. Ltd (Ogee Ltd.) [1940] 1 All E.R. 174 (K.B.).
[92] Sullivan v. Moody [2001] 183 A.L.R. 404, at 415 (H.C. Aust., per Hayne J.).

varying treatments of economic loss arising out of a defect of quality, about the relationship between contract and the duty of care in negligence.[93] Even if the particular parties are not bound to each other by contract, the nature and limits of contractual obligation may nonetheless have the implications for the existence of a tort duty of care between them. For instance, the argument may be made in cases of defect in quality, that apart from contract one has no right to an object of a certain quality and that, therefore, no duty of care regarding quality arises in tort. Contemporary courts disagree as to the success of this argument,[94] but, whether successful or not, it is an argument that pertains to the relationship between the parties without invoking any independent policy. This is because the parties to a tort suit are related to each other as legal persons—that is, as parties whose legal relationships are expressive of the systematic coherence of the entire law of obligations. Accordingly, they do not interact juridically apart from the whole ensemble of intertwined legal concepts and principles that governs their participation in the law's systematic nature.[95]

---

[93] Murphy v. Brentwood District Council [1990] 2 All E.R. 908 (H.L.); Winnipeg Condominium Corp. No. 36 v. Bird Construction [1995] 121 D.L.R. (4th) 193 (S.C.C.); Bryan v. Maloney [1995] 128 Aust. L.R. 163 (H.C.).

[94] Contrast the *Murphy* and *Winnipeg Condominium* cases, above n. 93.

[95] The Supreme Court of Canada in Cooper v. Hobart, above n. 60, also held that "different types of policy considerations are involved at each of the two stages" of the two-stage test; ibid., at 202. At the first stage policy goes to the definition of proximity in the circumstances of the case; it focuses on factors that arise out of the relationship between the parties. The court describes this enquiry as follows (ibid., at 204):

> Defining the relationship may involve looking at expectations, representations, reliance, and the property or other interests involved. Essentially, these are factors that allow us to evaluate the closeness of the relationship between the plaintiff and the defendant and to determine whether it is just and fair to impose a duty of care upon the defendant.

Then at the second stage "the question remains whether there are residual policy considerations outside the relationship of the parties that may negative the imposition of a duty of care." Ibid., at 203.

This distinction between relational and extra-relational policy considerations is welcome, and one can expect, if the second stage recedes in significance (as suggested above in section 4 of this chapter), Canadian courts in the future will put greater effort into elucidating the relational aspect of policy. The court, however, still has a confused conception of what the distinction really is. First, it seems to view both kinds of policy as involving a balancing of interests that legal reasoning embraces and yet conceals; above at n. 81. Moreover, factors that are properly relational it views as extra-relational. For example, it regards the effect of recognizing a duty of care on other legal obligations as an extra-relational policy consideration; ibid., at 206. Similarly, it regards as extra-relational the question of whether recognition of a duty of care would "create the spectre of unlimited liability to an unlimited class" (ibid.), whereas, because the liability should be limited by the scope of the right to which the duty is correlative, this properly belongs to the relational analysis.

The second notion of policy is merely a way of signaling the presence of a conception of the duty of care that becomes significant for particular cases through the exercise of practical judgment. Such an exercise may involve the casuistic consideration and comparison of cases in the light of the conception of duty that they instantiate, or it may involve a process of legal argument that elucidates the right and the correlativity of the wrong and that coherently integrates the conception of duty with the other norms in play in the circumstances of the case. Recourse to practical judgment is concomitant to the inherent generality and abstractness of the legal concepts, including the duty of care, out of which the relationship between the parties is juridically constructed. Policy in this sense differs from the first notion of policy suggested earlier, which referred to independent goals outside the relationship and to the balancing of interests where these goals are in tension. The practical judgment involved in casuistic analysis and legal argument does not actualize goals extrinsic to the parties' relationship as doer and sufferer of a wrong, but, rather, explicates the legal meaning of that relationship in its particular circumstances. Policy in this sense is not only consistent with but also required by the general conception of duty. For the very generality of that conception necessitates its being related to the particular case by an exercise of practical judgment. Through practical judgment the indeterminacy of the general conception of duty becomes determinate for the case at hand.

Thus, inasmuch as the general conception of duty is a constituent of the coherent legal relationship between the doer and the sufferer of the same wrong, it is only the first notion of policy but not the second that is inimical to it. Only the first notion of policy effaces the coherence of the parties' relationship in the name of external goals that favor (and may require balancing between) the interests of one party or the other. The second notion, by contrast, far from effacing that coherence, posits the exercise of practical judgment that renders it effective for a particular case.

Whence arises the mistaken idea that the duty issue, being (in Lord Denning's words) "at bottom a matter of public policy"[96] requires recourse to the first notion of policy? Perhaps the answer is that this idea is part of the *damnosa hereditas* of instrumentalist legal thinking. Confronted by legal concepts that are indeterminate, that is, that do

---

[96] Above n. 75

not immediately dispose of the particular issue at hand but require a further operation of legal argument or casuistic reasoning, instrumentalists assume that two alternatives are available: either these concepts deductively produce legal certainty, or they are merely the rhetorical cover for the identification and balancing of external goals. Because no deductive framework is available, all that remains is reasoning in terms of external goals. Having realized that the legal material does not allow judges to be conceived as automata devoid of freedom, they assume that the only way to exercise this freedom is to choose and balance goals.[97]

This conclusion is mistaken for two related reasons. First, it poses a false choice between deduction and instrumentalism. Deduction is not the exclusive—or even a very important—mode of reasoning internal to the determination of liability. It may well be the case that no interesting legal question can be approached deductively, with the major premise being provided by an unambiguous statement of the law, the minor premise by an unambiguous recital of the facts, and an instant and unshakeable conclusion emerging from the subsumption of the latter under the former. But to think that the absence of deduction leads inexorably to the necessity for identifying and balancing independent policies is to assume that deduction is the only move internal to the elucidation of legal relationships. Ignored is the possibility of the kind of reasoning included under the second notion of policy, where the judge either compares the relevant characteristics of one case with other cases that instantiate the same general conception or elucidates the meaning of the conception in question in a way that coherently construes both the legal relationship between the parties and the whole ensemble of legal concepts.

Second, the instrumentalist conclusion moves too quickly from the indeterminacy of the general conception of duty to the external goals

---

[97] In "Privilege, Malice and Intent," (1894) 8 Harv. L. Rev. 1, Oliver Wendell Holmes provides a classic example of this approach. In Holmes's view, adjudication involves decisions about questions of policy—that is, legislative questions concerning relative advantages to the community of liability and no liability. These questions have to be addressed by comparing the gain from permitting the impugned act with the loss that the act inflicts. Judges shy away from acknowledging that this is the true ground of their decisions, because "the moment you leave the path of merely logical deduction, you lose the illusion of certainty which makes legal reasoning seem like mathematics. But certainty is only an illusion, nevertheless." Ibid., at 7. Accordingly, judges present their decisions not as grounded in legislative policy but as "hollow deductions from empty general propositions" or as unexplained postulates about what constitutes a wrong.

that are supposed to ground the decision in a particular case. The fact that the general conception of duty does not immediately determine particular cases merely indicates the existence of scope for practical judgment. It does not imply that the general conception is without meaning, a mere mirage that vanishes when one focuses on it from close in, leaving an empty space that can be filled up by whatever the judge thinks is a good idea. Rather, in leaving scope for practical judgment, the general conception indicates what the judgment must be a judgment about. What Lord Atkin himself postulated was "a general conception *of relations* giving rise to a duty of care."[98] Accordingly, the exercise of practical judgment through which this general conception is brought home to a particular case involves reasoning that is relational, not reasoning about goals that are independent of the relationship. Such relational reasoning is precisely what is encompassed in the second notion of policy. The first notion of policy, in contrast, cannot determine the meaning of the general conception of duty in a particular case, because it does not address itself to that conception. Instead, by inquiring into the independent goals that might be forwarded by decisions about liability, it offers an answer to a question that the law of negligence does not ask, while ignoring the question that it does ask.

6. Conclusion

Lord Atkin's judgment in *Donoghue v. Stevenson* is one of the great monuments of the modern law of negligence. Sweeping aside the received idea that negligence law was comprised of a miscellany of particular duties, he suggested that there must be a general conception of duty based on the prospective injury to others from unreasonable risk-creation. This general conception implied coherence both among the particular duties and within the conception of duty itself. The argument in this chapter has been that this idea of coherence requires that the parties to a negligence action be understood as the doer and sufferer of a single wrong, and that the wrong must be seen as an integrated sequence in which prospect of the plaintiff's injury is a reason for considering the defendant's act negligent. The leading cases of the twentieth century on the duty of care and on proximate cause

---

[98] Above n. 1 (emphasis added).

developed this conception of a coherent civil wrong. By avoiding basing liability on one-sided justifications, this approach to the law of negligence was normatively coherent, consistent with the judicial role and judicial competence, and fair to both parties. In contrast, more recent cases, especially those that employ the two-stage test, are appealing to a notion of policy in which the promotion and balancing of external and independent goals is leading the law back to the disintegration of duty that Lord Atkin repudiated. There is, however, another notion of policy that, avoiding reference to external and independent goals, elucidates the relational significance of the wrong through an exercise of practical judgment. This second notion of policy merely reflects the fact that the coherence of its underlying justifications is itself the supreme policy of the law of obligations.

3
Remedies

1. Two conceptions of remedies

In this chapter I explore two ways of conceptualizing the relationship between the basis of the defendant's liability and the remedy—that is, between what Peter Birks termed the causative event and the response.[1] In the first way, originally formulated in Aristotle's account of corrective justice and later elaborated in the philosophical tradition of natural right, the causative event is the reason for the remedial response. In the second way, paradigmatically set out in Kelsen's pure theory of law, the causative event is the condition of the remedial response. For each of these two ways the causative event enters into the practical reasoning about the response in a different manner. In the first, the causative event is a condition of the response because it is the reason for it. In the second the causative event is the reason for the response because it is a condition of it.

Consider first the following observations from Aristotle's account of corrective justice about the function of the judge in a civil action:

When people have a dispute, they have recourse to the judge. To go to the judge is to go to what is just, for the judge means to be, as it were, justness ensouled ... The judge restores equality. As though there were a line segmented into two unequal segments, he takes away as much as the larger segment is greater than half the line and adds it to the smaller segment. And when the whole has been divided into two parts, only

---

[1] Peter Birks, *Unjust Enrichment*, 2nd ed. (2005), 21.

then, when they take what is equal, do they say that each has what is his own.[2]

Aristotle represents what properly belongs to each of the disputing parties as an equal segment of a line. The injustice—the causative event—consists of the defendant's having taken part of the segment that properly belongs to the plaintiff, thereby destroying the underlying equality. The judge remedies this injustice by reattaching to the plaintiff's segment the amount by which the defendant's part exceeds the half-line that each should have.

In this representation, the causative event is the reason for the particular response. What the defendant has done *to* the plaintiff determines what the judge requires the defendant to do *for* the plaintiff. The defendant is now obligated to return what the defendant unjustly took from the plaintiff. Because justice between the parties obtains when the line is equally divided between them, the disturbance of the equality counts as an injustice, which the judge undoes by restoring the initial equality. Just as the causative event for liability consists in the defendant's taking a segment of the plaintiff's line, so the remedy is the retaking of that segment from the defendant and reattaching it to the plaintiff's part of the line. If one were to ask Aristotle's judge why he redivided the line in this way, he would answer that this was the only just response to the defendant's action.

One can contrast Aristotle's conception of the remedy with the one formulated by Hans Kelsen. For Kelsen, the legal order stipulates the conditions under which certain coercive acts function as sanctions that react against illegal acts or omissions. What counts as a wrong or delict is an act or omission that the legal order makes the condition of the coercive act; conversely, what counts as the sanction is the coercive consequence that the legal order attaches to that act or omission. Thus, the relationship between causative event and remedy is solely that of condition and consequence: "Given, as condition, behaviour opposite that which the norm establishes, then a coercive act is to be forthcoming as consequence."[3]

Aristotle and Kelsen link the causative event to the remedy in entirely different ways. For Aristotle, the causative event is a reason for

---

[2] Aristotle, *Nicomachean Ethics*, V, 1132a19–29.
[3] Hans Kelsen, *Introduction to the Problems of Legal Theory*, tr. Bonnie Litschewski Paulson and Stanley L. Paulson (1997), 30.

the remedy because it is an injustice that the judge, as justness ensouled, must reverse. For Kelsen, the notion that "a moral value element is immanent in the concepts of delict and sanction"[4] is untenable, because only the positive legal order imbues an act or omission with the character of a delict. To put the point another way: for Aristotle, the causative event is the condition of a remedy because of the kind of event it is, whereas for Kelsen, the event counts as causative only because it is the condition of a remedy. In Kelsen's words:

[A] definite action or refrainment is not—as traditional jurisprudence assumes—connected with the coercive act because this action or refrainment is a delict, but a definite act or refrainment is a delict because it is connected with a coercive act, that is, with a sanction as its consequence. No immanent quality, no relation to a meta-legal natural or divine norm is a reason for qualifying a specific human behaviour as a delict; but only and exclusively the fact that the positive legal order has made this behaviour the condition of a coercive act—of a sanction.[5]

This juxtaposition of Aristotle and Kelsen brings out the contrast between relating the causative event to the remedy as a reason or as a condition. Aristotle and Kelsen are led to these differing conceptions by the differences in their projects. Aristotle's interest is in presenting the form of justice that is immanent in the relationship between the parties in private law. Integral to this form of justice is the idea that the direct relationship of the parties characterizes both the causative event and the remedy—indeed, that it characterizes the remedy because it characterizes the causative event. Thus, the reason for thinking that the defendant's act is an injustice to the plaintiff is also a reason for thinking that the remedy that corrects the injustice has to have the same relational structure as the injustice. Kelsen, in contrast, is concerned not with justice but with the posited nature of law. Because a norm can be legally valid even if it is thought to be unjust, the connection between the causative event and the remedy must be understood in terms of condition and consequence with respect to the coercion that the positive law mandates. Whereas Aristotle views the relationship of causative event to remedy as immanent to the structure of justice between the parties, Kelsen regards that relationship as

---

[4] Hans Kelsen, *Pure Theory of Law*, tr. Max Knight (1967), 111.
[5] Ibid.

exhibited through "an analysis of the immanent meaning of the legal order"[6] as a system of positive law. The injustice that is paramount for Aristotle is therefore irrelevant to Kelsen.

The sections of this chapter that follow develop some of the implications of each of these conceptions of remedies. I first elaborate, in section 2, corrective justice's conception of the relationship between the injustice and the remedy. Corrective justice integrates the injustice and its rectification by construing the latter as undoing the former. The injustice is not an occasion for a court to do what is best, all things considered, given the present situation of the parties. Rather, even after it has occurred, the injustice remains the decisive feature in the parties' relationship, because the injustice to be corrected determines the available range of remedies that can correct it. What is rightfully the plaintiff's is the subject matter both of the right and of the remedy, the right entailing a duty of non-interference, the remedy a duty of restoration or reparation. Because what is rightfully the plaintiff's remains constant throughout, the remedy is the continuation of the right; together they make up a single unbroken juridical sequence. In postulating so intimate a relationship between right and remedy, corrective justice merely draws out what the law takes for granted. Long ago Learned Hand formulated this relationship as a truism when he characterized a remedy as "an obligation destined to stand in place of the plaintiff's right, and be, as nearly as possible, equivalent to him for his rights."[7] My goal is to explicate the sense in which the remedy is equivalent to, limited by, and continuous with the injured right.

I then turn to the conception of the remedy as merely conditioned by the causative event. Kelsen's account of this conception is part of his elucidation of what it is for a norm to have the form of positive law regardless of the norm's content. This indifference to content means that one cannot extrapolate from his account anything that would address the lawyer's interest in what the legal system should look like. In this respect there is an asymmetry between Kelsen's account and Aristotle's. For, as we saw in Aristotle's treatment of the segmented line, Aristotle thinks that the remedy has to match the bipolar structure of the injustice that it corrects; accordingly, his approach reproduces, although at a very high level of abstraction, the

---

[6] Ibid., 112.
[7] Learned Hand, "Restitution or Unjust Enrichment," (1897) 11 Harv. L. Rev. 240, at 256.

lawyer's concern for the normative intelligibility of the law's content. For Kelsen, in contrast, the law is a posited order that can have any content. Kelsen allows that actual legal systems do have remedies that purport to right the wrong by requiring the defendant to repair the damage illegally inflicted upon the plaintiff,[8] but he considers these to exemplify a kind of logical error in which the way a person behaves (a statement of what is) is mistakenly taken to contradict a norm (an statement of what ought to be).[9] In Kelsen's view, from the standpoint of positive law the illegal act means nothing more than that the sanction ought to be forthcoming. Inasmuch as the sanction is an operation of the legal order, the illegal act should therefore be understood not as the negation of law but as its condition.

From the lawyer's standpoint Kelsen's observations may suggest an unpromising framework for considering the role of remedies within a system of private law. Sophisticated legal systems, after all, are not indifferent to their own content. Rather, they view that content as something that makes at least incipient sense from a suitably defined moral point of view. Within private law, events are causative of liability because they are thought to work some sort of injustice toward the plaintiff. Nonetheless, torn from its context within Kelsen's pure theory, the idea of the causative event as a condition of the remedy is no stranger to contemporary discussions of remedies. It surfaces whenever the remedy is seen not as normatively continuous with what makes the causative event an injustice, but as the locus of an independent enquiry. By breaking the normative connection that might exist between the remedy and the causative event, such an enquiry treats the latter as a condition but not a reason for the former.

To the extent that remedies exemplify this conception, they ignore or go beyond the injustice that calls them into being. Such remedies are not concerned—or at least not concerned only—with responding to whatever aspect of the parties' interaction forms the basis for liability. In the language of the old remoteness cases, what goes to culpability is viewed as distinguishable from what goes to compensation (or to other remedial impositions).[10] This disjunction between the injustice of the causative event and the remedial response creates

---

[8] Above n. 4, 109.

[9] Ibid., 113.

[10] The distinction between what "goes to culpability" and what "goes to compensation" was current in the law of negligence until overruled in Overseas Tankship (UK) v. Morts Dock & Engineering (The Wagon Mound, No. 1) [1961] A.C. 388 (P.C.).

a tension in which the injustice occasions the remedy without grounding it. On the one hand, the causative event is seen as some sort of injustice that requires a remedy; yet on the other, the remedy's operation is independent of the reason for thinking that the causative event was an injustice to begin with. Thus, so far as the remedy is concerned, the injustice of the causative event is both indispensable and superfluous.

Section 3 explores the problematic nature of this conception by reference to a conspicuous example of it, the indemnified injunction. This kind of injunction allows the plaintiff to bring a nuisance to an end only if the defendant is compensated for costs imposed by the injunction. Although absent from the traditional corpus of remedies and rarely invoked in practice, the indemnified injunction has received extensive attention in the economic analysis of law. It is sometimes even regarded as suggesting a new "grand theory of remedies":[11] by breaking the "sensible convention" of "not asking those in the right to pay when they are wronged,"[12] it is supposed to contribute to a more unified theory of remedies that combines rights, remedies, and bargains around those rights and remedies. Whatever its virtues on that score, the remedy operates independently of the injustice that lies at the root of the determination of liability, as its breach of the "sensible convention" shows. Indeed, the remedy obscures the very nature of the injustice that gives birth to it. In these respects it is characteristic of the conception of the remedy as merely conditioned by the injustice.

Finally section 4 aligns the distinction between these two conceptions with the recent contrast made by remedies scholars between monistic and dualistic approaches to remedies. The focus within corrective justice on the normative ground of the remedy may cast light on the tension—present in both monism and dualism—between the centrality of the infringed right to the remedy and the introduction of new considerations at the remedial stage. Corrective justice reconciles this tension by situating the right within the system of rights, thereby allowing systemic considerations to be introduced at the remedial stage. In this way, I shall suggest, the corrective justice conception may narrow the gap between these two approaches.

---

[11] Saul Levmore, "Unifying Remedies: Property Rules, Liability Rules, and Startling Rules," (1997) 106 Yale L.J., 2149.

[12] Ibid., at 2150.

2. The corrective justice conception of remedies

On what grounds does corrective justice posit a continuity of right and remedy?[13] This continuity flows from the mutually complementary ways in which corrective justice conceives of the structure and the content of the private law relationship.[14] The structure consists in the parties being correlatively situated as doer and sufferer of the same injustice. The content consists in the plaintiff's having a right and the defendant's being under a correlative duty, so that injustice occurs on the defendant's breach of a duty correlative to the plaintiff's right. The continuity of the remedy reflects the persistence of this structure and content in the aftermath of the injustice.

This structure and content go to the reasons for holding a particular defendant liable to a particular plaintiff. As a matter of structure, the normative considerations that appropriately govern finding of liability are those that implicate both parties in their relationship. As a matter of content, these considerations presuppose that the injury is to something to which the plaintiff has a right and with respect to which the defendant is under a correlative duty. Being juridical manifestations of the parties' self-determining freedom with respect to each other, right and duty are the ingredients, and not merely the conclusions, of legal argument about the terms of the parties' interaction. The task of private law is to work out the meaning of these rights and duties so as to make them coherent with one another, reflective of the idea of self-determining freedom, and applicable to the myriad concrete situations of human interaction.

In correcting an injustice, the remedy has the same correlative structure as the relationship itself, because a relational injustice cannot be corrected non-relationally. Accordingly, the remedy operates simultaneously against the defendant and in favor of the plaintiff. In an award of damages, for instance, the plaintiff is entitled to receive the very sum that the defendant is obligated to pay. If the law took money

---

[13] The continuity of right and remedy is explicit in German jurisprudence as the *Rechtsfortsetzungsgedanke*, the idea that "the injured right lives on in a claim for damages"; Walter van Gervan et al., *Common Law of Europe Casebooks: Tort Law* (2000), 753. The standard German legal textbook treats the idea of continuity as one aspect of—and therefore less comprehensive than—the idea of compensation (the *Ausgleichsgedanke*), because it views consequential damages as falling outside the idea of continuity; see Karl Larenz, *Lehrbuch des Schuldrechts*, Band I (Algemeiner Teil), 14th ed. (1987), 424. The implication of my argument in this chapter is that, from the theoretical perspective, continuity is the more fundamental idea.

[14] Above, chapter 1.

from the defendant without giving it to the plaintiff, the injustice suffered by the plaintiff would remain uncorrected. Similarly, if the law gave money to the plaintiff without taking it from the defendant, the injustice done by the defendant would remain uncorrected. And even if the law took money from the defendant and gave an equivalent amount of money to the plaintiff in separate operations (say, by requiring payment into one government fund and out of another), the injustice as something done by the defendant to the plaintiff—and therefore as being of relational significance between them—would still remain uncorrected. Structurally, the remedy is the mirror image of the injustice. Both feature the same movement from one pole of the relationship to the other, so that, to the extent possible, the relationship ends up as free of injustice as it was at the beginning.

The correction maintains not only the structure but also the content—the right and the correlative duty—of the parties' relationship. What is correctively just about a private law relationship is the absence of breaches of any duty correlative to another's right. Conversely, injustice lies in an inconsistency with the plaintiff's right that is imputable to the defendant. The point of the remedy is to eliminate this inconsistency. In this progression from justice to injustice and back again, the same right (and, of course, the same correlative duty) is the focus of the law's attention. The right survives the injustice and continues into the remedy, which is nothing other than the judicially crystallized post-injustice shape of the right.

Now one might think that identifying the remedy with the pre-injustice right (and its correlative duty) overstates the closeness of the connection between them. Suppose that the defendant has tortiously destroyed an object belonging to the plaintiff and now has to pay the plaintiff a sum equal to the object's value. Before the destruction the defendant was under a duty to abstain from exposing the object to an unreasonable risk. After the destruction the defendant cannot be under this duty, because the object no longer exists. The action now required of the defendant is not abstention from creating an unreasonable risk, but transfer to the plaintiff of a certain sum of money. A duty mandates a specific action, and if the specific actions mandated are different, so are the duties.[15]

---

[15] "[O]bligations ... are individuated according to the actions that they make obligatory," J. Gardner, "What is Tort Law For? Part 1: The Place of Corrective Justice," (2011) 30 Law and Philosophy 1, 35.

A similar argument can be made on the rights side. A right gives its holder the freedom to act within its bounds. Yet the actions permitted before the injustice may differ from those permitted after the injustice. For example, my right to bodily integrity cannot be alienated, but it may be possible for me, within restrictions set out by the positive law, to assign the damages claim that arises from the injury.[16] The fact that after the injustice one has the freedom to do actions unavailable previously indicates (so the argument would go) that the different freedoms reflect different rights rather than the continuation of the same right.

That the variety of actions prohibited or permitted attests to a variety of duties and rights is an appealing but misleading notion. It is not the case that if the specific actions mandated by the law are different, so are the legal duties. Different actions can be required by a single duty and a single action can be required by different duties. An example of the latter is that the same specific action may be required both contractually and delictually. As for the former, suppose that the defendant, being under a duty of care as a bailee with respect to an object belonging to the plaintiff, was obliged both to keep his car locked as he transported the object and to water the object regularly. The law would regard these two different actions as different ways of fulfilling the same legal duty, not as the fulfillment of two different duties. The fact that there are innumerable ways in which a duty could be breached does not mean that each possible breach is the breach of a different duty.[17]

A legal duty takes its character from the legal category that informs it, not from the specific action that it prohibits or requires. The same action required as a matter of both contract law and tort law is governed concurrently by two duties, one for each possible ground of liability. In my example of the bailment, the legal duty is that of a bailee, not that of a person who waters an object or transports it in a locked car.

Considered as a theoretical issue, the relation between right and remedy engages a still higher level of generality. Theory is concerned

---

[16] I owe this example to Lionel Smith.

[17] The distinction between a duty and a required specific action tracks Kant's obscure distinction between an obligation ("the necessity of a free action under a categorical imperative of reason") and a duty "that action to which someone is bound. It is therefore the matter of the obligation." Kant adds that "there can be one and the same duty (as to the action, although we can be bound to it in different ways." Immanuel Kant, *The Metaphysics of Morals*, tr. Mary Gregor (1996), [6:222].

not with particular grounds of liability and their respective remedies, but with the nature of liability as such and the corresponding conception of a remedy. As noted above, under corrective justice the injustice that gives rise to liability is an inconsistency with the plaintiff's right that is imputable to the defendant. At its most general, having a right in private law means that the right-holder is normatively so connected to the object of the right that another person is under a duty not to interfere with that object.[18] The legal system lays down the grounds for acquiring and holding rights of various sorts—offer and acceptance for contract, *animus donandi* and *factum donandi* for gift, and so on. As long as these grounds obtain, the relationship of right and duty continues regardless of what the defendant has done to the object of the right. Only actions consistent with the holder's right can terminate this normative connection, as when property is alienated or a contract is discharged by performance. Conversely, the right (and the duty correlative to it) always survives an injustice, which by definition is an inconsistency with the right.

Accordingly, the defendant who, in breach of her duty, destroys an object belonging to the plaintiff does not thereby destroy the plaintiff's right to the object. The plaintiff remains linked to the defendant through a right that pertains to the object as an undamaged thing. Although the defendant's wrong has modified the physical condition of the object embodying the plaintiff's right, the right remains intact as the normative marker of the relationship between them with respect to that object. Even if the object no longer exists as a physical entity, the parties continue to be related to each other through the object's normative connection to the plaintiff and the consequent duty on the defendant to act in conformity with that connection. Instead of being embodied in the object itself, the right and its correlative duty with respect to the object now take the form of an entitlement and have the defendant furnish the plaintiff with its value.

The survival of the right means that its correlative duty also survives. The defendant's breach of duty did not of course bring to an end the duty with respect to the plaintiff's right, for, if it did, the duty—absurdly—would have been discharged by its breach. To be sure, the specific action required of the defendant has been transformed by the defendant's tort. Just as the plaintiff's right is no longer

---

[18] "That is rightfully mine (*meum iuris*) with which I am so connected that another's use of it without my consent would wrong me." Ibid., at [6:245].

embodied in the specific object, which has been destroyed, but in an entitlement to receive the object's equivalent from the defendant, so the defendant's duty is no longer to abstain from its destruction, which has already taken place, but to provide the plaintiff with the object's equivalent. The specific action that the duty requires is different, but the defendant is not under a different duty. This is because, from a juridical point of view, what determines the nature of the duty is not the specific action that the duty requires but the right to which the duty is correlative. And what determines the right is the appropriate normative connection between the object of the right and the person holding it. So long as that connection persists, the right and correlative duty with respect to the object remain.

Thus, the right and its correlative duty continue to exist with different specific content before and after the injustice. Underlying the succession of specific characteristics of the right and its correlative duty is the relationship that the parties have through the plaintiff's connection with the object of the right. That relationship remains identical throughout the metamorphosis that the defendant's injustice has wrought in the object of the right. To put it in familiar philosophical terms, the diachronic identity of the right is merely a juridical exemplification of the category of substance as that which persists through change: during the legal relationship the existence of the right remains constant, but the way in which the right exists changes.[19] Just as a person has different characteristics at different times of life while yet remaining the same person, so a right and its correlative duty have different characteristics at different points in their existence while yet remaining the same right and duty. Juridically, the parties step twice into, or rather stand continuously in, the same river.

Blackstone summed up the relation between right and remedy by stating that remedies "redress the party injured, by either restoring to him his right, if possible, or by giving him an equivalent."[20] Blackstone's formulation is a paradigmatic expression of corrective justice. It implies three theses. The first is the thesis of identity, that the plain-

---

[19] "In all appearances, the permanent is the object itself, that is, substance as phenomenon; everything, on the other hand, which changes or can change belongs only to the way in which substance or substances exist, and therefore to their determinations. I find that in all ages, not only philosophers, but even the common understanding, have recognized this permanence as a substratum of all appearance, and always assume it to be indubitable." Kant, *Critique of Pure Reason*, tr. Norman Kemp Smith (1929), A184, B227.

[20] Blackstone, IV *Commentaries*, 9.

tiff's injured right and the right restored by the defendant are the same right or its equivalent. One cannot regard a right as being restored if it is other than the one that the defendant wronged. The second is the thesis of limitation, that the remedy restores *only* the plaintiff's right and does not give the plaintiff more than that right (or its equivalent). Thus, the reason for creating liability also limits it.[21] The third is the thesis of continuity, that the plaintiff's right survives the injury intact and continues to be the normative marker of the parties' relationship. Because the right continues to exist, plaintiffs can justly apply to courts for the restoration of what remains rightfully theirs.[22]

These three theses are interrelated. Rights could not be enjoyed as domains of freedom unless the law secured them against wrongs by requiring wrongdoers to restore what they have injured (the identity thesis). However, because the relationship between the parties is one of equal freedom, the plaintiff's freedom does not entitle the court to coerce the defendant into providing the plaintiff with a windfall over and above the restored right, for that, in turn, would be inconsistent with the defendant's freedom (the limitation thesis).[23] With the ideas of injury and restoration in place, one might wonder how the temporal gap between them is normatively bridged. For one might suppose

---

[21] Compare Warren A. Seavey, "Mr. Justice Cardozo and the Law of Torts," (1939) 39 Colum. L. Rev. 20, 34.

[22] Blackstone's terminology of restoring the plaintiff's right is not entirely felicitous, as it participates in the ambiguity of right as both something that a plaintiff has and a normative status that attaches to something that the plaintiff has. One should not think that the very description of the remedy as the restoration of a right shows that the plaintiff did not have what the remedy restores. Kant draws attention to this terminological imprecision in his discussion of external right. In Kantian terms, ownership involves possessing an object intellectually rather than empirically, because the essence of ownership is that it persists even when the owner is not in physical possession of the thing owned. For this reason, he writes, "it is not appropriate to speak of possessing a right to this or that object but rather of possessing it *merely rightfully*; for a right is already an intellectual possessing of an object and it would make no sense to speak of possessing a possess[ing]." Kant, above n. 17, [6:249] (translation slightly modified). In the same way here, the wrong is a deprivation of what is rightfully the plaintiff's and the remedy restores to the plaintiff what is rightfully hers. For an illuminating treatment of remedies from a Kantian perspective, see Arthur Ripstein, "As If It Had Never Happened," (2007) 48 Wm. and Mary L. Rev. 1957.

[23] As Kant observed in his comment about tort law:

I cannot acquire a right against another through a deed of his *that is contrary to right (facto iniusto alterius)*; for even if he has wronged me and I have a right *to* demand compensation from him, by this I will still only preserve what is mine undiminished but will not acquire more than what I previously had.

Kant, above n. 17, [6:271].

that the occurrence of the injury puts an end to the plaintiff's right, leaving the plaintiff without a basis for claiming what he no longer has. Perhaps all that the plaintiff can expect is an apology for the misfortune that the defendant caused.[24] The continuity thesis holds, in reply, that even after the injury the plaintiff continues to have the right to what was wrongly injured. From the normative point of view, no gap in the plaintiff's right-holding exists between the injury and the remedy.

One might object that this account of corrective justice implausibly effaces the significance of the wrong, because it entails that one is discharging one's duty to refrain from wrongdoing ex ante by compensating the victim ex post.[25] This is not the case. The continuity of right and remedy means that the same relationship of right and duty continues through a sequence of stages that, on the duty side, require different specific actions. A sequence is not a smorgasbord from which the defendant can mix and match. What counts as the discharge of the duty in any given stage is determined by the actions that the duty calls for at that stage, not at a previous or subsequent one. Accordingly, the defendant cannot satisfy the duty as it existed at one stage by performing the action called for at a subsequent stage. As a juridical instantiation of the category of substance,[26] the right and its correlative duty persist *through* change; they do not remain *un*changed. Just as my being a more mature version of the person I was as a child does not now require me to enroll in kindergarten, so the defendant who has committed an injustice can no longer satisfy his duty in its original form. The injustice committed earlier remains an injustice. The remedy vindicates the plaintiff's right by restoring what is rightfully his, thereby affirming rather than denying that the injustice occurred. Because the defendant has not complied with a duty owed to the plaintiff, the duty continues to exist in a new form that requires the performance appropriate to this new stage of the parties' relationship.[27]

---

[24] Stephen R. Perry, *Loss, Agency, and Responsibility for Outcomes: Three Conceptions of Corrective Justice, in Tort Theory*, ed. Ken Cooper-Stephenson and Elaine Gibson (1993), 24.

[25] Benjamin C. Zipursky, "Rights, Wrongs, and Recourse in the Law of Torts," (1998) 51 Vand. L. Rev. 1, 74.

[26] Above n. 19.

[27] Nor is the corrective justice account affected by the Austinian distinction between a primary duty and the secondary duty that arises out of a violation of a primary duty; John Austin, *Lectures on Jurisprudence*, 5th ed. (1885), 764. That distinction merely sets out different stages in the parties' relationship; it does not address the nature of the normative connection between them.

By regarding the remedy as a continuation of the injured right, corrective justice provides a unifying framework for understanding and assessing the various remedies that the law makes available. Corrective justice is a normative regime of rights and their correlative duties. In awarding a remedy the law aims to remove the inconsistency with the plaintiff's rights by having the defendant restore what is rightfully the plaintiff's. The diversity of the remedies reflects the different ways of impairing and restoring what is rightfully the plaintiff's.

Restoration of the plaintiff's right can take two forms: the qualitative and the quantitative. The qualitative form restores to the plaintiff the very thing that is the subject matter of the right, thereby allowing the plaintiff to have and enjoy "its specific qualitative character."[28] In such cases the law gives specific relief, such as specific delivery of a unique or unusual chattel, specific performance of a contractual obligation, or an injunction against a private nuisance or trespass. The quantitative form restores to the plaintiff, through an award of damages, the monetary equivalent of the injury. One of the tasks of the law of remedies, of course, is to work out which of these forms of restoring the plaintiff's right is available in what circumstances—an issue that different jurisdictions handle in different ways. Nonetheless, in accordance with corrective justice, both forms of restoration exemplify the continuity of right and remedy.

Now, one should not think that the availability of injunctive relief is inconsistent with corrective justice on the grounds that an injunction against future wrongdoing applies when there is yet no wrong to correct. Under corrective justice, the private law relationship is correlatively structured by the plaintiff's right and the defendant's duty. The remedy instantiates that structure by vindicating the plaintiff's right against the defendant's breach of the correlative duty. What matters is not the temporal relation between the injustice and the remedy, but the structure of the injustice and the consequent structure of the remedy. For instance, if (as I have argued elsewhere)[29] the norms against nuisances instantiate corrective justice, then so do the injunctions that prevent nuisances. Thus, corrective justice operates not only by requiring the defendant to repair a wrong once it has occurred, but also by

---

[28] Hegel, *Philosophy of Right*, tr. T. M. Knox (1952), s. 98R.
[29] Ernest Weinrib, *The Idea of Private Law* (1995), 190–96.

granting the plaintiff an injunction that prevents the defendant from extending the wrong into the future.[30]

The continuity of right and remedy also holds for the various kinds of damages that figure in the quantitative form of restoration: substitutive damages, nominal damages, consequential damages, gain-based damages, and aggravated damages. Let us briefly consider each of these in turn.

First, the right-holder is entitled to the physical integrity of the thing that forms the subject matter of the right.[31] Correspondingly, others are under a duty not to wrongfully interfere with that physical integrity. When such interference occurs, the right-holder's entitlement to an intact thing continues as against the wrongdoer. The wrongdoer then has a correlative duty to transfer the sum of money that leaves the right-holder with the equivalent of the thing's value in its intact state. Such damages have been termed "substitutive," in that they are awarded to the plaintiff as a substitute for the right that the defendant infringed.[32]

Second, when a right is infringed without impairing the physical condition of the object, a court awards nominal damages. The availability of nominal damages is the remedial affirmation that private law vindicates rights and does not merely repair losses. Just as no liability follows when a loss is not the wrongful infringement of a right, so conversely can a defendant be held liable, and required to pay nominal damages, for a wrong to the plaintiff's right that does not occasion a loss. The obligation to pay nominal damages is the continuation of the defendant's duty not to interfere with the plaintiff's right even when no loss results from such interference.

Third, the right-holder's entitlement to have the thing physically intact carries with it an entitlement to use the thing in its intact condition for his or her purposes. Accordingly, a wrongful interference with the thing's physical integrity may wrongfully interfere with the use, actual or prospective, to which the right-holder is putting or is likely to put the intact thing. The entitlement to use the intact thing imports a correlative duty not to wrongfully interfere with such use. This duty finds its remedial continuation in what the law terms

---

[30] Ibid., 144.

[31] For purposes of exposition I assume a wrong with respect to a corporeal object. The argument would not essentially change for non-corporeal objects, though it would be reformulated to accord with the non-corporeal nature of the subject matter of the right.

[32] Robert Stevens, *Torts and Rights* (2007), 60

"consequential" damages—that is, the monetary sum equivalent to the worth of the use of which the defendant wrongly deprived the right-holder.

Fourth, the right-holder has an exclusive entitlement to deal with the thing owned, and can realize the thing's value by charging for its use or by selling it. The gain from the use or the sale is as much the right-holder's as is the thing itself. Accordingly, the right-holder can claim restitution of such a gain from a wrongdoer who made it through a use or a sale that was unauthorized. This award of gain-based damages (and its historical antecedent in "waiver of tort") is the continuation of the right-holder's entitlement to the thing's value.[33]

Fifth, the common law recognizes that a wrongdoer may not only have injured the object of the right, but may also have done this so high-handedly as to injure the dignity of the right-holder. To compensate for such injuries to dignity the law awards aggravated damages, for a court may "take into account the motives and conduct of the defendant when they aggravate the injury done to the plaintiff."[34] This form of damages reflects the connection between the object of the right and the dignity that the law ascribes to the holder of the right. As a system of rights, the law presupposes a distinction between persons, (entities imbued with the dignity that attends the capacity for rights) and things (entities devoid of that dignity). The dignity that comes from the right-holder's connection to the object of the right is as much within the entitlement of the right-holder as the object of the right itself. Accordingly, the law awards additional damages, which it regards as compensatory, for a wrong committed in a way that imparts injury to the right-holder's dignity over and above the injury done to the object of the right itself. Such damages are the continuation of the dignity inherent in being the holder of a right.[35]

Corrective justice also provides a standpoint for criticizing the controversial practice of awarding punitive damages. This critical standpoint is the consequence of the theoretical aspirations of the corrective justice approach. Corrective justice explicates the internal structure and presuppositions of the private law relationship as found in sophisticated legal systems, in order to present at a high level of abstraction

---

[33] Below, chapter 4.
[34] Rookes v. Barnard [1964] A.C. 1129, 1221 (H.L., per Lord Devlin).
[35] On aggravated damages as reparation for injury to dignity, see Allan Beever, "The Structure of Aggravated and Exemplary Damages," (2003) 23 Oxford J. Legal Stud. 87; John Murphy, "The Nature and Domain of Aggravated Damages," (2010) 69 Cambridge L.J. 353.

what it means for private law to be fair and coherent on its own terms. Because sophisticated systems of private law strive—not always with success, of course—to be fair and coherent, they are composed of norms that might exhibit the specific meaning of corrective justice for a particular legal system or legal tradition. Conversely, corrective justice provides an internal standpoint for the criticism of norms that are not consonant with a liability regime's own aspiration to fairness and coherence. Accordingly, if the corrective justice arguments against the punitive damages are sound, then corrective justice has fulfilled its theoretical function of providing the internal standpoint for identifying unfair or incoherent doctrine.

Punitive damages are inconsistent with corrective justice for reasons both of structure and of content. So far as structure is concerned, corrective justice requires that the normative considerations applicable to the relationship between defendant and plaintiff reflect the parties' correlative standing as sufferer of and doer of the same injustice. Accordingly, it excludes considerations that refer to one of the parties without encompassing the correlative situation of the other. The standard justifications for punitive damages—deterrence and retribution—are one-sided considerations that focus not relationally on the parties as doer and sufferer of the same injustice, but unilaterally on the defendant (and anyone else who might be similarly situated) as doer. The place of such considerations is not private law but criminal law, because criminal law is concerned not with whether the accused has injured someone's particular right, but with whether the accused has acted inconsistently with the existence of a regime of rights in general.[36] In effect, punitive damages function as a defendant-financed reward for acting as a private prosecutor while subjecting the defendant to punishment without the protections of the criminal law.

So far as content is concerned, punitive damages are inconsistent with the role of rights in corrective justice. Punitive damages do not restore to plaintiffs what is rightfully theirs, but instead give them a windfall. Punitive damages based on deterrence and retribution thus violate what I earlier termed the limitation thesis, that the remedy should only restore the plaintiff's right and not give the plaintiff more than that right (or its equivalent).

Thus the corrective justice account, through the robust role that it assigns to rights and their correlative duties, provides a unifying frame-

---

[36] Below, chapter 5, section 4.

work for understanding both the relationship between right and remedy and the range of different remedies that the law makes available. All appropriate remedies reflect the reason for liability, that the injustice imputed to the defendant is inconsistent with the plaintiff's right. The different kinds of damages reflect the various kinds of entitlement that a right gives, including an entitlement to the intactness of the object of the right, to its use and value as an intact object, to its inviolability even in the absence of loss, and to the dignity that attaches to the right-holder. And the distinction between monetary damages and specific remedies such as injunctions reflects the different ways in which the injured right can be restored.

3. The causative event as a condition of the remedy

I now turn to the alternate conception of remedies, in which the causative event functions as a condition and not as a reason. As was mentioned at the outset, I want to focus on a conspicuous if rather unusual example: the indemnified injunction. Under an indemnified injunction the plaintiff is entitled to an injunction provided that the defendant is compensated for the damage that the injunction causes. This remedy was not known to exist until 1972. In that year it was coincidentally employed in the nuisance case of *Spur Industries v. Del E. Webb Development Co.*[37] and suggested in a celebrated article by Guido Calabresi and Douglas Melamed that has revolutionized academic thinking about remedies in the United States.[38]

Because compensating the defendant is manifestly at odds with the supposedly wrongful behavior that occasions the remedy, the indemnified injunction is an extreme example of this alternate conception of remedies. When an indemnified injunction is awarded, the causative event has to be understood not as the reason that grounds the remedy as a matter of justice but as the occasion that triggers the operation of a normatively independent remedial policy. This gap between response and the normative ground of the causative event means that the remedy obscures the nature of the injustice being remedied. Indeed, from the standpoint of corrective justice, such a remedy

---

[37] Spur Industries v. Del E. Webb Development Co., 494 P. 2d 700 (Arizona S.C., 1972)
[38] Guido Calabresi and A. Douglas Melamed, "Property Rules, Liability Rules, and Inalienability: One View of the Cathedral," (1972) 85 Harv. L. Rev. 1089.

works a new injustice to one or the other of the parties: it requires the defendant to do either too much (if the defendant's behavior was not really a wrong) or too little (if it was). In any event, the extreme nature of this instance makes it an apt illustration of what this alternate conception entails.

A. Spur v. Del E. Webb

Consider first the nuisance case.[39] The defendant was the operator of a cattle feedlot built in what had long been an agricultural district. The plaintiff was a real estate developer who had purchased land in the neighborhood of the feedlot in order to develop an urban area. As the development grew, it came closer and closer to the cattle feedlot, until the feedlot's smells caused the developer to encounter sales resistance from prospective purchasers and persistent complaints from past purchasers. The developer sued in nuisance. The court held that the developer was entitled to an injunction. It also held, however, that having brought into the previously agricultural area the population that makes the granting of an injunction necessary, the plaintiff should also indemnify the defendant for the damages it would sustain by having to move or cease operations under the injunction.

The striking feature of this remedy is that it makes it hard to discern the injustice of, or even to identify, the causative event. Indeed, because the remedy has two parts, the injunction for which the defendant is liable and the indemnification that the plaintiff provides in return for the injunction, it is not even easy to single out the party responsible for the causative event. Nor is it easy to identify the victim of the wrong, especially since the court took into account the interests not only of the parties but also of the residents in the development, who purchased their properties from the developer. On the facts of this case four possibilities suggest themselves: (1) the feedlot operator wronged the developer; (2) the feedlot operator wronged the residents; (3) the developer wronged the feedlot operator; (4) the developer wronged the residents. None of these possibilities, however, is completely satisfactory.

The first possibility, matching the roles of defendant and plaintiff in the case, is that the feedlot operator committed a wrong against the developer. On this possibility, which accords with the classic

---

[39] Above n. 37.

understanding of nuisance law,[40] the presence of the cattle feedlot prior to the activity of the developer does not exonerate the operator of the feedlot from what was otherwise a nuisance. The defendant cannot restrict the plaintiff from developing its land, and once the land is developed, the plaintiff's rights in the use of that land are protected by the law of nuisance. This protection includes the availability of an injunction to bring to an end the defendant's interference with the plaintiff's rights. But then it is hard to account for requiring the plaintiff to indemnify the defendant for the injunction. It seems odd that the victim of a wrong should have to indemnify the wrongdoer for exercising the remedy that the law grants to bring about the cessation of that very wrong.[41]

The second possibility, that it was the residents rather than the developer who were the victims of a wrong done by the feedlot operator, looks to the fact that the plaintiff can secure freedom from the smells only by purchasing that freedom. One might infer from this that the defendant did not really commit a wrong against the plaintiff in carrying on with its feedlot operations despite the harm that the smells inflicted on the approaching development. The court adopted this approach. It referred to cases of "coming to the nuisance" under which a use that is prior in time does not constitute a nuisance at all against parties who subsequently enter the neighborhood with inconsistent uses.[42] Had only the developer been harmed and not also the purchasers of the houses, it would have dismissed the case on this ground.[43] The plaintiff's entitlement to relief was based on the damage "to the people who have been encouraged to purchase homes" in the development.[44] Although the remedy is placed in the hands of the developer, the wrong was done to the residents. On this reasoning the court granted an injunction to a party that was not the victim of a wrong on the expectation that the remedy would be pursued for the benefit of the real victims. This means that, contrary to the ruling idea of tort law,[45] the plaintiff was awarded a remedy on the basis of a wrong done to someone else.

---

[40] Sturges v. Bridgman [1879] 11 Ch. D. 852 (C.A).

[41] This is the criticism of the court's treatment by Holohan J., dissenting in the subsequent case Spur Feeding Company v. Superior Court of Maricopa County, 505 P 2d 1377 (Arizona S.C., 1973).

[42] Spur v. Webb, above n. 37, at 707.

[43] Ibid., at 707.

[44] Ibid., at 708.

[45] Palsgraf v. Long Island Railroad Co., 162 N.E. 99 (N.Y. C.A., 1928).

The third possibility is that the developer, although entitled to an injunction, actually committed some sort of wrong against the feedlot operator. The court remarks that in bringing the development into proximity with the cattle feedlot the plaintiff is not "blameless."[46] The defendant's business was a lawful one, and the plaintiff was the cause of foreseeable detriment to it. The indemnification is appropriate, the court ruled, in a case in which the developer "has, with foreseeability, brought into a previously agricultural... area the population which makes necessary the granting of an injunction against a lawful business and for which the business has no adequate relief."[47] It is as if the court was postulating a notional wrong that consists in populating an area in a way that would foreseeably lead to an injunction against a pre-existingly lawful business. One problem with this is the implausibility of thinking that building on one's own property and then selling what one has built constitutes a wrong. Another problem is that an inherent element in such a wrong would be the entitlement of the supposed wrongdoer to an injunction, the securing of which would simultaneously be the assertion of a right and the commission of a wrong against the same person.

A fourth possibility is that the developer committed a wrong not against the feedlot operator but against the residents who were exposed to the feedlot's smells. As noted in connection with the second possibility, the court regarded the residents as the true victims of the nuisance, and it awarded the developer the injunction only because of the harm that they suffered. Moreover, as noted in connection with the third possibility, the court also regarded the developer rather than the cattle feedlot operator as the true cause of the feedlot's having to move. Putting these two points together, one might surmise that the developer was primarily responsible for the nuisance suffered by the residents.

That the court thought so is indicated by subsequent litigation. At the time of the case brought by the developer another action in nuisance brought by several hundred residents was also pending against the feedlot operator. The feedlot operator filed a third-party complaint against the developer, so as to be able to obtain indemnity from the developer for the damages for which it might be liable to the residents. The court dismissed the developer's contention that

---

[46] Spur v. Webb, above n. 37, at 707.
[47] Ibid.

the claim between the developer and the feedlot operator, having been definitively settled by the litigation between them, was res judicata. Consequently, the court concluded, "the [feedlot operator] is entitled to have litigated the conduct of [the developer] as to each of the [residents] and to have the question of indemnity litigated as to each of them."[48] This decision raised the prospect that the developer would have to compensate the feedlot operator for whatever remedy the residents might be awarded. This too seems an odd prospect. The entitlement that the residents had against the developer concerning the smells to which they would be exposed in the new homes they had purchased was a matter of contract.[49] If they had no such entitlement through their contracts, it seems strange that they could secure one by the indirect route of suing the feedlot owner in nuisance for harms for which the developer would ultimately have to pay.

From the consideration of these four possibilities emerges the difficulty of specifying the normative ground of the causative event to which the indemnified injunction is the response. The wrong is not the reason for the remedy, because no viable wrong can be established that would match so curiously structured a remedy. The court states the circumstances in which this remedy is available—the developer's bringing in of a population that makes the injunction foreseeably necessary—but these circumstances are merely the conditions that trigger the remedy without providing a normatively coherent reason for it.

Because a sophisticated system of private law aspires to make an intelligible connection between the causative event and the response, the following difficulty arises. On the one hand, the production of smells by the feedlot operator is considered to be a wrong of some sort because otherwise a court would have no occasion to formulate any remedy at all. On the other hand, once the remedy is formulated, no matching wrong can be located. The remedy is occasioned by a wrong about whose nature the remedy provides no testimony. Like a door swinging without the hinges that attach it to anything, the remedy is both conditioned by and normatively independent of the events that give rise to it.

---

[48] *Spur Feeding Company*, above n. 41, at 1379.

[49] The developer apparently advertised that purchasers would be able to enjoy the outdoor living that the properties afforded; Spur v. Webb, above n. 37, at 705.

B. The Calabresi–Melamed framework

That the award of an indemnified injunction obscures the injustice of the causative event is also evident from the analysis of Calabresi and Melamed.[50] In suggesting a unified remedial framework that encompasses both property law and tort law, they disclose the economic basis for a new way, corresponding to *Spur v. Webb*, of addressing the legal issues posed by pollution. Their analysis, however, is indifferent to the normative character of the entitlements involved.

Calabresi and Melamed argue that the indemnified injunction is necessary to complete the set of remedial possibilities applicable to nuisance claims. Take the conflict between a polluter who is claiming an entitlement to pollute and the victim who is claiming an entitlement to be free from pollution. Under the traditional remedial framework the victim's entitlement can be protected in two ways. An injunction protects the entitlement by what Calabresi and Melamed call a "property rule," so that in order to continue polluting the polluter must purchase the entitlement from the victim at a value to which the victim agrees. An award of damages protects the victim's entitlement by what they call a "liability rule," so that the polluter pays the victim the value of the entitlement as objectively determined by a court.[51] However, if the victim's claim cannot successfully be made, the entitlement to pollute remains in the hands of the polluter. The effect of this is that the polluter's entitlement is protected by a property rule, because then the victim will have to purchase freedom from pollution by buying out the polluter at the polluter's price. Thus, under the traditional framework, the victim's entitlement is protected by both a property rule and a liability rule, whereas the polluter's entitlement is protected by a property rule only. Stating the entitlement-protecting rules in this way shows, they argue, that something is

---

[50] Above n. 38.

[51] Richard Epstein gives a lucid definition of these rules and the difference between them:

A property right gives the individual the right to keep the entitlement unless and until he chooses to part with it voluntarily. Property rights are, in this sense, made absolute because the ownership of some asset confers sole and exclusive power on a given individual to determine whether to retain or part with an asset on whatever terms he sees fit. In contrast, a liability rule denies the holder of the asset the power to exclude others or, indeed, to keep the asset for himself. Rather, under the standard definition he is helpless to resist the efforts by some other individual to take the thing on payment of its fair value, as objectively determined by some neutral party.

Richard Epstein, "A Clear View of the Cathedral: The Dominance of Property Rules," (1997) 106 Yale L.J. 2091.

missing: a liability rule to protect the polluter's entitlement.[52] Under such a rule the victim could stop the polluter from polluting but would have to compensate the polluter on the basis of an objectively determined value. The contemporaneously decided *Spur* case illustrates this. There the developer could force the cattle feedlot operator to cease producing the smells only by indemnifying the feedlot operator for the disruption of its activities. In the terminology of Calabresi–Melamed, *Spur* protected the feedlot operator's entitlement with a liability rule.

The purpose of this additional rule—Rule 4 as it has come to be known—is to render the parties' positions completely symmetrical. The defect of the traditional framework is that the victim's entitlement, but not the polluter's, is protected by a liability rule. Under the Calabresi–Melamed framework both the property and the liability rules that apply to the victim have counterparts that apply to the polluter.[53]

The achievement of such symmetry is integral to the economic analysis that informs the Calabresi–Melamed framework. Economic analysis illuminates how the law assists the movement of resources to those who value them most. In the absence of transactions costs this movement is achieved through bargaining, which determines the fate of the resource regardless of the party to whom the law initially assigned it.[54] Because the parties bargain against the background of their respective opportunity costs rather than of the one's rights against the other, each is symmetrically the potential cause of the other's deprivation. Legal determinations matter only when transactions costs disrupt the possibility of bargaining. Inasmuch as the point of such

---

[52] Above n. 38, at 1116.

[53] Even if one is attracted, as Calabresi and Melamed are, to the elegance of a remedial framework in which every possibility on the victim's side had a counterpart on the polluter's side, it does not follow that a liability rule is missing on the polluter's side. Instead of adding a liability rule that protects the polluter's entitlement, one could also subtract the liability rule that protects the victim's entitlement, leaving the victim with the protection of a property rule only. Something like this is the position in the Commonwealth jurisdictions, where the plaintiff in a successful nuisance suit is entitled to an injunction except in very limited circumstances; Shelfer v. City of London Electric Lighting Co. [1895] 1 Ch. 287 (C.A.). For a long time this was also the position in U.S. jurisdictions (see Whalen v. Union Bag and Paper Co., 101 N.E. 805 (N.Y.C.A., 1916), until the change effected by Boomer v. Atlantic Cement Co., 257 N.E. 2d 870 (N.Y.C.A., 1970). This would prevent the oddity of an "entitlement" that others could expropriate at will provided they gave the owner its value; see the strong comments of Idington J. in Canada Paper Co. v. Brown, 63 S.C.R. 248 (1922).

[54] Ronald Coase, "The Problem of Social Cost," (1960) 3 J. Law & Economics 1.

determinations is to move the resource to its most valued use—that is, to replicate the result of bargaining in the absence of a process of bargaining—the law has to have available a set of remedies that situates the parties as symmetrically as they would have been as bargainers. Rule 4 accomplishes this symmetry for liability rules, thereby complementing the symmetry of property rules already present in the prevailing framework. With Rule 4 in place the polluter's entitlement is liable to be bought out by the victim, just as the prevailing framework allows the victim's entitlement to be bought out by the polluter. The result is that the remedy, be it a property rule or a liability rule, can be applied against the one party or the other, depending on the nature of the transactions costs.

The symmetry thus achieved deals with effects. It focuses on the point at which the court determines whether the defendant ceases to pollute, pays damages, is absolved from liability, or is indemnified for having to cease polluting. The premise is that whatever kind of effect the law can impose on the polluter for the protection of the victim's entitlement, it should also be able to impose on the victim for the protection of the polluter's. If the law protects the victim's entitlement with a property rule, it should also protect the polluter's entitlement with a property rule, as in fact it does under the traditional framework. If the law protects the victim's entitlement with a liability rule, it should also protect the polluter's entitlement with a liability rule, as it would be able to do under Rule 4.

The oddity of such symmetry of effect is that it operates despite the asymmetry in the normative character of the parties' entitlements. If the victim triumphs, the entitlement protected by the award of an injunction or of damages is, in Hohfeldian terms, a claim right.[55] In the law of private nuisance this is a right that the possessor of land has to be free from "an inconvenience materially interfering with the ordinary comfort physically of human existence."[56] The recognition of this right in the victim implies a correlative duty of non-interference for the polluter. The injunction or damages are then supposed to restore the victim to the enjoyment (or to its monetary equivalent) of the right with which the polluter was duty-bound not to interfere. In contrast, however, the polluter's success in staving off this suit does not

---

[55] Wesley N. Hohfeld, "Some Fundamental Legal Conceptions as Applied in Judicial Reasoning," (1913) 23 Yale L.J. 16, at 32.

[56] Walter v. Selfe, 4 DeG & S 315 (1851), at 322.

show that the polluter has a claim right against the victim. Nor is the victim under a correlative duty to continue to suffer from the pollution. If, for instance, the victim encased the property exposed to the pollution in a dome, so that the victim could no longer smell the polluting odors, no duty to the polluter would be violated.[57] The polluter's entitlement is merely a liberty[58]—that is, the recognition that no right of the victim is being infringed and that therefore the polluter is under no correlative duty to the victim. Accordingly, whereas the victim's entitlement is a claim right correlative to which is a duty on the polluter, the polluter's entitlement is to a liberty correlative to which is not a duty on the victim but the absence of a claim right. The term "entitlement" used by Calabresi and Melamed is therefore misleading. Its application to both the victim and the polluter within a symmetrical framework of protection masks the difference between a claim right and a liberty—and thus also the difference in their correlatives between being and not being under a duty.

By positing that a liability rule is symmetrically applicable to the entitlements of the polluter and the victim, the Calabresi–Melamed framework flattens the normative landscape in two ways. First, the award of damages against the polluter is no longer seen as the response to the violation of a duty correlative to the victim's right. Applying the notion of duty to the polluter's conduct would destroy the symmetry with the victim's payment—clearly not a matter of duty but rather a condition for getting an injunction—under the indemnified injunction. Instead, the damage award is regarded merely as giving the polluter an option to purchase the victim's entitlement at an objectively established price.[59] The polluter's violation of the victim's right is thereby treated as an allowable choice, rather than as a wrong. Second, in giving the victim a parallel option to purchase the polluter's entitlement in a case like *Spur*, the indemnified injunction distorts the victim's right. Instead of vindicating the victim's right against the polluter's wrongful conduct, the injunction operates only as the prelude

[57] For a similar point, see Henry Smith, "Exclusion and Property Rules in the Law of Nuisance," (2004) 90 Va. L. Rev. 965, at 1012.

[58] In Hohfeld's terminology, a "privilege"; above n. 55, at 33.

[59] Daniel Friedmann, "Rights and Remedies," in *Comparative Remedies for Breach of Contract*, ed. Nili Cohen and Ewan McKendrick (2005), 3, at 7. One of the results of the Calabresi–Melamed analysis is the growth of a complex literature treating liability rules as options. See Madeline Morris, "The Structure of Entitlements," (1993) 78 Cornell L. Rev. 822, at 851–56; Ian Ayres and Paul M. Goldbart, "Optimal Delegation and Decoupling in the Design of liability Rules," (2001) 100 Mich. L. Rev. 1; Ian Ayres, *Optional Law* (2005).

for the victim's option to purchase the polluter's abstention from pol-luting. In this way the Calabresi–Melamed framework of symmetrical liability rules substitutes parallel options for the correlative categories of right and duty.

In sum, then, Calabresi and Melamed put forward a remedial frame-work of symmetrical effects, even though these effects protect entitle-ments of differing normative characters. This is inconsistent with the idea that the point of the remedy is to match the injustice that moti-vates it. In the Calabresi–Melamed framework the response is based not on the normative character of the causative event, which it ignores and obscures, but on the efficiency gains that result from movement of resources to their most valued uses. As is typical of the second concep-tion of remedies, the Calabresi–Melamed analysis treats the causative event merely as the preliminary to a response that is independent of the reason for considering the event an injustice.

4. Monism and dualism

In recent years commentators on the law of remedies have distin-guished two approaches to the relationship between the causative event and the response.[60] The "monist" integrates the right and the remedy, treating the remedy as the mirror image or reflex of the right—in Peter Birks's words, "the same thing as the right, looked at from the other end."[61] The "dualist" separates the right from the rem-edy, postulating that the court in determining the remedy chooses from the basket of all potential remedies the context-specific one that is most appropriate in the circumstances. How does this distinc-tion between monism and dualism relate to the reason and condition distinction?

Obviously these two sets of distinctions overlap, with the corrective justice conception being monistic and the other conception dualistic. The former conception treats the remedy as merely the continuation of the plaintiff's right in circumstances in which the defendant has, or

---

[60] G. Hammond, "Rethinking Remedies: The Changing Conception of the Relationship between Legal and Equitable Remedies," in *Remedies: Issues and Perspectives*, ed. Jeffrey Ber-ryman (1991), 87, 90–91; Michael Tilbury, "Remedies and the Classification of Obligations," in *The Law of Obligations and Boundaries*, ed. A. Robertson (2004), 11, 17–24.

[61] Peter Birks, "Definition and Division: A Meditation on Institutes 3.13," in *The Classifica-tion of Obligations*, ed. Peter Birks (1997), 1, 24.

has done, something inconsistent with that right. In this sense the remedy is, as Birks said, the right "looked at from the other end."[62] Conversely, the dualistic approach allows for the possibility, characteristic of the latter conception, that "the remedy granted in any case may serve purposes unrelated to the reason(s) for the imposition of the liability in the first place."[63] The principal difference between of the two sets of distinctions is that the reason–condition distinction operates closer to the normative basis of liability. Its central concern is to conceptualize the relationship between right and remedy in terms of the reasons for thinking that justice requires that the defendant be held liable to the plaintiff. In contrast, the debate between monism and dualism focuses on adherence to or rejection of precedent, history, and established categories.[64]

However, corrective justice may assist in narrowing, or at least illuminating, the gap between dualism and monism. By presenting the remedy closer to its normative ground within a conceptual framework that is more abstracted from the particularities of precedent, corrective justice affords a more unobstructed vista of the issues that divide monism and dualism. In particular, corrective justice may point the way to dealing with a tension that exists in both monism and dualism, and thus to reconciling monism and dualism themselves.

Consider two features of dualism. The first feature is the dualist emphasis on the fact that the law brings into play at the remedial stage certain considerations that were absent earlier. This is especially the case with equitable remedies, where the determination of the remedy is leavened by various grounds for exercising discretion. In the dualist view, the introduction of these new considerations at the remedial stage makes it implausible to regard the remedy simply as the right viewed from the other end. The second feature is that the dualist does not posit the complete separation of the right from the remedy. When recommending the availability of *all* possible remedies, the dualist does not have in mind all the ingenious remedies that the fertile human mind can excogitate—for example, the indemnified injunction and its numerous notional relatives[65]—however disconnected they are from

---

[62] Ibid.

[63] Tilbury, above n. 60, at 19.

[64] J. D. Davies, "Duties of Confidence and Loyalty," (1990) Lloyd's Maritime & Commercial L.Q., 4, at 5.

[65] Saul Levmore lists sixteen remedies available within the Calabresi–Melamed framework; see Levmore, above n. 11, at 2173.

the normative ground of the cause of action. Even a dualist recognizes the "unbreakable relationship" between obligation and remedy, thereby acknowledging that "the nature of the obligation breached is the starting point and generally the most important factor (while not necessarily the only one) determining the appropriate remedy in any particular case."[66] Thus, the dualist maintains that the remedial stage involves considerations that are both different from and yet unbreakably related to the infringed right. How is the combination of these apparently incompatible features to be understood?

The monist position faces a parallel challenge. The monist wants to underline the second of these two features, the adamantine nature of the connection between right and remedy. Yet the first feature, that the remedy may be determined by considerations not present in the specification of the right and its infringement, seems also undeniable in the law's remedial practice. If the monist position is to be plausible, it too must find a way to combine these two features despite the apparent tension between them.

So far as corrective justice is concerned, the monist position that the remedy is "the same thing as the right, looked at from the other end"[67] has to be understood in a particular way. Under corrective justice the identity of right and remedy means that they form a single continuous normative sequence, so that the right both grounds and limits the remedy. The function of the remedy is to remove the inconsistency with the plaintiff's right that is imputable to the defendant. The plaintiff's right, therefore, is the reason both for the defendant's duty to abstain from doing or having something inconsistent with it and for the defendant's duty to eliminate any such inconsistency should it occur. These duties, being correlative to the same right, are conceptually the same duty, though the duty has a different content before and after the injustice. The right and its correlative duty thus persist through the causative event despite the change that the causative event works in the particular thing to which the plaintiff has a right and in the particular action that the defendant has a duty to perform. The identity of right and remedy, in other words, is not one of content but of normative ground. When one gazes at the right from the other end, one looks at the same thing even though what one may see is different.

---

[66] Tilbury, above n. 60, at 26; cf. also David Wright, "Wrong and Remedy: A Sticky Relationship," (2001) Sing. J. Legal Stud. 300.

[67] Above n. 61.

One kind of circumstance that may manifest a change in the content of the right at the remedial end is trivial. As was noted above in section 2, the causative event may have had effects in time or space that render the specific subject matter of the right irretrievable. For example, the plaintiff may have had a right to a specific thing that was destroyed or to contractual performance at a specific time that has passed. Nonetheless the right, as a marker of the normative relationship between the parties with respect to the specific thing or to the contractual performance at a specific time, remains intact. The court then requires the defendant to give the plaintiff a quantitative or qualitative equivalent. Although not physically or temporally identical with the original content of the right, this equivalent is from the normative standpoint nonetheless "the same thing as the right, looked at from the other end."[68]

More germane to the present discussion is another kind of circumstance, in which the law at the remedial stage refers to fresh considerations that pertain not to the physical or temporal landscape but to the normative one. These fresh considerations arise out of the relationship between the plaintiff's right and the entire system of rights. In this connection, three points have to be kept in mind.

First, rights are necessarily systematic. A right does not merely give a particular right-holder an entitlement to a particular thing. Rather, it exists normatively within a comprehensive system of rights. Rights are the juridical manifestations of the freedom of self-determining beings who interact with one another as equals. Accordingly, a person claiming a right necessarily acknowledges that others also have rights with which the claimant's right must systematically coexist.[69] There is no particular right divorced from its situation within a system of rights.

Second, rights have to be enforced by a court—that is, by a disinterested and impartial public authority. Because a claim of right involves the acknowledgment that others also have such claims within the system of rights, the obligations generated by any particular right can be treated as binding only insofar as there exists a public authority that interprets and enforces all the obligations contained in all the rights considered as a totality.[70] This authority does not give effect to

---

[68] Ibid.
[69] Kant, above n. 17, [6:255–56].
[70] Ibid.

the unilateral will of any particular right-holder or look at any right in isolation. Rather, it impartially and disinterestedly brings out the normative implications of the system of rights and applies them to each right within the system. Accordingly, a claim of right implies a judicial role in interpreting and enforcing the claim. The claim is, therefore, qualified both by the limits of judicial competence and by the exercise of judgment in accordance with public reason. In this way the court functions as guardian of the system of rights, preserving the rights of all in their juridical relationships with one another.

Third, the special responsibility of the court as the guardian of the system of rights becomes particularly salient at the remedial stage. The remedy is the point at which the coercive enforcement of the plaintiff's right directly impacts the defendant. It is at this point that a court must be particularly sensitive not only to the plaintiff as the claimant of the right, but also to its own institutional role within the system of rights and to the defendant as a participant in that system.

Thus, within corrective justice the infringed right that is the reason for the remedy has its being within a system of rights whose meaning is determined by a court exercising its judgment within its institutional competence. In being "the same thing as the right looked at from the other end"[71] as the monist claims, the remedy reflects the right considered not in isolation but as a component of the system of rights. This does not change the right at the remedial stage from what it was initially: the particular right always had normative significance—that is, it generated a duty that the defendant had to treat as binding—only because it belonged to the system of rights.

Seen in this light, the dualist contention that the remedy may "serve purposes unrelated to the reason(s) for the imposition of liability in the first place,"[72] can also be understood in a way that brings it within the corrective justice conception of remedies. If the reason for imposing liability refers to the infringed right taken in isolation, the remedy may appear to be unrelated to it. However, the moral significance of a right precludes taking the right in isolation from the system of rights as a whole. The system of rights—what Kant called "the sum of the conditions under which the choice of one can be united with the choice of another in accordance with a universal law of freedom"[73]—forms an

---

[71] Above n. 61.
[72] Above n. 63.
[73] Kant, above n. 17, [6:231].

objective normative order of which the right of the plaintiff is a particularized crystallization.[74] Thus, so long as it is intelligible within the system of rights, the remedy is not unrelated to the reason for imposing liability, even if it embodies considerations that did not figure in the imposition of liability in the first place.

Within a functioning system of law, in other words, systemic considerations are always implicit in the right even as initially regarded. In the determination of the remedy, however, the court has to exercise its coercive authority so as not to affect the defendant in a manner inconsistent with the system of rights and therefore with the defendant's status in the community of interacting rights-holders. The court therefore makes explicit the systemic considerations appropriate to the circumstances at hand. This difference, between the implicit and the explicit, accounts for the appearance of new considerations at the remedial stage, yet in a way that preserves the centrality of the right, as monists and dualists agree.

One example of the role of systemic considerations about rights, drawn again from the law of nuisance, will have to suffice. As is well known, in Commonwealth jurisdictions the successful plaintiff in a private nuisance suit is entitled, with rare exceptions, to an injunction. This injunction follows from the nature of the plaintiff's right. Because the wrong of nuisance is an interference with the plaintiff's use and enjoyment of property, the injunction forbidding the offending activity restores to the plaintiff the very thing of which the plaintiff was wrongfully deprived. Under the corrective justice conception of remedies, the granting of an injunction is straightforward.

But what about the rare exceptions where the plaintiff can get no more than damages for a continuing nuisance? The case of *Shelfer v. City of London Electric Lighting Co.*[75] provides the classic formulation of the circumstances in which a court may in its discretion substitute damages for an injunction. According to the judgment, four factors must all be present: a small injury to the plaintiff's rights, an injury capable of being estimated in money, adequate compensation by a

---

[74] The notion of "objective normative order" is drawn from German constitutional law (see the Luth decision, *Decisions of the Bundesverfassungsgericht—Federal Constitutional Court— Federal Republic of Germany*, vol. 2/I: *Freedom of Speech* (1998), 1–20) where the same issue arises of the relationship between a particular right and the system of rights. For treatment of this issue from the constitutional perspective see, Lorraine E. Weinrib, "The Postwar Paradigm and American Exceptionalism," in *The Migration of Constitutional Ideas*, ed. Sujit Choudhry (2006). I am grateful to Lorraine Weinrib for discussion of this aspect.

[75] [1895] 1 Ch. 287, at 222 (C.A.).

small monetary payment, and the oppressiveness to the defendant of an injunction. Under these circumstances the plaintiff is not restored to the use and enjoyment of the property, which is the plaintiff's right, but must instead accept the monetary equivalent of the wrongful injury. To that extent, as the dualist would claim, the remedy does not match the plaintiff's particular right but is rather the product of considerations present only at the remedial stage.

These considerations represent a specific conception of remedial fairness. On the one hand the plaintiff's injury is small, monetizable, and capable of being adequately compensated by a small monetary payment, so that the difference between damages and an injunction is minimal from the plaintiff's perspective. On the other hand, the injunction would be oppressive to the defendant, because it would inflict on the defendant a significant hardship from which the plaintiff would derive no substantial benefit. Under these circumstances the only point of seeking an injunction would be to damage the defendant rather than to promote any legitimate interest of the plaintiff. Accordingly, by not awarding an injunction the court prevents the plaintiff from using the judicial process to harm the defendant through a remedy that would not materially benefit the plaintiff. In the language of the civil law, the substitution of damages for an injunction prevents the plaintiff from abusing his or her right.[76]

The notion of abuse of rights is often regarded as introducing into the law considerations of social or moral good that are alien to the idea of rights.[77] A right provides an area of untrammeled freedom for the right-holder. The notion of abuse of right seems to contain the contradictory impulses of recognizing the right while yet limiting the

---

[76] A similar explanation would apply to the requirement at common law that the plaintiff mitigate his or her damages. It would also apply to some of the situations, exemplified by Patel v. Ali [1984] Ch. 283 (C.A.), in which hardship to the defendant prevents the court from issuing a decree of specific performance of a contract. Similar are situations of laches, in which the prejudice suffered by the defendant as a result of the plaintiff's delay in seeking specific performance is the basis for denying the remedy. These remedial considerations illustrate Tony Weir's observation that "we are not supposed to have any doctrine of abuse of rights (but it is only the doctrine which is lacking)." Weir, "The Staggering March of Negligence," in The Law of Obligations: Essays in Celebration of John Fleming, ed. Peter Cane and Jane Stapleton (1998), 99, at 124. See also Joseph M. Perillo, "Abuse of Rights: A Pervasive Legal Concept," (1995) 27 Pac. L.J. 37.

[77] S. Herman, "Classical Social Theories and the Doctrine of 'Abuse of Rights'," (1977) 37 La. L. Rev. 747; W. T. Tete, "Tort Roots and the Ramifications of the Obligations Revision," (1986) 32 Loy. L. Rev. 47, 68–72 (decribing Josserand's conception of abuse of right).

right-holder's freedom. Hence arises the impression that the normative basis of the limit is external to the rights perspective.

This impression, however, is mistaken. The idea that the law should
not legitimize the infliction on another of gratuitous harm is fully
consonant with the normative presuppositions of a system of rights.
Participants in the system of rights are conceived as persons with a
self-determining capacity for purposive action in their relations with
one another. Within this system all persons pursue their self-chosen
purposes, subject only to the constraint that their actions be capable of
coexisting with the purposiveness of others. This requires that one
pursue one's purposes as ends that one is trying to achieve for oneself,
not as an obstacle against what someone else is trying to achieve.
Actions for the sake of creating mutual obstacles against the actions of
others cannot systemically coexist.

As juridical manifestations of self-determining freedom, rights provide the space within which all the right-holders may pursue ends of
their own. Such ends are consistent with the self-determining freedom of others only if the point of pursuing them is independent of
the adverse effect on someone else. When all act to pursue ends of
their own in this sense, they all rank equally as persons whose activities can coexist within the system of rights. Conversely, if the freedom
to perform an act merely to frustrate the purposes of another were
legitimate, rights would be transformed from markers of mutual freedom to instruments of subordination. Accordingly, it would be inconsistent with what is normatively presupposed in the system of rights
to allow a right to operate in a way that would harm another without
promoting (in the language of the civilians)[78] a "serious and legitimate
interest" of the right-holder.

In awarding damages in lieu of an injunction to the victim of a
nuisance, the court is acting as guardian of the system of rights, keeping the remedial consequences of the infringement of a particular
right aligned with what is normatively presupposed in the system as a
whole. The plaintiff is ordinarily entitled to an injunction, as that
would restore to the plaintiff the use and enjoyment of the property
that makes up the content of the plaintiff's right. However, through its
determination of the remedy the court prevents the plaintiff's right

---

[78] Antonio Gambaro, "Abuse of Rights in the Civil Law Tradition," in *Aequitas and Equity: Equity in Civil Law and Mixed Jurisdictions*, ed. Alfredo Mordechai Rabello (1997), 632, at 637; A. N. Yiannopoulos, "Abuse of Right in Louisiana," ibid., 690, at 700.

from operating in a way that prejudices the defendant without forwarding an interest of the plaintiff. To grant an injunction under the conditions enumerated in *Shelfer* would be inconsistent with the normative grounding of rights in the coexistence of the parties' self-determining freedom. This latter consideration is systemically implicit in all rights, including the particular right infringed by the defendant. Thus, the award of damages rather than an injunction treats the infringed right not as free-standing but as situated within the system of rights that is required for the right's normative significance.

Similar observations about the systemic aspect of rights can be made about other circumstances in which new normative considerations are introduced at the remedial stage. Especially in exercising their discretion to grant specific performance, courts often invoke such factors as the difficulty of constant curial supervision, the futility of the remedy, the absence of mutuality, the plaintiff's failure to do equity, and the reluctance to enforce a decree of personal service. These factors refer to substantive and institutional aspects normatively presupposed in the system of rights, from the maintenance of the transactional equality of the parties to the avoidance of the court's exceeding its institutional competence. To be sure, the application of these factors to particular circumstances is controversial, as is evidenced, for instance, by the contention that the difficulty of judicial supervision has been overstated.[79] Nonetheless, however such factors ought to figure in particular circumstances, the point for present purposes is that, within the corrective justice conception of remedies, attention to the system of rights rather than merely to a given right in isolation opens up the normative space in which such factors can coherently be considered.

If this is so, the corrective justice conception of remedies may be able to reconcile, at least to some extent, the apparently competing insights of monism and dualism. From the monist perspective, the notion that the remedy is just the right looked at from the other end is maintained, but with the understanding that because a particular right participates in a system of rights, systemic considerations may modulate the remedy. From the dualist perspective, the systemic character of rights may introduce new considerations at the remedial stage while preserving the central importance of the infringed right and the remedy's unbreakable connection with it.

---

[79] Jeffrey Berryman, *The Law of Equitable Remedies* (2000), 175–85.

5. Conclusion

In presenting the two conceptions of remedies, this chapter has ultimately been concerned with how remedies might figure within a normatively coherent system of private law. The corrective justice conception maintains this coherence in two ways. First, it integrates the causative event and the response by treating the injustice as an inconsistency with the plaintiff's right that the remedy is supposed to eliminate. The remedy is thus continuous with the right, reflecting its structure and content. In contrast, the conception of remedies as merely conditioned by causative events fragments private law by making the remedy the locus of considerations that are independent of the injustice of the causative event. Second, corrective justice treats rights not as isolated entitlements but as members of a system of rights, so that the remedy conforms to what is normatively presupposed in the system as a whole. Accordingly, to be continuous with the right, the remedy also has to be continuous with the right's systemic aspects. Only by attending to these two dimensions of juridical coherence can a judge, in determining the remedy, live up to Aristotle's observation that "to go to the judge is to go to what is just, for the judge means to be, as it were, justness ensouled."[80]

[80] Above n. 2.

4

Gain-based Damages

1. Introduction

On what basis can damages for tortious conduct be measured by the defendant's gain rather than the plaintiff's loss? This question recently has received increasing attention for reasons that are not hard to see. Gain-based damages for torts implicate fundamental issues in our conception of private law. On the one hand, they open up the possibility of a more nuanced assessment of damages both by extending the long-established jurisprudence of waiver of tort and by linking tortious liability to the newly invigorated interest in restitutionary liability. On the other hand, they present an intellectual puzzle. If tort law is concerned with wrongful injury to the plaintiff, special arguments are required to explain why, as a matter of justice, the remedy should refer to the gains of the defendant. The reparation of injury seems satisfied by compensating the plaintiff for his or her loss. To place into the plaintiff's hands the defendant's gain in excess of that loss seems to confer a windfall.

My immediate excuse for revisiting this topic is to draw attention to the relevance of inquiring into the *plaintiff's* entitlement to damages measured by the defendant's gain. Many of the current treatments of gain-based damages for torts focus on the defendant's desert in the aftermath of wrongdoing or on the social good that can be achieved by compelling the disgorgement of the wrongdoer's gain. Hence commentators appeal to the idea that one should not profit from a wrong,[1] that disgorgement of wrongful gain is an effective deterrence for

[1] Andrew Burrows, *The Law of Restitution*, 2nd ed. (2002), 455.

potential wrongdoers,[2] or that gain-based damages are directed toward the protection of legal facilities in whose integrity the community has an interest.[3] However, the injustice or social inexpediency of the defendant's retention of the gain indicates only the party from whom the gain should be taken, not the party to whom it should be awarded. Thus, such accounts fail to provide a reason for the law to transfer the defendant's gain to the plaintiff, of all people.[4] If the basic difficulty with an award of gain-based damages is the supposed windfall of the plaintiff, an adequate treatment must show either that the award is justified despite being a windfall or that the award, where appropriate, is not really a windfall but damages that the plaintiff may of right demand from the defendant. The latter is the strategy that I will essay here.

More broadly, my aim in this chapter is to situate gain-based damages within the theoretical framework of corrective justice. Like any remedy, an award of gain-based damages presupposes a conception of the injustice that it remedies. Because corrective justice views damages as undoing an injustice, it is particularly sensitive to the connection between the remedy that the plaintiff can claim and the injustice that is imputed to the defendant. The significance of that connection for gain-based damages is the subject of this chapter.

Corrective justice embodies a notion both of the relationship of the remedy to the injustice that it remedies and of the relationship between the parties to that injustice. The two parties are correlatively situated as the doer and sufferer of an injustice that is itself undone by the corresponding remedy. Correlativity is inherent in the notion of liability, which treats the injustice done by the former as the very injustice suffered by the latter. Correlativity is also inherent in the idea of damages, which treats the plaintiff as entitled to receive the very sum that the defendant is obligated to pay. These instances of correlativity

---

[2] Peter Cane, "Exceptional Measures of Damages: In Search of a Principle," in *Wrongs and Remedies in the Twenty-First Century*, ed. Peter Birks (1996), 301.

[3] I. M. Jackman, "Restitution for Wrongs," (1989) 48 Cambridge L.J. 302. By "legal facilities" Jackman means "private property, relations of trust and confidence, and (with some qualification) contracts," which "require protection against those who seek to take the benefits of an institution without the burdens thereof." Ibid., 302.

[4] Burrows, above n. 1, 480, shows some sensitivity to this problem. He accordingly suggests that gain-based damages might be available in situations where the idea that one should not profit from one's wrong can be supplemented by additional reasons for restitution, such as the need to protect facilitative institutions and to deter cynical wrongdoing. The difficulty is that these additional reasons no more single out the plaintiff than the consideration they supplement. It is hard to see how a multiplicity of reasons for restitution that are not plaintiff-specific generate a recovery that is plaintiff-specific.

are mirror images of each other, with the plaintiff's entitlement to damages from the defendant reflecting the plaintiff's entitlement to be free from suffering injustice at the defendant's hands.

Because the remedy mirrors the correlative structure of the injustice, corrective justice disqualifies accounts of gain-based damages that focus solely on the wrongdoer. Among the accounts excluded on this basis are those that, under the banner of punishment and deterrence, focus on the past or future actions of defendants, thereby treating the plaintiff merely as a convenient conduit of social consequences rather as someone to whom damages are owed to correct the wrong suffered. Of course, this does not mean that explanations of gain-based damages must be oriented to the plaintiff as some are now oriented to the defendant. Corrective justice rejects all one-sided accounts, regardless of the particular side singled out. Rather, the parties must be seen as related through the injustice in such a way that the plaintiff can demand such damages as of right from the defendant. Accordingly, the justification for awarding such damages must include not only the reason for making the defendant pay but also the reason for entitling the plaintiff to receive them; indeed, the same reason must apply on both sides. Only then is the correlativity that marks the injustice carried forward into the account of the remedy.[5]

The corrective justice framework, then, makes salient the need to account for the plaintiff's entitlement to gain-based damages as a response to the defendant's having something, or having done something, inconsistent with the plaintiff's right. This chapter attempts to satisfy this need in the following steps. Section 2 deals with the radical proposal that would allow the plaintiff gain-based damages for any wrongful gain. The problem with this proposal, that it does not adequately link the damages to the normative quality of the wrongful act,

---

[5] The basic idea of this article is similar to the one animating the analysis of the *Eingriffskondiktion* in German law since the writings of Wilburg and von Caemmerer, that the availability of restitution for an interference with the plaintiff's right depends on the scope and purpose that the legal order attributes to the right. See B. S. Markesinis et al., *The German Law of Obligations*, vol. 1, *The Law of Contracts and Restitution: A Comparative Introduction* (1997), 744–45. This congruence of approach is hardly surprising, since the German approach proceeds from the assumption that both restitution and delict are informed by Aristotle's notion of corrective justice; see E. von Caemmerer, *Bereicherung und unerlaubte Handlung*, in *Festschrift fuer Ernst Rabel*, Band I (1954), 333, 335. Wilburg's comment that restitution in the *Eingriffskondiktion* "grows organically out of the mother-right, so to speak of itself" (quoted in John Dawson, *Indirect Enrichment*, in *Ius Privatum Gentium (Rheinstein Festschrift)*, vol. 2 (1969), 789, 798) is a graphic way of portraying the intimate connection that corrective justice posits between the injustice and the remedy.

leads in section 3 to an examination of the more traditional connection of gain-based damages with dealings with another's property. The virtue of the focus on dealings with another's property is that the idea of property includes within the proprietor's entitlement the potential gains from the property's use or alienation. Section 4 generalizes from the property cases to the conclusion that gain-based damages ought to be available only insofar as they correspond to a constituent element in the wrong that the defendant has done to the plaintiff. Section 5 discusses the relevance of the willfulness of the wrong insofar as it entails a denial of the plaintiff's right, not because of notions of punishment or deterrence. The final section deals with situations where, although the plaintiff's interest is not, strictly speaking, a proprietary one, the analysis of the property cases nonetheless applies.

2. The Goff–Jones principle

Requiring tortfeasors to disgorge their wrongful gains is an intuitively appealing idea. The tortfeasor's moral claim to retain the fruit of his or her own wrongdoing is a weak one. Permitting a wrongdoer to enjoy the benefits of the wrong might seem an additional victimization of the wronged party. Moreover, through the old "waiver of tort" cases, the law has long recognized the principle of disgorgement for certain torts, and the task of distinguishing torts that allow for disgorgement from those that do not has proved a difficult one. Indeed one might think that task misguided, on the ground that the morally relevant feature of the wrongdoer's gain is the commission of the wrong, not the kind of wrong committed.

Presumably these considerations lie behind the radical proposal of Lord Goff and Professor Jones that the victim of a tort should be allowed restitution of all wrongful gains. They formulate their proposal as follows: "If it can be demonstrated that the tortfeasor has gained a benefit and that benefit would not have been gained but for the tort, he should be required to make restitution."[6] This suggestion has the advantage of simplicity, for it offers a comprehensive principle that obviates the need to distinguish between wrongs that do and wrongs that do not admit of gain-based damages.

---

[6] Lord Goff of Chieveley and Gareth Jones, *The Law of Restitution*, 7th ed. (2007), 36–006.

Despite its simplicity and its intuitive appeal, the Goff–Jones principle has not been accepted by the courts. In the view of Professor Jones, this is because courts "fear the great unknown."[7] I would like to suggest a more charitable reason, arising out of an ambiguity in the notion of wrongful gain.

When we think of wrongful gains for restitutionary purposes, precisely how are the ideas of wrongfulness and gain connected? One possibility is that a gain is wrongful because of its history; that is, a gain is wrongful if it is the consequence of a wrongful act. Rather than pointing to a feature of the gain itself, "wrongful" is used to indicate that wrongful conduct by the defendant is a historical antecedent of the defendant's gain. The wrongdoing that underlies ascription of wrongfulness stands to the gain as cause to effect. "Wrongful gain," then, could be understood as shorthand for the more accurate description "gain resulting from a wrongful act."

The other and more restrictive possibility is that we call a gain "wrongful" by virtue of its inherent normative quality. Here the significance of the wrongfulness is not merely that it produces the gain, but that it survives into the gain and informs it. The gain's origin in wrong is a necessary condition for the gain's having this normative quality, but something further is required. For the gain to take on the normative quality of wrongfulness, it must be the materialization of a possibility—the opportunity to gain—that rightfully belonged to the plaintiff. Because it is an incident of the plaintiff's entitlement that the defendant has wrongfully infringed, the gain is not merely the result of a wrongful act, but is the continuing embodiment of the injustice between the parties.

The Goff–Jones principle rests on the assumption that the relevant understanding of wrongful gain is the historical one. Using language reminiscent of the factual causation test in negligence law ("the benefit would not have been gained but for the tort"), they formulate the relation between wrongfulness and gain solely in terms of cause and effect. In their view the fact that the plaintiff has been wronged by the defendant, plus the fact that the defendant has consequently realized a benefit, add up to the liability of the defendant to surrender the benefit to the plaintiff.

Why might one be reluctant, as Jones notes that courts are, to accept a principle that bases liability on the historical rather than the

---

[7] Gareth Jones, *Restitution in Public and Private Law* (1991), 77.

normative connection between wrongdoing and gain? I suggest that it is because the Goff–Jones principle challenges the internal coherence of private law. By this I mean not that the principle measures the plaintiff's injury by the defendant's gain (the waiver of tort cases show that this is not in itself unacceptable), but that the connection it posits between what the wrongdoer has done and what the victim recovers is at odds with the principle underlying the law's treatment of wrongful loss.

The phenomenon of compensatory damages for wrongful loss is the counterpart to gain-based damages for wrongful gain. In wrongful loss the same two conceptions of wrongfulness present themselves. A loss is wrongful by reference to its history if the occurrence of the loss was the result of the defendant's wrong. A loss is wrongful by reference to its normative quality if the potential for such loss is a reason for considering the defendant's conduct to have been wrongful in the first place.

The cases on duty and proximate cause in negligence illustrate the difference between these two ways of connecting wrongfulness and loss. In the famous case about duty, *Palsgraf v. Long Island Railroad*,[8] the plaintiff was injured by an act that negligently imperiled the property of someone else. The plaintiff's loss was wrongful in the historical sense, in that one of the historical antecedents of the loss was a wrongful act by the defendant. However, because the plaintiff was beyond the ambit of reasonably foreseeable injury, the prospect of her being harmed was not a reason for thinking that the defendant's conduct was wrongful. The conduct was thus not a wrong relative to her. Similarly, the *Wagon Mound* case holds that the requirement of proximate cause is not satisfied when the defendant negligently exposes the plaintiff to the risk of one kind of injury, but the plaintiff suffers an injury of a different kind.[9] Such losses are historically connected to the wrongful conduct, in that they would not have occurred without it, but they do not partake of the conduct's wrongful quality since they are not the losses by virtue of which the conduct is regarded as wrongful.

These doctrines show that in the context of compensatory damages for negligence, liability exists only when the connection between the wrongfulness and the loss is normative and not merely historical. That

---

[8] 248 N.Y. 339, 162 N.E. 99 (1928).
[9] *The Wagon Mound, No. 1* [1961] A.C. 388 (P.C.).

the negligent conduct is factually caused by the loss is not sufficient. To be recoverable, the loss must be within the risk the creation of which rendered the defendant's act unreasonable.

From the perspective of corrective justice, negligence law has good reason for insisting, through the doctrines of duty and proximate cause, that a loss should be considered wrongful by virtue of its normative quality rather than merely its history.[10] In negligence law, wrongdoing consists in the creation of unreasonable risk. When the plaintiff's loss is within the ambit of the very risk that renders the defendant's conduct wrongful, the parties stand to each other as the active and passive poles of the same injustice. Because freedom from this kind of loss is both the content of the plaintiff's right and the object of the defendant's duty, the parties are normatively linked through the wrongfulness of the defendant's risk-creation. Liability then obligates the defendant to eliminate the loss wrongfully imposed on the plaintiff, and thus to restore (to the extent that monetary damages can) the freedom from loss which was the plaintiff's original entitlement. In contrast, when the plaintiff's loss, although caused by the defendant's wrongdoing, is not within the ambit of what makes it wrongful, the defendant's conduct cannot be said to be wrongful with respect to that plaintiff's loss. Because the parties are then not related to each other as doer and sufferer of an injustice, the plaintiff lacks the normative standing to call upon the defendant to make good the loss.

Negligence law's treatment of wrongful loss undermines the Goff–Jones proposal concerning wrongful gain. To highlight the parallel between the two, one may say (echoing the Goff–Jones formulation) that negligence law rejects the principle that the tortfeasor must pay compensation "if it can be shown that the victim suffered a loss and that loss would not have been suffered but for the tort." The compensatory principle that negligence law rejects has the same structure as the gain-based principle that Goff and Jones propose. Both principles use factual causation as a sufficient condition for the damage award. The only difference between them is that whereas the compensatory principle deals with loss and compensation, the Goff–Jones principle deals with gain and restitution. Since it is the significance of factual causation that is at issue in each, the fact that one deals with compensation for loss and the other with restitution for gain is unimportant. If the law has good reason for rejecting factual causation as a sufficient

---

[10] Above, chapter 2, section 2.

condition of liability for wrongfully caused loss, then it also has good reason to reject it as the test for wrongfully caused gain. Accepting the Goff–Jones principle would introduce the inconsistency of allowing factual causation to be sufficient for restitution when it has been found to be insufficient for compensation.

The corrective justice analysis of compensation for wrongful loss applies, *mutatis mutandis*, to restitution for wrongful gain. If the wrongfulness consists in creating the prospect of a loss (as, let us assume for the moment, is the case with negligence), the fact that the defendant has realized a gain as well adds nothing to the plaintiff's case. Because the gain lies beyond the wrong done to the plaintiff, the plaintiff suffers no injustice through the existence of the gain. The parties do and suffer injustice only with respect to the loss, not the gain; the gain remains external to their relationship.

Accordingly, from the standpoint of corrective justice, factual causation no more suffices for liability on the gain side than it does on the loss side. What matters is not the historical connection of gain to wrong, but rather the nature of the wrong as an inconsistency with the plaintiff's right and whether the gain partakes of that inconsistency. Gain-based damages are justified when the defendant's gain is of something that lies within the right of the plaintiff and is therefore integral to the continuing relationship of the parties as the doer and sufferer of an injustice. Then the gain stands not merely as the sequel to the wrong but as its present embodiment, and the plaintiff is as entitled to the gain as he or she was to the defendant's abstention from the wrong that produced it. A gain that thus embodies the injustice done by the defendant to the plaintiff immediately implies restitution of that gain.

The Goff–Jones principle has the twin virtues of simplicity of formulation and comprehensiveness of application, but it also has the corresponding vices. On the one hand, the proposed principle obviates the need to distinguish among wrongs by using the simple test of whether the wrong factually caused the gain. On the other hand, the principle is insensitive to the limited significance of factual causation and to the need to forge a normative link between the wrong and the gain. Given that the restitution of the gain depends on the gain's normative quality, and that quality varies with the nature of the wrong, there is no alternative to the difficult task of distinguishing between the wrongs that do and the wrongs that do not admit of the restitution of their resulting gains.

Aside from highlighting the necessity for a normative connection between the defendant's wrong and the plaintiff's entitlement to the gain, the parallel between wrongful loss and wrongful gain suggests a more particular point: gain-based damages are especially appropriate when property rights are violated. The reason that negligence law requires the defendant to compensate the plaintiff for wrongful loss is that such loss is the materialization of an adverse possibility—the unreasonably created risk of harm—to which the defendant ought not rightfully to have exposed the plaintiff. Because the defendant then inflicts a loss from which the plaintiff is entitled to be immune, the loss constitutes an injustice between the parties that an award of compensatory damages reverses. Similarly, gain-based damages should be available when the defendant's gain is the materialization of a favorable possibility—the opportunity to gain—that rightfully belonged to the plaintiff. Then the gain to be nullified by the award of gain-based damages represents an injustice both committed by the defendant and suffered by the plaintiff. Since a proprietary right includes the opportunity to gain from what one owns, one may plausibly regard the defendant's dealings with the plaintiff's property as an occasion for gain-based damages. That, at any rate, is the argument of the next section.

3. Dealing with another's property

As has often been noted, the misappropriation of another's property is the paradigmatic example of an event that gives rise to gain-based damages.[11] Because property rights give proprietors the exclusive right to deal with the thing owned, including the right to profit from such dealings, gains resulting from the misappropriation of property are necessarily subject to restitution. Gains from dealings in property are as much within the entitlement of the proprietor as the property itself.

The disgorgement of these proprietary gains fits readily within the correlativity of corrective justice. Property consists simultaneously in a right of the proprietor and in a correlative duty on others to respect

---

[11] See especially Daniel Friedmann, "Restitution of Benefits Obtained through the Appropriation of Property or the Commission of a Wrong," (1980) 80 Colum. L. Rev. 504; von Caemmerer, above n. 5, 353.

that right. Just as the owner's right to set the terms on which property is used or transferred implies a correlative duty on others to abstain from using or selling it, so the owner's right to the profits from the use or transfer of the property imports a correlative duty on others to abstain from such profits. This correlativity of the proprietor's right and the wrongdoer's duty means that the realization of an unauthorized gain is an injustice as between them. The gain is the continuing embodiment of this injustice, and the injustice is undone when the gain is restored to the owner of the object from which the gain accrued.

Gain-based damages for dealing with another's property mirror the wrong and illuminate its nature. The law's focus on the benefits of ownership at the remedial stage presupposes the defendant's intention to act on the owned object at the stage of wrongdoing. In appropriating the benefits from using or alienating the object, the defendant implicitly asserts the ownership that alone would entitle the defendant to those benefits. Gain-based damages reverse the wrong by showing, through the return of the benefits, that the law considers the defendant's implicit assertion of ownership to be a nullity whose consequences are to be undone. The remedy is conditioned, therefore, not merely on the defendant's realization of a benefit but on the defendant's having treated the object as if it were his or her own. One treats an object in this way when one so directs one's attention to the object that its use or alienation can be regarded as an execution of one's purposes. In contrast, action that inadvertently produces an effect on the object does not qualify as an expression of one's will with respect to the object, and so is not the basis for gain-based damages. Thus, gain-based damages are available for intentional torts against property and not for harm to property that results from negligence.

From the perspective of corrective justice, gain-based damages for proprietary wrongs are an entitlement of the proprietor, and not merely a mechanism for protecting the integrity of property as a facilitative institution.[12] The argument for referring to property as a facilitative institution is that, because damages measured by the defendant's gain do not reflect an injury to the plaintiff personally, they must be justified by pointing to an institutional harm. The premise of this argument is false. The fact that the damages are gain-oriented does not exclude their reflecting an injury to the plaintiff personally. One's

---

[12] Jackman, above note 3.

rights provide the baseline for measuring injury. If those rights include the possibility of gain, then the defendant's gain measures the extent of the plaintiff's injury. The relevance of property is not that it is a facilitative institution, but that it connects the parties in such a way as to make the object owned—and thus the gain that dealings in that object can produce—the locus of a right and a correlative duty.

Two broad categories of dealings in property can give rise to profits that the wrongdoer is obligated to disgorge. The defendant either might purport to alienate that which belongs to the plaintiff, or might benefit by putting it to an unauthorized use. In either instance the plaintiff ought to be allowed damages measured by the defendant's gain.

The disgorgement of gains has long been uncontroversial in connection with purported alienations of property. The old waiver of tort cases allowed recovery of the proceeds realized from a thief's sale of the owner's goods, even if the proceeds exceeded the goods' market value. To accomplish this within the framework of an action in *assumpsit* for money had and received, the courts implied a contract to repay, ascribing to the thief a fictitious relationship of agency. Although such reasoning led to well-known difficulties and is no longer necessary, its basic normative impulse was sound. The language of agency expressed the implications of property. The idea behind the ascription of agency was that the only legal basis for selling what belongs to another is that the seller is acting as the owner's agent and therefore holds the proceeds on the owner's behalf.

The jurisprudence concerning gains realized through the use rather than the purported alienation of another's property is more complex. The notorious case of *Phillips v. Homfray*[13] is often taken to indicate that such gains are not recoverable.[14] In that case the plaintiff claimed wayleave rent for the use of underground passages through which certain minerals had secretly been conveyed. Because of the death of the defendants, the established doctrine that *actio personalis moritur cum persona* barred an action for tort. Accordingly, the plaintiff based his claim not on his own wrongful loss but on the defendant's wrongful gain through the free and unauthorized use of the passageways. The English Court of Appeal dismissed the claim. In the court's view, one could

---

[13] [1883] 24 Ch. D. 439 (C.A.).
[14] But see William Swadling, "Phillips v Homfray (1883)," in *Landmark Cases in the Law of Restitution*, ed. Charles Mitchell and Paul Mitchell (2006), arguing that the usual interpretation is mistaken.

recover only for wrongful gains in the form of property or the proceeds or value of property withdrawn from the plaintiff and added to the estate of the defendant. Here the defendant's profit in using the plaintiff's passageways consisted merely in the saving of an expense, not in bringing into the estate any additional property, or proceeds or value of property, belonging to the plaintiff.

The notion that the use of another's property is not a benefit is now universally reprobated by restitution scholars. Even under the doctrine of the day, the unauthorized use of another's land was compensable by the assessment of a wayleave rent, as is shown by other episodes in the protracted litigation of this plaintiff's claim.[15] Moreover, from the gain-based standpoint it seems odd to distinguish between the enrichment that the estate would have achieved positively by having its assets swollen by the proceeds or value of property, and the enrichment it achieved negatively by not having its assets diminished by the payment of a wayleave rent.

Perhaps the best that can be said about the case is that it deals with a narrow point that arose out of the positive law of the time. On the death of the tortfeasor, the *actio personalis* rule necessitated a distinction between actions to repair a wrongful loss, which were barred, and actions to recover a gain, which were allowed. In cases of the unauthorized use of another's property, the action often can be conceptualized either way, since the use, in and of itself, is both a benefit to the defendant and a loss by the plaintiff of an opportunity to exploit a potentially profitable asset.[16] In the *Phillips* case the tortfeasor, by using the passageways without authorization, was spared the expense of negotiating for the plaintiff's consent or making arrangements that would avoid the need to trespass on the plaintiff's property. This, however, was merely "a negative benefit . . . acquired by saving himself the expense of doing his duty."[17] There are few breaches of duty that could

---

[15] W. M. C. Gummow, "Unjust Enrichment, Restitution, and Proprietary Remedies," in *Essays on Restitution*, ed. P. D. Finn (1990), 47.

[16] Cf. Strand Electric and Engineering v. Brisford Entertainments [1952] 2 Q.B. 246 (C.A.), where two members of the court analyzed the claim in terms of loss and one judge analyzed it in terms of gain. See also Robert J. Sharpe and S. M. Waddams, "Damages for Lost Opportunity to Bargain," (1982) 2 Oxford J. of Legal Stud. 290 for the argument that damages for the use of another's property are compensatory rather than gain-based, in that they compensate for the deprivation of the amount for which the plaintiff would have bargained away the right.

[17] Phillips v. Homfray, 24 Ch. D. at 465 (Lord Justice Bowen uses this language to explain one of the cases on which he is relying).

not be avoided by undertaking some expense. All interferences with property, for instance, can be seen either as wronging the owner or as sparing the wrongdoer the expense of purchasing the owner's consent. If the *actio personalis* rule barred actions for the former but allowed actions for the latter, its scope would be nugatory. The saving of the expense of doing one's duty, in other words, was not a benefit distinct from the wrongfulness of the loss, but was rather that wrongfulness itself, formulated in terms of a benefit. The court, anxious to preserve the integrity of the *actio personalis* rule (in the words of Lord Justice Bowen, "[i]t is part of the law, and while so, ought not to be frittered away"[18]), in effect held that the rule caught any gain that was indistinguishable from a wrongful loss.

Be that as it may, in emphasizing the importance of property or its proceeds or value, the *Phillips* case in effect distinguishes, with respect to the availability of gain-based damages, benefits realized through use from benefits realized through alienation. This distinction should have no further vitality. If the key to the recovery of gain-based damages is that the defendant has dealt with the plaintiff's property, the availability of such damages should not depend on whether the dealing took the form of a use or an alienation. It is true, as noted above, that the damages in cases of the unauthorized use of property often can be seen to be loss-based, because the defendant's use of the plaintiff's asset deprives the plaintiff of the opportunity to realize profits through it. Some cases, however as where the defendant uses an object that has been stored[19] or that is part of a discontinued business[20]—are harder to construe as involving a loss, since the defendant's unauthorized use cannot realistically be said to have deprived the plaintiff of money that the plaintiff would otherwise have had. The damages in such cases may more easily be regarded as based on the gain that the defendant realized by not paying for the use. Whether seen as quantifying a wrongful loss or a wrongful gain, gain-based damages for unauthorized use are justified because they restore the value of the owner's pre-existing right. Indeed, what ultimately matters is not the semantic exercise of designating the damages as gain-based or loss-based, but the normative task of connecting the damages to the infringed right.

---

[18] Ibid., at 456.
[19] Olwell v. Nye and Nissen, 173 P.2d. 652 (Wash. 1946).
[20] Penarth Dock Engineering v. Pounds [1963] 1 Lloyd's List L. Rep. 359 (Q.B.D.).

The difference between unauthorized use and purported alienation goes not to the availability of gain-based damages but to the way in which they usually are computed. In the case of unauthorized use, the measure of the damages is the value of the use; in the case of alienation, the plaintiff can choose either the value of the thing alienated or the price the defendant received. This difference implies no principle that would bar gain-based damages in cases of use, but merely reflects the contingency that, in contrast to alienation, unauthorized use does not necessarily involve the defendant in a further exchange of the plaintiff's property. Were such an exchange to take place (for instance, if the defendant charged a fee purportedly to license the use to a third party), the plaintiff presumably could choose to have the defendant disgorge this fee.[21]

From the perspective of corrective justice, two aspects of these damages call for comment: the role of the notion of value and the option of the plaintiff to insist on disgorgement if there has been an exchange.

The notion of value fits into corrective justice in the following way. Corrective justice deals with interacting parties correlatively as doer and sufferer of an injustice. Inasmuch as it governs interaction, corrective justice applies to parties who impinge upon each other by acting on particular things in the world pursuant to their specific needs and wants. But inasmuch as it embraces the two parties as correlatively situated, corrective justice abstracts to a common standpoint from the particularity of these things and from the specificity of these needs and wants. Value is the economic notion that fulfills this abstracting function.[22]

By making objects quantitatively comparable, value enables corrective justice to apply to property despite the heterogeneity of persons' specific needs and wants. Because corrective justice is concerned with the correlativity of the doing and suffering of an injustice, it does not regard something owned merely as a particular thing used to minister to the specific needs and wants of the particular person who owns it. Its interest is in the thing as a factor in the juridical relationship between the owner and others. Value provides the means for quantitatively comparing the owner's wants to other wants and the owner's thing to other things, thereby enabling the possible uses

---

[21]   Cf. Edwards v. Lee's Administrator, 96 S.W. 2d.1028 (Ky. Ct.App. 1936).

[22]   On value, see below chapter 6, section 2.

of a thing to figure in the interactional framework of a juridical relationship.

When a property right is violated, corrective justice requires the wrongdoer to undo the wrong perpetrated against the proprietor. Neither the specific wants satisfied by the defendant's wrongful use nor the specific wants frustrated by the unavailability to the plaintiff of the thing used can be reversed in their specificity. Value, however, presents the quantitative equivalent of that use or that thing from a standpoint that both parties share. Thus, seen in the light of the value of the thing taken or used, the defendant's infringement of the plaintiff's right becomes capable of a remedy in accordance with corrective justice. By awarding the value of the use, a court reverses the injustice that consists in the use. Similarly, by awarding the value of the thing alienated, a court reverses the injustice that consists in the alienation.

Also in accordance with corrective justice is the owner's option to recover the wrongdoer's gains from selling the thing at a higher price than the market. Because value arises from specific needs and wants, it includes the possibility of a purchaser who is willing to pay more than the market price. This possibility is as fully within the owner's entitlement as the thing itself and its value. For such a possibility to be the owner's, the payment that happens to realize the possibility must also be the owner's. Otherwise, the owner would have a possibility that is juridically incapable of fulfillment—which is no possibility at all. A lawyer may justify this conclusion by saying that it does not lie in the mouth of the wrongdoer to deny that the owner could have made the sale. What such a formulation points to, however, is not the empirical likelihood that the owner would have made this sale, but the irrelevance of who made it given that ownership carries with it an entitlement to the proceeds. Of course, the recovery of the proceeds remains merely an option that the owner need not exercise when the proceeds are less than the market value. This option is the continuation of every owner's entitlement either to retain the thing owned and its value or to dispose of it for the price that a willing buyer will pay. Thus, consistently with corrective justice, the plaintiff's option replicates at the remedial stage the content of the plaintiff's substantive right.

In sum, gain-based damages are justified where there are dealings in—use or alienation of—another's property. Because property includes the possibility of gains, the plaintiff may as of right reclaim a gain realized through the defendant's use or alienation of the property. Contrary to the suggestion of *Phillips v. Homfray*, the distinction between use and alienation makes no difference in principle for the availability of gain-based damages. These damages quantify the value of the plaintiff's right, so that when the defendant encroaches on this right, gain-based damages respond to and undo the injustice between the parties.

4. Indirect benefits

In denying the plaintiff's claim to sue for the unauthorized use of his passageways in *Phillips v. Homfray*, Lord Justice Bowen emphasized that the gain realized through the wrongdoer's trespass was an indirect or negative benefit that consisted in the expense saved from not paying a wayleave rent. The significance of this for Lord Justice Bowen was that the gain from the wrong did not increase, but merely avoided decreasing, the wrongdoer's estate. As noted above, this distinction makes no sense from a gain-based standpoint. Nonetheless, I suggest that Lord Justice Bowen was struggling—not without insight—with the necessity to distinguish recoverable from irrecoverable gains. This necessity is present even if one acknowledges, as Lord Justice Bowen did not, that the plaintiff should be able to recover the defendant's gain from the wrongful use of property. For then the question arises: what counts as the relevant benefit for purposes of assessing the gain-based damages?

The case of *Olwell v. Nye and Nissen*[23] is an apt illustration of the need to be attentive to this issue. After selling his egg-packing business to the defendant, the plaintiff stored his egg-washing machine in an adjacent space. Subsequently, without the plaintiff's knowledge or consent, the defendant took the machine out of storage and began to use it. When the plaintiff discovered this, he offered to sell the machine to the defendant, but the negotiations fell through. The plaintiff then sued. The Washington Supreme Court held, following the waiver of tort cases, that since the defendant had benefited from his wrong, the plaintiff could elect to sue for restitution. Although the case involved unauthorized use of another's property, *Phillips* was effectively rejected in favor of the proposition from the Restatement of Restitution that "[a] person confers a benefit on another . . . not only where he adds to the property of another, but also where he saves the other from

---

[23]   Olwell v. Nye, 173 P.2d 652 (Wash. 1946).

expense or loss."[24] The court then approved an assessment based on the expense that the defendant would have incurred had the eggs been washed by hand during the period that the machine was in use.

The court's reasoning seems attractive. An action for loss-based damages runs into the difficulty that the defendant's conduct neither damaged the machine nor, since it was in storage, deprived the plaintiff of the income that it might generate. Gain-based damages, in contrast, allow reference to the defendant's enrichment regardless of what the plaintiff lost. The enrichment includes the saving of expense. Here the defendant was saved the expense of having the eggs washed by hand. Therefore the damage award is for the cost of having the eggs washed by hand.

Yet something has gone wrong in the court's analysis. In the negotiations for the sale of the machine, the plaintiff had asked for $600 and the defendant had counter-offered $25. The court, after considering the number of hours it would take to wash the eggs and the hourly wages of the washers, awarded $900. Remarkably, the plaintiff recovered 50 per cent more from the use of the machine than the highest price he wanted from its sale.[25]

The court committed two interrelated conceptual errors. First, it rejected the correct formulation of the benefit. The defendant had argued that the damages "should be based on the use or rental value of the machine." The court thought this measure of damages was unsuitable because it was loss-based and the plaintiff had suffered no loss from the defendant's use of a machine that was not in the stream of commerce. However, as we have seen, damages geared to the value of the use can be gain-based as well as loss-based. One usually may characterize the avoidance of rental costs indifferently as an expense saved by the defendant or as income lost by the plaintiff. Even if on the *Olwell* facts the loss-based characterization is implausible, the gain-based characterization remains pertinent, since the opportunity for gain is within the owner's entitlement. Second, in focusing on the expense of hand-washing the eggs, the court accepted an incorrect formulation of the benefit. It may well be the case that without the machine the defendant would have had the eggs washed by hand. But

---

[24] § 1(b), at 12.
[25] The full facts of the case were even more egregious. The expense of hand-washing the eggs came to $1,560, but that amount turned out to be more than the plaintiff had claimed, and therefore was reduced on appeal.

that is no concern of the plaintiff. The plaintiff's only interest in the defendant's egg-washing operation is in the use of this particular machine, not in how the defendant would have operated his business without it. Therefore, the court should have based the calculation of damages on the value of the use of the machine.

Corrective justice illuminates the court's errors. Corrective justice requires that the remedy undo the inconsistency on the part of the defendant with the plaintiff's right. The role of damages in *Olwell* is to make good the breach of the defendant's duty not to violate the plaintiff's right. Because the remedy should reflect the duty correlative to the plaintiff's right, basing the damages on the cost of hand-washing the eggs implies that the defendant was under an obligation to the plaintiff to wash the eggs by hand. This is absurd. The plaintiff had a right in the machine but no right to have the defendant hand-wash the eggs. The only relevant duty that the defendant owed the plaintiff was not to use the machine. Accordingly the damages should have been set at the value of the use as reflected by the rental value of the machine.

One should observe that this criticism of calculating the damages by reference to the cost of hand-washing the eggs involves a conceptual point, not an empirical one. The criticism does not suppose that the defendant was in fact unlikely to have had the eggs hand-washed. The point is rather that, whatever the alternatives to using the machine and however probable their employment, none of them forms the basis for calculating the damages, because in principle none is directly relevant to the injustice between the parties. Assume the situation most favorable to the plaintiff, that in the absence of the machine there was no alternative to hand-washing the eggs if the defendant was to stay in business. Such an absence of alternatives presumably would have increased both the value of the machine and the value of the machine's use. The basis of the gain-based damages, however, would still be the value of the use (increased by the necessity for hand-washing without it) rather than the cost of the hand-washing as such.

These deficiencies of the *Olwell* case illustrate a general point. Gain-based damages, like other remedies in private law, must correct the injustice that the plaintiff has suffered at the defendant's hand. Such damages, accordingly, must correspond to the elements constitutive of the juridical relationship between the parties. Factors absent from the law's conceptualization of the defendant's duty to the plaintiff, and therefore external to that relationship between the parties, ought not to be the basis for the calculation of damages. If, as in *Olwell*, the injustice consists in the unauthorized use of the plaintiff's property, the damages are to be calculated with reference to the value of the use. Since the alternatives to that use are external to the juridical relationship and their performance is not a duty owed to the plaintiff, the benefits of the savings from not having recourse to those alternatives also are not owed to the plaintiff.

This analysis suggests that Lord Justice Bowen's reference in *Phillips v. Homfray* to indirect benefit is not completely off the mark. He was aware that the saving of expense does not in and of itself constitute a benefit that invariably gives rise to gain-based damages. However, he formulated indirect benefits in terms of a contrast with benefits that increase the wrongdoer's assets. He ought to have formulated these benefits in terms of a contrast with benefits, including those involving the saving of an expense, that are within the ambit of the plaintiff's entitlement.

Understood in this way, the notion of indirect benefits applies to other situations besides the unauthorized use of property. The law of nuisance, for example, imposes an obligation not to interfere with the use and enjoyment of another's property. Take the example of a polluter who fails to install anti-pollution equipment costing x and causes discomfort assessed at y, and assume x is greater than y. The plaintiff cannot recover x. The defendant is under a duty to avoid causing the plaintiff the discomfort, which is quantified at y. How the plaintiff achieves this end is no business of the defendant. Of course, if the defendant had made expenditure x, the plaintiff would not have suffered the discomfort; but the tort consists in causing the discomfort, not in saving the expense that would have avoided the discomfort.[26]

The same applies to negligence law, where the defendant is under a duty not to create an unreasonable risk. Here recovery of the defendant's benefit is almost unheard of, even though the defendant might have avoided the unlawful risk by undertaking certain expenditures. Assume that the risk, which caused the plaintiff damages of y, could have been avoided had the defendant expended x on precautions, and that x is greater than y. Again, the plaintiff does not recover x. It is true that the defendant realized a benefit by not taking the precautions and that the injury would not have occurred had those precautions been

---

[26] Cf. Kirk v. Todd [1882] 21 Ch. D. 484 (C.A.).

taken. The duty owed, however, was to avoid imposing the risk, not to undertake the expenditures.

Distinguishing the duty from the contingent means to avoid violating it fits within corrective justice in three related ways. First, corrective justice highlights the juridical connection between the plaintiff and the defendant. Because the juridical connection is forged through the correlativity of the plaintiff's right and the defendant's duty, the remedy is determined by the precise contours of the right and its correlative duty. The steps that the defendant can take to avoid violating the duty owed to the plaintiff do not in themselves juridically connect the defendant to the plaintiff. They are merely factual possibilities that pertain to the defendant's situation.

Second, in emphasizing the plaintiff's right and the defendant's correlative duty, corrective justice sets its face against consequentialist understandings of private law. The consequentialist assumes that what matters is the state of affairs that exists at the end of the day. Accordingly, from the consequentialist standpoint there is no reason to distinguish the defendant's duty from actions that produce the situation that will obtain if the duty is discharged. Corrective justice, in contrast, focuses on the normative dynamics internal to the interaction between the right-holder and others. What matters is not the situation at the end of the day, but whether the defendant acted wrongfully with respect to the plaintiff's right.

Third, the duties of corrective justice result from the moral capacity of rights to put others under obligations. The fact that these are duties relative to rights rather than to other possible normative categories (for example, maximizing human welfare or fostering virtue) means that these duties are negative in nature: they function as prohibitions against wrongful interferences with another's rights rather than as positive commands to do particular acts, even if those acts promote another's good. The common law reflects the essentially negative nature of private law duties by denying the existence of duties in situations of nonfeasance;[27] in such situations the actor's behavior, however morally reprehensible, merely fails to promote another's interest but does not interfere with another's rights. Accordingly, tort and other private law duties are defined negatively in terms of non-interference

---

[27] This statement is subject to exceptions that are not relevant here and that, in any case, do not undermine the principle at stake. See Ernest J. Weinrib, *The Idea of Private Law* (1995), at 153–54.

with rights rather than positively in terms of particular acts that are obligatory.[28] In view of this, a requirement in the examples discussed here to do a particular act, such as having eggs hand-washed or installing antipollution equipment or undertaking the burden of precautions, would be inconsistent with the structure of private law norms. Thus, the line between wronging the plaintiff and failing to do something that would result in the plaintiff's not being wronged, far from being adventitious, is both essential to the definition of duty within corrective justice and confirmed by the organization of the common law.

The key, then, to the availability of gain-based damages lies in aligning the remedy with the injustice it corrects. Through the assessment of damages, the law transforms the plaintiff's right and the defendant's correlative duty not to interfere with that right into their monetary equivalent. Thus, what the defendant owes the plaintiff at the remedial stage of their relationship corresponds to what the defendant owed the plaintiff at the stage of conduct. One must distinguish, however, between the duty itself and the measures that would avoid a breach of the duty. Only the former defines the legal relationship between the parties; the latter are merely the contingent ways to prevent transforming that relationship into a wrongful one. The defendant may owe the plaintiff a duty not to convert the plaintiff's egg-washing machine or not to commit a nuisance or not to create an unreasonable risk; and it may well be true that hand-washing the eggs or purchasing antipollution equipment or undertaking precautions would in the circumstances have avoided the breach of these duties; and it may also be true that the defendant is better off for not having done these actions. But these latter actions were not constitutive of the duties incumbent on the defendant by virtue of the plaintiff's right. Consequently, what the defendant gained by not performing these actions also is not within the plaintiff's right.

The damages for the value of using another's property stand on a different footing. The reason that the court in the *Olwell* case should have assessed damages at the rental value of the egg-washing machine is not because renting the machine was obligatory on the defendant. The defendant's only duty—and the duty that was breached—was not

---

[28] Even contractual obligations are not an exception: the promisor is obligated to perform the particular acts specified by the contract only because the contract has made the performance of those acts a right of the promisee.

to use the machine. Damages set at the rental value do not quantify a contingent means of preventing the wrong from occurring. Rather, they quantify the wrong that did occur. By owning the machine, the plaintiff is also entitled to the value that could be realized from using it. Since that value is an incident of the plaintiff's proprietary right, it is also an element in the duty correlative to that right.

These reflections provide theoretical support for what many commentators have observed, that dealing with another's property is the paradigmatic case for gain-based damages. From the standpoint of corrective justice, dealing with another's property is paradigmatic because the idea of property weaves the plaintiff's entitlement to gain into the fabric of the juridical relationship with the defendant. In other situations the gains that a wrongdoer might realize are at best indirect, forming not an element of the plaintiff's right but a benefit realized from the non-performance of the duty correlative to it.[29]

5. Innocent and willful wrongdoing

I mentioned at the outset of this chapter that, because it focuses on the bipolar relationship between the parties, corrective justice is unreceptive to justifications like punishment and deterrence that consider the defendant independently of the plaintiff. To some, this starting point may appear peremptorily to cut off a promising line of exploration, that gain-based damages respond to deliberate or outrageous conduct. Such conduct is intuitively offensive to our moral sensibilities, and ideas like punishment and deterrence seem particularly well suited to the analysis of its legal consequences. Conversely, my emphasis on

---

[29] The idea that a gain-based award responds to an interference with the plaintiff's proprietary right receives its logical development in the German *Eingriffskondiktion*, which von Caemmerer argued should be classed with such property-protecting devices as the *vindicatio*; above n. 5, at 353. Strictly speaking, what matters for the *Eingriffskondiktion* is not the wrongfulness of the defendant's interference but the scope and purpose of the plaintiff's right, and thus whether the defendant's gain was within that scope and purpose; Markesinis et al., above n. 5, 745. The common law, in contrast, generally protects property not directly but through the law of torts. Accordingly, for the common law the issue of gain-based damages is usually thought to arise in the context of restitution for wrongs. The decisive question should, nonetheless, remain whether the defendant's gain rightfully belongs to the plaintiff as an incident of the plaintiff's property. This may be the case even in situations in which no tort claim against the defendant is available; see Daniel Friedmann, "Restitution for Wrongs: the Basis for Liability," in *Restitution Past, Present and Future: Essays in Honour of Gareth Jones*, ed. W. R. Cornish et al. (1998), 133, 133–38.

rights and their correlative duties may seem less felicitous, since the rights of the plaintiff do not seem to be affected additionally by the deliberateness with which the defendant violated them.

To a certain extent the law reinforces these doubts about my dismissal of punishment and deterrence. The law presents instances where the deliberateness or innocence of the wrongdoing affects the plaintiff's remedy. One set of instances (discussed in this section) concerns dealings in another's property, where gain-based damages are uncontroversial but the extent of the damages depends on whether the wrongdoing was innocent or deliberate. Another set of instances (discussed in the following section) concerns wrongs that are not proprietary, so that gain-based damages seem unavailable on the approach suggested above, but where additional damages are nonetheless awarded on a gain-based or punitive basis. Can such instances be comprehended within corrective justice?

An example of the law's differentiating innocent from willful wrongdoing is the defendant's wrongful removal from the plaintiff's realty of some valuable resource, such as timber or minerals, that the plaintiff intends to exploit. The severance enhances the value of the resource, and the general (though not invariable) rule is that the plaintiff recovers the enhanced value.[30] Such recovery is a straightforward application of gain-based damages to dealings in another's property, and poses no special theoretical problem. Of particular interest, however, is the relevance of the trespasser's willfulness to the question of whether the defendant is credited with the expense of severing the resource or of otherwise making it more marketable. An innocent trespasser (one who mistakenly thought that taking the resource was not a violation of the plaintiff's right) is allowed to deduct such expenses; a willful trespasser is not.

The higher damages that willfulness attracts, however, do not signal the presence of punitive considerations in the law's treatment of the trespasser.[31] The law can be explained through the standard

[30] A leading House of Lords case, however, Livingstone v. Rawyards Coal, 5 App. Cas. 25 (1880), awarded the owner of land from which coal was taken only the royalty value of the coal while it was in the ground. The court emphasized the special features of the case: both parties thought that the trespasser had the right to take the coal, and the owner's plot was so small and so completely surrounded by the trespasser's holdings, that only the trespasser could have extracted the coal.

[31] Cf. James Edelman, *Gain-Based Damages: Contract, Tort, Equity and Intellectual Property* (2002), 137–38, who claims that these cases exemplify what he calls "disgorgement damages," which, in his classification, are always based on deterrence (ibid., 83).

conceptual tools in the law of unjust enrichment—itself consistent with corrective justice.[32]

From the standpoint of the law of unjust enrichment the rules concerning severed resources make sense. As noted above in section 3, the proprietor has an entitlement to any increase in the value of what is owned. With respect to the enhanced value, the innocent and the willful trespasser stand on the same footing, since even the fact that the trespass was innocent does not create for the trespasser a proprietary interest. Their situations are different, however, with respect to the expense of severing the resource. By undertaking this expense, the willful trespasser improved property known to belong to someone else. Under the law of unjust enrichment, the improver of property known to belong to another is considered to have willingly taken the risk of losing the value of the benefit conferred on the owner.[33] The owner's retention of this benefit is, therefore, not an injustice. Accordingly, the owner who reclaims the property does not have to credit the willful trespasser with the expenditure that improved it. In contrast, the expenditure by the trespasser who mistakenly thinks that he or she is entitled to sever the resource cannot be construed as a voluntary risk-taking. Rather, by innocently anticipating the plaintiff's own intended severance and exploitation of the resource, the expenditure can be considered an incontrovertible benefit—that is, a non-gratuitous enrichment that, because of the practical inevitability of the severance, can be returned without unduly interfering with the proprietor's autonomy.[34] Accordingly, the proprietor cannot claim from the innocent trespasser the enhanced value clear of the expenditure necessary to produce it.[35]

These rules disclose no trace of a punitive impulse.[36] They merely apply, in the context of increased value through trespass, the usual considerations at play in the restitution of unrequested benefits under the principle of unjust enrichment. The key questions are whether the

---

[32] See below, chapter 6.

[33] Peter Birks, *An Introduction to the Law of Restitution* (1989), 102–3.

[34] Ibid., at 116–24. Birks suggests that the argument of incontrovertible benefit is available to any defendant sued for damages, because then the claim turns the improvement into money and prevents the defendant from subjectively devaluing the benefit (ibid., at 122). If this suggestion is correct, the plaintiff in a severance case will have to credit the defendant's expenses even if the plaintiff did not intend to exploit the resource.

[35] Hugh Evander Willis, "Measure of Damages when Property is Wrongfully Taken by a Private Individual," (1908–09) 22 Harv. L. Rev. 419, 425–26.

[36] But see Lord Diplock's observation in Broome v. Cassell [1972] A.C. 1027, 1129.

benefit conferred by the trespasser plausibly can be regarded as gratuitous, and, if it cannot, whether restitution would be consistent with the owner's proprietary right. Because one cannot unilaterally create an obligation by marking another person out for a benefit for which one expects recompense, the law understands the willful trespasser's knowing improvement of another's property as the manifestation of a donative intent. Consequently, justice between the parties allows the proprietor to keep what has thus been given gratuitously. In contrast, the innocent trespasser lacks a donative intent, and can recover the value of the benefit if the benefit to the plaintiff is incontrovertible in light of the plaintiff's anticipated exploitation of the resource. Then the plaintiff cannot retain what the defendant did not intend to give. In both situations the law works out the circumstances under which the enrichment of one right-holder at the expense of the other constitutes the doing and suffering of an injustice. The idea of punishment, with its one-sided focus on the defendant, is entirely absent.

Indeed, from an explanatory standpoint the corrective justice account is superior to the invocation of punishment or deterrence with respect to the treatment of the expenditures of the willful trespasser. A notable feature of the treatment of willful trespass is that the trespasser is disqualified from deducting the expenses, whatever they are. No attempt is made to calibrate the unrecouped costs to the trespasser's desert. From a punitive standpoint, this is odd, since the amount of the supposed punishment is not necessarily related to the trespasser's culpability.[37] From a deterrence perspective also, this appears difficult, though perhaps some elaborate economic story could be told of why, despite the overall gain in utility through the creation of enhanced value, neither disgorgement of the net gain nor the imposition of an additional penalty greater or less than the amount of the expense would create the proper incentives. Corrective justice avoids these difficulties because it looks to the normative implications of the parties' interaction without orienting that interaction to any external end that might be forwarded by punishment or deterrence. Corrective justice calls for no assessment of culpability apart from the fact of willfulness, because that fact in itself allows the implication that the defendant's conduct is donative, given his awareness of the plaintiff's right. Similarly, corrective justice is not concerned with deterring potential trespassers, but with making the remedy correspond to the

---

[37] Dan B. Dobbs, *Law of Remedies*, 2nd ed. (1993), 511.

wrong. For corrective justice the expenses as such, regardless of their relationship to any other policy, pertain to the interaction of the parties, and so the remedial consequence of the wrong—the absence of the trespasser's entitlement to recoup them—can attach to the expenses as such.

6. Property-like rights

So far I have emphasized the significance of property for a corrective justice approach to gain-based damages for tort. Since such an approach highlights the correlativity of the injustice done by the defendant and the injustice suffered by the plaintiff, it conditions liability on the requirement that the defendant's conduct be wrongful with respect to the plaintiff's right. If the plaintiff is to recover gain-based damages, that right must include an entitlement to the profit from whatever embodies the right. Proprietary rights contain this entitlement.

Strictly speaking, a proprietary right has two features. First, a proprietary right can be asserted against the world, and therefore the right carries with it a correlative duty, incumbent on everyone else, not to interfere. The proprietor's entitlement to the profit from what is owned derives from the power to determine the object's use, including the conditions under which it can be alienated, to the exclusion of everyone else. Since the proprietor must agree to the terms on which the object can enter the stream of commerce, the proprietor also owns whatever can be realized through use or alienation.

Second, the subject matter of a proprietary right has to be capable of being acquired and alienated. For example, an incident of a person's bodily integrity is not the subject of a proprietary right. One's body is not what one owns but what one is; it is the organism through which humans as self-conscious and purposive beings express themselves in the world. One does not come to be entitled to one's body by any act of acquisition, and one cannot alienate it to someone else. The right to one's body is so intimately connected to the person whose body it is that it lacks the moral possibility of being externalized and passing into the possession of someone else. Similar considerations apply to other aspects of one's dignity—to what Hegel compendiously termed "those goods, or rather substantive characteristics, which constitute my own private personality and the universal essence of my self-consciousness."[38] Such interests in physical integrity and dignity are, of course, legally protected with the status of rights, but they are not considered to be rights of a proprietary kind.

Under certain circumstances, gain-based damages are justified even if either or both of these features are absent. Although gain-based damages do not then respond to the violation of what is strictly speaking a proprietary right, the relationship between the parties can give rise to an interest sufficiently property-like to allow this kind of award.[39] These relational property-like wrongs can be grouped into two broad categories. In the first category, a gain-based remedy emerges from the pre-existing relationship between the parties, so that the remedy is available only against the defendant and not against the whole world. In the second, the remedy emerges as a response to the defendant's particular conduct.

The violation of a fiduciary duty is the paradigmatic example of the situation in which a gain-based remedy can emerge from the objective nature of the relationship. From the perspective of corrective justice, a fiduciary relationship reflects the Kantian idea that private law as a system of rights supposes persons to be ends in themselves rather than means to the ends of others.[40] Accordingly, a relationship such as that between fiduciary and beneficiary, the legal structure of which makes one person's interests entirely subject to another's discretion, must have as one of its incidents the duty of loyalty owed by the latter to the former. The fiduciary's duty of loyalty then becomes for purposes of this relationship an entitlement of the beneficiary. Since the meaning of this duty of loyalty is that the fiduciary cannot profit from the relationship,

---

[38] G. W. F. Hegel, *Philosophy of Right*, tr. T. M. Knox (1952), § 66. Cf. Immanuel Kant, *The Metaphysics of Morals*, tr. Mary Gregor (1991), [6:237] (describing innate right as something "belonging to every man by virtue of his humanity").

[39] The danger, of course, is that the possibility of calling something "property-like" may appear to provide a convenient black box into which to stuff the residual instances that do not fit what a property-based approach requires. However, I think that the property-like aspects of these situations are salient enough to bring them within the approach I have suggested. Peter Birks writes that "[i]t is not helpful . . . to say that gain-based damages should always be available for a 'proprietary' tort. The difficult questions will merely be transferred to the definition of property." Peter Birks, *Civil Wrongs: A New World* (1990–1), 98. While the fear is well founded, the truth is that, as with every interesting legal issue, difficult questions are unavoidable. The basic issue is whether property is the appropriate concept, not whether the concept is completely determinate in its application. See Weinrib, above n. 5, at 222–27. In any case, property seems to be a more manageable criterion than the one Birks proposed, namely that one ask whether there is sufficient justification for giving the plaintiff a windfall and for tolerating the suppression of economic activity.

[40] Kant, above n. 38, at [6:236].

gains can be regarded as the material embodiment of the breach of duty—what the fiduciary has, as it were, sold out the duty for—and the beneficiary is as entitled to these profits as he or she was to the duty for which they were exchanged. Courts occasionally refer to the opportunity to profit from the relationship as the beneficiary's "property"[41] though, because it entails the right to exclude only the fiduciary and not the whole world, it "is not property in the strict sense."[42] Seen in this light, the fiduciary's liability to disgorge profits is not an example of a policy of deterrence impacting the relationship from the outside, but is rather the remedial consequence that reflects the nature of the obligation owed by the fiduciary to the beneficiary.

The other property-like wrongs are those characterized by action of the defendant that implicitly or explicitly treats the plaintiff's right as an asset whose value the defendant can appropriate.[43] For things that can be acquired and alienated, value belongs to the owner as an aspect of property; as noted above in section 3, the wrongdoer who deals with such things can be liable for the market value or for the realized gains. In the case of property-like wrongs, the same liability is available for wrongs done with respect to things, like physical integrity, that cannot be acquired and alienated. Compared to the victim of a true proprietary wrong, the plaintiff is not placed in a worse position by virtue of the fact that the right was too intimately connected with the plaintiff's being and dignity even to rank as proprietary. Because the defendant acted with knowledge of the plaintiff's right and with the intent to appropriate its value, the law ascribes a proprietary quality to the right so far as the relationship between the defendant and the plaintiff is concerned. In doing this, the law merely holds the defendant to the implications of his or her own conduct. Since the plaintiff's right was treated as a commodity whose value was available to the defendant, the plaintiff is allowed to recapture the gain that was realized through it. Thus, once the wrong is construed as a property-like one for purposes of the parties' relationship, the plaintiff has available the gain-based damages that attend a dealing with another's property.

Consider the example posed by Professor Birks of the thug hired to beat someone up.[44] The thug cannot resist a claim by the victim of

---

[41] See, e.g., Boardman v. Phipps [1967] 2 A.C. 46, 107, 115 (H.L.).

[42] Ibid., at 102.

[43] See Peter Benson, "The Basis for Excluding Liability for Economic Loss in Tort Law," in *Philosophical Foundtions of Tort Law*, ed. David Owen (1995), 427, 457.

[44] Birks, above n. 33, at 319.

the beating for gain-based damages on the basis that the wrong was a bodily injury and thus too closely connected to the victim to count as property. In these circumstances the battery is part of a process of illegitimate commodification. Having treated the plaintiff's bodily integrity as an item that the thug was in effect selling for a price, the thug cannot take refuge in the argument that bodily integrity is really an inalienable pearl beyond price. Although bodily integrity is not in itself property, the thug's relationship to the defendant's bodily integrity has become property-like through the thug's conduct. Consequently, the thug is liable for gain-based damages, as he would be for any dealing with another's property.

The idea that special remedial consequences attend the defendant's profiteering from another's right finds its most general expression in Lord Devlin's second category of punitive damages, which applies to conduct calculated by the defendant to make a profit that may exceed the compensation payable to the plaintiff.[45] Lord Devlin ascribed to this category of damages the admonitory function of teaching the wrongdoer that tort does not pay, rather than the restitutionary function of causing the disgorgement of the gain. Nonetheless, given that disgorgement is a way of preventing the wrongdoer from profiting, the two functions are not easily kept separate.[46] Lord Devlin himself noted the connection between this category of punitive damages and the misappropriation of property when, instancing defamation, he remarked that "no man should be allowed to sell another man's reputation for profit."[47] Indeed, gain-based damages have been recommended as a way of introducing greater specificity into the punitive idea.[48] And even in jurisdictions that do not follow the approach to punitive damages set out by Lord Devlin, courts may factor gain-based considerations into their punitive awards.[49]

Despite their similarity, gain-based damages differ from punitive damages in their conception of the plaintiff's role. Commenting on

---

[45] Rookes v. Barnard [1964] A.C. 1129, 1227 (H.L.).

[46] In Broome v. Cassell [1972] A.C.1027, 1129 (H.L.), Lord Diplock notes the analogy of this category of punitive damages to the restitution of an enrichment.

[47] Ibid.

[48] Jeff Berryman, "The Case for Gain-based Damages over Punitive Damages: Teaching the Wrongdoer that Tort Does Not Pay," (1994) 73 Canadian Bar Rev. 320; John Glover, "Gain-based Principles in Tort: Wrongful User of Property and the Exemplary Measure of Damages," (1992) 18 Monash U. L. Rev. 169.

[49] Austin v. Rescon Construction [1989] 57 D.L.R. (4th) 591 (B.C.C.A.); Huff v. Price [1990] 76 D.L.R. (4th) 138 (B.C.C.A.).

this category of punitive damages, Lord Diplock once observed that, because their purpose is merely to prevent the wrongdoer from obtaining a reward for his wrongdoing, "the plaintiff is the accidental beneficiary of a rule of law based on public policy rather than on the reparation of private wrongs."[50] Punitive damages are oriented toward striking the gain from the hand of the defendant; the plaintiff is nothing but the contingent recipient of a windfall. Gain-based damages, in contrast, allow us to focus on the juridical relationship between the parties. Even in the property-like cases, we can work through the implications of the defendant's wrongful treatment of the plaintiff to a remedy that reverses that wrong. Just as the plaintiff has a right not to be wronged, so the plaintiff has an entitlement to the damages that undo that wrong.

7. Conclusion

The reawakening of interest in restitution has given gain-based damages a new salience. Now that the significance of restitution for private law is widely recognized, the question arises: what is the conceptual framework within which gain-based damages are to be understood?

To this question, corrective justice supplies an old answer. Corrective justice treats the defendant as the doer and the plaintiff as the sufferer of the same injustice. Corrective justice therefore highlights the correlativity of right and duty that characterizes the norms connecting the parties. From the perspective of corrective justice, the point of a legal remedy is to undo that injustice, and so the remedy must mirror the structure of the injustice. Corrective justice thereby ties both the defendant to the plaintiff and the remedy to the injustice. Under this approach, gain-based damages are available when the potential for gain is an incident of the right that the wrongdoer violated. Hence the paradigmatic case for the availability of gain-based damages is the defendant's violation of a property (or property-like) right held by the plaintiff.

With this understanding of gain-based damages comes a repudiation of the notion that they are occasions for the promotion of social

---

[50] McCarey v. Associated Newspapers Ltd. (No. 2) [1965] 2 Q.B. 86, 107 (C.A.) (Diplock L.J.).

purposes extrinsic to the relationship between the parties. Purposes such as punishment or deterrence (or broader purposes such as the promotion of economic efficiency or of other goals), even if they otherwise seem desirable, cannot be accommodated to the correlative nature of private law justifications and, therefore, cannot explain the most characteristic and pervasive features of private law. Thus, in this context as in others, corrective justice breaks free of the instrumentalist modes of explanation that over the last decades have so brilliantly obscured private law.

5

Punishment and Disgorgement as Contract Remedies

1. Introduction

For corrective justice the remedy corrects the injustice suffered by the plaintiff at the defendant's hands. This chapter examines the implications of this simple statement for contract damages. The focus will be on two kinds of damage award for breach of contract: punitive damages and damages that require the disgorgement of gains. The fact that over the last decades these two kinds of damage award have received notable elaboration by the highest courts in Canada, England, and Israel[1] attests to the continuing relevance of the issues that they raise.

In private law the idea that compensation is an appropriate remedy is generally accepted. The award of compensation reflects the plaintiff's entitlement to recover at least the loss that the defendant's wrongful act has caused. More problematic is the issue of whether compensation is also the limit of what the plaintiff can be awarded. Damages that go beyond compensation and aim at punishment or disgorgement operate in circumscribed situations and are subject to special, often controversial, justifications.

Contract law, however, poses a special difficulty. Here the very notion of compensation is uncertain and its primacy disputed. The standard measure of damages for breach of contract is the expectation measure, which puts the plaintiff in the position in which the plaintiff would have been had the contract not been breached. In their classic article on contract damages Fuller and Perdue denied that this measure, which reflected the value of something that the promisee did not yet

---

[1] Whiten v. Pilot Insurance Co. [2002] 209 D.L.R. (4th 257 (S.C.C.)); Attorney-General v. Blake [2000] 4 All E.R. 385 (H.L.); Adras Building Material v. Harlow & Jones [1995] Restitution L.R. 235 (Supreme Court of Israel, 1988).

have, was compensatory.[2] Expectation damages, they suggested, might better be viewed as having the quasi-criminal purpose of penalizing the promisor for breaching the contract.[3] This suggestion raises the possibility that a punitive impulse is present even in the most routine award of contract damages. On this view, truly compensatory assessments of contract damages are comparatively rare, whereas non-compensatory damages merely extend and make more explicit the non-compensatory policies already pervasive in contract damages.

At the heart of these issues about remedies lies the more fundamental issue: what is the nature of the right to contractual performance? So far as corrective justice is concerned, the remedy is merely the continuation at the remedial stage of the correlativity of right and duty that defines the parties' relationship. Accordingly, the first step to specifying the plaintiff's remedy against the defendant is to identify the right that contract law gives the plaintiff and the correlative duty that it lays upon the defendant. I turn to this in section 2, presenting a contrast between the function that Fuller and Perdue assign to the contract remedy and Kant's now largely forgotten treatment of contractual right. The Kantian account also casts light, as I contend in section 3, on the inaptness of requiring the disgorgement of gains resulting from contract breach, despite the superficial attractiveness of preventing wrongdoers from profiting from their wrongs. In section 4, I turn to punitive damages, addressing first the preliminary question of how corrective justice and punishment—and the institutions devoted to them coexist and are differentiated in a legal order based on rights. Finally in section 5, I discuss the difficulties that emerge from the elaborate but ultimately unsatisfying recent attempt in Canada to work out a coherent treatment of punitive damages for contract breach.

2. Contractual right

What, then, is the nature of a contractual right and how does an award of damages undo the violation of that right?[4] The basic rule of contract

---

[2] L. L. Fuller and William R. Perdue, "The Reliance Interest in Contract Damages," (1936) 46 Yale L.J. 52, 373.

[3] Ibid., 61.

[4] The most detailed contemporary application of corrective justice to contact law is found in the work of Peter Benson; see especially Benson, "The Unity of Contract Law," in *The Theory of Contract Law: New Essays*, ed. Peter Benson (2001), 118.

damages is that damages are awarded on the expectation measure: the plaintiff is to be put in the position that the plaintiff would have been in had the contract not been breached. Is there the internal connection that corrective justice requires between the injury to the promisee's contractual right and what the award of expectation damages restores? In other words, are expectation damages consistent with corrective justice?

This question was the starting point of the celebrated article on contract damages by Fuller and Perdue, who answered it in the negative.[5] In their view the purpose of corrective justice is "the maintenance of an equilibrium of goods among members of society."[6] This the law accomplishes by awarding compensatory damages "to heal a disturbed status quo."[7] In the contracts context, corrective justice can be seen to be at work in the protection accorded to the restitution and reliance interests; the equilibrium of goods represented by the status quo has been disturbed in the former both by a gain for the defendant and an identical loss for the plaintiff, and in the latter by a loss for the plaintiff. Expectation damages, they argue, are different. Such damages protect a future expectancy—"something [the plaintiff] never had"—rather than a loss already suffered. "[T]his seems on the face of things a queer kind of 'compensation.'"[8] And so they contend that "[i]n passing from compensation for change of position to compensation for loss of expectancy we pass...from the realm of corrective to that of distributive justice."[9]

Having discarded corrective justice, Fuller and Perdue then locate the rationale for expectation damages in considerations of policy. They suggest that expectation damages are an effective means of protecting the reliance interest. Expectation damages function not only as compensation for reliance losses (for reliance can consist in loss of the opportunity to enter other contracts) but also as a quasi-penal prophylaxis against breaches of contract that occasion reliance losses. Moreover, expectation damages promote and facilitate business agreements, which in turn stimulate economic activity, especially within a credit

---

[5] Above n. 3. My treatment of the article by Fuller and Perdue has been much influenced by Peter Benson, "Contract," in *A Companion to Philosophy of Law and Legal Theory*, ed. Dennis Patterson, 2nd ed. (2011), 29, 30–34.

[6] Above n. 2, 56

[7] Ibid.

[8] Ibid., 53.

[9] Ibid., 56.

economy. In this way expectation damages attest, in their view, to the intertwining of legal institutions and the economic system.

The Fuller–Perdue account of expectation damages stands at the confluence of two conclusions. The first is that corrective justice, although appropriate for rectifying the gains and losses associated with the restitution and the reliance interests, is inapplicable to the award of expectation damages. The second is that expectation damages are to be justified in terms of remedial policies concerning the indirect protection of the reliance interest and the promotion of commerce in a credit economy. These two conclusions are related. Having rejected the applicability to expectation damages of corrective justice, which internally connects the injustice to the remedy, Fuller and Perdue have recourse to considerations of remedial policy that present such damages as instrumental to the desirable social goals of protecting reliance and facilitating business agreements.

The basic presupposition of this account is that corrective justice does not operate in the absence of a disturbance of the status quo's equilibrium of goods among members of society. Unless there is a loss (as occurs with detrimental reliance) or a gain that corresponds to a loss (as when the restitution interest is in play), an award of damages cannot be construed as the working of corrective justice. Expectation damages, Fuller and Perdue argue, are not truly compensatory: by breaching the promise, the defendant merely withdraws a future good without inflicting a present loss. Only when the plaintiff relies on the prospect of receiving this good and thereby puts the future to some present detrimental use does the plaintiff suffer a loss that grounds a claim for compensation.[10] Of course, by awarding expectation damages the law signals its willingness to treat the promise as creating something of present value. But one cannot deduce the justification of expectation damages as compensating for the loss of a present value from their mere existence. Apart from policies like the protection of reliance and the promotion of commerce (so Fuller and Perdue claim), there is no argument, independent of a circular appeal to the consequences that the law attaches to a breach, for regarding the promise as creating a present right in the expectancy.[11] In and of itself, they assume, a contractual undertaking does not suffice to do so.

---

[10] Ibid., 59.
[11] Ibid., 59–60.

Crucial to this reasoning is the idea that contract itself does not transfer the subject matter of the contract to the promisee. If contract did so, expectation damages would lose their mystery: given that the subject matter of the contract would belong to the promisee, its value would of course determine the level of compensation owed when the promisor withholds it through breach. Since Roman times, however, the law has distinguished between contract and conveyance.[12] At common law, only specific kinds of contracts, such as contracts of sale, effect an immediate transfer of title. Thus an agreement to sell (as contrasted with a contract of sale) gives the purchaser not a property interest in the object to be sold, but only the expectation of owning such an object in the future. Yet if the vendor breaches, the purchaser is nonetheless, under the rule of expectation damages, entitled to the object's value. This seems strange. Usually one's entitlement to the value of something stems from one's ownership of the thing that has that value. The rule of expectation damages thus presents the paradox that the law, by requiring that the promisor make good the value withheld through the breach of the contract, treats the promisee as entitled to the object's present value even though it does not yet regard the promisee as owner of the object itself.

To resolve this paradox, it is worth considering Immanuel Kant's account of the distinction between *in rem* and *in personam* rights. This account provides a response to the kind of position subsequently put forward by Fuller and Perdue.[13] In Kant's understanding, law is a system of universal reciprocal freedom that includes the freedom to acquire rights to what is external to the interacting parties as self-determining agents. Such external rights mark a relationship between the right-holder and the object of the right that imposes a correlative duty on others. The different kinds of external rights reflect the categories of the understanding that deal with relations. Accordingly, the distinction between rights *in rem* and rights *in personam* expresses juridically the epistemological distinction between the relational categories of substance and causality respectively.[14] An *in rem* right relates the holder of the right to substance—that is, to something that all others are obligated to leave intact; an *in personam* right relates the

[12] Barry Nicholas, *An Introduction to the Study of Roman Law* (1962), 103.

[13] The difficulty to which Kant was responding was not dissimilar to that raised by Fuller and Perdue; see Helge Dedek, "A Particle of Freedom: Natural Law Thought and the Kantian Theory of Transfer by Contract," (2012) 25 Can. J. L. & Juris L, 313.

[14] Immanuel Kant, *The Metaphysics of Morals*, tr. Mary Gregor (1996), [6:247].

holder of the right to a causality—that is, to an act that a promisor is obligated to perform because of the relationship with the promisee. A relation to substance is necessary for an *in rem* right to be good against the whole world; a relation to causality is necessary for an *in personam* right to be good against a particular person.

Kant is explicit about the nature of a contractual right. It is not a right to the subject matter of the contract. Nor is it a right to the situation that would result from the performance of the promised act. Rather, it is a right merely to the performance of that act, to what Kant calls "another's choice to perform a specific deed."[15] Kant formulates this important conclusion as follows:

By a contract I acquire something external. But what is it that I acquire? Since it only the causality of another's choice with respect to the performance he has promised me, what I acquire directly by a contract is not an external thing but rather his deed, by which that thing is brought under my control so that I make it mine.—By a contract I therefore acquire another's promise (not what he promised), and yet something is added to my external belongings; I have become *enriched (locupletior)* by acquiring an active obligation on the freedom and means of the other.[16]

Thus, Kant continues, what the promisee acquires through a contract is not a right to a thing but a right against the specific person obligated to perform the requisite act.[17]

This Kantian account of contractual entitlement provides a basis in corrective justice for the expectation measure of damages. By breach-

---

[15] Ibid., [6:402].

[16] Ibid., [6:424].

[17] In Kant's view, the acquisition of a thing by means of a contract involves two conceptual steps: the contract that makes a certain act (delivery of the thing) obligatory, and then the delivery that accomplishes the transfer of property by putting the promisee into possession of the thing (ibid., [6:424–26]). While it is true that the contract to deliver something makes the promisee's acquisition of the subject matter of the contract a "rightfully necessary *result* of it" (ibid., [6:432], emphasis in original), that result is the consequence of the promisor's discharge of the obligation, not "a part of the contract" (ibid.)—that is, not constitutive of the obligation itself. Kant here is following a principle of Roman law that survived in Germany, that the contract of sale (*emptio venditio*) does not itself transfer property; that happens only through a subsequent conveyance, such as delivery (*traditio*); see Fritz Schultz, *Classical Roman Law* (1951), 526–33. In holding this view, Kant implicitly disagreed with Grotius and Pufendorf, both of whom rejected the principle of Roman law, that contract does not convey property; see Hugo Grotius, *De Jure Belli ac Pacis Libri Tres*, 2 vols., tr. Francis W. Kelsey (1925), vol. 2, 308–9; Samuel Pufendorf, *De Jure Naturae et Gentium Libri Octo*, 2 vols., tr. C. H. and W. A. Oldfather (1934), vol. 2, 610–11.

ing the contract, the defendant unjustly deprives the plaintiff of the performance to which the plaintiff is entitled. The law undoes that injustice by restoring to the plaintiff either the specific performance that has been lost or the value of that performance. This value, in turn, reflects the value of the subject matter of the contract. Hence the plaintiff is entitled to damages that put the plaintiff into the position that the plaintiff would have been in had the contract not been breached. This is so not because the plaintiff has acquired an entitlement to (in Kant's formulation) "what was promised," that is, the thing that was the subject matter of the contract, but rather because the plaintiff has acquired the promise itself, that is, the act that the defendant is obligated to perform. The value of the thing promised is merely a way of measuring the value of the promise itself. The plaintiff has not acquired the thing promised "directly" (as Kant notes),[18] but the thing figures indirectly in the plaintiff's entitlement because the entitlement's value reflects the value of the thing.

This account resolves the Fuller–Perdue perplexity, that expectation damages seem to be "a queer kind of compensation" in that they give the plaintiff something that the plaintiff never had.[19] It is true that the plaintiff never had the thing promised; its loss is therefore not something for which the plaintiff can rightly claim compensation. But the plaintiff did have an entitlement to the performance itself; it is for the infringement of this entitlement that expectation damages compensate. Kant thereby answers the question that implicitly troubles Fuller and Perdue, "How can the law treat the plaintiff as entitled to the thing's value if the plaintiff is not entitled to the thing?" The plaintiff turns out to be entitled to the thing's value because that value determines the value of the performance to which the plaintiff *is* entitled. Both the Kantian account and the Fuller–Perdue critique of expectation damages presuppose the disjunction between contractual performance and ownership of the subject matter of the contract. But this very feature of contract that is problematic for Fuller and Perdue is what for Kant characterizes contract as a distinct kind of right.

The two accounts employ different conceptions of what is involved in providing a justification for the rule about expectation damages. For Fuller and Perdue justification consists in identifying the social purposes that the rule serves. Indeed, they regard this conception of

[18] Kant, above n. 14, [6:424].
[19] Above n. 8.

justification as so well established that it has achieved a pervasive trite-ness.[20] Therefore, once they dismiss the suggestion that expectation damages maintain the equilibrium of goods among members of soci-ety, they are free to rummage through the repertoire of social pur-poses until they alight on the protection of reliance and the promotion of commerce. Kant, in contrast, working in the tradition of corrective justice, does not justify legal concepts by reference to a social purpose, because that would involve the law's treating the parties as means rather than as agents who interact as ends in themselves. Instead, Kant views justification as immanent in a system of rights. Because a system of rights requires that the action of one self-determining person be consistent with the freedom of another, a rule is justified simply inas-much as it manifests this consistency. Conversely, a restriction of self-determining activity for any reason except consistency with the freedom of others (for example, a refusal to give legal recognition to contractual entitlement) would *eo ipso* be unjustified. Thus, once a rule can be understood as the juridical manifestation of self-determining agency in one person's interaction with another, no further work remains for justification to do. The rule is justified by virtue of its expressing the self-determining freedom of the interacting parties. This freedom forms the baseline from which deviations count as injustices. And then the undoing of such injustices in accordance with corrective justice partakes of the normativeness immanent in the sys-tem of rights and duties as a whole.

A virtue of the Kantian account of contractual entitlement is that it is consonant with the compensatory function that law itself implicitly assigns to expectation damages. In awarding the plaintiff the value of what the contract would have given, the law treats promisees as enti-tled to the expectancy that breach deprives them of. In contrast, a long and complicated narrative—which Fuller and Perdue attempted to provide—is needed to divert expectation damages from their osten-sibly compensatory role to the remedial policies identified by Fuller and Perdue. Although the classification of interests that Fuller and Per-due offered has taken hold, their account of expectation damages and the reconceptualization of contract law that this account entails have, on the whole, had little effect on the law.[21] The interest in securing

[20] Above n. 2, at 52.
[21] Daniel Friedmann, "The Performance Interest in Contract Damages," (1995) 111 Law Q.R. 628, 646–54.

the promised performance or its equivalent remains "the only pure contractual interest."[22] This interest in performance as the distinctive feature of contractual entitlement is the focus of Kant's attention. In providing a theoretical account that allows us to understand expectation damages for what they purport to be—that is, as compensation to the plaintiff for an injustice suffered at the defendant's hands—Kant's treatment of contract exemplifies the commitment of corrective justice to understand the basic structure of private law in the law's own terms.

3. The disgorgement of gains from breach

Whereas expectation damages, whatever their proper theoretical basis, are well established in the law, awards based on the plaintiff's gains are more controversial. The question of whether the promisee is entitled to what the promisor has gained from the breach has been called "devilishly difficult."[23] Favoring gain-based awards are strong ethical intuitions that promises should be kept and that those who breach their contracts should not profit from their wrongs. On the other hand, the difficulty in working out the applications of a new gain-based principle reinforces the suspicion that the traditional approach may be justified after all.

In many contract situations gain-based awards lie at the margins of the law's traditional compensatory framework. One such situation occurs when the defendant's gains may be used as a means of measuring the plaintiff's losses. For example, when the defendant competes with a plaintiff to whom the defendant has given an exclusive license to sell or manufacture a certain commodity, the usual approach is to treat the defendant's gain as evidence of the profit that the plaintiff lost through the breach.[24] Another such situation occurs when defective performance saves the promisor an expenditure without ultimately causing the promisee a further loss. Then the promisee can deduct what the promisor saved from the agreed price in order to bring the payment into line with what the promisee received, thus preventing what

---

[22] Ibid., 629.

[23] Andrew Burrows, "No Restitutionary Damages for Breach of Contract," (1993) Lloyd's Maritime & Commercial L.Q. 453.

[24] John Dawson, "Restitution or Damages?," (1959) 20 Ohio St. L.J. 175, 189.

turns out to be an overpayment.[25] Yet another such situation occurs when the promisor builds in breach of a negative covenant with the promisee but without causing the promisee financial loss. The promisee's entitlement to receive, in lieu of an injunction, the amount that reasonably would have had to be paid for securing a relaxation of the covenant can be interpreted either as gain-based or as compensatory.[26] A fourth such situation occurs when the breach of contract is also the breach of a fiduciary duty, when the aggrieved fiduciary can secure an accounting of the principal's profits, which would have been unavailable from a mere breach of contract.[27] A fifth such situation occurs when a purchaser breaches a provision of the contract of sale that limits the price at which the item can be resold.[28] Disgorgement to the original seller of the purchaser's excess profit on resale can perhaps be justified on the ground that, so far as the purchaser is concerned, the seller retained the value of the item above the price limit.

It is tempting to regard such miscellaneous instances of gain-based recovery not as particular applications of traditional categories, but as the scattered embers of a general conception of gain-based damages, to be collected into a new and explicit principle of disgorgement for breach of contract. An appealing analogy from the law of torts beckons. For centuries the owner of an object that the defendant converted and sold has been able, by "waiving the tort," to recover the proceeds of the sale from the defendant, even when this would give the owner more than the value of the lost object.[29] The gain based award that is controversial for breach of contract is universally accepted for the misappropriation of property. This difference, one might suppose, is entirely a product of history rather than reason. For why should profiting from another's contractual right be treated less severely than profiting from another's proprietary right?

---

[25] Samson and Samson v. Proctor [1975] 1 N.Z.L.R. 655 (S.C.) (builder, in breach of building contract, puts insufficient steel reinforcing into house which is sold at a price undiminished by the defect; court holds that a deduction from the contract price is not a departure from the fundamental principle of compensation). See also *Blake*, above n. 1, at 398.

[26] Wrotham Park Estate v. Parkside Homes [1974] 1 Weekly L. Rep. 798. (Ch. D.); see the different interpretations of this case in *Blake*, above n. 1, at 395–97, 410.

[27] E. Allan Farnsworth, "Your Loss or My Gain? The Dilemma of the Disgorgement Principle in Breach of Contract," (1985) 94 Yale L.J. 1339, 1354–60.

[28] British Motor Trade Association v. Gilbert [1951] 2 All E.R. 641 (Ch. D.).

[29] Lamine v. Dorrell, 92 Eng. Rep. 303 (1705). See Daniel Friedmann, "Restitution of Benefits Obtained through the Appropriation of Property or the Commission of a Wrong," (1980) 80 Colum. L. Rev. 504; Graham Virgo, *The Principles of the Law of Restitution*, 2nd ed. (2006), 454.

In recent years two important cases, one from Israel and the other from England, have provided the most extensive discussions favoring the disgorgement of gains from contract breach. In *Adras Building Material v. Harlow & Jones*[30] the defendant had agreed to sell steel to the plaintiff, but when the price of steel spiked, the defendant instead sold the steel stored for that purpose to a third party. Because the plaintiff did not purchase substitute steel at a higher price before the market receded to its former level, no loss was proved. The Supreme Court of Israel awarded the plaintiff the gain that the defendant realized by selling its steel to the third party above the contract price. In *Attorney-General v. Blake*[31] a former employee of the intelligence service, who had been convicted of spying and had escaped from prison, breached his contract of employment with the Crown by publishing his memoirs. Although he was not a fiduciary and the published information was no longer confidential, the House of Lords held that the Crown was entitled to the money owed to him by the publisher, on the ground that in the circumstances the Crown had a legitimate interest in preventing him from profiting from his breach of contract.

The basis of disgorgement in such cases is the sentiment that one should not profit from one's wrongdoing. This sentiment has obvious moral resonance. It treats the breach of contract as a wrong—that is, as an act that the promisor was morally obliged not to commit. By striking the gains of contract-breach from the hand of the promisor, disgorgement gives teeth to the long-standing principle that promises are to be observed (*pacta sunt servanda*).

In this respect disgorgement is at odds with the notion of efficient breach. Efficient breach, a dominant idea in the economic approach to contract theory, postulates that a contract breach from which the promisor gains more than the value of the promisee's expectancy is economically efficient.[32] By allowing the promisor to gain more than

---

[30] Above, n. 1; see Daniel Friedmann, "Restitution of Profits Gained by Party in Breach of Contract," (1988) 104 L.Q.R. 383.

[31] Above, n. 1. The parallel case in the United States, Snepp v. United States, 100 S. Ct. 763 (1980), differs in that the promisor in *Snepp* was held to be a fiduciary. On the other hand, it is hard to resist the impression that, in ordering the disgorgement, the court in *Blake* was aiming not merely at the promisor's breach of contract in publishing his memoirs, but at the traitorous activities that gave him the notoriety that made his memoirs profitable—an aspect not present in *Snepp*.

[32] A clear formulation of this much-discussed notion appears in Richard A. Posner, *Economic Analysis of Law*, 5th ed. (1998), 131. See also David W. Barnes, "The Anatomy of Contract Damages and Efficient Breach Theory," (1988) 6 S. Cal. Interdisc. L.J. 397.

would be sufficient to redress the promisee's loss, the breach moves the subject matter of the contract to its most valued use. In this way, the self-interested preferences of the parties tend to the production of the greatest social good. From the economic point of view, therefore, no reason exists for the law to discourage such a breach. Conversely, requiring the promisor to disgorge gains made through the breach discourages the promisor from engaging in this wealth-maximizing step.

How do these matters stand from the perspective of corrective justice? Corrective justice of course has no more interest in the promotion of efficiency than it has in the promotion of any other goal extrinsic to the interaction of the parties as the doer and sufferer of an injustice. Indeed, the theory of efficient breach conceptualizes the breach of contract not as an injustice to the promisee, but as an option available to the promisor within the system of incentives that the law makes available for the forwarding of efficiency. The breach of contract is simply a way of channeling resources to their most valued use; the normative status of a contract as imposing an obligation on the promisor plays no role. In contrast, corrective justice shares with the disgorgement principle the supposition that breach of contract is a wrong.

On the other hand, disgorgement involves the following difficulty from the standpoint of corrective justice. The fact that the promisor has profited from committing a wrong appears to supply an intuitively plausible reason for requiring the promisor to surrender the gain, but not for transferring that gain to the promisee. The taint that attaches to the promisor's gain by the wrongful manner of its acquisition does not in itself make the promisee rather than someone else the justified recipient of that gain. To be sure, the gain was realized through a breach of contract with the promisee, but the question that corrective justice raises is whether this breach establishes not merely the historical origin of the gain—its cause in fact, to use tort terminology—but also the normative connection between the gain and the promisee's entitlement to it.[33] This normative connection is present only when the gain represents something to which the promisee had a right of which he or she was deprived by the promisor's wrongful act. Only then would the gain be a constituent of the rights and correlative duties obtaining between the parties, and only then would the award of the gain render unto the promisee what was the promisee's. It is not

---

[33] On the difference between historical and normative connection, see above, chapter 4, section 2.

immediately apparent, however, on what grounds the gain can be considered an entitlement of the plaintiff.

For an award of damages to be consistent with corrective justice not only must the breach of the contract be a wrong to the promisee but the damages must be the measure of that wrong. Otherwise, there is no reason for the damages to be awarded specifically to the promisee for the injustice suffered. The Kantian account of contractual right, which highlights the promisee's entitlement to the promisor's performance, shows why a breach of contract can be viewed as a wrong to the promisee within the framework of corrective justice. That account, however, carries us no further than the promisee's entitlement to compensation for the loss of the value of the performance. Even though the gain realized by the promisor resulted from the wrong to the promisee, it does not seem to be part of that wrong.

Accordingly, from the standpoint of corrective justice, it is not enough for the proponent of disgorgement to dismiss the economic theory of efficient breach as indifferent to the normative dimension of contract law. If that normative dimension is to be fully respected, it is also necessary to indicate the positive ground for thinking that the gain is within the promisee's entitlement as quantifying the wrong that the promisee has suffered. The fact that efficient breach is incompatible with disgorgement does not entail the conclusion that disgorgement follows from the rejection of efficient breach.

Neither the Israeli nor the English disgorgement case succeeds in showing the promisee's particular entitlement to the gain that the promisor is made to disgorge. In the *Adras* case Justice Barak explicitly referred to the theory of efficient breach, rejecting it with the following observations:

Moreover, it seems to me that the economic approach does not give enough weight to considerations which cannot be measured in economic terms. The law of contract is not only meant to increase economic efficiency but also to enable society to lead a proper life. Contracts are there to be performed, whether or not damages to be payable on breach, an approach by which we encourage people to keep their promises. Promise keeping is the basis of our life as a society and a nation.[34]

---

[34] *Adras*, above n. 1, at 272. Similarly Justice S. Levin, at 241, acerbically remarked that "the approach of the economic school of law ignores in cases like this the fact that we are dealing with people with moral feelings and not with robots."

With these words Justice Barak rightly emphasized that contract has a normative dimension that the economic approach ignores. However, the vindication of the morality of promise-keeping against the amorality of economically efficient breach is insufficient to ground a legal entitlement in the promisee to the promisor's gains. What is needed to sustain the decision is reference not to the social morality of promising, but to contract as a juridical regime of rights and correlative duties that renders the promisor's breach (and, in particular, the realization of profit through breach) an injustice to the promisee. Justice Barak's allusion to the role of promise-keeping in the proper life of society makes it seem that the promisor's profiting from the breach was not specifically a wrong against the promisee, but more generally a subversion of the collective effort to preserve promise-keeping as the basis on which social and national life rests. This view of the profit in turn leaves unexplained why the promisee is entitled to recover for what was a wrong against society as a whole.

Blake, the English case concerning the profits from the former spy's memoirs, has a parallel difficulty. In ordering disgorgement Lord Nicholls, while acknowledging that disgorgement is an exceptional remedy not subject to fixed rules, offers as a general guide "whether the plaintiff has a legitimate interest in preventing the defendant's profit making activity and, hence, in depriving him of his profit."[35] The legitimate interest included the need to preserve the trust of informants and to uphold the morale of secret service officers, apparently even with respect to information that was no longer confidential. These considerations, however, do not address the question of why the plaintiff was entitled to the profits, even assuming the defendant was not. This absence of any entitlement to the gain on the part of the plaintiff is perhaps why the dissenting judge, Lord Hobhouse, pointing out that the defendant's gain was not made at the plaintiff's expense, stigmatized the claim as being of an "essentially punitive nature."[36]

The reasoning in both *Adras* and *Blake* is directed to the pursuit of social goals rather than to the justice intrinsic in the parties' interaction. The plaintiffs in these cases are awarded the profits realized from the defendants' breaches of contract not because the plaintiffs can show their respective entitlements to these profits, but because they are conveniently situated for assisting in the accomplishment of cer-

---

[35] *Blake*, above, n.1, at 398.
[36] Ibid., 407.

tain social goals. In *Adras* the goal is to encourage the socially important practice of keeping promises. In *Blake* the goal is to forward the
effective functioning of the secret service. These considerations focus
on the desirability of preventing the defendants from keeping what
they might gain from breaching their contracts. The goals as such are
indifferent to the question of who might get the profits thus struck
from the defendants' hands. Instead of treating the gain as the locus of
an injustice done by the defendant and suffered by the plaintiff, the
reasoning points one-sidedly to the inadmissibility of the defendant's
profit. The position of the plaintiffs is adventitious; they are connected
to their respective defendants through their contractual entitlements
even though the profits that they are awarded are not themselves
constituents of those entitlements. In this respect the reasoning in the
cases is incompatible with the correlative structure of corrective
justice.[37]

As was indicated in the previous chapter, disgorgement to the plaintiff of profits made by the defendant is the appropriate response, so far
as corrective justice is concerned, to the unauthorized alienation by
the defendant of something to which the plaintiff had a proprietary
right. By virtue of ownership the owner is entitled to all the profits
that accrue from the alienation of what is owned. Just as the owner's
exclusive right to the object implies a duty on others to abstain from
it, so the owner's right to the profits that accrue from its alienation
imports a correlative duty in others to abstain from such profits or, if
there was a failure to abstain, to yield these profits to the owner. The
profits are the owner's as surely as the object that produced them. The
correlativity of the owner's right and the wrongdoer's duty means that
the wrongful gain is an injustice as between them. The injustice
embodied in this gain is undone when the gain is restored to the
owner of the object from which the gain accrued. The proprietary
nature of what was alienated makes the realization of profits a

---

[37] Once the exercise is conceived instrumentally as the forwarding of extrinsic goals, the
choice of certain goals at the expense of others becomes significant. What, for instance,
makes the promotion of promissory good faith more important than the promotion of economic efficiency (as the Supreme Court of Israel assumes)? Hanoch Dagan, for example, has
suggested that both are important and the profits should be split to reflect this; see Dagan,
"Restitutionary Damages for Breach of Contract: An Exercise in Private Law Theory," (2000)
1 Theoretical Inquiries in Law 115, at 151. This natural consequence of instrumental analysis
would produce the incoherence of two considerations (efficiency and promissory good
faith) each artificially limiting the reach of the other. On the problematic normative structure of such incoherence, see Weinrib, *The Idea of Private Law* (1995), 32–44.

correlatively structured wrong that accounts for the role of both parties in the remedy.

This suggests that in the contracts context the promisee should be
awarded the promisor's profits if the breach of contract can be construed as the alienation of what belongs to the promisee. The Kantian
account of contractual entitlement, however, reveals the implausibility
of regarding the breach as the wrongful alienation of the promisee's
property. The difficulty is to identify the property alienated through
breach. There are only two possibilities. In the first of these there is no
property; in the second there may be property in some sense, but there
is no alienation.

The first possibility is that the promisee owns the object promised
in the contract. However, on the Kantian view the promisee is entitled
to performance but does not have property in the object of the contract. In the *Adras* case, for instance, the contract to ship a certain
quantity of steel to the promisee did not in itself transform any of the
defendant's steel into the property of the plaintiff. The plaintiff, therefore, should have had no claim to the profits made by the sale to the
third party, even if the steel would otherwise have been shipped in
fulfillment of the contract. To the contrary: the defendant simply sold
its own steel to the third party and was accordingly entitled to the
profits from the sale by virtue of its ownership of what it sold.

The other possibility concerns the contractual performance itself,
which, in the Kantian account, constitutes the promisee's contractual
entitlement and promisor's correlative obligation. To be sure, the entitlement to contractual performance can be treated as a species of property for certain purposes (for example, classification as a chose in
action, assignment, constitutional protection).[38] However, the promisor's breach cannot plausibly be regarded as a purported alienation of
this entitlement, so as to give the promisee a claim to the profits in the
promisor's hand. The *Adras* case is illustrative. The promisor's obligation was to perform a certain act—that is, to deliver steel to the promisee. The breach consisted in not delivering the steel, which had been

---

[38] For example, in a discussion of contract damages Daniel Friedmann suggests that,
because contractual rights enjoy the constitutional protection of property for purposes of the
takings clause of the constitution of the United States, property includes contractual rights;
Friedmann, "The Efficient Breach Fallacy," (1989) 18 J. Legal Stud. 1, 16. However, one cannot conclude that because the state compensates for the taking of contractual rights, the
promisor should be liable for non-compensatory damages for breaching a contract. The compensatory norms of constitutional law are irrelevant to the private law's treatment of non-
compensatory awards.

sold to a third party. This breach can hardly be construed as the promisor's alienation of something that can be conceptualized as "the delivery of steel as owed to the promisee." What it sold to the third party
was the steel that would have fulfilled its contract with the promisee;
it did not sell the act of delivery that was owed by the promisor to the
promisee. Nor did it alienate the promisee's entitlement. The third
party contracted with respect to the steel, not with respect to the
promisee's entitlement. Nor, finally, did the promisor alienate the obligation correlative to the promisee's entitlement; by buying the steel,
the third party did not become obligated, as the promisor was and
remained, to deliver steel to the promisee. The breach of the contract
is not an alienation of something that the promisee owned.

Some have contended that, although sound when the subject matter of the contract is indefinite, this conclusion does not apply, even
on Kantian grounds, when the subject matter of the contract is specific or unique.[39] If the promisee's entitlement was to the delivery of a
horse, then the promisor's sale of his only horse, Bessie, to a third party
is not the alienation of the promisee's right, because the promisee's
right did not specifically include Bessie. This is essentially the situation
in *Adras*, where disgorgement was, accordingly, not justified. If, however, the promisee's entitlement was to the delivery of Bessie, then the
act of delivering Bessie to someone else "is identical to the act which
has already been transferred to the [promisee]."[40] Selling this act of
delivery to a third party then represents a misappropriation by the
promisor of what belongs to the promisee. The profit thereby obtained
is rightfully the promisee's.

This argument hinges on the identity of what was promised to the
promisee and what was sold to the third party. Only if this identity
exists can the promisor be construed as selling to the third party what
already belonged to the promisee. It is crucial to the argument's Kantian character that this identity consists not in the horse delivered (the
horse named "Bessie") but in the act of delivering the horse; the specification of the horse as Bessie merely allows the two acts of delivery
to be identified as the same act, so that the second can be regarded as
a misappropriation of the first. However, the argument confines the

---

[39] Peter Benson, "Disgorgement for Breach of Contract and Corrective Justice: An Analysis
in Outline," in *Understanding Unjust Enrichment*, ed. Jason Neyers, Mitchell McInnes, and
Stephen G. A. Pitel (2004), 311, at 329; Andrew Botterell, "Contractual Performance, Corrective Justice, and Disgorgement for Breach of Contract," (2010) 16 Legal Theory 135.

[40] Benson, above n. 39.

specification of the act to the specification of the object transferred. This limitation is artificial. Once the specification of the required act is expanded to include all the terms of the respective transactions, the identity between the two acts disappears. The two transactions may call for acts of delivery at different times and places. Moreover, the specification of delivery will inevitably refer to different recipients. Accordingly, what was sold to the third party was not the act of delivery that belonged to the promisee, but a different act of delivery inconsistent with the first one. This new act of delivery made breach of the contract unavoidable, thereby exposing the promisor to damages, but it was not the misappropriation of an act of delivery identical to, and therefore owned by, the promisee. The effect of insisting on the importance of specification but confining this specification to the object of the contract ("Bessie") is to transform—inconsistently with the Kantian argument—the contractual right to performance into a right to the thing.

Thus, a breach of contract is not tantamount to the alienation of a proprietary right. Because a proprietary right imposes a duty of non-interference on the whole world, it has a juridical significance that is independent of any particular wrongdoer. This independence means that the duty correlative to the proprietary right has to be defined in terms of a particular object that is separate from the indefinite number of juridical relationships in which it figures. That object is therefore available for misappropriation in a transaction between one non-proprietor and another, with consequent liability to the owner for the proceeds of this transaction. In the waiver of tort cases involving the unauthorized alienation of property, the thing misappropriated is indeed identical to the content of the owner's right. Formulated in terms of Kantian theory, the stable identity of the proprietary right with respect to the duties it imposes on the whole world brings such a right under the Kantian category of substance. Breaches of contract are different. Contractual performance falls under the Kantian category of causality—that is, of a relationship of consequence and ground, because performance is a normative consequence of the nexus between the two contracting parties. The required performance is defined by the contract between the parties. The obligation to do the contracted-for act is particular to that contractual relationship. By breaching the contract the promisor infringes the promisee's right but does not alienate it. The subject matter of the promisee's entitlement— which is always the promisor's act and not the thing required for the act—has not been and cannot be passed on to a third party by the promisor's breach. Accordingly, the profits that the promisor has realized from the breach do not come within the entitlement of the promisee.

In the *Blake* case, the significance of the difference between contractual and proprietary entitlement was a matter of dispute between the judges. Lord Hobhouse, dissenting, was in favor of dismissing the claim for the disgorgement of profits on the ground that "that is a remedy based on proprietary principles when the necessary proprietary rights are absent."[41] Lord Nicholls, on the other hand, remarked in allowing the claim that "it is not easy to see why, as between the parties to a contract, a violation of a party's contractual rights should attract a lesser degree of remedy than violation of his property rights."[42] Lord Nicholls's assumption was that the only difference between a contractual and a proprietary right is a quantitative one, that the former obligates only on one person whereas the latter obligates an indefinite number of persons.[43] Lord Nicholls therefore concluded that "it is not clear why it should be any more permissible to expropriate personal rights than it is permissible to expropriate property rights."[44]

Lord Nicholls's conclusion is suspect for a number of reasons. First, given that breach of contract is the violation of a right, the issue is not one of the relative permissibility of the defendant's conduct, but of the remedial response appropriate to that conduct. Secondly, a breach of contract is not helpfully characterized as an expropriation; breach does not involve the taking of an object that can exist independently of the relationship between the parties or the extinction of an entitlement owing to the plaintiff. Moreover, Lord Nicholls's conclusion proves too much: if proprietary and contractual entitlement did not differ, disgorgement would be the standard remedy when the promisor profitably breaches, rather than the extraordinary one that even Lord Nicholls treats it as. Most importantly, the difference between proprietary and contractual entitlement is not merely quantitative. In *Adras*, for instance, the promisee did not have a contractual right that

---

[41] *Blake*, above n. 1, 410.

[42] Ibid., 395.

[43] This assumption is developed in the article on which Lord Nicholls expressly draws; see Lionel Smith, "Disgorgement of the Profits of Breach of Contract, Property, Contract and 'Efficient Breach,'" (1994–95) 24 Canadian Business L.J., 121, 130–2.

[44] *Blake*, above n. 1, 395.

consisted in owning the steel with only the promisor being subject to a correlative obligation, in contrast to a proprietary interest in the steel that created a correlative obligation for the whole world. The promisee in *Adras* did not own the steel at all; all that the promisee was entitled to was a certain performance. The difference between a proprietary and a contractual right is qualitative; the former goes to an object, the latter to an action.[45] The result of this is that nothing is available for the promisor to expropriate or alienate, since these verbs are inapplicable as descriptions of what the promisor does with respect to an entitlement that consists in his own actions. The upshot of this is that, as Lord Hobhouse saw in dissent, disgorgement is an inappropriate remedy for contract breach.

Is this conclusion affected by whether the remedy to which the promisee is entitled is specific performance? For instance, in contracts for the sale of land, where the purchaser is entitled to specific performance, courts may describe the vendor as a trustee and the purchaser as the equitable owner, and hold the vendor liable for the profits realized from reselling the land to the third party at a higher price.[46] One may be tempted to regard such instances as evidence that, even though disgorgement is not generally a remedy for contract breach, the availability of specific performance transforms the promisee's contractual entitlement into a proprietary one so as to allow the promisee to claim the promisor's profits from sale. In this way of considering the promisee's entitlement, the supposed transformation of the contractual entitlement into a proprietary one is merely a terminological shorthand for anticipating the availability of specific performance;[47] the conclusion about property is the result of the premise about the remedy.

This approach to the entitlement is inconsistent with corrective justice's conception of the relation of right and remedy. For corrective justice the right is conceptually prior to the remedy that responds to the right's infringement. Of course, if the system of private law is well ordered, the remedy will reflect the kind of entitlement that the plain-

---

[45] In Kant's terminology, proprietary and contractual obligations deal with objects of choice that come within different categories: property deals with substance (an external thing) and contract deals with causality (another's choice to perform a specific deed); see Kant, above n. 14, at [6:402].

[46] Timko v. Useful Homes Corporation, 168 A. 824 (N.J. Ch., 1933); Lake v. Bayliss [1974] 1 Weekly Law Rep. 1073 (Ch. D.).

[47] Dawson, above n. 24, 186.

tiff has. The remedy, however, does not determine the nature of the underlying right. Whether the entitlement is proprietary or not depends on the concepts internal to the juridical relationship between the parties (such as the connection between the alienation of property and the claim to proceeds). It does not depend on the court's response to the defendant's injustice. The remedy, therefore, cannot transform into a proprietary right what is not already one before the remedy is fixed.[48]

Thus, the general picture that emerges from the present discussion is as follows. Making the promisee disgorge his or her gains to prevent profiting from a wrong has intuitive appeal. Corrective justice, however, requires that the parties be treated as correlatively situated through the right of the plaintiff and the corresponding duty of the defendant. One-sided attention to the defendant's gains does not reflect this correlativity. If disgorgement for contract breach is to

---

[48] At common law, specific performance is available where damages are inadequate due to the real or (as in the case of land in traditional contract doctrine) deemed uniqueness of the subject matter of the contract. The consequence of this uniqueness is that the market cannot reliably determine the value of what the promisee has lost through the breach. Only by granting specific performance or by treating the promisee as equitable owner and therefore entitled to the proceeds can the law ensure that promisor is awarded what he or she has been unjustly deprived of. Accordingly, cases such as those mentioned above in n. 46 above need not be considered as examples of disgorgement rather than compensation.

Even the fact that in a given jurisdiction (for example, in Israel) specific performance is the default remedy should not affect the argument about disgorgement. In the *Adras* case, the Supreme Court of Israel thought that the institution of specific performance as the default remedy for contract breach in Israel marks a fundamental difference from the common law that makes disgorgement more plausible; see *Adras*, above n. 1, at 241, 271. This, however, is not necessarily the case. All that the status of specific performance as the primary remedy indicates is that the Israeli system takes very seriously the idea that the promisee is, as corrective justice affirms, entitled to performance; it does not necessarily change the subject matter of the performance into a proprietary right. The temptation to slide from the former to the latter should be resisted. For example, at p. 271 Justice Barak writes:

> The injured party has a right not only to compensation for breach of contract, but also to specific performance... Therefore, under Israeli law, a buyer in a contract of sale is entitled to receive the subject matter of the sale, and an enrichment of the seller which infringes this right is an unjust enrichment at the buyer's expense... When there is a contract for the sale of a horse, the buyer has the right to receive the horse, not damages for non-delivery. If the seller receives a benefit from selling the horse to a third party, he... takes from the buyer a right to which the buyer is entitled.

There is an equivocation here about the right to which the last sentence refers. A right to receive the horse is not the same as a right to the horse (to which the language of "taking" might be applicable). The former right is to the performance of an act, the latter is to a particular thing. The former is contractual, the latter proprietary. The enhanced role of specific performance does not change the categorical difference between what Kant, above n. 45, called substance and causality.

conform to corrective justice, the promisor's profit must be understood as proceeds from the alienation of the promisee's property. Given the Kantian account of contractual entitlement, an alienation of property cannot be made out. Disgorgement of the gains from contract breach awards to the promisee something that the promisee was not deprived of.

To a large extent this conclusion coincides with the result favored by the theory of efficient breach. However, this convergence in result masks a fundamental divide between the two approaches. As its critics have emphasized,[49] efficient breach abstracts from the normative dimension of contract to the promotion of efficiency. In contrast, corrective justice, by exhibiting the immanently normative structure of the contract relationship as a nexus of rights and correlative duties, is normative through and through. Instead of disavowing (as the economic approach does) an interest in the duty of contractual performance, corrective justice maintains that the nature of that duty is precisely what excludes the notion of disgorgement. Thus, its rejection of the disgorgement of gains from contract breach comes not in the pursuit of an external goal like economic efficiency, but as an internal implication of the very idea of contractual entitlement.

4. Punishment and corrective justice

I now move to the possibility of punitive damages for breach of contract. This possibility has lurked in the background of the preceding discussion of expectation damages and disgorgement. Once one assumes that a given head of damages is not compensatory, one is tempted to ascribe to it a punitive purpose. Thus, Lord Hobhouse, dissenting in *Blake*, maintained that a claim for disgorgement had an "essentially punitive nature."[50] Similarly, Fuller and Perdue at one point suggested that, in the absence of a plausible compensatory justification for them, expectation damages might be viewed as having the implicit quasi-criminal purpose of penalizing the promisor's breach for the sake of protecting the reliance interest.[51] Such observations about implicit purpose raise the question of whether an explicitly

---

[49] See especially Friedmann, above n. 38.
[50] *Blake*, above n. 1, at 407.
[51] Above n. 2, 61.

punitive component should be added to the damage award. The two sections that follow address this question by considering from the standpoint of corrective justice first, the theoretical relationship between punishment and liability and then, the use of punitive damages specifically for contract breach.

At the juncture of punishment and liability lies the issue of punitive damages. Such damages are encased in controversy. Formally unrecognized in the civil law jurisdictions but widely accepted in the common law world, punitive damages have been especially contentious over the last several decades. Developments in both the United States and England have contributed to this. In the United States, the relatively unstructured discretion of the jury to determine damages has led to concerns that the standards for awarding punitive damages are too vague and that the awards themselves may be excessive.[52] In England a more fundamental development occurred: the House of Lords, unequivocally repudiating punitive damages as anomalous, restricted their scope to the minimum allowed by precedent, a position in turn rejected by courts in the old Commonwealth.[53]

The House of Lords was of the view that almost the only circumstance when punitive damages were available at common law in a dispute between private parties was when the wrongdoer's conduct was calculated to make a profit that would exceed the compensation payable to the victim.[54] Lord Reid termed the traditional broader conception of punitive damages a "form of palm tree justice" and he characterized the objections to it as "overwhelming." He explained:

To allow pure punishment in this way contravenes almost every principle which has been evolved for the protection of offenders. There is no definition of the offence except that the conduct punished must be oppressive,

---

[52] David G. Owen, "The Moral Foundations of Punitive Damages," (1989) 40 Ala. L. Rev. 705, 727–38.

[53] The House of Lords cases are Rookes v. Barnard [1964] 1 All E.R. 367 (H.L.) and Cassell v. Broome [1972] App. Cas. 1027 (H.L.). The leading cases in the Commonwealth reaction are Uren v. John Fairfax [1966] 117 C.L.R. 118 (H.C. Aust.); Fogg v. McKnight, [1968] N.Z.L.R. 330 (S.C.); Lamb v. Cotogno [1987] 164 C.L.R. 1 (H.C. Aust.); Vorvis v. Insurance Corporation of British Columbia [1989] 1 Sup. Ct. Rep. 1085; *Whiten*, above n. 1 (S.C.C.).

[54] The House of Lords also allowed punitive damages where they are authorized by statute and where there was oppressive, arbitrary, or unconstitutional action by government employees. These categories are not relevant to the present theme. On the second of these, see Kuddus v. Chief Constable of the Leicestershire Constabulary [2000] 2 Weekly Law Rep. 1789 (H.L.).

high-handed, malicious, wanton, or the like—terms far too vague to be admitted to any criminal code worthy of the name. There is no limit to punishment except that it must not be unreasonable. The punishment is not inflicted by a judge who has experience and at least tries not to be influenced by emotion: it is inflicted by a jury without experience of law or punishment and often swayed by consideration which every judge would put out of his mind. And there is no effective appeal against sentence.[55]

Critics of the English approach have responded that the institutional distinction between criminal law and private law does not dictate so exclusive an allocation of punishment to the criminal law.[56]

This controversy raises two fundamental issues. The narrower issue concerns the role of punishment, as expressed through an award of punitive damages, within private law. In dealing with this Lord Reid adverted to the significance of the procedural distinctions between tort law and criminal law. This in turn implicates the second and broader issue of determining the nature of the demarcation between civil and criminal liability. How does corrective justice stand with respect to these two issues?

The first of these two issues can be briefly treated. That corrective justice renders punitive damages problematic is obvious on its face. Corrective justice insists that the normative considerations applicable to the relationship between defendant and plaintiff reflect the parties' correlative standing as the sufferer and doer of the same injustice. Accordingly, it excludes considerations, regardless of how appealing they otherwise might be, that refer to one of the parties without encompassing the correlative situation of the other. Punishment is a one-sided consideration of this sort. Punishment focuses not relationally on the parties as doer and sufferer of the same injustice, but unilaterally on the defendant as doer. From a punitive standpoint, we do not ask what would restore to the plaintiff what he or she was deprived

---

[55] *Cassell*, above n. 53, at 1087.

[56] Nicholas McBride, "Punitive Damages," in *Wrongs and Remedies in the Twenty-First Century*, ed. Peter Birks (1996), 175; Peter Cane, *The Anatomy of Tort Law* (1997), 118. For an assessment of the controversy, see Andrew Burrows, "Reforming Exemplary Damages: Expansion or Abolition," in *Wrongs and Remedies in the Twenty-First Century*, ed. Peter Birks (1996), 153. In England the Law Commission under Burrows's direction recommended the expansion of punitive damages; see "Aggravated, Exemplary and Restitutionary Damages," Law Comm. No. 427 (1997). Also favoring punitive damages is James Edelman, *Gain-Based Damages: Contract, Tort, Equity and Intellectual Property* (2002), 9–21.

of by the defendant, but rather what punishment is deserved in view of the defendant's behavior. Accordingly, damages at private law that are the vehicle of punishment are a windfall to the plaintiff because they do not represent anything that the plaintiff has been wrongly deprived of. Instead of measuring the plaintiff's entitlement, punitive damages in effect function as a reward for providing the socially useful service of acting as a private prosecutor.[57]

The second and broader issue is the difference between civil and criminal liability. Although corrective justice is a regime of rights and their correlative duties, the denial of the relevance of punishment to corrective justice is not a denial of punishment's place in a right-based legal order. Instead, the point is that from the standpoint of corrective justice, this place must be located within criminal law rather than within the private law relationship. Since corrective justice brings out the distinctiveness of the private law relationship, it illuminates Lord Reid's differentiation between criminal and civil liability and his insistence that punishment is the concern of the former and not the latter. From the standpoint of corrective justice, the relationship between compensation and punishment, and between the legal institutions of private law and criminal law that correspond to them is, I suggest, as follows.

Corrective justice rectifies injustices that operate on the parties in a transactionally specific way. This transactional specificity involves linking two specific parties through the injury by one of them of a right held by the other. For example, the defendant may have tortiously injured the plaintiff as a result of acting inconsistently with the plaintiff's right to physical integrity or to a specific item of property that the plaintiff owns. Kant's account of contractual entitlement includes the promisor's performance under a valid contract among the particular rights that a specific person might have. Or the defendant may have been unjustly enriched by the plaintiff's having transferred value that rightfully ought to be restored. Such unjust losses or gains relate to rights that a specific plaintiff is entitled to vindicate against a specific defendant as a matter of corrective justice. When one's right is injured, one is entitled to restoration of the right or to its monetary equivalent.

Punishment is different. It is state action that inflicts an adverse consequence on the wrongdoer without restoring the right of a wronged

---

[57] *Whiten*, above n. 1, para. 36.

party. When the state punishes, it acts not to rectify a wrong that is transactionally specific to the plaintiff and the defendant, but to vindicate its own standing as the public guarantor of rightful order. The underlying idea is that the actualization of rights requires that they be publicly guaranteed, so that their establishment, delineation, and enforcement do not reflect the merely unilateral will of any particular person.[58] Rights cannot be enjoyed in a world lacking public institutions—a condition that Kant termed a "state of nature." Accordingly, everyone is obligated to be and to remain subject to what Kant called public right—that is, a condition in which public institutions lay down norms that guarantee the rights of all. The consequence of this is that the state, as the juridical manifestation of public right, has an interest of its own, distinct from the interest of any particular party, in having its norms respected. Whereas each person's interest is to prevent or rectify an injury to one's rights, the state's interest is to prevent a defection from the condition of public right into the state of nature. Thus arises the possibility of a wrong that is not transactionally specific: it is relative to the condition of public right, rather than relative to a particular plaintiff. Punishment is the response to this kind of wrong.

The role of public right accounts for two defining features of punishable wrongs. Because the wrong is a defection from public right, its vindication lies at the hand not of a particular right-holder (as would be the case with corrective justice), but of the state. Hence the state, acting through its public prosecutors, has the role of initiating and carrying the legal process that determines the guilt and consequent punishment of the accused wrongdoer. Moreover, the intention with which the act was performed is crucial to assessment of the actor's guilt. Because the offense signals that the offender has, at least to the extent of the offending act, exempted himself from the requirements of public right, it must be intentional. Otherwise, the offense would not reflect the reason for the state's interest in the actor's behavior. This accounts for the salience of *mens rea* in the criminal law.

Thus, intent plays a double role within a system of rights. On the one hand, the defendant's intention to injure the plaintiff constitutes the element of culpability linking the defendant's wrongful action to the plaintiff's wrongful injury. Indeed, if the act is performed with malevolence sufficient to injure the plaintiff's dignity, the plaintiff may be awarded aggravated damages. This role is transactionally specific and therefore

---

[58] Arthur Ripstein, *Force and Freedom: Kant's Legal and Political Philosophy* (2009), 145.

within the scope of corrective justice. On the other hand, the wrongful intent also goes to the offender's self-exemption from the norms of public right. This role is not transactionally specific, because, although the injustice takes place within a transactional context in which a specific person may be[59] injured, the deliberateness has significance beyond that injury. Because of this double role, intent can figure both as the mental element of an intentional tort and as the *mens rea* of a criminal act.

The difference between wrongs relative to another and wrongs relative to public right provide the conceptual ground for regarding civil liability and punishment as distinct. This distinctiveness works in both directions. The punitive arrangements of criminal law are not rendered superfluous by the existence of a system of civil liability; that system deals merely with transactionally specific violations of rights rather than with transactionally non-specific challenges to public right. Nor can punishment coherently be stuffed into the framework of civil liability, for then lawsuits that have a transactionally specific structure, in which a specific plaintiff sues a specific defendant to restore a particular right or its equivalent, would have to deal with the transactionally non-specific aspect of the wrong. The result of this would be an award of punitive damages, which inevitably gives a windfall to the plaintiff on the basis of considerations that go one-sidedly to the deliberateness of the defendant's conduct.

Lord Reid's repudiation of punitive damages, quoted above,[60] picks up the institutional implications of this incoherence. Because a deliberate self-exemption from the regime of public right is more serious than the infringement of a particular right and because conviction carries the stigma of criminality, criminal law insists on express definition of offenses and of possible punishments. Criminal law also entrenches procedural safeguards (such as the benefit of a more stringent burden of proof) for those who are accused, which would be out of place in a civil trial because the advantage they would give to defendants would be incompatible with the notional equality of the parties as the alleged doer and sufferer of the same injustice. Lord Reid's criticism of punitive damages as involving a form of palm tree justice, as well as his almost complete rejection of punitive damages,

---

[59] I say "may be" rather than "is" because the challenge to the regime of rights does not necessarily require that someone actually be injured. This, I would suggest, is why there are attempted crimes but not attempted torts.

[60] Above at n. 55.

thus give legal expression to the conceptual difference between corrective justice and punishment and to the institutional roles that each has within a rights-based approach to law.

5. Punitive damages in contract

With these general considerations about punitive damages in hand, I want to turn more specifically to punitive damages in contract law. In contrast to the situation in tort law, where such damages have historically been well entrenched and the controversy has been whether the legal order ought to restrict them, contract law was traditionally hostile toward punitive damages. One can ascribe this hostility to the fear of disturbing the certainty of commercial dealings by introducing a damage component that floated free of the value of the contractual performance to which the parties had agreed. In England this hostility remains. In the United States, however, the rule against awarding punitive damages for breach of contract has been eroding for the past century. Beginning with an exception that punitive damages could be allowed when the breach was accompanied by a fraudulent act,[61] the present majority position in the United States is that punitive damages can be awarded if the conduct constituting the breach of contract is also a tort for which punitive damages can be given, with some state courts allowing such damages on even more expansive grounds.[62]

Perhaps the most dramatic recent developments have occurred in Canada. In 1989 the Supreme Court of Canada, signaling its rejection of the restrictive English approach to punitive damages, recognized that punitive damages were available (though it did not in fact award them) for breach of contract.[63] There matters stood until 2002, when in *Whiten v. Pilot Insurance*[64] the court upheld a punitive damage award

[61] Welborn v. Dixon, 39 S.E. 232 (S.C. Sup. Ct., 1904); see Simpson, "Punitive Damages for Breach of Contract," (1959) 20 Ohio St. L.J. 284.

[62] Dodge, "The Case for Punitive Damages in Contracts," (1999) 48 Duke L.J. 629, 636–51. The majority United States position is of limited interest in a discussion of contract damages, because it merely prevents the fact that there was a breach of contract from precluding the concurrent tort remedies.

[63] Vorvis v. Insurance Corporation of British Columbia [1989] 1 Sup. Ct. Rep. 1085.

[64] *Whiten*, above n. 1. At the same time the court issued a companion judgment applying *Whiten* and concluding that, in the circumstances, an award of punitive damages for contract breach was not justified; Performance Industries Ltd. v. Sylvan Lake Golf & Tennis Club Ltd. (22 February 2002, S.C.C.).

against an insurer who attempted to evade honoring a fire insurance policy. The plaintiff in *Whiten* had insured her house with the defendant insurer. When her house burned down, the defendant's denied her claim under the policy, alleging without basis that the plaintiff had committed arson. For two years the defendant persisted in hostile and groundless opposition to the claim. In the meantime, because the insurance claim was substantially her sole asset, the plaintiff's financial situation deteriorated. The defendant's conduct was deliberately designed (so it was found) to starve the plaintiff into an unfair settlement. The court upheld a jury award that gave the plaintiff not only the insurance proceeds to which she was entitled under the policy, but also an additional million dollars as punitive damages.

In coming to this conclusion the court dealt comprehensively with the issue of punitive damages. The court emphasized that both the decision to award punitive damages and the determination of the quantum had to be rational in the light of the objectives of punitive damages. The amount awarded also had to be proportionate to the accomplishment of those objectives. While punitive damages were the exception rather than the rule, they nonetheless could be employed when compensatory damages and the law's other sanctions were inadequate to achieve the retribution that the defendant deserved, the deterrence that would prevent similar conduct in the future, and the denunciation that would mark the community's collective condemnation. Retribution, deterrence, and denunciation are the objectives of punitive damages; so long as an award was not so disproportionate as to exceed the bounds of what is rational for the achievement of these objectives, the award could stand.

As a result of this development the Canadian jurisprudence now provides one of the most extensive recent discussions in the common law world of punitive damages in contract law. Like many Commonwealth jurisdictions, Canada has definitively repudiated the idea (which corrective justice supports) that punitive damages have no place in private law. Instead the court has affirmed that "[p]unishment is a legitimate objective not only of the criminal law but of the civil law as well."[65] The question that arises is whether, having dispensed with the coherence imparted by corrective justice, the court has nonetheless succeeded on some other basis in working out a coherent role for punitive damages in relation to breach of contract.

---

[65] *Whiten*, above n. 1, para. 36.

The threshold issue is what are the circumstances in which punitive damages may be awarded for breach of contract. On the one hand, something more than a breach of contract, even if deliberate, is required. On the other hand, it would have been inappropriate simply to award the plaintiff in *Whiten* the insurance proceeds; some account had to be taken of the abusive manner in which the defendant had dealt with her claim. The defendant insurer's high-handed treatment of the plaintiff made it liable to the payment of a premium over and above the amount that would have satisfied its contractual obligation had it paid promptly. What is the legal basis of the obligation to pay this premium?

When this issue originally came up in the earlier case in 1989, the court had been divided between two alternatives. The minority favored simply assessing whether the conduct was "deserving of punishment because of its shockingly harsh, vindictive, reprehensible or malicious nature."[66] The majority feared that such exclusive reliance on what has been called "the whole gamut of dyslogistic judicial epithets"[67] would open the door to subjective judgments on the basis of emotive adjectives. Although the court rejected the restrictive English approach, it was nonetheless sensitive to the institutional concerns that the House of Lords had articulated. If punitive damages were to be allowed, they had to operate within a recognizable set of legal constraints. Once it was detached from the criminal law and imposed as occasion demanded by the institutions of civil law, punishment required a legally objective form of justification:

It must never be forgotten that when awarded by a judge or a jury, a punishment is imposed on a person by a Court by the operation of the judicial process. What is it that is punished? It surely cannot be merely conduct of which the Court disapproves, however strongly the judge may feel. Punishment may not be imposed in a civilized community without a justification in law.[68]

Unwilling to accept the sufficiency of reference to the manner of the defendant's conduct, the court formulated an additional substantive requirement: to be liable for punitive damages for breach of contract, the defendant must have committed an actionable wrong.[69]

[66] *Vorvis*, above n. 63, at 1130.
[67] Lord Diplock in *Cassell*, above n. 53, at 1129.
[68] *Vorvis*, above n. 63, at 1105.
[69] Ibid. That the requirement of actionable wrong is an addition to the requirement of reprehensible and high-handed conduct is evident from *Vorvis*, ibid., at 1108 and from *Whiten*, above n. 1, para. 83.

This requirement was satisfied in the *Whiten* case. The insurer had not only refused to pay the proceeds as due. It had also breached the contractual duty of good faith it owed to its insured. Although the duty of good faith and the duty to pay the loss were both contractual, they were independent of each other. The breach of the duty of good faith thus constituted the actionable wrong that could trigger an award of punitive damages.[70]

This is a laudable attempt to accommodate a punitive function for private law to the ideal of legality. However, it raises a number of difficulties that are variants of the same question: why should an accumulation of actionable wrongs lead to punitive damages rather than to an accumulation of compensatory damages for the various wrongs suffered?

The court assumed that compensation would be exhausted by payment of the insurance proceeds and that, therefore, any award above this amount that was based on the defendant's obstructionist processing of the claim had to be punitive.[71] The court's specification of the defendant's breach of its duty of good faith as a further actionable wrong shows that this assumption was mistaken on the court's own reasoning. For if the defendant's conduct not only breached the contractual duty to pay the proceeds but also constituted the further actionable wrong of breaching the defendant's good faith obligation as an insurer, then there must be some sum, however notional, that would provide compensation for that actionable wrong.

Indeed, this is only one of the alternatively available ways of having compensatory assessments take care of what the defendant owed for its high-handed treatment, over and above its liability to pay the insurance proceeds. Another way flows from the court's repeated characterization of the fire insurance policy as a homeowner's "peace of mind" contract.[72] If the defendant's obstruction of the claim breached its contractual obligation with regard to the plaintiff's peace of mind, then that could have been the subject of a compensatory assessment. A third way would have been to claim aggravated damages for the harm that the defendant's outrageous conduct caused to

---

[70] *Whiten*, above n. 1, paras. 79–83. As the court noted, by not insisting that the actionable wrong be tortious, the Canadian position is more expansive than the parallel provision of the Restatement on the Law of Contracts (Second), 255.

[71] *Whiten*, above n. 1, para. 129.

[72] Ibid., paras. 4, 115, 129.

the plaintiff's feelings and sense of self-worth.[73] Thus, even though the defendant should have been made to pay more than the insurance proceeds it withheld, the court's assumption that punitive damages were therefore necessary was based on its ignoring the compensatory implications of its own description of good faith and peace of mind as aspects of the contract.[74]

This failure to make a comprehensive assessment of the compensatory damages leads to another difficulty. In the court's view, punitive damages are to be awarded only where compensatory damages are insufficient to accomplish the punitive purposes.[75] The court regards even compensatory damages as forwarding the punitive objectives of denunciation, retribution, and deterrence,[76] so that the punitive damages are understood as residual to the compensatory ones from the standpoint of punishment itself. Punitive damages, therefore, are additional to compensatory damages without being independent of them: punitive damages are merely the continuation of the aspect of punishment already present in the award of compensation. Thus one cannot tell whether or to what extent punitive damages are needed to supplement the compensatory damages until all the compensatory damages are in view. The court regards this sequencing, in which punitive damages are considered only after compensatory damages are seen to be insufficient, as an important device for preventing immoderate

---

[73] In *Vorvis*, above n. 63, the court recognized the possibility of awarding aggravated damages for breach of contract. See John Swan, "Extended Damages and Vorvis v. Insurance Corporation of British Columbia," (1990) 16 Can. Bus. L.J. 213, 216–21 Bruce Chapman, "Punitive Damages as Aggravated Damages: The Case of Contract," (1990) 16 Can. Bus. L.J. 269.

[74] A compensatory claim along one of these lines would have yielded significantly less than the punitive damages that the plaintiff received. In the case itself the plaintiff was awarded approximately $318,000 in insurance proceeds, a similar amount in legal costs, and $1 million in punitive damages. It is inconceivable that compensation for breach of the duty of good faith or for infringing her contractual interest in peace of mind or for the aggravated damage would have amounted to $1 million. The insurer's duty of good faith in processing the insurance claim would presumably not have been assessed at more than thrice the value of the claim itself. Nor would her peace of mind about her home have been assessed at more than thrice the value of the home itself. Nor would the damage to her sense of self-worth have been evaluated at so much more than the maximum that the Canadian courts allow ($100,000 in 1978 Canadian dollars) for non-pecuniary damages in personal injury cases; see Andrewes v. Grand & Toy Alberta [1978] 83 Dom. L. Rep. (3d) 456 (S.C.C.); Lindal v. Lindal [1981] 121 Dom. L. Rep. (3d) 263 (S.C.C.). Of course, had the plaintiff been awarded a smaller compensatory amount rather than the large punitive one, she would not have been able to complain; from the plaintiff's standpoint the punitive award is always a windfall.

[75] Above n. 1, paras. 74, 94, 123, 129.

[76] Ibid., para. 94.

awards.[77] The consequence of the court's insistence that punitive damages are awarded if and only if compensatory damages are insufficient should be that punitive damages are unavailable in the absence of a full compensatory reckoning.[78] Thus, the absence in *Whiten* of a comprehensive compensatory assessment undermines, according to the court's own reasoning, the appropriateness of the award of punitive damages that the court approved.

Furthermore, the requirement that punitive damages need to be triggered by a further actionable wrong is inconsistent with the idea that punitive damages are to be awarded only if compensatory damages are insufficient. Under this idea, in seeking punitive damages the plaintiff in *Whiten* should have claimed compensatory damages for the defendant's breach of its duty of good faith. But then the breach of that duty could not have served as the further actionable wrong in accordance with the requirement the court lays down, for that wrong would have been something for which she was seeking compensation. She would then need to locate yet another actionable wrong. However, if that actionable wrong were another breach of contract, it too would have been something for which she should have claimed the compensation that would have prevented it from being regarded as a further actionable wrong, and so on ad infinitum. The point at which this sequence stops would be the point at which punitive damages could not be awarded for lack of an independent actionable wrong to trigger them. It thus turns out that (at least so long as all the actionable wrongs are breaches of contract, as in *Whiten*) were the plaintiff to claim compensatory damages for all actionable wrongs suffered, then punitive damages could not be awarded. In other words, the requirement of a further actionable wrong, in combination with the notion that punitive damages are given only if compensatory damages are insufficient, renders impossible the very award that the requirement is supposed to condition.

Now the idea that punitive damages are awarded only when compensatory damages are insufficient is itself part of a more comprehensive idea that punitive damages are awarded only if *all* other penalties, including criminal and regulatory sanctions, have been taken into account and

---

[77] Ibid., para. 74.

[78] In *Whiten*, there was no consideration of aggravated damages because the plaintiff did not claim them; ibid., para. 91. But it is odd that the plaintiff could expose the defendant to a punitive fine simply by not claiming under a compensatory head of damages.

found to be inadequate to accomplish the objectives of retribution, deterrence, and denunciation.[79] These other sanctions are relevant but not a bar to the award of punitive damages. The court explains:

The prescribed fine, for example, may be disproportionately small to the level of outrage the jury wishes to express. The misconduct in question may be broader than the misconduct proven in evidence in the criminal or regulatory proceeding. The legislative judgment fixing the amount of the potential fine may be based on policy considerations other than pure punishment.[80]

Thus, the assessment of contract damages can rank as the final determinant of the sum total of the punitive consequences visited on the defendant.

This is odd. It will be recalled that the reason for introducing the requirement of an independent actionable wrong was to prevent the decision to award punitive damages from being subjective. But on the issue of the quantum of damages, such subjectivity is allowed (provided that it is not so egregious as to violate vague notions of rationality and proportionality). Criminal and regulatory proceedings, which are devoted to punishment, have standard legal constraints on subjectivity, such as the absence of common law crimes, the procedural and evidentiary protections for the accused, and the prohibition of double jeopardy. But the judge or jury determining the quantum of punitive damages, operating free of those constraints, can impose an additional penalty out of a higher feeling of outrage or conclusions reached on a lower burden of proof or a judgment that the legislated level of punishment was inadequate. It is little wonder that the dissenting judge in *Whiten* warned against "a sort of private criminal law, devoid of all the procedural and evidentiary constraints which have come to be associated with the criminal justice system."[81]

---

[79] *Whiten*, above n. 1, para. 123.
[80] Ibid.
[81] Ibid., para. 158. A notable feature of *Whiten* is that, despite the court's elaborate treatment of rationality and proportionality, there is little indication of what placed this specific punitive damages award of $1 million within the acceptable range. Aside from observing that the judges below thought that this sum was not unreasonable and that there had been an analogous increase in the size of the punitive damages award for defamation (ibid., paras. 135–40), the court twice mentioned the fact—which it acknowledged to be irrelevant under the test of rationality that it was formulating—that the award was less than two times the total of compensatory damages and legal costs (ibid., paras. 4, 132).

Moreover, the court's own view of punishment makes this cavalier attitude toward other legal processes more questionable. The court specifies the objectives of punishment as retribution, deterrence, and denunciation. These objectives are indeterminate in two ways. First, there is an indeterminacy about what penalty would achieve any of these objectives considered on its own. But, second, there is also an indeterminacy about what would achieve all of them in combination. This is because the three objectives rely on considerations that are at least partly inconsistent with each other.[82] There can be no single correct view of what penalties or ranges of penalties would achieve these three divergent objectives. All that a legal system can hope for is that its institutions of positive law make determinations that are general, transparent, authoritative, responsible, and based on the appropriate specialized expertise and institutional competence. One would think that the judge or jury in a contracts trial would be institutionally the least qualified to decide the final amount of the defendant's punishment. To have the judge or jury determine as part of a contracts case whether other institutions specifically charged with punishing have indicated the appropriate outrage or had access to adequate evidence or legislatively formulated the appropriate punishment does not seem consistent with a well-ordered legal system.

These reflections bring us back to the criticisms of punitive damages voiced by the House of Lords, that punitive damages are institutionally misplaced in private law. It should be apparent that the recent Canadian developments have not satisfactorily obviated those criticisms. Nor, having rejected the approach consistent with corrective justice, has the Supreme Court of Canada yet established a plausible approach for punitive damages in the contracts context. Perhaps future elaboration will alleviate the inadequacies of the court's present jurisprudence.[83] Or perhaps, with the passage of time, these inadequacies will be recognized as the inevitable consequence of the incoherence

---

[82] Bruce Chapman and Michael J. Trebilcock, "Punitive Damages: Divergence in Search of a Rationale," (1989) 40 Ala. L.R. 741, 779–86 (cited in *Whiten*, above n. 1, at para. 43). For example, as Chapman and Trebilcock observe at 797, deterrence would favor and retribution would oppose grossing up the penalty to reflect the fact that the probability of its enforcement is less than one.

[83] In subsequent cases claiming punitive damages for breach of contract, the Supreme Court of Canada held that the conduct in question was not sufficiently reprehensible to merit punitive damages (Fidler v. Sun Life Assurance Co. of Canada [2006] 2 S.C.R. 3; Honda Canada Inc. v. Keays [2008] 2 S.C.R. 362).

of introducing punitive objectives into the contract law's framework of corrective justice.

6. Conclusion

Starting with the basic idea of corrective justice, that the remedy corrects the injustice suffered by the plaintiff at the defendant's hand, this chapter has examined the significance of various conceptions of contract damages. Its conclusions can be briefly stated. Despite the contentions of Fuller and Perdue, expectation damages are justified as compensation for the promisor's breach of contract in accordance with corrective justice. Expectation damages represent the value of the promisor's performance; the promisee's entitlement to this performance is illuminated by the Kantian account of contract, which construes the doing of the contractually required act as the content of the promisee's entitlement. Kant's insistence that "what I acquire directly by contract is not an external thing but rather his deed"[84] also indicates the deficiency of requiring the promisor to disgorge the gains from the breach. The plaintiff is entitled to the disgorged gains only if the gains came from the alienation of the plaintiff's property; the alienation of property, however, is not a concept applicable to the promisor's failure to perform a contractually obligatory act. Nor does it make sense to regard disgorgement (or, as Fuller and Perdue thought, expectation damages) as punitive in nature, in view of the categorical distinction between liability and punishment. Moreover, as the Canadian experience shows, even when damages are expressly punitive, they seem incapable of being coherently integrated into the fabric of contractual liability.

At the heart of this argument lies the identification of the nature of the contractual entitlement. So far as corrective justice is concerned, right and its correlative duty are the legal concepts that mark the doing and suffering of an injustice. Unless the contractual right is properly identified, the law's interest in awarding expectation damages becomes obscure, as the classic discussion by Fuller and Perdue shows. Conversely, the nature of the contractual right has implications for how disgorgement is to be viewed. In particular, the identification of the contractual entitlement with the performance of an act reveals the

---

[84] Above n. 16.

inappositeness of assimilating contract breach to the alienation of property, and thus also the inappositeness of disgorgement.

From the standpoint of corrective justice, private law is a distinct form of practical reason, in which justification reflects the correlative situation of the parties as doer and sufferer of the same injustice. One-sided considerations, no matter how appealing, such as that the party in breach should disgorge profits made from its wrong or should be punished for its malevolent conduct, do not conform to this correlativity. Such considerations can be incorporated only if private law is willing to countenance unfairness as between the parties and the disturbance of the law's internal coherence. Perhaps sensing this, the common law traditionally did not use damage awards to punish the breaching party or to force disgorgement of the gains from breach. In recent decades both courts and commentators have been willing to reconsider. If the argument presented here is correct, the law has to that extent become more flexible but less just.

6

Unjust Enrichment

1. The theoretical challenge

"A person who has been unjustly enriched at the expense of another is required to make restitution to the other."[1] In the past few decades, this principle of liability has recently become as firmly established in the common law jurisdictions as it has long been among civil law systems. Being a relatively new basis of liability, unjust enrichment is now the most dynamic of all areas of private law. Nonetheless, skeptical voices continue to be heard. Scholars have contended that unjust enrichment adds little to the traditional arsenal of private law categories;[2] that the idea of unjust enrichment is either hopelessly circular or is a conclusion based on unmentioned normative values that do the real work;[3] and that the principle of unjust enrichment submerges within a common framework types of claims that should be governed by diverse principles.[4] Despite being recognized as never before, unjust enrichment remains the most embattled of the bases of liability in private law.

Two interrelated theoretical puzzles have fueled such expressions of skepticism. First, at the heart of unjust enrichment lies the mystery of what makes an enrichment unjust. This question concerns not merely the positive law, but the normative theory implicit in it, exposing a

[1] Restatement of Restitution (1937), s. 1.
[2] Steve Hedley, *Restitution: Its Division and Ordering* (2001).
[3] Hanoch Dagan, *The Law and Ethics of Restitution* (2004), 19.
[4] Peter Jaffey, "Two Theories of Unjust Enrichment," in *Understanding Unjust Enrichment*, ed. Jason W. Neyers, Mitchell McInnes, and Stephen P. A. Pitel (2004), 39; Christopher T. Wonnell, "Replacing the Unitary Principle of Unjust Enrichment," (1996) 45 Emory L.J. 153.

gap through which seep doubts about the nature and scope of the principle of unjust enrichment. Even proponents of unjust enrichment acknowledge the absence of a viable theory of the unjustness that grounds this form of liability.[5] For many years the development of unjust enrichment was impeded by the suspicion that, once recognized as a category of liability, it would direct judges away from traditional legal reasoning to the amorphous exercise of legal discretion on unspecified grounds that vary according to one's personal sense of justice.[6] How, then, can the unjustness of the enrichment be conceptualized in a juridically disciplined manner?

Second, how do the principle's three elements (that the plaintiff has been "enriched," that the enrichment has been "at the defendant's expense," and that the enrichment was "unjust") as well as the defense of change of position fit together to form a coherent basis of liability? Historically, the prime impetus for the development of unjust enrichment has been to bring together various instances of restitutionary liability that the common law had assigned to separate compartments. This drive for unity across different kinds of transactions, however, would be pointless unless the principle provided unity within each transaction. For if the elements of liability are merely a potpourri of mutually inconsistent or indifferent considerations, liability would depend on the particular way in which the various considerations are balanced and combined in any given case or group of cases. Unjust enrichment would then provide merely a common label, not a common pattern of reasoning. Only by combining in a coherent set could the elements of unjust enrichment impart the unity of an overarching

---

[5] A distinguished commentator on the law of restitution has lamented:

Lurking beneath the surface is an awkward question that needs to be answered by jurists: what is it that makes a particular enrichment unjust? It is a question which has not been answered in modern writing on the law of restitution. Indeed, most modern writing on the law of restitution is notable for its apparent indifference to theoretical issues. What is the notion of justice which underpins the law and its development? If this area of law is to be restyled the law of unjust enrichment, surely it cannot avoid openly addressing questions that relate to the conception of justice which underpins the law? Writers avoid the issue . . .

Ewan McKendrick, "Taxonomy: Does it Matter?" in *Unjustified Enrichment: Key Issues in Comparative Perspective*, ed. David Johnston and Reinhard Zimmermann (2002), 627, 654.

[6] "[T]he adoption of this concept . . . would clothe judges with a very wide power to apply what has been described as 'palm tree justice' without the benefit of any guidelines. By what test is a judge to determine what constitutes unjust enrichment? The only test is his individual perception of what he considered to be unjust." Martland J., dissenting, in Pettkus v. Becker [1980] 117 D.L.R. (3d) 257 (S.C.C.). A similar note was sounded decades earlier in W. S. Holdsworth, "Unjustifiable Enrichment," (1939) 55 L.Q.R. 37, at 49.

principle to the various situations that contemporary scholars of restitution claim fall under it.

Moreover, only when they are coherently unified do the individual elements themselves have a stable meaning. What counts as an "enrichment" of the defendant cannot be determined independently of what renders the enrichment "unjust" and "at the expense of the plaintiff." The idea of an enrichment presupposes a normatively relevant baseline against which the enrichment is measured, and what is normatively relevant has to refer to something to which the appropriate considerations of unjustness can intelligibly apply, and vice versa. The same is true of what it means for the enrichment to be realized "at the expense of" the plaintiff. As with other bases of liability, the meaning of each element conditions, and is conditioned by, the meaning of all the others. Each element is intelligible not on its own but through its place in the principle of unjust enrichment conceived as a unified whole.

The theoretical idea that reflects this concern with the inner unity of the principle of unjust enrichment, as well as of other principles of private law, is corrective justice. Indeed, in a recent judgment the Supreme Court of Canada remarked: "Restitution is a tool of corrective justice. When a transfer of value between two parties is normatively defective, restitution functions to correct that transfer by restoring their parties to their pre-transfer positions."[7] Such an observation testifies to the intuitive plausibility of understanding liability for unjust enrichment as an instantiation of corrective justice. Unjust enrichment at another's expense seems to be an obvious example of an injustice as between the parties, which a finding of liability then corrects by requiring restoration of the enrichment.

However, it is one thing to assert the intuitive plausibility of connecting unjust enrichment to corrective justice, and another to provide an adequate theoretical account of the connection. Such an account must show how liability for unjust enrichment manifests the three interwoven features that make up corrective justice.[8] First, corrective justice, reflecting the bipolar nexus of plaintiff and defendant, signifies a normative structure in which the parties are correlatively situated. Second, because this structure requires a content that is itself informed by correlativity, the organizing features of the parties'

---

[7] Kingstreet Investments v. New Brunswick (Department of Finance) [2007] 1 S.C.R. 3, para. 32.

[8] Above, chapter 1.

relationship are the plaintiff's right and the defendant's correlative duty. Third, rights and their correlative duties imply a conception of the parties as persons who interact with each other as free and equal agents, without the law's subordinating either of them to the other. Accordingly, as an instantiation of corrective justice, liability for unjust enrichment should exhibit the correlative structure of the parties' relationship, vindicate the plaintiff's right as against the defendant, and affirm the parties' freedom and equality. And so the question arises: how are these features of corrective justice implicit in liability for unjust enrichment?

In the recent scholarship on unjust enrichment, doubts about corrective justice flow from difficulties that supposedly pertain to the second of these features, the correlativity of right and duty. On the duty side, the difficulty rests on the defendant's being obligated to make restitution despite his or her passivity in receiving the enrichment. This passivity means that the recipient cannot plausibly be regarded as a wrongdoer— that is, as someone who is to be subjected to liability as a consequence of having breached a duty owed to the plaintiff. One consequence of this is that liability in unjust enrichment is "strict" or without fault, and therefore at odds with the corrective justice account of tort law.[9] Even this, however, understates the difficulty. In fact, the recipient has not merely done no wrong, but has not done anything at all: "there is no sense in which the defendant is the agent of the plaintiff's misfortune."[10] Nor does it seem possible to say that the injustice consists in the act of withholding restitution. That would be an injustice only if the defendant were already under an anterior duty to make restitution. This is the duty that corrective justice is alleged to be incapable of grounding.

A parallel difficulty emerges in connection with the plaintiff's right. Cases of unjust enrichment deal with the transfer of money or goods or with the provision of services. In none of these cases does the plaintiff retain a proprietary right to the subject matter of the enrichment. Corrective justice postulates that liability vindicates some right of the plaintiff's. In cases of unjust enrichment, however, the enriching transaction seems to have wiped away that right, leaving the plaintiff with nothing to vindicate.[11]

---

[9] Mitchell McInnes, "The Measure of Restitution," (2002) 52 U.T.L.J. 163, 186–96.

[10] Dennis Klimchuk, "The Structure and Content of the Right to Restitution for Unjust Enrichment," (2007) 57 U.T.L.J. 661, 677.

[11] A sophisticated statement of this difficulty is found in Klimchuk, ibid.

The challenge concerning the plaintiff's right moves from the premise that the unjust enrichment leaves the plaintiff without a proprietary right to the conclusion that the plaintiff has no right at all. This conclusion does not follow. The plaintiff may well have a non-proprietary right—that is, a right not *in rem* but *in personam*. Such a right, consisting in an entitlement against a particular defendant rather than against the world in general, is established through a transaction in which both parties participate. A paradigmatic instance is the right to contractual performance, which arises through a course of dealings (offer, acceptance, and so on) between the parties and runs in favor of a particular promisee and against the particular promisor. In pointing to this instance of an *in personam* right, I am not proposing a revival of the pernicious view that a claim in unjust enrichment is based on an implied contract. However, I am suggesting that perhaps the reason that unjust enrichment could have been assimilated to contract for so long is that both bases of liability are of a kind that do not rest on a proprietary claim. Of course, one can make good on this suggestion only by specifying (as I hope to do) the elements in the parties' dealings that perform for unjust enrichment the function that such concepts as offer and acceptance do for contract.

The purpose of this chapter is to elucidate unjust enrichment as an *in personam* basis of liability that conforms to corrective justice. As in the case of contract, the parties to liability in unjust enrichment (so I shall argue) establish the correlative right and duty through the interaction in which they both participate. Being interactionally established, the *in personam* right stands in contrast to an *in rem* right, which the right-holder has prior to and independently of the defendant's wrong. With respect to both *in rem* rights and *in personam* rights, corrective justice undoes an injustice that consists in an inconsistency with the plaintiff's right that is imputable to the defendant. But there is this difference between them. The *in rem* right imposes a duty on the whole world; the defendant's particular duty arises out of membership in that world. The *in personam* right imposes a duty specifically on the defendant; this duty is the product of a right-establishing interaction with the plaintiff. To be sure, the *in personam* right is not a creation *ex nihilo*. It arises out of what is rightfully the parties': the parties to a contract, for example, have pre-existing rights to what they are exchanging. However, the juridical effect of the parties' interaction is to transform these pre-existing rights into components of a new relationship of right and duty.

How, then, does an unjustly enriching interaction establish a correlative right and duty of restitution? As the Supreme Court of Canada observed, unjust enrichment occurs "[w]hen a transfer of value between two parties is normatively defective."[12] My focus is on the role of value in a corrective justice account of unjust enrichment. I intend to trace how value starts out as an entitlement of the plaintiff's that is transferred to the defendant in a normatively defective way, with the result that the value must be retransferred to the plaintiff.

2. The juridical significance of value

What is value and what is involved in its transfer? To address these questions I start with the account of value in Hegel's *Philosophy of Right*. This account continues a tradition of enquiry about value that stretches back to Aristotle and was subsequently carried forward by Marx and others. Hegel's remarks are particularly illuminating for issues of liability, because he treats value initially not as an economic concept but as a juridical one.

Hegel regards value as an incident of property. One is entitled to the value of something by virtue of one's ownership of the thing that is the locus of the value. Hegel's description of value as an object of ownership reflects commonplace notions drawn from contract and tort law, respectively, that the owner of anything alienable is entitled to realize its value through exchange[13] and to be compensated to the extent of its value in the event of wrongful injury or deprivation.[14] The owner of the thing owns the value in the sense that ownership of the thing carries with it an entitlement to something equivalent when the thing is exchanged or injured. Value is thus the potentiality that is actualized through a set of legal operations—exchange and liability—with respect to things that one owns. Indeed, unless it were possible to conceive of this potentiality as an entitlement of the thing's owner, the transformation of an entitlement to what one owns into an entitlement to what is substituted for it through exchange or liability would make no sense. The entitlement to value thus marks the continuity through the process of exchange and the determination of liability of the owner's entitlement to the thing owned.

[12] Above, n. 1.
[13] G. W. F. Hegel, *Philosophy of Right*, tr. T. M. Knox (1952), s. 77.
[14] Ibid., s. 98.

After dealing with the right to use one's property, Hegel makes the following observations about the notion of value:

A thing in use is a single thing, determined quantitatively and qualitatively and related to a specific need. But its specific utility, being *quantitatively* determinate, is at the same time comparable with [the specific utility] of other things of like utility. Similarly, the specific need which it satisfies is at the same time need in general and thus is comparable on its particular side with other needs, while the thing in virtue of the same considerations is comparable with things meeting other needs. This, the thing's universality, whose simple determinate character arises from the particularity of the thing, so that it is *eo ipso* abstracted from the thing's specific quality, is the thing's *value*, wherein its genuine substantiality becomes determinate and an object of consciousness. As the full owner of the thing, I am *eo ipso* owner of its *value* as well as of its use.[15]

Hegel here draws attention to three characteristics of value. First, value is quantitative. This is apparent from the contrast between value and use. Use involves reference to the specific qualities that a thing has that allow it to satisfy the specific needs of the specific person using it. I can make use of my shoe, for example, because my shoe has certain qualities: a concave shape into which my foot fits, a flexible material that will bend as I lift and lower my foot, a slightly curved sole that facilitates locomotion, and so on. Only with such qualities can the shoe satisfy the needs of movement and protection that the shoes serve. In contrast, when I enquire into the value of the shoe, my interest is entirely quantitative: to how many units of something else is the shoe equivalent? The movement of our attention from use to value is thus a movement from quality to quantity.

Second, value is relational. As is indicated by the enquiry into the number of units of something else to which the shoes are equivalent, value relates a thing to other things by quantitatively comparing them. The value of my shoes is not at issue so long as these shoes are considered exclusively on their own. Attention shifts to the shoes' value when I compare the shoes, say, to food by wondering how many loaves of bread the shoes equal.[16] Value is thereby a quantitative representation of the relation between the shoes and the loaves.

---

[15] Ibid., s. 63.
[16] The example is Aristotle's: *Nicomachean Ethics*, V, 1133a23.

Third, such quantitative comparison presupposes abstraction from the particular uses to which the compared items are put and from the particular needs that they serve. Nothing can have value that another cannot put to some particular use or that does not serve another's particular need. When quantitatively compared, however, these diverse uses and needs implicitly share a common dimension of commensurability as instances of usefulness and need generally. For instance, shoes and loaves of bread serve the particular needs of ambulatory comfort and nutrition respectively, which, qua particular needs, are not intrinsically related to each other. In their particularity they are incomparable. Accordingly, if so many shoes are to be treated as equivalent to so many loaves, then the needs served by shoes and bread, or the uses that satisfy these needs, figure in this equivalence only through the general idea of need or usefulness in which they participate as instances. Abstraction from the particularity of need and use is the presupposition of value's functioning as a medium of quantitative comparability between qualitatively different things.

These three characteristics of quantity, relation, and abstraction are reciprocally entailed in the idea of value. The presence of each is demanded by the presence of the other two. Value's quantitative character requires abstraction from one thing's particular use to the usefulness that allows that thing to be quantitatively compared to another. If the value of shoes is represented by the formula that so many shoes equal so many loaves, each characteristic of value pauses on a different aspect of the shoes' valuation. Quantity looks to the numbers modifying the things being compared. Relation looks to the fact that the quantification of shoes is here stated comparatively by reference to the number of loaves that the shoes equal. Abstraction from the particularity of need and use looks to what is presupposed in conceiving of the relation between two particular items, such as shoes and loaves, in terms of their quantitative equality.

Value refers to the possibility of exchange and is concretized through the process of exchange. In exchange the owners of things of value determine what is to be exchanged for what and how many units of one thing are to be given for how many units of the other. They thereby give expression to the relational and quantitative characteristics of value. They do so, however, not merely in fulfillment of their own particular needs or in anticipation of the particular uses they will make of what they receive through exchange, but as participants in a world of value that abstracts from those needs and uses.

Because value treats particular needs and uses as instantiations of need and usefulness in general, the quantitative comparison between the two things being exchanged is systematically linked to quantitative comparisons between these things and other things. By abstracting from the particularity of need or use, value becomes indifferent to the particularity of the things being exchanged and can therefore be expressed through the comparison of anything of value with any other thing of value. If I wish to exchange a pair of shoes for loaves of bread, the number of loaves that I receive is a function not merely of the relationship between shoes and loaves, but also of the relationship between shoes or loaves and anything else for which they might possibly be exchanged. Even if I want bread and someone else wants shoes at the end of the day, we can each reach our desired destinations through a series of exchanges involving other commodities. The value of my shoes and the value of another's bread exist in equilibrium with the value of other things. The formula that so many shoes equal so many loaves can be expanded to include the equality of these numbers to so many of any other thing of value. Value thus reflects the possibility of equalizing all things of value with one another, and equating any given thing of value with all other things of value.[17]

Consequently, the quantification of equivalents in exchange is beyond the power of the exchanging parties alone. The value to be attached to things that they exchange is determined not by either the party's subjectivity or by the relationship between their respective subjectivities. Rather, value reflects the relationship between all possible exchanging parties with respect to all possible exchangeable things. Equivalence in exchange is an objective rather than a subjective idea. In the formula "so many shoes equal so many loaves," the quantities do not represent merely what the owners of the shoes and the loaves, as persons who wish to satisfy their particular needs, accept from each other. Given the abstracting characteristic of value, the quantities of shoes exchanged for loaves represent what the shoes and the bread are objectively worth relative to each other.

Value is thus the medium for measuring whether what was received is quantitatively equivalent to what was given. The difference between these two marks the extent to which one party gave the other something for nothing. Only if there is such a difference does the transaction constitute a transfer of value.

[17] I. I. Rubin, *Essays on Marx's Theory of Value* (1972), 109.

The reason for this is as follows. When dealing with transfers, one must distinguish between things that have value and value itself. The transfer to another of a thing that has value does not necessarily mean that there has also been a transfer of value. Take the example of exchange. When I exchange a certain quantity of shoes for a certain quantity of food, I no doubt have transferred something of value, the shoes, and received something of value in return, the food. But if the food is of equal value to the shoes, no value has been transferred. Exchange on such terms features the reciprocal transfer of things of value but not the transfer of value itself, since it keeps constant the value to which each party is entitled. Exchange demonstrates that value "is distinct from the external things which change owners in the course of the transaction,"[18] because in an exchange external things are transferred but value is not. To be sure, I would not engage in this exchange unless the food I received was more useful or valuable to me than the shoes I surrendered. But the value that is expressed in and through the exchange abstracts from me as a particular person with a particular preference for this amount of food rather than that amount of shoes. What matters to value in exchange is not the value to me in isolation, but value as determined by the intrinsically relational process of exchange among those trading shoes and food.

Only to the extent that the transfer is gratuitous—that is, involves no receipt of equivalent value—does the transfer of a thing of value become a transfer of value as well. If I transfer shoes but receive in return nothing or food of less value (like the Homeric hero who foolishly "exchanged gold armor for bronze armor, a hundred oxen's worth for nine"),[19] then I have transferred not only the shoes as things of value but value itself. In contrast to what happens in an exchange, the transaction does not preserve intact the amount of value that I have, because there is no equivalence of value in what was given and received. Through this gratuitous transfer the value of what is rightfully mine has been diminished and the value of what is rightfully the transferee's has been increased by the amount of value that has been transferred without reciprocation. In the language of unjust enrichment, the transferee has been enriched at my expense. This does not mean, of course, that the transferee is obligated to return the enrichment. That further consequence depends on whether the retention of

---

[18]   Hegel, above n. 13, s. 77.
[19]   Homer, *Iliad*, vi, 235–36.

that enrichment is unjust—that is, whether the transfer occurred under conditions that generate an obligation to restore the transferred value.

Being unreciprocated, the transferred value of the shoes thus has a double aspect. On the one hand it is an incident of the transferee's proprietary right in the shoes. As is the case with every owner, the transferee who becomes the owner of the shoes also thereby becomes entitled to their value. If the transferee sells the shoes, the transferee is entitled to keep the value realized through the sale. If the shoes are tortiously destroyed or converted, the transferee is entitled to receive from the wrongdoer their equivalent value as compensation. Because the transferee's right to the shoes (and the consequent entitlement to their value) is good against the whole world, I am not differently situated with respect to this value than is everyone else.

On the other hand, the transferred value in the shoes is also a component of the normative relationship, unshared by anyone else, between me as transferor and the transferee. Even if the transfer of the shoes (and therefore of their value) is valid from a proprietary standpoint, the gratuitousness of the transfer raises a distinct issue of justice between us as parties to the transaction. Because the law assumes that persons generally act to further their own ends rather than another's, it seeks to ensure that I truly intended the transfer to be gratuitous. And conversely because the law does not allow obligations to be created behind another's back, restitution of the transferred value has to be consonant with the free will of the transferee. Thus, aside from the passage of title in the shoes, the question arises whether the circumstances of the gratuitous transfer of the value in the shoes are such that the transferee is under an obligation to restore this value to me. These circumstances pertain to the relationship between the two of us as participants in the transfer of value rather than the relationship between the transferee, as the new owner of the shoes, and everyone else. Put more technically, although I have lost the *in rem* right to the shoes (and thus to their value), one can still ask whether the conditions of transfer were such that I now nonetheless have, as against the transferee, an *in personam* right to their value. It is this aspect of the transferred value that engages the principle of unjust enrichment.

Exchange and transfer of value are thus mutually exclusive notions. Exchange features a movement of things of value from each party to the other. It does not, however, feature any movement of value. In contrast, a transfer of value occurs when one party gives the other something of value, but in return receives nothing or something of lesser value. This transaction transfers not only a thing of value, but also value itself, for through this interaction one party loses and the other party gains value.

This contrast between a transfer of value and a transfer of a thing of value is the consequence of the inherently relational nature of value. Characterized as it is by quantitative comparability that abstracts from the qualitative differences between things of value, value equates an amount of one thing to an amount of another. Value is not concerned with anything on its own but with the quantitative relationship between one thing and another. Whether a transfer of value has occurred thus depends not on the movement of any single thing of value, but on whether that movement has been matched by the reciprocal movement of some other thing of equivalent value. This reciprocal movement is a contingent matter. When it occurs, one has an exchange in which things of value have been transferred but not value itself. When it does not occur, one has a transfer of value.

3. The transfer elements of liability

I now turn to the juridical significance of treating unjust enrichment as involving a transfer of value, understood as the giving of something (whether objects or labor) for nothing. How is the idea of a transfer of value actualized through the requirements for liability? These requirements reflect the idea to the extent that it provides a structure to which they conform. They also construct the idea by endowing with legal specificity what would otherwise be an abstraction. Several points deserve notice.

First, at the most general level the idea of a transfer of value is reflected in two of the requirements for liability under the principle of unjust enrichment, that the defendant be enriched and that the enrichment be at the expense of the plaintiff. Understood as aspects of a transfer, these two requirements are not mutually independent elements but the integrated moments of a single bilateral phenomenon. Unjust enrichment deals not with maintaining the wealth of one party or another against an increase or decrease in the value of their respective resources, nor even with a matching increase and decrease in each party's wealth, but with a relationship between the parties that can ground the liability that one of them may have to the other. The idea of a transfer establishes the requisite relationship by pointing to an enrichment that has moved from the plaintiff to the defendant. Accordingly, the "enrichment" and "expense" mentioned in the principle of unjust enrichment are terms of mutual relation, each requiring the other in order to function as constituents of liability. They refer not to gains and losses *simpliciter*—that is, to one person being better off and another person being worse off than before, but to the connection of each to the other through the giving and receiving of value.

Second, enrichment at the expense of another should be understood as structured by the immediacy of the link between the parties as transferor and transferee of value. The notion of a transfer thereby defines the ambit of liability, preventing liability that is either too restrictive or too expansive. Liability is too restrictive when the plaintiff's claim is disqualified on the grounds of absence of enrichment even though value has been transferred to the defendant. An example is the now fading suggestion that the plaintiff's passing on to third parties of the loss from the transfer excludes recovery of the value from the transferee.[20] Liability is too expansive when the plaintiff's claim is allowed even though the parties are not related as transferor and transferee. An example is the view that the relationship between the parties can be indirectly established through the remotely causal stages of the enrichment's transmission.[21]

Third, not every benefit realized from the action of another involves a movement of value. For value to move, the enriching action must be directed toward something that is the defendant's. If the purpose and intended effect of the action refer only to the plaintiff and the plaintiff's property, the value remains with the plaintiff even though the defendant has been advantaged as a result. The absence of liability for incidental benefits illustrates this. In a typical case of incidental benefit, the plaintiff acts with reference to what is his or her own property or in the exercise of his or her own rights but in the process happens to confer a benefit on a neighbor. Classic examples are the cutting down of a wood that obscures a neighbor's prospect or building a wall that happens to shield a neighbor's house from windstorms.[22] Because the

---

[20] For criticism of the "passing on" defense, see Michael Rush, *The Defence of Passing On* (2006).

[21] Peter Birks, "'At the Expense of the Claimant': Direct and Indirect Enrichment in English Law," in *Unjust Enrichment: Key Issues in Comparative Perspective*, ed. David Johnston and Reinhard Zimmermann (2002), 493, 518.

[22] Ruabon Steamship v. London Assurance [1900] A.C. 6, at 12 (H.L.).

work was done not on the defendant's property but on the plaintiff's property and for the plaintiff's own purposes, nothing has occurred that can be construed as a transfer of value from the plaintiff to the defendant.[23] One can phrase this conclusion in the terms of the principle of unjust enrichment by saying that the defendant's enrichment has not come at the plaintiff's expense.[24] What this means is that by virtue of the labor having been expended on the plaintiff's property and for the plaintiff's purposes, the value of the labor has been retained by the plaintiff and has not passed to the defendant.[25]

Fourth, conceiving of the enrichment as a transfer of value casts doubt on the appropriateness of terms like "subjective devaluation" and "incontrovertible benefit." In the current treatment of unjust enrichment, these terms qualify the segment of the analysis that deals with enrichment. "Subjective devaluation"[26] suggests that a benefit may not qualify as an enrichment if a defendant can plausibly assert that, despite the benefit's objective value, he or she subjectively attaches no value to it. Once enrichment is understood as signaling a transfer of value, however, subjective devaluation cannot pertain to the determination of whether there has been an enrichment. Because value abstracts from the parties' particularity, neither value nor its transfer is determined subjectively. Whether a person who gives another something of value has in return received something of equivalent value is an objective question, the answer to which is systemically determined by market exchanges. Value, therefore, cannot be subjectively devalued. Nor can subjective devaluation be defeated by subjectively revaluing the benefit on the ground of its incontrovertibility. At bottom, subjective devaluation is not about the nature of the enrichment, but about the transferee's freedom to make his or her own choices.[27] This is of course an important consideration, but it concerns not the existence of an enrichment but the justness of the defendant's retaining it.

---

[23] Daniel Friedmann, "Unjust Enrichment, Pursuance of Self-Interest, and the Limits of Free Riding," (2003) 36 Loy. L.A. L. Rev. 831, at 845 ("recovery is denied simply because the nature of the benefit consists of an increase in value without a transfer of property or labor").

[24] Edinburgh and District Tramways Ltd. v. Courtenay [1909] S.C. 99, at 106.

[25] "When a person does something on somebody else's property, in the mistaken idea, it may be, that it is his own, then the *jactura* is obvious enough. He has expended money, or something else, which has passed into other persons' property. But here nothing has passed." Ibid.

[26] Peter Birks, *An Introduction to the Law of Restitution* (1985), 109.

[27] Mitchell McInnes, "Enrichment Revisited," in *Understanding Unjust Enrichment*, ed. Jason W. Neyers, Mitchell McInnes, and Stephen P.A. Pitel (2004), 175.

Fifth, because one can transfer only that to which one has a right, the notion of a transfer of value recognizes that the transaction enriched the defendant with what was initially within the plaintiff's entitlement. Recall Hegel's observation that "as full owner of the thing, I am *eo ipso* owner of its value as well as of its use."[28] The enrichment is at the plaintiff's expense not merely because the transaction had an adverse effect on the plaintiff, but because that effect operates on value as an incident of what the plaintiff owned on entering the transaction.[29] The plaintiff's right to the value at the inception of its transfer is the precondition of the claim that the value should be retransferred to the plaintiff once the transfer is shown to be defective.[30]

Sixth, although it originates in the plaintiff's pre-transfer right to the thing of value, the plaintiff's claim is to the retransfer of the value independently of that thing. Ownership of the thing of value involves a relationship between the transferee and the rest of the world; the claim to the value independently of the thing of value involves a relationship between the transferee and the transferor. The bilaterality of the transfer endows the value with a juridical significance that is separate from the one it has as an incident of a thing of value. This is because, due to its quantitative, relational, and abstract character, value is transferred not through the movement of any particular thing from transferor to transferee, but through the absence of a reciprocal movement of something of equivalent value from the transferee to the transferor. What is crucial is the giving of something for nothing, not the title to what was given. This is why the plaintiff's lack of a proprietary right to the thing that embodied the value does not undermine the claim to the value's retransfer.

Seventh, the idea that enrichment at the expense of another denotes a transfer of value casts light on what renders an enrichment unjust. As

---

[28] Above n. 13.
[29] Conversely, the plaintiff cannot complain of the diversion to the defendant of a benefit that lacked this status—for example, customers' patronage for which the defendant successfully competes; James Gordley, *Foundations of Private Law* (2006), 425.
[30] See Brian Fitzgerald, "Ownership as the Proximity or Privity Principle in Unjust Enrichment Law," (1995) 18 U. Q. L. Rev. 166, at 172:

> If the plaintiff did not own the property in which the value inhered and emanated before the unjust enriching event, then it is incomprehensible...to say that value has been subtracted from P and transferred to D. Ownership, then, is the starting point of any claim in unjust enrichment because it tells us who holds value at the start and in turn who can come into court and claim loss of value.

noted at the outset, a perennial apprehension raised by opponents of unjust enrichment is that "unjust" is too amorphous a qualifier of enrichment to yield a juridically manageable basis of liability. This apprehension is unfounded. Once the enrichment is understood as a transfer of value, the familiar idea of a transfer determines the nature of the applicable unjustness. A transfer of value is unjust if its conditions are not consistent with the norms of justice that govern transfers generally. Unjust enrichment is, on this view, concerned not with justice at large, but with the specific and narrowly legal issues of just transfer. To be sure, the fact that the object of the transfer is value rather than some particular asset introduces special considerations; just as value's being the object of transfer implies a special notion of what a transfer is—the non-receipt of an equivalent—so it also implies special notions of what makes such a transfer normatively defective. Such special considerations, however, do not make the enquiry into the justness of the enrichment amorphous. The law's task remains that of drawing out the legal implications of justice in transfer, given the object of the transfer. To this task I now turn.

4. Justness in the transfer of value

What considerations make a gratuitous transfer defective? I propose to address this question by comparing gifts and unjust enrichment. The two are similar in that both feature the giving of something for nothing, gift through the requirement of delivery, and unjust enrichment through the notion of enrichment at another's expense. They are, however, dissimilar in several respects. A gift involves the transfer of a particular object, whereas unjust enrichment involves the transfer of value. Value is the antithesis of particular objects, in that it abstracts from their particularity to the quantitative comparison between them. Moreover, defectiveness in the transfer of a gift prevents a change in property rights, leaving intact the *in rem* relationship between the owner of the object and everyone else, whereas defectiveness in the transfer of value creates in the transferor an *in personam* right to have the transferee restore the value. Defectiveness in the transfer of gifts is well understood from the long and settled jurisprudence about gifts. Defectiveness in the transfer of value is more mysterious, and its jurisprudence more fluid and controversial. Accordingly, it makes sense to begin with the conception of defectiveness operative for gift, and then focus on how that conception is modified when applied to transfers of value.

So far as gifts are concerned, justice in transfer requires that the gift manifest the will of both the donor and the donee. "In order to make it a gift, it must be made out not only that it was given as a gift but that it was received as a gift."[31] On the donor's side, the delivery of the gift must be accompanied by a donative intent; on the donee's side, the gift must be accepted as donatively given. The giving of the gift for nothing forms the terms of the transfer, which is effective only if both parties subscribe to them. However, if (for example) the transferor really intended a loan rather than a gift, or if the transferor intended a gift but the transferee treated it as a loan[32] or refused to accept it, then the transfer is normatively defective, so that the proprietary right remains with or reverts to the transferor.[33]

Donative intent and acceptance are thus the legal concepts through which justice in transfer expresses the freedom of both of the parties. To be effective, a transfer must connect the parties in a way that they both consent to. The donor is entitled to what is his or her own until freely parting with it. Similarly, the donee is entitled not to be subjected even to the beneficence of another unless he or she finds such beneficence acceptable. Of course, one can usually presume acceptance of the conferral of a benefit. However, if the evidence shows that the intended transferee does not accept the transfer as gratuitous, the law does not force a conferral against the transferee's will. The transferee may graspingly desire the gift of something for nothing, and the transferor may benevolently desire to give something for nothing, but neither of them can impose his or her will on the other party. They each remain free from subjection to the purpose of the other unless they accede to that purpose.

Accordingly, in the case of gifts, the unwillingness of either party renders the transfer defective. A transfer purports to move the ownership of a specific object from the transferor to the transferee. This movement can be interrupted by a lack of the relevant intent as the object purports either to exit the transferor's ownership or to enter the transferee's.

I turn now from the gratuitous transfer of a specific object dealt with by the law of gift to the transfer of value, also gratuitous, dealt

---

[31] Hill v. Wilson, L.R. 8 Ch. App. 888 (1873).
[32] The situation in *Hill*, ibid.
[33] J. Hill, "The Role of the Donee's Consent in the Law of Gift," (2001) 117 L.Q.R. 127.

with by the law of unjust enrichment. Here too donative intent figures in justice in transfer. If the transferor intended a transfer of value,
that is, intended to benefit the transferee for nothing, then (assuming,
as is almost invariably the case, that the benefit is acceptable to the
transferee) the transfer complies with justice, and cannot be reversed
on the ground of unjust enrichment. It is not unjust for value donatively transferred to be irretrievable.[34] In the terminology of the Canadian jurisprudence, donative intent counts as a "juristic reason" for the
enrichment.[35] Another such juristic reason is that the benefit was conferred in fulfillment of a valid obligation owed to the transferee or in
the settlement of an honest claim made by the transferee, for it is not
inconsistent with justice in transfer for the transferee to retain what
the transferor was obligated to give.[36] Thus, when donative intent is
present, the transfer of value conforms to justice in transfer no less
than does the transfer of a specific object through gift.

However, in the absence of donative intent by the transferor, justice
in transfer requires that the transfer of a specific object through gift be
treated differently from the transfer of value. The absence of donative
intent is sufficient to render a gift defective because the failure of the
object rightfully to leave the ownership of the donor keeps intact the
transferor's entitlement to what was given. For transfers of value, however, the absence of donative intent is not sufficient to render the
transfer defective. Because a transfer of value involves the transfer of a
thing of value without receiving an equivalently valued thing in
return, the thing that embodies the value—and therefore the value
that is an incident of owning that thing—has already irrevocably

---

[34] Donative intent includes risk-taking—that is, the conferral of a benefit under circumstances in which the transferor hopes for remuneration but knows that the transferee is not
obligated to give it.
[35] Peter v. Beblow [1993] 1 S.C.R. 980, at 987.
[36] In *Peter*, ibid., McLachlin J. listed the following considerations among those going to
juristic reason:

    (i) Did the plaintiff confer the benefit as a valid gift or in pursuance of a valid common law,
       equitable or statutory obligation which he or she owed to the defendant?
    (ii) Did the plaintiff submit to, or compromise, the defendant's honest claim?

The presence of a valid obligation is a ground for supposing that, despite the brilliance of the
judgment, Moses v. MacFerlan, 97 E.R. 676 (K.B., 1760) was incorrectly decided, as subsequent cases held; see Dublin v. Building and Allied Trade Union [1996] 2 I.L.R.M. 547 (S.C.).
If one excludes the possibility of MacFerlan's contractual obligation, Moses was in effect a
risk-taker who, by incurring the obligation entailed in endorsing the notes, gave MacFerlan
the benefit of his own potential liability under circumstances in which MacFerlan was not
obligated to abstain from availing himself of that liability.

entered the ensemble of the transferee's entitlements.[37] Unlike the defectiveness in the case of gift, which interrupts the movement of a specific object from transferee to transferor, defectiveness in the case of a transfer of value creates a claim that value that has already moved with the thing that embodies it be restored to the transferor. If the claim succeeds, it has to be satisfied out of assets that rightfully belong to the transferee. In contrast to gifts, the transferor's claim is not that the transferee never received the value but that, having received for nothing what was not intended to be gratuitously given, the transferee is not entitled to retain the value. Consequently, the duty of the transferee to restore value cannot be determined solely by one-sided reference to the absence of donative intent on the part of the transferor.

In dealing with the defectiveness of a transfer of value, the law has to observe a strict equality in its treatment of plaintiff and defendant.[38] The basis of the plaintiff's claim is that, in the absence of donative intent on her part, the transfer of something for nothing has deprived her of value that belonged to her without her having freely parted with it. If the plaintiff's lack of donative intent were to suffice for liability, defendants in turn would be deprived of what belongs to them without their having freely parted with it. The principle of justice in transfer, that one is entitled to what one owns until one freely parts with it, would thereby be inconsistently asserted for plaintiffs and denied for defendants. To vindicate justice in transfer, the law must apply it equally to both parties.

5. Acceptance

Accordingly, a finding that the defendant cannot retain an enrichment made at the plaintiff's expense has to be based on considerations that implicate both of the parties in their relationship to each other. In this connection two ideas, one normative and the other contextual, are relevant. The normative idea is that, with respect to the beneficial transfer, the wills of the two parties are so related to each other as to converge on the reason for not allowing the defendant to retain the benefit. On the plaintiff's side, this reason consists in the absence of an

---

[37] Similarly, in the case of pure services, the transfer of value has left no residue that is independent of the totality of the transferee's entitlements.

[38] For an exposition of this point, see Abraham Drassinower, "Unrequested Benefits in the Law of Unjust Enrichment," (1998) 48 U.T.L.J. 459, at 477.

intention (or of an obligation) to give the defendant something for nothing. On the defendant's side, the reason consists in the defendant's acceptance of the benefit as non-gratuitously given. Acceptance here refers not to an express affirmation by the defendant but to the integration of the benefit into the defendant's purposes. It is present when the beneficial transfer is consonant with the defendant's projects, so that the defendant can plausibly be regarded as satisfied with the non-donative transfer of value. If the plaintiff did not intend to give something for nothing, and if the defendant accepted the benefit as not having been given for nothing, then an obligation to restore the value arises. The plaintiff cannot retain gratis what was neither given gratis nor accepted as given gratis.

The contextual idea is that of entanglement. Entanglement occurs when the benefit can no longer be separated from what the defendant is otherwise entitled to. The provision of a service is a paradigmatic example. A benefit, once entangled, can no longer be an independent object of the defendant's choice. Nor can the benefit be returned to the plaintiff in its disentangled state. Because the benefit has merged into the defendant's entitlements, the defendant can no more be required to part with it or its value than she can be required to part with whatever else she owns. The only circumstance in which this does not hold is if defendant has accepted the benefit as non-donatively transferred. Then the wills of the parties converge on the non-donativeness of the transfer, precluding the defendant from retaining it as if it were a gift.

The classic instance of entanglement appears in a famous statement by Chief Baron Pollock: "One cleans another's shoes; what can the other do but put them on? . . . The benefit of the service could not be rejected without refusing the property itself."[39] In this graphic example, the benefit has been so completely entangled in the recipient's property, that the cleaning of the shoes cannot be treated as an object of choice that is independent of his use of them. If one assumes, as Chief Baron Pollock clearly does, that the shoes were cleaned without the owner's knowledge, to compel the owner to make restitution of the value of the cleaning would be to hold her liable for owning shoes whose condition was changed without her consent. Nor can the mere wearing of the shoes count as an acceptance, for this would derogate from the pre-existing entitlement of the owner, as having exclusive

[39] Taylor v. Laird [1856] 156 E.R. 1203.

dominion over the shoes, to owe nothing to anyone else through their lawful use. Entanglement means not merely that the transferred value has been absorbed into the totality of the defendant's entitlements—this happens to all unjust enrichments—but that within that totality it cannot be separated from the other components, as here the cleanness of the shoes cannot be separated from the shoes themselves.

Entanglement sets the context within which acceptance operates to link the parties' wills to the non-donative transfer. Once entanglement occurs, the defendant can be held liable only if the non-donatively transferred benefit was accepted. In contrast, the situation prior to entanglement allows for an additional option, at least in theory. Although acceptance may also be present prior to entanglement, as where the defendant requests a benefit or acquiesces in its conferral, this is not the sole circumstance of liability. So long as the benefit remains disentangled, the defendant can be held liable even if the defendant's situation or conduct can be construed as a rejection of the benefit. Because the rejected benefit is still separately available for return without affecting what the defendant is otherwise entitled to, no impediment exists to returning the value that neither party wants transferred.

Leaving aside the unusual case of rejected benefit, one may say that there are two obligation-creating conditions for liability. The plaintiff-oriented condition is that the benefit was non-donatively transferred. The defendant-oriented condition is that the benefit was accepted as non-donatively given. Although these obligation-creating conditions are each oriented to a different party, they share a common focus that normatively links the plaintiff as transferor of value and the defendant as transferee of value. Because a transfer of value is the giving of something for nothing, the common focus is on how the parties stand with respect to the gratuitousness of what one gave and the other received. The point of these two conditions is that their joint presence renders the obligation to restore the transferred value consonant with the free will of both parties.

These two conditions do not refer to disconnected moments. Rather, to accept the benefit is to accept it as given. In the movement of the value from the plaintiff to the defendant, the non-gratuitousness with which the plaintiff transfers the value is completed by the defendant's acceptance of the transfer as non-gratuitous. Because acceptance is relevant to liability as a relational phenomenon, the juridically pertinent notion of acceptance is of the benefit considered not on its own, but as it has arisen through the parties' interaction. The absence of donative intent in the plaintiff is crucial to that interaction. Accordingly, acceptance establishes a relationship not of the defendant to the benefit, but of the defendant to the plaintiff though the benefit. If the benefit has been given as a gift, the acceptance of it is as a gift, and no liability follows. But if the benefit has been non-donatively given, the consonance of the benefit with the defendant's will marks an acceptance as non-donatively given.

When the benefit is accepted by the defendant on the same non-donative basis with which the plaintiff gave it, the defendant cannot justly retain it as if it had been given and accepted as a gift. The two obligation-creating conditions thereby have an analogous function in the law of unjust enrichment to that of offer and acceptance in the law of contract: they link the wills of the parties to each other through the subject matter of the transaction, so as to establish an *in personam* legal relationship between them. In the contractual context, the parties' wills converge on the contractual performance offered by the promisor and accepted by the promisee, with the effect of creating a contract between them. In the unjust enrichment context, the parties' wills converge on the non-gratuitous transfer of value, with the effect of creating not a contract, but a right to the retransfer of the value. Because it connects the defendant's will to the intention of the plaintiff in conferring the benefit, acceptance is a relational idea.

In accordance with their relational significance, the two obligation-creating conditions have reference to the juridical world of public meaning that the two parties share. On the plaintiff's side, the notion of donative intent is an extended one. It goes beyond subjective intent to include situations in which, whatever the transferor's subjective intent, the background legal categories justify the imputation of an intention to bestow a gift. In this extended sense, donative intent draws on the public meaning that the plaintiff's action has in the relationship between the parties. Imagine, for example, that the plaintiff makes an unrequested improvement to property that he knows belongs to another in the hope of being compensated for his labor. Subjectively, he may have no intention of giving a gift. But because his action takes place within a legal regime under which, as he knows or ought to know, only the owner has the right to determine whether to improve one's property, the improver can be taken to know that his action cannot obligate the owner to pay for the improvement. Accordingly, the law treats his action as the bestowal of a gift. The background legal category of property, which recognizes in the owner the exclusive power to improve the condition of what is owned, justifies the law's viewing the improvement as the expression of a donative intent. In this example the imputation of donative intent is based not on what is subjectively within the plaintiff's mind, but on how the plaintiff's conduct is to be publicly understood and categorized in relation to the defendant's property. Accordingly, one can conclude that having transferred the value free of any obligation on the transferee, the improver is a risk-taker with respect to the hoped-for compensation.[40] Conversely, however, if the improver mistakenly thinks that the property is his own or that he is improving it at the owner's request, donative intent can no longer be imputed to him. Because the improver is unaware that his improvement was not authorized, he cannot be held to what is implied by the knowledge that the power to improve property is exclusively the owner's. For the improver who acts out of mistake or ignorance, an obligation-creating condition is in place.

On the defendant's side also, acceptance of the enrichment as non-gratuitously given refers to the absence of donative intent in the transfer of value. It imbues this absence of donative intent on the plaintiff's part with a relational significance by connecting it to an imputed expression of the defendant's free will. The non-gratuitousness of the transfer—the consideration at the heart of unjust enrichment—thereby embraces and normatively links the parties. If the defendant can be regarded as having accepted a benefit as non-gratuitously given, then in fairness the benefit cannot be retained gratis. Nor can the defendant be compelled to give something in exchange for that benefit as if there were a contract between the parties, since the benefit was not given as part of an enforceable exchange or with the intention to create a contractual relationship. All that the defendant can do is return the value, so as to avoid keeping as a gift what was neither given nor accepted as a gift.

Acceptance is thus a relational notion. It refers to what is to be imputed to the defendant in the light of the plaintiff's non-gratuitous transfer of value. Although it is defendant-oriented, it does not treat the defendant in isolation from what the plaintiff did. It is not one "unjust factor" in a list of unjust factors. Nor does it point to a moral failure consisting in the defendant's unconscientious receipt of something for

---

[40] Birks, above n. 26, 101–3.

which he or she wants to avoid payment.[41] Rather, as a member of the conceptual sequence that unites the transferor and transferee of value within an obligation-creating relationship, it is a structural feature of liability for unjust enrichment. Within that relationship the defendant's acceptance of the beneficial transfer as non-gratuitous and the plaintiff's lack of donative intent are correlatives.

As with donative intent, the idea of acceptance draws on the public meaning of the parties' interaction. What matters is not the defendant's inner psychological state, but the judgments and assumptions about the parties' interaction that can reasonably be made against the background of the legal structure in which they operate.[42] In particular, the defendant who receives something for nothing has no reason to assume that the benefit was given gratuitously. Private law is a legal regime through which parties act for their own purposes without subordinating to others their freedom or the means for realizing it. The law does not presume—and therefore those subject to the law are not entitled to presume—that someone has chosen to transfer value gratuitously, thereby surrendering the means for pursuing one's own ends. To be sure, a person may on occasion identify another's interest with one's own and therefore confer gratuitous benefits on the other. However, such donative intent must be established for each particular case, and not assumed to be the general rule. Except when the enrichment was intended and accepted as a gift, the defendant can be regarded as assuming that no benefit is given gratuitously, even if the defendant has not turned his mind to this issue.

Acceptance is imputed when the law can reasonably regard the beneficial transfer as something that forwards or accords with the defendant's projects. The imputation of acceptance thereby connects the law's construction of the defendant's will both to the transferred value and to the terms on which it was transferred. In this context the will—the capacity to set and pursue one's own purposes—is a juridical, not a subjective or psychological notion: what matters is the purpose not as internally formed but as externally pertinent to the relationship of plaintiff and defendant. Awareness of the benefit and acting with respect to it are sufficient but not necessary to indicate

---

[41] For "free acceptance" as an unjust factor or as a signal of unconscientious receipt, see Birks, ibid., 114, 266; Peter Birks, "In Defence of Free Acceptance," in *Essays on the Law of Restitution*, ed. Andrew Burrows (1991), 105.

[42] Compare Deane J.'s reference to "a benefit actually or constructively accepted" in Pavey & Matthews Proprietary Ltd. v. Paul [1986] 162 C.L.R. 221, at 257.

acceptance; a benefit can be consonant with the defendant's purposes even if these are lacking. Acceptance goes, accordingly, not to the defendant's particular psychological state, but to what the law can reasonably impute to the defendant, given the defendant's purposes and the law's background assumptions about the significance of donative intent. Of course, any defendant might subjectively prefer to keep the transferred value rather than return it to the transferor. Nonetheless, by imputing acceptance of the enrichment as non-gratuitously given, the law indicates its view of how the defendant's will can reasonably be regarded as standing with respect to what was received, with the implication that the defendant has no right to retain it for the service of his projects as if it had been given gratuitously.

One might think that, because acceptance can occur subsequent to receipt of the benefit,[43] ascribing a structural role to acceptance is inconsistent with the cause of action being complete upon receipt. This, however, misapprehends the effect of acceptance. What the recipient accepts is not the benefit conceived statically at the time that the acceptance becomes operative, but rather the benefit *as transferred*. This includes not only the transfer's non-donativeness but also its occurrence at a particular point of time. The acceptance, in other words, is of the transfer whose subject matter is the benefit, not of the benefit standing alone, for it is the transfer that links the parties to each other. Thus, even when the acceptance comes after the benefit's receipt, its effect is retrospective to the time of the receipt. This is why the moment of enrichment can reasonably be regarded as the time from which judgment interest[44] and the statute of limitations[45] run.

6. Situations of acceptance

The consonance of the benefit with the defendant's purposes can arise in three ways: through action by the defendant with respect to the benefit, through a specific project of the defendant's that the benefit forwards, or through a benefit—money—that fits with any project that the defendant might have. These different ways form the various situations in which acceptance can be imputed to the defendant.

---

[43] For example, McDonald v. Coys of Kensington [2004] 1 W.L.R. 2775 (C.A.).
[44] Woolwich Equitable Society v. Inland Revenue Commissioners [1993] A.C. 70.
[45] Robert Goff and Gareth Jones, *The Law of Restitution*, 7th ed. (2009), ss. 43-004–006.

In the first situation the defendant knows or takes the risk that the benefit is non-gratuitously given and yet requests it or acquiesces in it by foregoing the opportunity to refuse it. Some of the best-known cases in the law of restitution illustrate this: the plaintiff performs a service for the defendant under an unenforceable contract, which serves as evidence both of the defendant's request for the service and of the plaintiff's non-donative intent in providing it;[46] or the defendant has been enriched by the plaintiff's labor in a quasi-spousal relationship although he knew or ought to have known that the benefit was given to him not as a personal gift but as an reflection of the full integration of their economic well-being;[47] or the owner "lies by" when he knows that another is expending money to improve the property on the mistaken supposition of his own title.[48] The same holds if after receipt the defendant refuses to restore a non-gratuitously given benefit that is easily returnable.[49] In such cases, the defendant's action or inaction in the face of the non-gratuitous conferral can be regarded as an acceptance of those benefits as given without donative intent.[50]

By failing to take the opportunity to reject a benefit, one both expresses one's free will with respect to it and assumes responsibility

---

[46] Deglman v. Guarantee Trust Co. and Constantineau [1954] S.C.R. 725; *Pavey & Matthews*, above n. 42.

[47] Pettkus v. Becker [1980] 117 D.L.R. (3d) 257, at 274:

> [W]here one person in a relationship tantamount to spousal prejudices herself in the reasonable expectation of receiving an interest in property and the other person in the relationship freely accepts benefits conferred by the first person in circumstances where he knows or ought to know of that reasonable expectation, it would be unjust to allow the recipient of the benefit to retain it.

[48] Ramsden v. Dyson [1866] L.R. 1 H.L. 129.

[49] McDonald v. Coys of Kensington [2004] 1 W.L.R. 2775 (C.A.); at paras. 37–38, Mance L.J. describes the defendant's action in keeping the personalized mark as a choice and as the exercise of a deliberate preference.

[50] It is sometimes thought that this notion of acceptance through inaction is in tension with the absence of tort liability for omissions; see G. Mead, "Free Acceptance: Some Further Considerations," (1989) 105 L.Q.R. 460, 463–64; Andrew Simister, "Unjust Free Acceptance," (1997) Lloyd's Maritime & Commercial L.Q. 103, 118–20. Properly understood, however, the absence of tort liability is not about inaction as such but about conferring a benefit to which the recipient has no right; see Peter Benson, "The Basis for Excluding Liability for Economic Loss in Tort Law," in *Philosophical Foundations of Tort Law*, ed. David G. Owen (1995), 427, 447–49. In the unjust enrichment context, the imputed acceptance through the defendant's inaction does not reflect a duty to bestow a gratuitous benefit on the plaintiff, but goes rather to whether the defendant's non-gratuitously given benefit can be treated as non-gratuitously accepted. Indeed, there is a deep harmony between the absence of liability for nonfeasance and the requirement of acceptance: both actualize the parties' freedom of choice by expressing the law's antipathy to gratuitous benefits that are not gratuitously intended.

for the implications of its non-gratuitous nature. Accordingly, by compelling a retransfer of the value, the law is not acting inconsistently with the defendant's will; such liability does not fall foul of Lord Justice Bowen's famous dictum that "[l]iabilities are not to be forced upon people behind their backs."[51] Rather, the law is merely following through on how the defendant's will is related to the plaintiff's through the transfer of value. For example, a defendant who is aware that another is bestowing an apparently gratuitous benefit and does not intervene to prevent it takes the risk that donative intent is absent. By allowing the enrichment to occur, the defendant manifests his volition with respect to it. If it turns out that the plaintiff indeed had no donative intent (for example, if the plaintiff was improving the defendant's land on the mistaken impression that it was his own), then the defendant's failure to prevent the transfer can be considered an acceptance of that benefit as non-gratuitously given.

In the second situation for imputing acceptance, the law treats the defendant as having accepted the beneficial transfer because, given the nature of the defendant's activities and projects, the defendant has no reason not to accept it. For example, the defendant holds property destined for a particular use or disposition that is forwarded by the benefit that the plaintiff non-gratuitously conferred;[52] or the plaintiff discharges an obligation owed by the defendant;[53] or a director exercises his skill to the advantage of the corporation although in breach of his fiduciary duty.[54] In such instances the issue is not whether the defendant as a rational maximizer is better off with the benefit in some global sense, but whether the benefit forwards the specific purposes implicit in the defendant's antecedent activities. If it does, then requiring restitution of the transferred value is, from the public standpoint of the parties' relationship, consistent with the defendant's free will.

Under the heading of "incontrovertible benefit" this second situation is conventionally treated as establishing the enrichment rather than the unjustness of retaining it. In this respect incontrovertible benefit is the counterpart of subjective devaluation. But as with subjective

[51] Bowen L.J. in Falcke v. Imperial Insurance Co. [1886] 34 Ch. D. 234 (C.A.).
[52] Lac Minerals v. International Corona Resources [1981] 64 D.L.R. (4th) 14 (S.C.C.) (defendant developed mine and constructed mill on plaintiff's mining property); Greenwood v. Bennett [1973] 1 Q.B. 195 (C.A.) (improvements to a car that was to be sold).
[53] Brooks Wharf & Bull Wharf v. Goodman Bros. [1936] 3 All E.R. 696 (C.A.).
[54] Phipps v. Boardman [1967] 2 A.C. 46.

devaluation, the considerations for postulating an incontrovertible benefit go not to whether a transfer of value has taken place but to whether the defendant's retention of the transferred value is consonant with the parties' free will. The point of invoking incontrovertible benefit is to show that imposing an obligation to make restitution would not violate the defendant's freedom of choice: "[t]he principle of incontrovertible benefit...exists when freedom of choice as a problem is absent."[55] If this is the case, it should be situated where it structurally belongs: as an obligation-creating condition pertaining to value transferred without donative intent.

A difference between these two situations is that in the first, but not in the second, the entanglement of the benefit with the defendant's entitlements is a barrier to recovery. The reason for this is that the two situations relate the defendant's will to the benefit received in different ways. In the first situation, instanced by request or acquiescence, the defendant's acceptance has to be referable to the benefit as such without cutting into the use that the defendant is otherwise entitled to make of what she owns. Therefore, the defendant's will has to be specifically directed to the benefit independent of the defendant's use of the owned thing. Once the benefit becomes entangled in the defendant's entitlements without indication of the defendant's acceptance, the defendant is not liable for enjoying the benefit through the use of what belongs to her. In the second situation, in which the benefit is incontrovertible, the acceptance is imputed because the benefit forwards the use that the defendant would otherwise have made. Unlike the first situation, here the actual or prospective use shows the consonance of the benefit with the defendant's projects, and is therefore the reason for regarding the benefit as accepted. Because the will need not be directed to the benefit independently of the use, the benefit's inextricable entanglement with what the defendant is otherwise entitled to use poses no barrier to liability. Thus, the distinction between the two situations is that in the first, acceptance is independent of use and, accordingly, cannot operate on an entangled benefit, whereas in the second, acceptance occurs through use, thereby rendering entanglement irrelevant.

Finally, the third situation for imputing acceptance is the non-donative payment of money. The peculiarity of money is that, as the

[55] Regional Municipality of Peel v. Her Majesty the Queen in the Right of Canada [1992] 98 D.L.R. (4th) 140 (S.C.C.), quoting J. R. M. Gautreau, "When Are Enrichments Unjust?" (1988–89) 10 Advoc. Q. 258, at 271.

universal medium of exchange,[56] it forwards any and every specific purpose that the defendant might have. The payment of money, therefore, is an incontrovertible benefit.[57] To be sure, in unusual circumstances a defendant might reject such a benefit—for example, if the mistaken payment makes the defendant ineligible for means-based government services.[58] But until spent, money is not entangled in the defendant's other entitlements and so can be returned even if rejected. Thus whether it is accepted or rejected, the defendant is under an obligation to make restitution.

Aside from such unusual circumstances, money is an incontrovertible benefit. As such it differs in two ways from the non-monetary instances of incontrovertible benefit. First, acceptance is imputable for a non-monetary benefit only if, given the benefit's particular qualities, it forwards some particular project that the recipient has. In contrast, except in unusual circumstances, money forwards the recipient's projects, whatever they are. Second, whereas in the case on non-monetary benefit the imputed acceptance arising from the benefit's incontrovertibility operates despite being entangled in the defendant's other entitlements, money has no such entanglement. However, the receipt of the money may lead the recipient to spend it on projects that she would not otherwise have undertaken—that is, to make the extraordinary expenditure that constitutes a change of position.[59] Accordingly, a benefit that subjects the defendant to liability while in the form of money may, when spent, become entangled in the defendant's entitlements. The imputation based on money's being the universal medium of exchange is then no longer appropriate. As long as the money is unspent, the defendant's position is no different than what it would be in the second situation. Once the defendant changes position by making an extraordinary expenditure that entangles the benefit in the defendant's entitlements, the defendant's position is not different from that of the person with the cleaned shoes in the first situation.

This account requires that change of position through expenditure, like incontrovertible benefit, should be regarded as going to the

---

[56] B.P. Exploration Co. (Libya) v. Hunt (No. 2) [1979] 1 W.L.R. 783, at 799 (Goff J.).
[57] Graham Virgo, *The Principles of the Law of Restitution*, 2nd ed. (2006), 75.
[58] Consider the situation in Ontario (Ministry of Community & Social Services) v. Henson [1987] 28 E.T.R. 121 (Ont. Dist. Ct.), affirmed on appeal (1989) 36 E.T.R. 192 (Ont. C.A.). I am grateful to Jason Neyers for pointing this out.
[59] Rural Municipality of Storthoaks v. Mobil Oil Canada [1975] 55 D.L.R. (3d) 1 (S.C.C.).

unjustness, not the existence, of the enrichment. Change of position is now conventionally explained in terms of enrichment, that the defendant has been "disenriched."[60] The explanation is not without difficulty. The consumption of the value is the exchange of the transferred value for some good to which the consumer attaches a still greater value. At the general level one may ask why such consumption negates the legal effect of the original transfer. Nor is the idea of disenrichment unambiguous. If I have spent the mistaken payment on a trip around the world,[61] I am still enriched by what I did with the money—I now have the recollection of adventure and discovery, the slides and photographs, the seemingly inexhaustible store of conversational material—even though the money is no longer in my bank account. What has occurred is a transformation of the enrichment, not its disappearance.

A more particular form of this difficulty is that the defense of change of position sometimes applies even when one can still discern the enrichment among the defendant's assets. Say that the defendant, having received a mistaken payment from the plaintiff, makes the extraordinary expenditure of throwing out her old shoes and buying a shining new pair. If the defendant had no notice of the mistake at the time of the purchase, the defense of change of position is available even though the defendant seems to remain enriched.[62] The argument to this conclusion on enrichment grounds is that—the defendant's choice to buy new shoes having been vitiated by her mistaken belief about her resources—she can subjectively devalue the shoes.[63] This preserves the relevance of the defense to enrichment, at the cost, oddly, of saying that the defendant can subjectively devalue what she decided was worth purchasing.

Even in its own terms this argument, with its reference to the vitiation of the defendant's choice, is about freedom of choice, not enrichment. The impression that the change of position in this instance is about enrichment is the product of the idea that subjective devalu-

---

[60] Birks, above n. 26, 208; at 261 Birks allows that there may turn out to be "very rare" examples of unjust-related change of position.

[61] Lord Templeman's example in Lipkin Gorman v. Karpnale [1992] 4 All E.R. 512, at 517.

[62] Cf. RBC Dominion Securities v. Dawson [1994] 111 D.L.R. (4th) 230 (Nfld. C.A.). I have substituted new shoes for new furniture in order to bring the case close to Pollock C.B.'s famous comment.

[63] Peter Birks, "Overview: Tracing, Claiming and Defences," *Laundering and Tracing*, ed. Peter Birks (1995), 289, at 331–32 .

ation is also about enrichment. At bottom, however, subjective devaluation is (as is widely acknowledged) really about freedom of choice.
Clarity about the structure of unjust enrichment requires that issues
of freedom of choice be treated as going to the unjustness of retaining
the value rather than to the occurrence of the transfer. This applies
also to change of position through expenditure, which constitutes a
defense not because it disenriches but because it precludes an
obligation-creating condition.[64]

Accordingly, the legal consequences of a mistaken payment can be
conceptualized as follows. A payment made by mistake lacks donative
intent, thereby fulfilling the first obligation-creating condition. Given
that money forwards any purpose that the recipient has, the recipient
is incontrovertibly benefited and (except in unusual circumstances
that do not affect the final result) has no reason not to be viewed as
accepting it. However, subsequent events can confirm or disconfirm
the acceptance that would have been imputable on payment. Once
the recipient is made aware that the unspent money was given by mistake, acceptance of the money as non-gratuitous becomes conclusive
because the recipient now has notice of the very circumstances that
grounded its imputation. Notice to the defendant that the payment
was mistakenly made cuts off the possibility of the defendant's subsequently spending the money in a way that would constitute a change
of position, because the defendant would be spending money that she
knew or should have known she was obligated to return to the plaintiff.

Conversely, when the recipient changes position prior to knowing
the payer's mistake, the circumstances supporting the imputation of
acceptance that was available previously no longer obtain. Change of
position operates as a defense insofar as the spending of the enrichment entangles it in the recipient's entitlements. If it has been spent to
purchase something separate from the defendant's other entitlements,
the value remains disentangled; restitution can be made of the second-
hand value of what was purchased.[65] If, however, the expenditure has

---

[64] The notion that change of position involves the defendant's disenrichment is more
apposite to the case of the innocent recipient of a mistaken payment that is subsequently
stolen or lost. There the defense is applicable even if the defendant had knowledge of the
mistake. See National Bank of New Zealand Ltd. v. Waitaki International Processing (NI)
Ltd. [1999] 2 N.Z.L.R. 211, 228–29 (C.A.).

[65] This is Lord Templeman's example of the purchased automobile in Lipkin Gorman v.
Karpnale [1992] 4 All E.R. 512, at 517.

consumed the value in such a way that nothing separately ascribable to it remains, then the enrichment is irrecoverable. Whether the defendant has spent the money on getting her old shoes cleaned or on replacing the old shoes with a new pair of clean shoes, her situation is no different from that person whose shoes are mistakenly cleaned by another. An obligation to restore such an enrichment would not be consistent with the defendant's freedom of choice. Pollock C.B.'s observation, that the benefit could not be rejected without refusing the property itself, applies.

The three situations described in this section correspond to the three ways of aligning the defendant's projects with the benefit bestowed by the plaintiff. The first aligns the project with a specific benefit that the defendant wishes to attain either by request or by non-rejection. The prospect of the benefit is what causes it to be incorporated into the defendant's purposes. The second is the converse of this: it aligns the benefit with a specific project that is otherwise evident in the defendant's activities. Because of the defendant's particular purposes the benefit that forwards them is regarded as accepted. The third deals with money as the all-purpose means for forwarding any project and with the consequences of transforming the money received through expenditure on a specific project.[66] In all of these situations, the benefit that the plaintiff non-donatively gives fits the purposes that the defendant pursues. This fit is the basis for imputing acceptance to the defendant.

One might object that only in the first kind of situation, and not in situations of incontrovertible benefit, is acceptance genuinely present. If so, acceptance cannot be a general feature of liability for unjust enrichment. Acceptance (so the objection would go) involves acting out of awareness of the existence or potential existence of the benefit. This is how acceptance operates in cases of request or acquiescence. In situations of incontrovertible benefit, in contrast, the defendant can be held liable even if unaware of the benefit. If the

---

[66] These different ways of aligning the benefit bestowed by the plaintiff and the projects pursued by the defendant seem to constitute a more or less exhaustive taxonomy. The only addition necessary for completeness is the converse of the third situation. The third situation features a possible movement from the universality of money to the specificity of change of position through expenditure. The converse is a movement from the specificity of the benefit to a transformation of the benefit into money. This last possibility corresponds to Birks's view that a benefit becomes incontrovertible when realized in money; Birks, above n. 26, 221.

point of acceptance is to implicate the defendant's will so that, in the words of Lord Justice Bowen's famous dictum mentioned earlier, "[l]iabilities are not to be forced upon people behind their backs,"[67] the defendant's ability to choose whether or not to take the benefit cannot be dispensed with. Acceptances that are constructed or imputed on the basis of the consonance of the benefit with the defendant's projects will not do.

The answer is that in this context the will has a relational, and not merely an interior, significance. Only on this basis is it appropriate to corrective justice, which conceives of liability's norms as interactional, rather than as unilaterally applicable to one or the other of the two parties. Accordingly, the role of the benefit in motivating the defendant's conduct is not the sole relevant factor. What matters is the connection between the defendant's will and the benefit bestowed by the plaintiff. This connection can take different forms. There is no reason why the difference between aligning purpose with benefit (situation one) and aligning benefit with purpose (situations two and three) should matter to the plaintiff's liability. What is relationally significant is the idea that includes all three situations: the benefit that the plaintiff non-donatively gives fits the purposes that the defendant pursues. The imputation of acceptance merely expresses the relational significance that all the situations share.

As for Lord Justice Bowen's dictum about not forcing liability behind a person's back, the objection proves too much. If the dictum is understood as applying only to situations in which the defendant was aware of the benefit, then incontrovertible benefit would not give rise to liability at all, regardless of whether incontrovertible benefit was seen as going to enrichment or unjustness. But although doubt is sometimes cast on the soundness of the doctrine of incontrovertible benefit on the grounds that it amounts to a forced exchange,[68] the doctrine is now solidly entrenched in the law. Consequently, unless one thinks that either the dictum or the doctrine of incontrovertible benefit is wrong, the two have to be brought into harmony. This harmony is achieved if one recognizes that, because liability for an incontrovertible benefit is based on the defendant's purposes, it does not operate behind the defendant's back.

---

[67] Above n. 51.
[68] Andrew. M. Tettenborn, *Law of Restitution in England and Ireland*, 2nd ed. (1993), 20–22.

7. The sequence of elements

The obligation-creating conditions of lack of donative intent and acceptance echo the conditions for the defectiveness of gift, with the exception that they are cumulatively necessary for rendering the transfer defective rather than alternatively sufficient. As noted earlier, to make out a gift, what is given as a gift has to be received as a gift.[69] When these two conditions are present, the donee acquires the right to the gifted object; when either of them is absent, the object remains the donor's. Unjust enrichment has aptly been called the law of non-gifts.[70] An obligation to make restitution arises when what is given as a non-gift is accepted as a non-gift—that is, when the plaintiff's unintended transfer of something for nothing is matched by the defendant's acceptance of what was transferred as something that was not intended to be given for nothing. This non-gratuitousness on both sides of the relationship between the transferor and the transferee of value triggers a reversal of the transfer, because the transferee cannot retain the value on terms other than those on which it was given and accepted.

So understood, the elements of liability form a sequence. The first stage in this sequence is to determine whether the plaintiff gave the defendant something for nothing—a stage formulated legally as the defendant's enrichment at the plaintiff's expense and theoretically as a transfer of value. If something was indeed given for nothing, one then moves to a series of questions that address the justice of the defendant's retaining what was given. The first of these questions is whether the plaintiff intended either a gift or the discharge of an obligation to the defendant.[71] An affirmative answer means that the claim is defeated.

---

[69] Above n. 31.

[70] Drassinower, above n. 38, at 478.

[71] The obligation at issue must be one that is owed to the defendant and not to some third party. Because the law's interest is in the relationship between the transferor and the transferee of value, only the plaintiff's discharge of an obligation to the defendant entitles the defendant to retain the benefit. Accordingly, Owen v. Tate [1976] 1 Q.B. 402 (C.A.) was wrongly decided. As a favor to a friend, the plaintiff substituted his personal guarantee for security given by the friend for a bank loan to the defendant, and then unsuccessfully sued for reimbursement when the security was applied to part of the debt. The plaintiff intended to benefit his friend, not to give a gift to the defendant. Moreover, since the plaintiff's obligation on the guarantee was to the bank not the defendant, it supplied no reason for the defendant to be entitled to retain the benefit of having its debt to the bank reduced to the extent of the plaintiff's payment.

A negative answer, concluding that the plaintiff gave something for nothing but had no donative intent, leads to the final question in the sequence: did the defendant accept the transferred value as non-donatively given? An affirmative answer to this question means that the defendant cannot justly retain the enrichment and is under an obligation to restore it to the plaintiff.

The leading Canadian case of *Deglman v. Guarantee Trust Co. and Constantineau*[72] illustrates this sequence. The plaintiff agreed to perform incidental services for his aunt in return for an oral promise that in her will she would leave him her house. The aunt died without doing so. The aunt's promise was unenforceable under the Statute of Frauds. Nonetheless, the nephew succeeded in getting restitution of the value of the services provided. The first stage was satisfied because the performance of the services at the aunt's request was a transfer of value. Turning to the question of justice in transfer, one might be tempted to think that, on the sequence that I have suggested, the claim should have been dismissed on the ground that this transfer of value was in fulfillment of a contractual obligation to the aunt, an obligation that was not voided but merely rendered unenforceable by the statute. However, for purposes of unjust enrichment, the relevant question is not whether the plaintiff was obligated to do certain acts, but whether he was obligated to transfer value—that is, to do those acts without receiving their quantitative equivalent in return. Although the nephew was contractually obligated to provide the services, he was not contractually obligated to provide them for nothing, as if he had made a gratuitous promise under seal. When the aunt died without leaving the house to the nephew, what the parties intended as an exchange of services for property was revealed to be a transfer of value, to which the nephew had not obligated himself. Nor did the plaintiff transfer the value donatively. Although the unenforceable contract could not be the basis for compelling performance, it showed that the services were not provided gratuitously.[73] Similarly (although the court did not expressly make this point), the contract showed that the aunt accepted the services on the assumption that she was not getting them

---

[72] [1954] S.C.R. 725.

[73] "[T]he services were not given gratuitously but on the footing of a contractual relation: they were meant to be paid for." Justice Rand, ibid., at 728; compare Justice Deane's observation in the parallel Australian case that "it will ordinarily be permissible for the plaintiff to refer to the unenforceable contract as evidence, but as evidence only, on the question whether what was done was done gratuitously." *Pavey & Matthews*, above, n. 42, at 257.

for nothing.[74] Because the aunt accepted as non-gratuitous the services that the nephew performed on a non-gratuitous basis, her estate could not retain their value as if they had been given for free.

Compared to the conventional understanding, this description of the structure of unjust enrichment shifts considerations usually associated with enrichment (subjective devaluation, incontrovertible benefit, change of position) to the obligation-creating conditions that make retention of the enrichment unjust. A consequence of the conventional placement is that the overloading of the "enrichment" slot within the principle of unjust enrichment involves the emptying of the "unjust" slot. It is then hardly surprising that the nature of the unjustness becomes a mystery. Once the "unjust" slot has been refilled in the way I have suggested, the meaning of unjustness in the context of unjust enrichment follows from the nature of enrichment at another's expense as a transfer of value. A transfer of value is the giving or doing of something for nothing. The issue of justice as between the parties that arises from a transfer of value centers on the normative defectiveness of a transfer in which the transferee retains for nothing what was both given non-gratuitously and accepted as non-gratuitously given. The question of what renders an enrichment unjust is, therefore, an enquiry not into justice at large but into the justice that is specific to the transfer of something for nothing.

8. The Kantian conception of the *in personam* right

Liability for unjust enrichment reflects the plaintiff's *in personam* right to have the defendant retransfer the value. In this section I explore the *in personam* nature of this right, drawing on Kant's taxonomy of private law. As was noted in the first section of this chapter, the identification of the plaintiff's right in cases of unjust enrichment has aroused considerable perplexity, especially among those who are skeptical about the relevance of corrective justice to unjust enrichment. Although Kant never discussed (and was presumably unaware of) unjust enrichment as a ground of liability, his account of the *in personam* right might assist in dissolving the perplexity.

To what does the plaintiff assert a right in an action for unjust enrichment? Since liability entails a retransfer of value, two possible

---

[74] Ibid.

answers are available, depending on how one thinks of the relationship between the retransfer and the value. On one view, the plaintiff asserts a right to the value, with the retransfer being merely the mechanism for getting it. On the second view, the plaintiff asserts a right to the retransfer, with the value being merely the object of the retransfer.

On the first view, the plaintiff simply asserts his or her right in the value as originally owned, on the ground that this right survives the defective transfer, just as the donor's right in what is given survives the defective gift. The action for unjust enrichment would be conceived as a kind of action for conversion or as a kind of *vindicatio* of a special asset that consists in the value. It would then turn out that liability for unjust enrichment refers not to a distinctive principle but to a novel kind of asset.[75]

I think that this is not the best way to conceptualize the plaintiff's right. The value returned to the plaintiff is not, as the subject matter of a right, identical to the value that the plaintiff originally held: the original value was an incident of the thing of value, whereas the value returned to the plaintiff is independent of the thing of value, which now rightfully belongs to the defendant. Moreover, one cannot conclude that the defectiveness of the transfer of value means that the value remains the transferor's, as in the case of gift. In the gift context, defectiveness of transfer refers to the role of *either* party's will in blocking the movement of title in the object of the gift. In contrast, in the unjust enrichment context, defectiveness of transfer refers to the joint role of *both* parties' wills, precisely in order to take account of the movement of title in the thing of value. Indeed, if the transferor had a continuous right to the value, it is hard to see why the transferee's acceptance of the benefit should be indispensable to the transferor's assertion of that right. In view of this dissimilarity between gift and unjust enrichment in what makes a transfer defective, one cannot straightforwardly argue that defectiveness of transfer means that what was purportedly transferred, whether a specific object or value, continues to be owned by the transferor.

Instead of looking at value as a static object of ownership that remains the transferor's through the defectiveness of the transfer, I suggest that one regard value more dynamically, as the content of a process of transfer and retransfer. The significance of the plaintiff's entitlement to the value at the inception of the transaction is that

---

[75] Klimchuk mentions this possibility, above n. 10, at 680.

value counts as the possible object of a transfer, and—if the obligation-creating conditions are present—as the possible object of a
retransfer, thereby making justice in transfer applicable to value. The
normative defectiveness that compels a retransfer itself partakes of the
dynamism of the process of transfer and retransfer, because the transfer-
or's right to have the value retransferred is established not by reference
to the transferor's intent alone, but through the convergence of the
parties' wills on the transfer's non-gratuitousness.

In unjust enrichment the plaintiff's right is not to the value as such,
but to a retransfer of the value. The object of the right is an action by
the defendant, not a thing. The right arises through the will-to-will
relationship of the parties—that is, through the unity of their wills
when the plaintiff's unintended transfer of something for nothing is
matched by the defendant's acceptance of the transfer as an unintended giving of something for nothing. When this non-gratuitousness
appears on both sides of the relationship between the transferor and
the transferee of value, the law reverses the transfer, because the transferee cannot retain the value on terms other than those on which it
was given and accepted. The reversal of the transfer in response to the
obligation-creating conditions is the plaintiff's right and the defendant's correlative duty.

This right to have the defendant perform an act can be presented in
Kantian terms. The matter of the plaintiff's right in the unjust enrichment context is what Kant called a causality of the defendant's will,
and its form is a *ius personale* (or, as we would put it, a right *in personam*).[76] I now want to set out more fully what this means.

Kant's conception of the *in personam* right emerges from two layers
in his classification of rights. The first is the division between innate
and acquired right. Innate right is the right that one has by virtue of
one's very existence, so that one does not have to do anything to
acquire it.[77] One's physical embodiment is a manifestation of this right.
One does not acquire one's body through the performance of any act
of acquisition. Indeed, the notion of such an act would be self-contra-
dictory. Because an act involves the use of one's body, the act of acquiring one's own body would presuppose that one had a right to one's
body prior to the act that acquired it. Kant specifies that the only
innate right is one's freedom—that is, one's independence from

---

[76] Immanuel Kant, *The Metaphysics of Morals*, tr. Mary Gregor (1996), [6:259–60].
[77] Ibid., at [6:237–38].

constraint by the action of another, though this right has several aspects (bodily integrity, freedom of speech and thought, immunity from reproach until one has wrongly affected another's rights, the innate equality of not being bound by others more that one can in turn bind them, and so on). The ensemble of the aspects that constitute one's innate right comprises what is internally one's own in one's relations with others.

In contrast, acquired rights are rights to objects external to the person, which become one's own through an appropriate act of acquisition. Because these objects are distinct from the person and are acquired through an act of the will, Kant calls them "external objects of choice."[78] Through the acquisition of an external object of choice one becomes connected with the object in such a way that another's action with respect to it can count as an infringement of one's rights. An acquired right is thus a relation between a right-holder and an external object of choice that places others under a duty to the right-holder with respect to that object of choice. Whereas there is only one kind of innate right, there are as many kinds of acquired rights as there are ways of relating a person to an external object of choice.

Within acquired right, then, a further division can be made into the kinds of relations that can link a person to an external object of choice. This division expresses the concepts of the understanding that are exercised in judgments about relation. Kant holds that there are three such concepts: substance, causality, and community.[79] Substance is that which subsists through the variations of the properties that inhere in it, as an apple subsists through its alterations in color as it ripens and then decays. Causality is unidirectional determination of a consequence by its ground. Community is the reciprocal determination of the different parts of a whole. Consequently, every right that connects a person to an external object of choice must be a right either to a substance or to a causality or to a community.[80]

First, substance is the object of a right *in rem*. A right *in rem* is a property right, which by connecting the right-holder to a substance puts all others under a correlative duty to abstain from that substance. Because it is a right to a substance, the entitlement of the right-holder remains intact whatever changes are undergone by the object of the right; if I

---

[78] Ibid., at [6:247].
[79] Immanuel Kant, *Critique of Pure Reason*, tr. Norman Kemp Smith (1929), A80/B106.
[80] Kant, above n. 76, at [6:247].

own the apple, it remains mine even when it turns from green to red and from red to brown. A property right is good against the whole world because it presupposes a general will of all under which everyone recognizes the legitimacy of anyone else's rightful acquisition.[81] Acquisition restricts the freedom of others with respect to the acquired object; it therefore cannot be achieved simply by the acquirer's unilateral action on that object. Accordingly, a notionally universal consent to the system of property rights is required for rightful acquisition under the category of substance. Thus, a property right imposes a correlative duty on everyone to adhere to the general will recognizing a system of property rights; the generality of the duty merely reflects the generality of the will that any particular property right presupposes.

Next, causality is the object of a right *in personam*. Contract is the paradigmatic example of a right to a causality.[82] What the promisee acquires through contract is the right to the promisor's performance of a particular deed—that is, a right to the causality of the promisor's will. The capacity to determine performance of this deed becomes part of the promisee's patrimony. In Kant's words, the promisee acquires "an active obligation on the freedom and means of the other."[83] Thus, the contract provides the rightful basis for the unidirectional determination of the promisor's will in fulfillment of the promisee's right. Such a right does not arise through the initiative of either party alone, as that would be inconsistent with the freedom of the other. Rather, the contractual right is jointly established by both parties through contract-forming steps—the promisor's making and the promisee's acceptance of the promise[84]—that express their united will. Unlike the general will of all that is presupposed in proprietary rights, the united will that establishes a right to the causality of another's deed creates a duty that runs between the two parties whose wills are united. Accordingly, the distinction between an *in rem* and an *in personam* right lies not solely in the number of persons that they respectively bind[85] but in the different relational categories of substance and causality that they respectively instantiate.

---

[81] Ibid., at [6:256, 261].

[82] Ibid., at [6:271–74].

[83] Ibid., at [6:274].

[84] These are Kant's terms (ibid., at [6:272]) for what common lawyers call offer and acceptance.

[85] Wesley Newcomb Hohfeld, "Fundamental Legal Conceptions as Applied in Judicial Reasoning," (1971) 26 Yale L.J. 710, at 718 (distinguishing between "paucital" rights *in personam* and "multital" rights *in rem,* with the latter made up of a great number of the former).

Finally, community: the object of this kind of right is another person's status, insofar as one has the right to make arrangements about that person.[86] Among Kant's examples are relationships between spouses and relationships between parents and children. In these relationships there is a reciprocal determination of rights and duties. The parent, for instance, has a right to manage and develop the child, but the parent is simultaneously under a duty to care for the child until the child matures. The right and the duty are not independent of each other, but are the mutually entailed aspects of the same relationship. A contemporary example of such status-based reciprocal determination is the fiduciary relationship; the fiduciary has the right to make arrangements about another, but because of that very right is subject to the obligation not to profit from the relationship or to allow interest to conflict with duty.

Kant regarded these three categories as exhausting our understanding of relation. When these categories are applied to law, a right in what is external to oneself places others under a correlative duty by being either an *in rem* right to a particular substance, an *in personam* right to cause the other to perform a deed, or a status right of a community within which rights and duties are reciprocally determining.

Within this taxonomy, liability for unjust enrichment is an instance of the plaintiff's *in personam* right to a causality of the defendant's will. The causality in question—the deed whose performance is the content of the plaintiff's right—is the defendant's retransfer to the plaintiff of the value. This right is established through the unity of the parties' wills with respect to the non-gratuitousness of the original transfer. Just as the promisor's making and the promisee's acceptance of the promise establish a right to contractual performance, so the plaintiff's non-donative transfer of value and the defendant's acceptance of the value as non-donatively given establish the plaintiff's right to the value's retransfer.

This understanding of unjust enrichment views liability under the category of causality, not substance. The basis of the liability is not that the plaintiff has retained ownership in the transferred value, but that the plaintiff has acquired a right to have the defendant retransfer the value.

---

[86] Kant, above n. 76, at [6:259, 276–84].

Value plays a double role for external objects of choice. On the one hand, value inheres in a thing of value considered as a substance, so that the transfer of the thing of value is also a transfer of the value that inheres in it. Unjust enrichment is indifferent to this value, which can be recovered only through the assertion of a property right to the thing of value. On the other hand, value is the content of a process of transfer in which something is given for nothing. This transfer gives rise to a relationship particular to the two parties to it. When neither of them treats the value as the content of a transfer—that is, when the transferor does not intend to make value the content of a transfer and when the transferee accepts the value as not having been the content of a transfer—then the law undoes the process of transfer by requiring restitution of the enrichment. The point of the liability is not that value, as an attribute inhering in the substance of what was given to the defendant, did not pass. It *did* pass along with the substance in which it inheres. Rather, the basis of liability is that the process of giving something for nothing was intended by neither party and therefore has to be reversed. The convergence of the parties' wills with respect to the non-gratuitousness of the transfer establishes the transferor's right to a retransfer, which is a causality of the transferee's will.

In the light of the Kantian categories of relation, one can understand as follows the opening words of the Restatement of Restitution, that "[a] person who has been unjustly enriched at the expense of another is required to make restitution to the other."[87] Enrichment at the expense of another refers to the transfer of value. The unjustness refers to the non-donative terms on which the plaintiff has given and the defendant has accepted this transferred value. This non-donativeness on both sides signifies the relationship of will to will that establishes the plaintiff's *in personam* right (and the defendant's correlative duty) to the retransfer of the value. The Restatement calls the duty to retransfer the value a "require[ment] to make restitution." Making restitution is the performance that constitutes the content of the *in personam* right as a causality of another's will.[88]

---

[87]   Restatement of Restitution, above n. 1.

[88]   Compare Ross B. Grantham and Charles E. F. Rickett, *Enrichment and Restitution in New Zealand* (2000), 470:

> In a case of subtractive enrichment, where the relevant right is defined in terms of the principle of restorable enrichment, the primary right *must* be the right to restitution. Where a restorable enrichment occurs, the plaintiff's primary right is to restitution from the defendant.

9. Corrective justice revisited

I mentioned at the outset that corrective justice has three interwoven features: the correlative structure of the parties' relationship, the presence of a right and a correlative duty, and the conception of the parties as free and equal persons. In this section, I sum up by noting how the account of unjust enrichment that I have offered conforms to all these features of corrective justice.

The challenge to corrective justice in the unjust enrichment context revolves around supposed difficulty of formulating the right and the correlative duty. In response, I have suggested that the normatively defective transfer of value relates the parties as will to will regarding the gratuitousness of the transfer, so as to establish in the plaintiff an *in personam* right (and to impose a correlative duty on the defendant) to have the value retransferred. Liability signifies that the defendant's retention of the value in the face of the two obligation-creating conditions that render the transfer defective is inconsistent with this right. Such retention makes the defendant and the plaintiff the active and passive poles, respectively, of an injustice between them.

In this conception of liability the parties are conceived as free and equal persons. The point of liability is to assure that the transfer and retransfer of value is in accordance with the parties' freedom of will. Hence the law construes as normatively defective a transfer of value in which the transferor did not intend to give something for nothing and in which the transferee accepted what was transferred as not having been given for nothing. These obligation-creating conditions treat the parties as equals by insisting that both of them are entitled to what rightfully belongs to them until they freely part with it.

Moreover, both the notion of a transfer and the circumstances under which the retention of what was transferred is unjust display the requisite correlativity. First, the requirement that the defendant's enrichment has to be at the plaintiff's expense constructs the transaction between the parties as a transfer of value from the plaintiff to the defendant. The notion of a transfer links the parties to each other by situating them in correlative positions as transferor and transferee. Liability undoes this transfer by obligating the defendant to restore the value to the plaintiff. Transfer thus marks out the two particular parties to the legal relationship by establishing between them the nexus of value given and received.

Second, the notion of unjustness with respect to the transfer is also correlatively structured. Whether the transferee's retention of the value is unjust depends on how the parties' wills are related to each other through the gratuitousness of the transfer. The transferor's giving of value without donative intent and the transferee's acceptance of that value as non-donatively given triggers the obligation to restore the value, because the transferee cannot retain for nothing a benefit that was neither given nor accepted as gratuitous. Thus, the enquiry into whether the enrichment was unjust situates the parties correlatively as transferor and transferee of what was not gratuitously transferred. Consequently, the interaction between the parties as the non-gratuitous transferor and transferee of value establishes a correlative right and duty of restitution.

The notion of a transfer and the circumstances under which the retention of what was transferred is unjust are conceptually linked. The unifying thread lies in the idea that a transfer of value consists in giving something to another for nothing. Only because what is transferred is value—that is, something for which the transferor receives nothing in exchange—does the issue of the injustice of its retention revolve around whether the value was given and received non-donatively. Thus, the correlativity both of the transfer and of its normative defectiveness come together in an integrated ensemble of liability-creating elements.

The correlative situation of the parties is also observed through the way that liability works to remedy the lack of justice in transfer. Just as the unjustness of the enrichment lies in normative defectiveness of the transfer of value, so the correction of this injustice consists in the retransfer of the value. The retransfer that rectifies the injustice has the same subject matter, the same correlative structure, and the same correlatively situated parties as did the defective transfer.

The consequence of these considerations is that liability for unjust enrichment fully conforms to corrective justice. This should astonish no one. Corrective justice is nothing more than a theoretical account of the obvious normative link between the parties within a regime of liability. This link, of course, is present in unjust enrichment no less than in other areas of liability.

Indeed, corrective justice has always been implicit in the revival of interest in unjust enrichment throughout the common law world. Decades ago the formulators of the first Restatement of Restitution justified their project on the ground that unjust enrichment unifies a variety of doctrines under a legal concept that works justice between the parties.[89] Corrective justice is merely the theoretical construct that reflects this justification for the development of the law of unjust enrichment. Corrective justice does this by capturing the fairness and coherence of justice between the parties and by providing the unifying structure under which various doctrines can be understood as instantiations of a single principle. To the extent that the development of the law of unjust enrichment has remained true to the Restatement's aspirations, an elucidation of the corrective justice of this basis of liability does no more than confirm in theory what everybody already assumes in practice.

[89] Warren Seavey and Austin Scott, "Restitution," (1938) 54 L.Q.R. 29.

7

Incontrovertible Benefit
in Jewish Law

1. The case of the planted trees

At some point in the early third century of the Common Era, a man
in Babylonia went into another's field and, without the owner's permission, planted trees there. The question then arose: under Jewish law
was the owner liable for this unsolicited improvement to his property?
The case was brought before Rav, the pre-eminent Jewish jurist of the
time. The Talmud gives the following account of the proceedings:[1]

A man came before Rav. Rav said to the owner of the field, 'Go and make
an assessment for him.' The owner said, 'I do not want the trees.' Rav said,
'Go and make an assessment for him, and he shall have the lower hand'
[that is, on the standard interpretation, the improver shall be entitled to the
lesser of his expenses and what the owner would pay to have the trees
planted]. The owner said, 'I do not want the trees.' Subsequently, Rav saw
that the owner had built a fence around the field and was guarding it. Rav
said to the owner, 'You have revealed your view that you are pleased with
the trees. Go and make an assessment for him, and he shall have the upper
hand.'

This ancient incident brings together features familiar to modern students of the law of restitution. On one side is the improver, who claims
remuneration for the benefit, albeit unrequested, of the planted trees.

---

[1] Babylonian Talmud, Baba Mezia, 101a (throughout this chapter the translations are my
own). On Rav, see Ephraim E. Urbach, *The Halakha: Its Sources and Development* (1986),
295–302.

On the other side is the owner, who (anticipating the modern notion of subjective devaluation)[2] repeatedly denies that this is a benefit that he wants. Rav, adjudicating the dispute, indicates the measure of the owner's payment with various formulations, but makes a decisive ruling only when the owner's behavior shows that he was satisfied with the trees after all. Pervading the whole account is familiar tension between the owner's freedom to determine the use of his own property and the prevention of enrichment at the improver's expense.

Rav's treatment of the planting of these trees represents one of the fundamental building blocks of the Jewish law's jurisprudence about unrequested improvements. This jurisprudence is extraordinarily complex and sophisticated. The dictum about the common law—that it has been "fined and refined by an infinite number of Grave and Learned Men"[3]—is even more apposite to the development of Jewish law. But because its long history has been accompanied by wide geographical dispersion and a largely decentralized structure of legal authority, legal doctrine has often been fluid and evolving within the stable framework provided by the Talmud, the system's basic text. Accordingly, although the jurisprudence of unrequested improvements originates in the brief Talmudic segment that centers on Rav's case, centuries of commentaries, responsa, and codifications have produced varied understandings of the legal elements of the problem and different suggestions of how those elements are to be combined. To examine, or even refer to, all the possibilities is beyond the scope of this chapter. I hope, instead, to highlight issues that run parallel to those found in the common law.

This chapter thus contributes to the burgeoning comparative literature that the revival of restitution in the common law world has stimulated.[4] From the standpoint of the common law, this literature has an obvious attraction. Although the modern common law of

---

[2] Peter Birks, *An Introduction to the Law of Restitution* (1985), 109–16.

[3] Thomas Hobbes, *A Dialogue between a Philosopher and a Student of the Common Laws of England*, ed. Joseph Cropsey (1971), 55.

[4] Especial attention has been paid to German law. See, for example, Thomas Krebs, *Restitution at the Crossroads: A Comparative Study* (2001); Gerhard Dannemann, "Unjust Enrichment by Transfer: Some Comparative Remarks," (2001) 79 Texas L. Rev., 1837; B. S. Markesinis, W. Lorenz, and G. Dannemann, *The German Law of Obligations*, vol. I, *The Law of Contracts and Restitution: A Comparative Introduction* (1997), 710–816; Reinhard Zimmermann, "Unjustified Enrichment: The Modern Civilian Approach," (1995) 15 Oxford J. Legal Stud. 403; Reinhard Zimmermann, *The Law of Obligations: Roman Foundations of the Civilian Tradition* (1990), 834–901.

restitution has antecedents that stretch back several centuries, only within the last decades have scholars and courts made a sustained effort to develop a set of distinct principles of unjust enrichment. Attention to the sophisticated older European traditions about unjust enrichment not only exposes further possibilities of analysis, but also contributes to the intellectual self-consciousness necessary for productive reflection about unjust enrichment as a juridical concept. However, scholars of restitution have had little opportunity to consider Jewish law, as is understandable given its obscurity and inaccessibility. Nonetheless, as the episode involving Rav indicates, issues of unjust enrichment have engaged the attention of the leading figures of the Jewish legal tradition for almost two millennia. This makes Jewish law the locus for the world's oldest uninterrupted and continuing discussion of unjust enrichment.

Although the Jewish law of unrequested improvements developed without apparent attention to Aristotle's conception of corrective justice, my exposition of Rav's case is nonetheless informed by that conception.[5] Corrective justice, with its insistence on the correlative structure of the private law relationship, is a theoretical idea for understanding the fairness and coherence of private law. It is not itself a notion explicitly invoked in the formulation of legal doctrine. However, inasmuch as a sophisticated regime of private law—as Jewish law assuredly is—aspires to deal fairly with both parties and to work out coherent doctrine, one should not be surprised if its norms are intelligible in the light of corrective justice.

Corrective justice also serves as a framework for the comparison of legal doctrine across legal systems. Scholars of comparative law are divided about whether to emphasize the commonalities or the differences between legal systems.[6] Corrective justice accommodates both commonality and difference. At the level of commonality it directs attention to the correlative structure of the parties' relationship, and thus to the most pervasive characteristic of legal doctrine insofar as it is fair and coherent. At the level of difference, it acknowledges the diversity of the ways in which legal systems construct and actualize

---

[5] For a brief treatment from an economic perspective contending that Jewish law converges with efficiency, see Aaron Levine, *Free Enterprise and Jewish Law: Aspects of Jewish Business Ethics* (1980), 78–83.

[6] Daniel Visser, "Unjustified Enrichment in Comparative Perspective," in *The Oxford Handbook of Comparative Law*, ed. Matthias Reimann and Reinhold Zimmermann (2007), 969, 972–73.

correlatively structured relationships.[7] As a theoretical idea, corrective justice orients us within the conceptual space of fair and coherent legal doctrine. It thereby alerts us to considerations that are inappropriate to a private law relationship because they are so structured that they could not possibly come within that space. However, corrective justice does not usurp the role of specific legal systems in working out the doctrines that are intelligible in its light. This allows the comparative examination of the different ways in which different legal systems formulate the doctrinal requirements of a common conceptual framework.

My especial focus is on the interplay between the improver's claim to remuneration for the benefit bestowed and the owner's freedom from having to pay for an unwanted improvement. From the standpoint of the idea of unjust enrichment, this interplay raises the issue of whether the owner's enrichment at the improver's expense is unjust. Within the framework of corrective justice, which conceives of unjust enrichment as involving a transfer of value that the transferee is obligated to restore, the lack of justice in the enrichment refers not to injustice at large but to injustice regarding the transfer of value.[8] Inasmuch as value is transferred only if the transferor has given something for nothing, the absence of justice in transfer revolves around how the parties' wills are related to each other through the gratuitousness of the transfer. Accordingly, in determining whether an enrichment was unjust, two issues regarding the justice of the transfer arise. The first is whether the transferor intended to give the value gratuitously. If the transferor had donative intent, justice in transfer is achieved. The transferred value cannot be recalled by claiming that the enrichment was unjust, because there is no injustice in the transferee's retention of what the transferor willingly gave him. If, however, the transferor did not intend to give the value gratuitously, a second issue arises: did the transferee accept the value as non-gratuitously given? An affirmative answer triggers the obligation to restore the value, because the transferee cannot retain for nothing a benefit that he accepted as non-gratuitously given. Thus, the enquiry into whether the enrichment was unjust situates the parties correlatively as transferor and transferee of value that was not gratuitously transferred.

---

[7] Ernest J. Weinrib, *The Idea of Private Law* (1995), 222–29.
[8] Above, chapter 6.

The transferor's lack of donative intent and the transferee's accept-ance are structural components of liability for unjust enrichment within the corrective justice framework. As a functioning system, however, the law of unjust enrichment must render this framework specific and concrete. From what is the transferor's donative intent to be inferred? Under what circumstances can acceptance of the benefit be imputed to the transferee? Different systems of law address the issues raised by these questions in different ways. The consequence is that Jewish law and the common law may differ in the way each han-dles unrequested improvements and yet, despite the absence of his-torical connection between the two systems, may implicitly share a framework of thought that conforms to corrective justice. Such com-monality would merely reflect the aspiration of each to fairness and coherence in their respective constructions of their regimes of private law.

In its treatment of unrequested improvements Jewish law pays considerable attention to the aspect of acceptance. Indeed, as I hope to show, the history of Jewish law in this context is the history of the shifting conceptions of acceptance. Speaking broadly and ignor-ing the details for the moment, one can say that the treatment of the issue in Jewish law will seem familiar to someone conversant with the common law. The common law employs two notions of accept-ance. Acceptance of a benefit can be imputed to the recipient either because the recipient has acted in a way that reveals an acceptance (for example, by acquiescence) or because, given the recipient's activities and projects, he has no reason not to accept it (cases of "incontrovertible benefit"). Parallels to both notions of acceptance appear in Jewish law. In the incident of the planted trees, for instance, the fencing and guarding were taken by Rav to be acts that revealed an acceptance even though the owner denied that he wanted the trees. More importantly, Jewish law crafted different conceptions of incontrovertible benefit, based on a working and reworking of the Talmudic material. These various conceptions are the subject of this chapter.

This chapter, accordingly, proceeds in the following stages. Sec-tion 2 explains the different measures of remuneration ("having the upper hand" and "having the lower hand") to which, in the opin-ion of subsequent commentators, the Talmudic account of Rav's case refers. These different measures are tied to the suitability of the property to the activity of the improver. As section 3 then outlines, the notion of suitability was the basis of the earliest conception in Jewish law of what we would term "incontrovertible benefit." The basic idea was that the owner of a field that was suitable for planting trees could be compelled to pay for them on the higher measure because the owner would not be averse to having the field brought to its optimal use. This idea depended on interpreting Rav's case as involving a field that was not suitable for trees. Section 4 outlines the collapse of this interpretation of Rav's case in favor of the view that, regardless of whether the field was or was not suitable for planting trees, owners retained their liberty to reject the improvement. Nonetheless, simultaneous with this collapse, a different basis for incontrovertible benefit arose, from which modern commentators derived two different conceptions of the conditions under which the owner could not reject an improvement. Section 5 discusses these different conceptions. Finally, section 6 offers some brief concluding reflections.

2. The measures of remuneration

Rav's case appears in a section of the Talmud, extending less than twenty lines, that deals with unrequested improvements. The section discusses two situations in which the improver acts for the owner's benefit but without the owner's permission. In the first, the improver plants trees in another's field, and the Talmud discusses the quantum that the owner is to pay for this improvement. In the second, the improver rebuilds another's dilapidated structure, and the Talmud discusses the improver's right to remove his materials. Rav's case is the final element in the discussion of the first of these situations.

The Talmud's conclusion in the first situation is that the amount to be paid by the owner depends on whether the field was "suitable for the planting of trees."[9] Where trees are a more profitable use of the field than the crops that otherwise would be there, the improver is entitled to a higher level of remuneration. Rav formulated the different levels of remuneration in terms of whether the improver had "the upper hand" or "the lower hand."[10] What precisely he meant by this was a matter of dispute among subsequent commentators.

---

[9] Babylonian Talmud, Baba Mezia, 101a.
[10] Ibid.

By the Middle Ages the most accepted view was as follows.[11] The practice was that persons who were employed by others to plant on their behalf were paid a proportion, determined by local custom, of the appreciation in the yield produced by their efforts. The unrequested improver, of course, had not been employed by the owner. Nonetheless, if the field was suitable for trees, the improver got either his expenses or the customary share of the yield, whichever was greater. By being entitled to the more advantageous of these alternative measures of remuneration, the improver "had the upper hand."

The reason for this treatment of a field that was suitable for trees is that the planting of trees brought the field to its optimal use. Accordingly, the improver did what the owner would have done in any case, and therefore the owner can be treated as if he wanted the trees planted. To arrive at the improver's remuneration, "one assesses how much a man would give to have this field planted."[12] Such an owner would have been willing to allot to the improver a share of the yield in accordance with the usual practice of the locality. Moreover, if the planter's expenditures exceeded his prospective share of the yield, the owner would have at least reimbursed those expenditures; otherwise the trees would not have been planted, because the improver would not have agreed to do it at a loss.[13] Therefore, once one treats the owner as desiring the improvement, the improver becomes entitled to

---

[11] Rashi (Rabbi Solomon Yitzhaki, France, 11th century) on "gilita adaatech deniha lach," Babylonian Talmud, Baba Mezia 101a; Ramban (Rabbi Moses ben Nahman, Spain, 13th century), *Milhamot HaShem* on Baba Mezia 101a; Rosh (Rabbi Asher ben Yehiel, Spain, 14th century) on Baba Mezia, chapter 8, 22. This view was described by Rashba, who disagreed with it (see below n. 17), as held by most of the commentators; Rashba (Rabbi Solomon ben Abraham Adret, Spain, 13th century), *Hiddushei HaRashba* on Baba Mezia 101a. Rabbi Joshua ben Alexander HaKohen Falk (Poland, 16th–17th century), *Sefer Meirat Einayim*, on Shulhan Aruch 375, n. 7 summed up the view as follows: "Know that according to the opinion of Rashi and the Rosh in several places that 'he has the upper hand' means that if the appreciation exceeds the expenditure he takes part of the appreciation like the other planters in the city, and if the expenditure exceeds the appreciation, he takes all the expenditure even though the owner got no benefit from it." There were many controversies concerning the details of this and similar approaches. What distinguishes these approaches from the minority view mentioned below at 239 is that they involve a comparison of expenditure and appreciation. *Encyclopedia Talmudit*, v. 23 s.v. "Yored lenichsei haveiro shelo midaato," chapter 2, gives a catalogue of the various interpretations.

[12] Samuel's formulation of the improver's remuneration in Babylonian Talmud, Baba Mezia 101a.

[13] Falk, *Sefer Meirat Einayim*, above n. 11, observes about Rav's award of the upper hand to the improver: "If he had not planted the field, the owner himself would have planted it and expended this amount on it."

the expenses or the planter's customary share of the appreciation, whichever is the greater.

If the field is not suitable for planting trees, the situation is different. Although the owner has benefited, the trees do not represent the optimal use of the field, so that the reason for treating the owner as wanting the improvement falls away. All that remains is the benefit itself, which is valued as the lesser of the cost of creating it and the appreciation that accrues from it. On the one hand, the value transferred from improver to owner is the value of the efforts expended in improving the property. On the other hand, the improver's expenditure does not enrich the owner beyond the appreciation in the yield; indeed, if the improver could charge the owner for expenses that exceed the value that his efforts added to the yield, he would be impoverishing rather than enriching the owner. Accordingly, the increase in the yield's value functions as a ceiling in the calculation of the quantum of the benefit received by the owner from the improver. Hence, the classic explanation of what it means for the improver to have the lower hand is that "if the appreciation is greater than the expenditure, he gets the expenditure, and if the expenditure is greater than the appreciation he gets no more than the appreciation."[14]

For improvements to non-agricultural properties such as buildings, where the notion of a yield was not relevant, the notional comparison of expenditure and appreciation worked in a slightly different way. Having the lower hand gave the improver the lesser of the expenditure and the increased value of the property.[15] However, the improver who had the upper hand was entitled to what the owner would have paid to have the work done, even if this exceeded the increase in the value of the property. The difference between the lower and the upper hand is that in the former the appreciation set the upper limit of the improver's remuneration, whereas in the latter improvers were entitled to the cost of the improvement without limit.[16]

Thus, the accepted view of the contrast between the improver's having the lower hand and having the upper hand involves a difference in the principle on which the remuneration is assessed. When

[14] Rashi on "yado al hatahtona," Babylonian Talmud, Baba Mezia 101a.

[15] The same rule is mentioned by the Roman jurist Celsus in his treatment of inadvertent improvements; Justinian, *Digest*, 6.1.38 (Celsus).

[16] Alfasi (Rabbi Isaac Alfasi, Morocco, 11th century) *Sefer HaHalachot* on Baba Mezia 101a; Rabbi Yosef Haviva (Spain, 15th century), *Nimukei Yosef*, on Alfasi, *Sefer HaHalachot* on Baba Mezia 101a.

the improver has the upper hand, the assessment is quasi-contractual. Because the improvement moves the property to its optimal use and is thereby equated to one that the owner desires, the assessment is based on a reconstruction of what the owner would have agreed to pay an improver to achieve the desired improvement. In contrast, when the improver has the lower hand, the assessment is restitutionary. Because the planting of trees benefits the owner without moving the property to its optimal use, the confidence in the owner's desire for the improvement is absent. What matters then is not what the owner would have agreed to pay, but rather the value of the benefit that was transferred to the owner through the improver's efforts.

Some commentators in the Middle Ages found the accepted interpretation of the upper hand implausible regardless of whether the expenditure or the appreciation was greater.[17] If the share of the appreciation was greater than the improver's expenses, the accepted view, by giving him the customary share of the appreciation, treated him like a person who had been hired to plant the trees. But this, so the objection went, treated a non-consensual transaction as if it were a consensual one. Moreover, giving the improver more than he expended meant that what the improver received exceeded the benefit that was attributable to him.[18] On the other hand, awarding the improver his expenses, no matter how large they were, even if those expenses exceeded the appreciation in the yield's value, would also entail having the owner pay for more than he benefited. The most that could be awarded to the improver is the expenses up to the value of the appreciation, since anything above that is a loss that the improver inflicted on himself.[19] The accepted view of the upper hand, in other words, remunerated the improver on a contractual measure despite the non-existence of a contract, while failing properly to measure the benefit that was the basis of the improver's claim.

---

[17] Rezah (Rabbi Zerahia Halevi Gerondi, France, 12th century), *Hamaor Hagadol,* on Alfasi, *Sefer HaHalachot* on Baba Mezia 101a; Rashba, *Hiddushei HaRashba* on Baba Mezia 101a; see also Rabbi Yosef Karo (Israel, 16th century), *Beit Yosef,* Hoshen Mishpat 375, 3.

[18] As Rashba puts it, above n. 11, "[on the standard view] the owner gives him what the planters of the city get, meaning, even more than the expenditure; this view is surprising, for on what basis will the owner give the improver more than the latter has benefited him?" Rashba is presumably assuming that the enrichment that the improver can claim consists only in the amount that quantifies his efforts, not in a share of the yield's appreciation, since the yield belongs to the owner unless he freely parts with it.

[19] Rezah, above n. 17.

Instead these commentators suggested a different view of the contrast between having the upper and the lower hand. What mattered for them was not the comparison of expenditure and appreciation, but different ways of measuring the expenditure:

The meaning of 'he has the upper hand' is as in the superior kind of hiring, when a man says to his fellow, 'Build on this land of mine, or plant this field of mine, so that I myself won't have to bother with it,' for this certainly is of conspicuous benefit to him. And the meaning of 'he has the lower hand' is as with the inferior kind of hiring, when the inferior workers treat it cheaply.[20]

The owner for whose field the planting of trees is the optimal use can be presumed to want the work done and to be willing to hire a more able contractor and pay him at a high rate to have the planting properly executed. The owner benefits by being spared the trouble of attending to this desired project himself; in particular he does not have to bother with bringing in various workmen to attend to the various stages of the work.[21] In contrast, the owner for whose field the planting of trees is not optimal would be satisfied to have it done at the minimal cost using the cheapest labor. The benefit consists simply in having someone put trees where there were none before. Thus, according to this view the benefit received by the owner varies with the kind of field he has. With respect to both kinds of field, the analysis is oriented to the enrichment that accrued to the owner, and the amount of the remuneration is conceptualized in what we would consider to be restitutionary terms.

We can now return to Rav's case and set it into its Talmudic context. The Talmud introduces the case to show Rav's view of the remuneration to be paid to the improver. Immediately before the Talmud's account of the incident, the Talmud mentions an apparent dispute between Rav and his contemporary Samuel with respect to the unsolicited planting of trees. Rav had said that the planter has the lower hand, whereas Samuel had said that the planter receives what the

---

[20] Ibid.
[21] As Ritva (Rabbi Yom Toi ben Abraham Ishvili, Spain, 14th century) explained in glossing Rezah's idea, "One estimates how much a person would be willing to pay to someone who will undertake to do this as a single project, so that the owners will not have to bother with it by arranging for workmen to come and go; for a person would gladly pay a lot of money for this." Ritva, *Hiddushei HaRitva* on Baba Mezia 101a.

owner would have been willing to pay to have the field planted. The Talmud then cites an opinion that these sages do not disagree; their stated views simply apply to different kinds of fields: Rav's statement applies to a field not suitable for planting, whereas Samuel's statement applies to a field suitable for planting. That Rav does not disagree with Samuel is inferred from the incident that came before him, where Rav envisages two measures of remuneration, the lower hand that the Talmud had previously attributed to him and the upper hand that is equivalent to the view attributed to Samuel. In dealing with the tree-planting, Rav makes three interventions. He first orders remuneration but without specifying its measure, to which the owner replies that he does not want the improvement. He then orders remuneration with the improver having the lower hand, which is the measure appropriate to a field that is not suitable for planting. The owner then repeats his insistence that he does not want the improvement. Finally, when Rav notices that the owner, by fencing and guarding the trees, has demonstrated that he wants them despite his earlier denials, Rav tells him to remunerate the improver with the improver having the upper hand—that is, at the higher level appropriate to a field suitable for planting.

3. Incontrovertible benefit

The special significance of a field that is suitable for planting is reminiscent of the common law's notion of an incontrovertible benefit. An incontrovertible benefit is one that would not have been declined even if the owner would have had the opportunity to choose.[22] For the determination of whether an improvement is incontrovertible, the nature of the improved property and the necessary or optimal use of it are relevant.[23] Jewish law takes the suitability of a field for the planting of trees as paradigmatic of optimal use; what is necessary to produce this optimal use then becomes the measure of the improver's remuneration, as the party who "has the upper hand."

To equate the field's suitability for trees with the incontrovertibility of the benefit at common law would, however, be premature. The

[22] Regional Municipality of Peel v. Her Majesty the Queen in Right of Canada [1993] 98 D.L.R. (4th) 140, 156 (S.C.C.).

[23] LAC Minerals v. International Corona Resources Ltd. [1989] 61 D.L.R. (4th) 14, 53 (S.C.C., per LaForest J.): "on the assumption that Corona had acquired the Williams property, it would of necessity have had to develop the mine."

incontrovertibility of the benefit goes to the owner's liability to make restitution of an unrequested benefit. In contrast, our discussion of the kinds of field has gone not to the owner's liability but to the measurement of the improver's remuneration. To this point the upper hand and the lower hand function merely as default rules for quantifying what the improver receives for the improvement. Whether the owner can be legally compelled to pay is another issue.

In the Jewish legal literature this issue arises in the following way. The short Talmudic section on unrequested improvements deals with two problems. The first is the remuneration of the person who plants trees without the owner's permission. The second is whether a person who reconstructs a dilapidated building without the owner's position can change his mind and remove his materials. The answer that the Talmud gives is that the improver can remove building materials from a structure but not trees from a field.[24] There are two reasons for this. The first, applicable only to the land of Israel, is that the special value of settling the land would be undermined by removing the trees. The second is that because trees are nourished by the earth, removing them would weaken the owner's soil. But what if it is the owner, not the improver, who wants the trees or the building materials removed? Can the owner reject the improvement by telling the improver to take his materials and go? The Talmudic text does not explicitly deal with this issue.

In the absence of explicit treatment, post-Talmudic commentators looked to the implications of the Rav story. Two features of this story attracted their attention. First, Rav told the owner to "go and make an assessment for him and he shall have the lower hand."[25] This mention of the lower hand indicates that the field in question was not suitable for planting trees. Second, when the owner then repeated his statement that he did not want the improvement, Rav did nothing in the face of this apparent defiance until the owner revealed his true sentiments by fencing and guarding the trees. From Rav's failure to compel the owner to obey him, commentators concluded that, so far as that particular field was concerned, the owner was within his rights to refuse the improvement, at least until his conduct contradicted his professed rejection.

---

[24] Babylonian Talmud, Baba Mezia 101b.
[25] Above n. 1.

Having thus determined that the field was not suitable for planting trees and that no obligation to pay arose from an improvement to such a field, the commentators reconstructed the various stages in the Rav incident as follows.[26] When the case was brought to Rav initially, he did not know whether the field was suitable for planting or not. He accordingly required an assessment without indicating whether the improver was to have the upper or the lower hand. When the owner declared that he did not want the trees, Rav inferred that the owner was unwilling to pay on the higher measure for having trees planted in a field that was not suitable for that use. Rav therefore told him that he should pay only on the lower measure, as was appropriate for a field not suitable for trees. The owner then repeated his assertion that he did not want the trees. Rav interpreted this as implicitly requiring the improver to remove the trees. Thus, Rav's inaction in the face of the owner's statement led to the conclusion that the owner of a field that was unsuitable for trees could require the improver to remove the improvement. Subsequently, by fencing in and guarding the trees, the owner revealed that he did want them after all. This expression of the owner's desire allowed the field to be treated as if it was one that was suitable for planting. Rav accordingly ordered him to pay for the trees on the higher measure.

Accordingly, on this interpretation, the owner could refuse to accept the trees if the field was not suitable for that use. Although the trees might well be a benefit from an objective point of view, the freedom of the owner of such a field to assert that he preferred not to have them was untrammeled.

The converse, however, also obtained. This interpretation emphasized that the field in Rav's case was not suitable for planting. Had the field been suitable for that purpose, the owner would not have been able to refuse the trees and would have had to pay for them on the higher measure. Just as Rav finally compelled the owner who fenced and guarded the trees to pay, with the improver having the upper hand, so the owner of a suitable field could be forced to accept and pay on the higher measure for trees planted without his authorization.

It is worth emphasizing the radical nature of this conclusion from the standpoint of the common law. Common lawyers are familiar

---

[26] Ramban, *Hiddushei HaRamban* on Baba Mezia 101a; Rashba, above n. 11; *Nimukei Yosef*, above n. 16; Ritva, above n. 21.

with—and often troubled by—cases where the owner is made to pay for an improvement by someone who mistakenly thought he owned the object improved.[27] This interpretation of Rav's case, however, imposes on the owner an obligation to remunerate the improver who knowingly plants trees in another's field, provided that the field is suitable for planting. The improver in Rav's case did not make a mistake of title or of any other kind.[28]

This contrast between the common law and Jewish law reflects differing premises about the volunteer. The common law views a person who improves property that he or she knows belongs to another as a volunteer who is making a gift. The improver's expectation of remuneration merely indicates that in bestowing this gift, the improver is also taking the risk that the owner will pay for it. The common law sees no reason to reverse the gift or reallocate the risk through an award of restitution.[29] Because the improver knows that only owners have the right to determine the condition of what they own, the improver is taken to know that the improvement cannot obligate the owner to pay for it. Hence the improvement counts as nothing more than a donative act. However, when the benefit is conferred by mistake, the argument that the improver was acting with donative intent evaporates. Then the issue becomes whether it is truly a violation of the recipient's freedom to compel payment and thus to treat the recipient as accepting the benefit. When considered as an incontrovertible benefit, for example, the improvement is one where—given the nature of the property, its necessary or optimal uses, or the owner's plans for it—the owner can be viewed as having every reason consistent with his or her own autonomy to accept it.[30]

---

[27] Greenwood v. Bennett [1973] 1 Q.B. 195 (C.A.); Gidney v. Shank [1995] 5 W.W.R. 385 (Man. Q.B.), reversed [1996] 2 W.W.R. 383 (Man. C.A.); Matthews, "Freedom, Unrequested Improvements, and Lord Denning," (1981) Cambridge L.J. 340.

[28] Moreover, the liability obtains even where Jewish law sees no difficulty in detaching the improvement from the improved property. The Talmud itself indicates that building materials can be detached from a reconstructed building, at least at the instance of the builder. Nonetheless, on the argument to this point, if the ruined building had been suitable for reconstruction, the owner would be legally compelled to remunerate the stranger for restoring the building. Compare the suggestion of Richard Sutton that the owner should owe restitution if he or she could have allowed the improver to remove the improvement; Sutton, "What Should be Done for Mistaken Improvers?," in *Essays on Restitution*, ed. Paul Finn (1996), 252–54.

[29] Birks, above n. 2, 101–3; Graham Virgo, *The Principles of the Law of Restitution*, 2nd ed. (2006), 39–40.

[30] Incontrovertible benefit is usually understood as negating the possibility of subjective devaluation by the defendant and thus going to the existence of the enrichment; Birks, above n. 2, 116. My account here varies from this understanding for reasons set out in chapter 6.

In contrast, Jewish law does not assume that the improver who knowingly acts on another's property does so with donative intent. "We do not say that simply because he went down into another's field, his intention was just to give a gift."[31] The general principle relevant to all unrequested benefits is that "if any person does an action or benefit for another, one cannot say to him that 'you did it for me gratuitously because I did not ask you to do it,' but one must give him his remuneration."[32] The person who planted the trees did so in order to get paid by the owner.[33] Jewish law treats this as a purpose worth giving effect to. Rather than disqualifying him as a volunteer or an officious intermeddler, the improver's knowing operation on another's property is the basis of his claim, which is inescapable (on the present interpretation of the Rav story) when the property is suitable for the improvement.

In this context both the common law and Jewish law are individualistic, but they exhibit different conceptions of individualism.[34] For the common law, the individualism resides in the institution of property and in the juridical construction of the social understandings to which property gives rise. Because the improver can be taken to know that only owners have the right to change the condition of their property, the improver is understood as giving a gift and, accordingly, is not eligible for restitution. For Jewish law, the individualism resides in giving effect to the improver's non-altruistic motivation. In the absence of evidence of a donative intent, improvers are treated as forwarding their own self-interested purposes.

From the standpoint of the common law, the approach of Jewish law has a paradoxical implication. Whereas for the common law the improver's knowledge of another's ownership weakens the improver's case, for Jewish law this knowledge strengthens it. The improver's claim to be remunerated on the higher measure presupposes that the improver has acted to improve another's land, for only if the improver's intention was to have another pay for his work can he be paid what (in Samuel's words) "a man would give to have this field

---

[31] Rashba, *Hiddushei HaRashba* on Nedarim 33b.

[32] Rema (Rabbi Moses Isserles, Poland, 16th century), *Shulhan Aruch* on Hoshen Mishpat 264, 4.

[33] Ramban, *Milhamot HaShem* on Baba Batra 4b.

[34] For a provocative comparison of Jewish and American law in another restitutionary context, see Hanoch Dagan, *Unjust Enrichment: A Study of Private Law and Public Values* (1997), 50–57, 109–29.

planted."[35] Accordingly, if he mistakenly thought that he was working his own land, he can be remunerated only on the lower measure, even if the field is one that was suitable for planting trees.[36]

The absence in Jewish law of the common law notion of a volunteer exposed owners to the possibility that, if their property was suitable for the improvement in question, they would be compelled to pay the improver for effecting it. How could this apparent indifference to the autonomy of owners to determine the use of their own property be justified? This question did not present itself explicitly; for those who interpreted the Rav story to lead to this result, the Talmudic origin of the rule was justification enough. Nonetheless, three general observations are in order.

First, the premise was that, if the field was suitable for planting, the improver was doing something that the owner wanted done. "The person who knowingly improves another's field thinks that the owners are pleased with it."[37] Conversely, the owner has no liability for the improvement if he has warned the improver not to do the work. A ruling to this effect in the thirteenth century included the comment that this was "in order to prevent everybody from forcing someone else to plant and to build."[38] Owners could protect their autonomy over their property by telling improvers that they did not want the contemplated improvement.

Second, some commentators based the higher measure of remuneration on a notion of acquiescence. "Because the field was suitable for planting and the owners knew and kept quiet, it is certain that they were pleased with his work, and he is like a person who made the improvement with their knowledge."[39] When this explanation of

---

[35] Above, n. 12.

[36] Ramban, *Hiddushei HaRamban* on Baba Mezia 40a; Rivash (Rabbi Isaac ben Sheshet, Spain, 14th century), *Responsa of the Rivash*, 515. This resembles the rule in Roman law, that if I improved another's property thinking it was my own, I have no *actio negotiorum gestorum* for reimbursement, "because I did not intend to obligate anyone to me"; *Digest*, 10.3.14.1 (Paulus).

[37] Rivash, *Responsa of the Rivash*, 515.

[38] Rashba, *Responsa of the Rashba*, 4, 54.

[39] Ritva, above n. 21; *Nimukei Yosef*, above n. 16 (cf. also *Nimukei Yosef* on Alfasi, *Sefer HaHalachot* on Baba Batra 4b); Rosh on Baba Batra 7. For a different view of the significance of the owner's silence, see Shalom Albeck, *Dinei Hamamonot Batalmud* (1976), 193. Albeck suggests that the silence operates as a retrospective consent once the owner discovers the improvement. This implies the effectiveness of a protest made against an improvement discovered after being completed, which seems inconsistent with the view of Ritva and *Nimukei Yosef* that the owner can be compelled to accept the improvement if the land is suitable for planting trees.

the improver having the upper hand is combined with the owner's inability to refuse the improvement, the picture that emerges is not unlike the recent suggestion of a common law doctrine of free acceptance.[40] On the one hand, the improver acts (and is assumed by Jewish law to act) not gratuitously but with the expectation of payment. On the other hand, the owner, knowing this and allowing the work to proceed without protest, cannot subsequently treat the improvement as undesired, especially since the improvement is consonant with the optimal use of the property. This notion of acquiescence can be regarded as an extension of the owner's power to warn away the potential improver: because at any moment the owner's protest puts an end to the potential improver's claim, omission to make the protest can be construed as free acceptance of the improvement.[41]

Third, because liability is not confined to situations where "the owners knew and kept quiet,"[42] a more comprehensive basis for liability must be postulated. The common law notion of incontrovertible benefit is a formulation, applicable to Jewish law, of this more comprehensive basis. Given that liability depends on the status of the land as suitable for planting trees, the improvement must be regarded as a benefit that the improver has no reason not to accept. By bringing the land to its optimal use, the improver has done what the owner wants done and, accordingly, what the owner cannot repudiate when done by another. It is not merely that the improver has made the owner better off in some general way; if that were all that were necessary, owners on this reading of the Rav story would be liable—as they are not—for improvements even to land that was not suitable for planting trees. Rather, the land's suitability for trees frames the legal construction of what owners can be assumed to want. By differentiating their wealth into specific pieces of property that have particular characteristics, owners can be regarded as signaling the terms on which they are prepared to accept improvements. Thus, although one cannot conclude that they are willing to remunerate an improver for producing

---

[40] Birks, above n. 2, 277–79; Peter Birks, "In Defence of Free Acceptance," in *Essays in the Law of Restitution*, ed. Andrew Burrows (1991), 105.

[41] Writing several centuries later than the authorities mentioned in n. 39 above and without referring to those texts, Maharit (Rabbi Yosef of Trani, Turkey, 17th century), *Responsa of the Maharit*, I, 106, denied that an owner could incur liability for an unsolicited improvement by knowing about it and keeping quiet. He contended that, unlike fencing and guarding, silence does not constitute a manifestation of the owner's view that he is pleased with the improvement.

[42] Above, n. 39.

general increases in their wealth (such increases might take forms incompatible with owners' specific projects), having property of a certain sort can be taken to indicate their willingness to have this property developed in accordance with its optimal use. An improvement consonant with the specific nature of a piece of property is a benefit that the law assumes the owner has no reason to reject. On this view, the nature of the property itself indicates what the owner of the property wants and is willing to pay for, thereby supposedly reconciling the owner's freedom of choice with the improver's entitlement to remuneration.

An example of such reasoning appears in a responsum of the early seventeenth century.[43] The author is commenting on the view of an earlier authority that, whereas the owner of a field suitable for planting trees could be compelled to accept the improvement, the owner of a dilapidated structure that was suitable for building could not.[44] He finds the argument in the earlier authority convoluted,[45] but he suggests that the distinction between an improved field and an improved structure might be supported in a more straightforward way:

Even the commentators who differed about whether we listen to the owner of a field suitable for planting when he says 'Take your trees and go' can acknowledge that we do listen to the owner of a house even though it is suitable for rebuilding. And the reason for this is that in the case of a field suitable for planting trees it is well known that a field of trees is worth more than a field of grain, and an unplanted field is available for being

---

[43] Maharit, above n. 41.

[44] *Nimukei Yosef*, above n. 16.

[45] The convoluted argument in the *Nimukei Yosef* is based on three elements. The first is that the implication of Rav's case is that the owner of a field suitable for planting trees cannot refuse the improvement but the owner of a non-suitable field can. The second is the Talmud's explicit statement at Baba Mezia 101b that the improver can remove his materials in the case of a building but not in the case of a field. The third is that the early post-Talmudic Babylonian academies were of the view that there was reciprocity between the owner and the improver, in that the owner can have the materials removed in any situation in which the improver can have them removed. From this the *Nimukei Yosef* argued that it followed from the first of these considerations that issue of removal mentioned by the Talmud applied only to properties that were suitable for the improvements (since we know from Rav's case that owners could have improvements removed from properties that were not suitable); that it further followed from the second and third of these considerations that the owner can have the improvement removed only in the case of suitable buildings but not of suitable fields; and that it further followed from the first of these considerations, that such removal could apply even to buildings that were suitable for rebuilding, but not to fields that were suitable for planting trees.

planted with trees, and because the improvers have made the field more valuable, one needs to give restitution for this surplus. But in the case of courtyards and fields, even if they are suitable for building, nonetheless not every person is ready to squander his wealth and to busy himself with buildings, which impoverish their owners, as the Talmud says, 'Repair and you will not have to rebuild.'[46]

The difference is that improving a field by planting trees in it is an unequivocal benefit, but improving a dilapidated structure involves a commitment to continuing efforts and expenditures that the owner might not want. Fields thus signal the acceptability of improvements in a way that buildings do not.

In sum, Rav's case was initially interpreted as allowing the owner of the field to repudiate the improvement only if the field was not suitable for the planting of trees. It was because Rav was dealing with a field of this sort that the owner could with impunity declare that he did not want the improvement, even after Rav had told him to pay on the lower measure. The owner, however, would have been compelled to remunerate the improver if the field had been suitable for trees. In this liability of the owner one can discern the Jewish equivalent of the common law notion of incontrovertible benefit.

4. The demise and rebirth of incontrovertible benefit

Although this interpretation of Rav's case attempts to bring the improver's claim for remuneration into harmony with the owner's freedom of choice, the truth is that the optimal use of the field can serve only as a rough surrogate for the desires of the owner. It is easy to imagine cases in which planting trees in a field used for grains interferes with the owner's autonomy, even though it increases the owner's wealth. The owner may be leading a life that is interwoven with the field's unimproved state: he may want to feed himself and his family with grain grown by his own hands, or he may be knowledgeable about growing grain but not about managing trees, or he may simply

---

[46] The reference is to Babylonian Talmud, Yevamot 63a: "Rav Papa said: '. . . Plug the hole and you will not have to repair; repair and you will not have to rebuild; for whoever engages in building becomes poor.'"

be unable to afford the improvement.[47] Thus, although non-optimal, the particular use may satisfactorily match his particular projects, which would be disrupted by the obligation to accept the improvement imposed by a stranger. If the owner could not reject the improvement, "it would turn out that any person could compel another to transform his field into an orchard and his courtyard into buildings."[48]

In the fourteenth century, Rosh, a leading authority in Jewish law, proposed a different interpretation of Rav's case that avoided this result.[49] As we have seen, the accepted view until then was that Rav was dealing with a field that was not suitable for planting, as is indicated by his ordering the owner to pay on the lower measure; the fact that Rav did not react to the owner's assertion that he nonetheless did not want that improvement led to the inference that the owner of a field not suitable for trees could not be compelled to pay the improver. Rosh contended that this reading of the incident was mistaken.

Rosh made two interpretive arguments. The first argument noted that Rav twice told the owner to pay, not specifying the measure of remuneration the first time and specifying the lower measure the second time. If the field was one that was not suitable for planting, the first order would have implied remuneration on the lower measure, thus making the second order a pointless repetition of the first. In Rosh's view, the field in question was one that was indeed suitable for planting trees, and the owner had the right, even for such a field, to refuse the improvement. When Rav told the owner to pay on the lower measure, he was not implying that the field was not suitable for planting. He was merely saying that "if the owner acquiesces in the improvement, let him pay the improver so much."[50] In other words, Rosh thought that Rav was merely proposing a settlement that might appeal to both parties: to the owner, because he would be getting the improvement for which his field was suited at a lower price than if he employed someone to plant the trees, and to the improver because he would get something for the trees instead of having to remove them.

---

[47] These examples are taken from Rabbi Abraham Karelitz (1878–1953), *Hazon Ish*, Hoshen HaMishpat, Baba Batra 2, 3.

[48] Maharit, above n. 41 and Rabbi Yosef Karo, *Beit Yosef*, above n. 17, 375, 2 (citing the students of Rashba).

[49] Rosh (Rabbi Asher ben Yehiel, Spain, 14th century), Baba Mezia 8, 22.

[50] Ibid.

Rosh's second argument noted that after Rav saw that the owner had fenced in and guarded the trees, Rav compelled the owner to pay on the higher measure. This disposition creates a puzzle if one thinks that the field in question was not suitable for planting. Remuneration for planting a non-suitable field should have been on the lower rather than the higher measure. To be sure, the owner's actions can be taken to show that his earlier denial that he wanted the trees was untruthful; but, given that the level of remuneration depends on the status of the land, it is hard to see why the fact that he really does want the trees should change the amount he has to pay for them. If, however, the field was suitable for planting trees (as Rosh thought), then the mystery about the award on the higher measure disappears.

With this transformation of the story, any semblance of liability for an incontrovertible benefit falls away from it. Rav's inaction after the owner repeated that he did not want the improvement shows that an owner could not be compelled to accept an improvement even if that improvement accorded with the optimal use of the property. All that the difference between the upper and the lower hand does is mark the different default measures of remuneration

if the owner is willing to keep the seedlings in his field. But if he is not willing to keep them, he can tell the improver to take his seedlings and go even if the field is suitable for planting trees, for he can say that 'as far as I am concerned, it is more satisfactory for me to have a field of grain'... It makes no sense at all for the owner of the field to have to pay the improver as a hired planter when he does not want the seedlings.[51]

In the story the owner ends up paying on the higher measure, but this is because, having shown through his actions that he wanted to keep the trees, he became liable to pay at the appropriate default level. If he really had not wanted the trees, he could have insisted that the improver remove them even though his field was suitable for planting. Rosh thus sees the story as reflecting the unbridled freedom of the owner to determine the use of his own property. In Rosh's interpretation of the case, what is paramount is the autonomy of the owner, not the status of the land.

Although Rosh's interpretation of Rav's case became the accepted one, it turned out not to be the end of the notion of incontrovertible

[51] Ibid.

benefit in Jewish law. For simultaneously with shutting off this avenue involving the planting of fields, Rosh opened or kept open another involving the building of structures.

Because of the Talmud's omission to deal with the matter expressly, disagreement had arisen among Rosh's predecessors about the right of the owner to refuse an improvement that consisted in the building or rebuilding of a structure, even if this structure was the land's optimal use.[52] This right to refuse the improvement, if it existed, would be expressed by the owner's telling the improver to remove his materials, thus restoring both parties to the position they were in before the improver's activities. One of the strands in this disagreement was the view that the owner had no such right, because building materials lose part of their value by being incorporated into a structure. Accordingly, by ordering the improver to remove his materials, the owner would be harming the improver rather than merely restoring the status quo.[53]

This disagreement stands in the background of Rosh's treatment of the owner's right to refuse the improvement. So far as fields were concerned, Rosh championed the view that even if the field was suitable for planting trees, owners did not have to keep the trees if they did not want them. Structures, however, were different from trees. In the case of trees, the Talmud had ruled that the improver could not remove his trees, because once they received nutriments from the earth, their

---

[52] For one facet of this disagreement, see above n. 44.

[53] Ravad (Rabbi Abraham ben David, France, 12th century), Comments on Alfasi, *Sefer HaHalachot* on Baba Mezia 101a, in *Shitah Mekubetzet* on Baba Mezia 101a. The Talmud had dealt expressly only with the instance of the improver who wanted to remove his materials; it had been silent about whether the owner could order the materials removed. The rule stated in the Talmud was that the improver could remove his materials in the case of a structure but not in the case of a field; above, n. 24. The early post-Talmudic Babylonian academies were of the view that whatever rule about removal applied to the improver also applied to the owner, with the result that the owner of the structure could order the improver to remove the materials; but see above n. 45. Ravad contested this view. The controversy is summed up by Ravad's follower Meiri (Rabbi Menahem ben Solomon, France, 13th century) as follows:

The Talmud does not mention what the rule is if the owner of the land tells the improver to take his wood and stones. The heads of the academies agreed to treat the improver and the owner equally, and because the improver can say 'I am taking my wood and stones,' so the owner can say 'Take your trees and stones.' Nonetheless, the greatest of the commentators disagree with this, because in the latter case there is a great loss. When the improver says 'I am taking my wood and stones,' we listen to him because he is waiving his loss. But in the case of an owner who says 'Take your wood', it is appropriate to say that we do not listen to him but we allow the improver to occupy the structure until the owner reimburses his expenses or gives him what we assess for him.

removal would weaken the owner's soil.[54] This ruling does not apply to the owner's requesting the removal of the trees, because the owner can decide to accept the weakening of his own soil. Nor is this weakening something about which the improver can complain; the improver gets his trees back unimpaired. However, the situation is reversed if the improvement involves building materials. In this case it is the improver who suffers from the depreciation of his materials. If the improver wishes to remove the materials and accept this loss, the owner cannot complain—which perhaps accounts for the Talmud's ruling that improvers can remove building materials but not trees. But the owner cannot impose a loss on the improver by requiring the materials to be removed.

Accordingly, Rosh ruled that although owners could not be forced to accept trees, they could be forced to accept structures. However, instead of merely adopting the conclusion that the owner could not require the improver to suffer a loss by removing the building materials, Rosh also outlined the conditions under which this conclusion applied. Rosh was insistent that the consideration of the harm to the improver not be at the expense of harm to the owner. He therefore asserted that the owner is barred from having the improvement removed only if the improvement did not cause him a loss. Thus, commenting on the view that the owner causes a loss by requiring removal of the building materials from a rebuilt ruin, he remarked:

This consideration makes sense where the owner was not using the ruin and he had his own place, because it is appropriate to build a structure like this when it does not impair the owner's livelihood, because [if the owner then requests removal of the materials] he is really seeking a pretext to inflict loss on the improver, and so we do not listen to him.[55]

On the surface Rosh's reasoning seems delictual rather than restitutionary. His reason for preventing the owner from having the materials removed is that the owner cannot gratuitously inflict loss on the improver,[56]

---

[54] Above n. 24.

[55] Rosh, Baba Mezia 8, 23.

[56] Rosh's statement that the owner seeks a pretext to inflict loss on the improver is presumably related to the recognition in Jewish law of a doctrine of abuse of rights. On this doctrine, see Aaron Kirschenbaum, *Equity in Jewish Law: Formalism and Flexibility in Jewish Civil Law* (1991), 185–252.

rather than that the improver is entitled to have the owner give restitution for a benefit. Nonetheless, in this context the delictual cannot be disentangled from the restitutionary. Rosh's formulation sets out what he regards as the conditions in which the owner is not adversely affected by—and therefore cannot complain about—the improvement. Under these conditions, the owner's freedom to determine the use of his own property no longer obtains, and the owner must pay for the improvement on the higher measure. Although the reasoning is not explicitly restitutionary, it has a restitutionary dimension.

This restitutionary dimension reflects the principle implicit in Rosh's formulation. Rosh's view is that owners can be compelled to keep the improvement when it does not leave them worse off than they would otherwise have been. An owner who is left worse off by the improvement could hardly be described as "seeking a pretext to inflict loss on the improver"; by having the materials removed in those circumstances all that the owner would be doing is avoiding his or her own loss. In other words, only if the improvement can be regarded as a benefit that the owner has no reason to reject does the preclusion against inflicting loss on the improver get off the ground. In this way, incontrovertible benefit, which was expelled in Rosh's account of trees, returns in his treatment of buildings.

5. Two conceptions of incontrovertible benefit

But what counts as an incontrovertible benefit in Rosh's line of reasoning? Given that Rosh holds that planting trees in a suitable field does not obligate the owner to pay for the improvement, incontrovertible benefit can no longer refer to the optimal use of the property. What sort of benefit, then, is implicit in Rosh's thinking? Modern authorities who have addressed this question have offered a restrictive and an expansive suggestion.

The restrictive suggestion appears in the codification of Rabbi Yehiel Michal HaLevi Epstein.[57] The owner could not refuse a benefit

where the court sees that it is necessary for the builder to build in this place according to the owner's circumstances and the circumstances of the city,

---

[57] Rabbi Yehiel Michal HaLevi Epstein (Poland, 1829–1908), *Aruch HaShulhan*, Hoshen Mishpat (1892), 375, 10–16.

and the owner himself would have built there, and the builder built it properly, in a way that the owner himself would not have improved upon.[58]

The benefit must be accepted only when the improver merely anticipates what the owner necessarily and inevitably would have done. This consideration is independent of the optimal use of the property. An owner can tell the improver to remove trees planted even in a field suitable for trees, because it is always possible that the owner prefers to grow grain.[59] The fact that the field is suitable for trees does not make trees necessary. As long as the owner can plausibly point to some other use for the property than the one exemplified by the improvement, the improvement can be rejected. Epstein thus allows the improver to interfere with the owner's freedom to determine the use of the property only when that interference matches what the owner would do in any case.

Epstein illustrates the distinction between necessary and unnecessary improvements with a responsum authored by Rosh himself. This instructive responsum is worth quoting almost in full:[60]

Reuben owned some houses, but travelled away from his city. Simeon came and lived in them and saw that the house was tottering and about to collapse. He reconstructed it and reinforced it and saved it from the danger of falling and plastered and paneled it. When Reuben returned, he wanted to evict Simeon from his house, saying that his initial entry was unauthorized. Does Reuben have to reimburse Simeon ...? Answer: Because it was tottering and close to collapsing, Reuben cannot evict him until he reimburses all the expenditures that Simeon made to reinforce the house and save it from collapsing, but what Simeon built that was not necessary, like making rooms and plastering and paneling, he did for his own benefit, and

---

[58] Ibid., 11. By "the circumstances of the owner" Epstein means that the owner has to be able to afford the improvement. If the owner does not have the resources to pay for the improvement, the owner can require the improver either to remove the materials (ibid., 12) or to buy the property at its pre-improved value (ibid., 14–15). By "the circumstances of the city" Epstein means that the building has to be conform to the "useful building appropriate to that courtyard as is the custom of that place." Maimonides, (Egypt, 12th century) *Mishneh Torah*, Laws of Robbery and Loss, 10, 6; Rabbi Joseph Karo, *Shulhan Aruch*, Hoshen Mishpat, 375, 7.

[59] Epstein, above n. 57.

[60] The responsum is available in the work of Rosh's son, Rabbi Jacob ben Asher, *Tur Hoshen Mishpat*, 375.

Reuben does not have to pay him for that but he tells him 'Take your wood and your stones,' and this assessment will be according to builders who will determine what Simeon had to expend to avoid the house's collapse, and they will assess him, and when Reuben gives this to Simeon, then Simeon will vacate Reuben's house.

The questioner asked further, Let our rabbi teach us: why do we not take into account the usefulness of the construction apart from the danger of collapse, especially since the houses had previously been plastered, and beneath the plaster the wall was mouldy and tottering, and Simeon had to destroy the plaster in order to fix the wall, and he fixed it to its previous state, and he fixed gates and windows and leaky roofs and locks? The answer: For any construction that is not to deal with the danger that the building could not continue to exist and remain standing and be kept from collapsing out of decay, why should we obligate the owner to pay? He can say, 'I do not want to spend my money on it, because the house could continue to exist without this construction. If you built it for your benefit, take your wood and your stones.'

This responsum draws a sharp distinction between the existence and the condition of the improved object. One cannot be sure that the owner wants a change in an object's condition, even if the improvement restores the object to the previous condition from which it deteriorated. The fact that the house had previously been plastered and that the plaster had to be removed to save the house from collapsing does not mean that the improver can charge the owner for replastering. The owner is therefore free to insist that the improver undo this aspect of the renovation, even though, since plaster cannot be reused, this causes the improver a loss. However, the owner can be compelled to pay for those aspects of the renovation that preserved the house. This benefit is incontrovertible, so that it would be abusive for the owner to make its conferral the reason for harming the improver. As Epstein remarks in glossing the responsum:

The court determines whether it was necessary for the owner to do this, and makes an assessment for him with the improver having the upper hand, because although the improvement was without authorization, the improver nonetheless conferred a benefit on him, and so why should he suffer a loss?[61]

⁶¹ Epstein, *Aruch HaShulhan*, 375, 12.

Rosh, and Epstein following him, think that one can safely ascribe to owners a desire to have their properties preserved, so that then they have no legitimate reason to harm improvers by compelling the removal of the materials. Because the owner necessarily realizes a benefit from the preservation of the property, the improver is entitled to be reimbursed for the expenses entailed in achieving that end. This responsum shows that, although in the case of structures Rosh did not nullify the notion of incontrovertible benefit (as he did in the case of trees), he narrowed the basis for the improver's claim to circumstances in which the interference with the owner's freedom of choice is not significant, because the owner is merely paying for work that in any case had to be done if the structure was to be saved from collapsing.

So much for Epstein's narrow construction of incontrovertible benefit. In contrast stands the more expansive view of Rabbi Abraham Karelitz.[62] Karelitz's argument is that the owner must accept and remunerate the improver at the higher level for any improvement that increases the value of the property, unless the owner has a bona fide reason for not accepting it. Whereas Epstein restricts what common lawyers would think of as the benefit's incontrovertibility to what was necessary in the circumstances, Karelitz broadens it to include whatever adds value without genuine inconvenience to the owner.

Karelitz's view of the circumstances under which the improvement must be accepted arises from a reconceptualization of what it means to say that a field is suitable for planting trees. A field is considered suitable for planting not because trees are its optimal use, but because a field with trees is worth more than a field with grain. In his view, the difference between a plantable and non-plantable field is simply a matter of the objectively higher economic value of the former. If the improvement increases the value of the field, the owner is assumed to want the improvement and must remunerate the improver at the higher rate. Similarly, if the owner reveals that he actually wants the improvement—as was the case with the owner who fenced and guarded the trees in the dispute that came before Rav—then the owner must pay on the higher measure even if improvement does not add value to the property. What is decisive is the benefit to the owner, whether that benefit is manifested in the increased value of the property or in conduct revealing the owner's desire for the improvement even though it does not increase the property's value.

[62] Rabbi Abraham Karelitz (1878–1953), *Hazon Ish*, Hoshen HaMishpat, Baba Batra 2, 3.

To this notion of benefit objectively manifested through value or conduct, Karelitz adds an important qualification: an owner who has a bona fide reason for not wanting an improvement that increases the property's value can refuse to pay and can have the materials removed. This qualification too involves an objective inquiry into the circumstances and motivations of the owner. Karelitz would have had little sympathy for the suggestion that the possibility of the owner's subjective devaluation of the benefit immunizes the owner from liability.[63] For Karelitz Jewish law does not, and never did, attach any significance to the owner's rejection of the benefit on the strength of "private reasons of his own."[64] The freedom of the owner to determine the use of his or her property is not absolute; it must reflect a plausible reason for rejecting a benefit that increases the value of the property. "Everything is according to what appears to the eye of the judge, as to whether the increased value is truly not to the benefit of the owner, or whether the owner is just saying so to put the improver off."[65] Karelitz reinterprets even the dispute between Rosh and his predecessors about whether the owner of a plantable field had to accept the trees as involving not a difference of legal principle but a distinction on the facts. Rosh's predecessors, who held that the owner of a field suitable for planting could be compelled to pay for the improvement, were merely referring to a situation where

the owner has no excuse or reason for why he would not want to plant the field, and we see his response 'Take your seedlings' as being merely for the sake of angering the improver, as if to say 'Neither I nor you will get anything,' or as evading payment; but if we see that it is actually the truth that he does not want the seedlings and he wants them uprooted, then we treat him as having field that is not suitable for planting.[66]

Similarly, when Rosh allows the owner to reject the improvements, he is dealing with a situation in which the owner has a genuine reason for preferring his land in an unimproved state.

Karelitz accordingly regards Rosh's statement about the rebuilt ruins[67] as illustrative of these principles. It will be recalled that Rosh

---

[63] Birks, above n. 2.
[64] Karelitz, above n. 62, second para.
[65] Ibid., Baba Kama 22, 6.
[66] Ibid., Baba Batra 2, 3.
[67] Above n. 55.

held that, although the owner generally could have the improvement removed, the owner of a ruin rebuilt without authorization could not order the improver to remove his materials if he was really seeking a pretext to inflict loss on the improver. Karelitz noted that Rosh indicated two circumstances that presented genuine reasons for not wanting the rebuilt structure. The first was that the owner was already using the ruin for something else, so that the pre-existing use could be taken as a manifestation of his genuine desires concerning the property. The second was that the rebuilding impaired his livelihood, which Karelitz interpreted as meaning that the owner could not afford to pay for the improvement. If, however, despite such considerations, the owner moved into the rebuilt ruin and began to live there, this conduct could be taken as a manifestation of his acceptance of the benefit, triggering an obligation to remunerate the improver on the higher measure.[68]

In sum, Jewish law refers to three different conceptions of what common lawyers regard as incontrovertible benefit. The earliest is that the owner can be compelled to accept an improvement that moves the property to its optimal use. This conception was destroyed by Rosh, who held that, regardless of the nature of the property, the owner is at liberty to order the improver to remove the improvement. In qualifying this with the observation that the right to order the removal of building materials cannot be turned into a pretext to cause loss to the improver, Rosh allowed incontrovertible benefit to be reborn. One form of this rebirth was the stringent view that the owner was barred from rejecting the improvement only if the improvement was necessary. The other form was the more liberal view that the owner had to accept any improvement that increased the value of the property, except if the owner had a genuine reason for rejecting it.

---

[68] Karelitz, above n. 62, at 2, 6. Karelitz's view has one additional complexity that I wish merely to mention for the sake of completeness. Having reconceptualized the suitability for planting trees in terms of an increase in the property's value, Karelitz was faced with the difficulty of explaining why the Talmud and the legal tradition to this point distinguished between fields that were or were not suitable for planting trees. For on Karelitz's view what matters ultimately is not the kind of field it is but whether the owner receives a benefit manifested either through value or conduct. Karelitz's solution to this difficulty was that even if the owner did not want the improvement and had genuine reason to reject it, the owner might nonetheless be willing to put up with it. Then whether the field was suitable for planting trees (that is, in Karelitz's view, whether the trees increased the value of the land) would determine the rate of the improver's remuneration; Karelitz, above n. 62, at 3, 4.

6. Conclusion

In this chapter I have traced the main lines in the development of the Jewish law governing unrequested improvements. The point of departure for this development is the story in the Talmud of Rav's dealings with the owner whose field was planted with trees. From this story emerge subsequent discussions of the difference between having the upper and the lower hand, of the significance of an improvement that puts the property to its optimal use, and of the conditions under which the owner could be compelled to accept the benefit.

At first blush, the Talmud's account of the trees planted in another's field and the jurisprudence that flows from it might, from the standpoint of the common law, seem peculiar on a number of grounds. The most important of these is that throughout the Talmudic passage Rav seeks, with eventual success, to have the owner pay for the improvement. In the eye of the common law, this solicitude for the improver seems misplaced. By planting trees in what he knew was another's field, the improver was the most unappealing of restitutionary claimants, a mere volunteer or officious intermeddler. Conversely, the owner should surely be able to determine for himself whether to plant trees in his own field. Right from the beginning Rav's assumption that the owner should be assessed for the trees seems eccentric.

A second peculiarity is that Jewish law gives the knowing improver a preferential position over an innocent one. Only the improver who knows that the property being improved belongs to another can claim remuneration on the higher measure, which under some circumstances gives the improver a share of the yield and under other circumstances allows the improver to recover expenditures in excess of the property's increased value. This is because the basis of such remuneration is what the owner would have paid to have the improvement, a quasi-contractual measure that presupposes that the improver is rendering a service to someone else rather than merely being mistaken about the extent of one's own ownership.

A third peculiarity is that situations in which the materials for the improvement (the trees in the field example, the wood and stones in the building example) can be removed are paradigmatic for the discussion of unsolicited improvements. English law encapsulates its concerns in Chief Baron Pollock's famous question, "One cleans another's shoes; what can the other do but put them on?",[69] because it assumes that the benefit has been irretrievably entangled in the owner's property. Jewish law, in contrast, expresses the owner's rejection of the benefit through the owner's telling the improver to "take your materials and go." In part this reflects the idea that even after the materials have been affixed to the owner's land or structure, the owner acquires property in them only on signaling acceptance of the improvement by offering to pay.[70] More deeply, however, it reflects a commitment to restoring the parties to their positions before the improvement, or at least to preventing the owner from ostensibly rejecting the benefit while continuing to enjoy it. When the Jewish jurists turned their attention to unremovable benefits (the classic example was dyeing someone else's wool), they adopted an approach similar to the one that governed removable ones: the owner had to pay unless there was reason to suppose that the improvement was not in fact a benefit.[71]

Perhaps from the perspective of systems other than the common law, some of these peculiarities might not seem all that eccentric after all. The possibility of removing an enrichment for which the owner is not liable was mentioned by the Roman jurist Celsus in the second century, is present in contemporary German law, and has been suggested for the common law as well.[72]

Be that as it may, the differences between Jewish law and the common law mask an important similarity. Although the particular moves about unrequested improvements in each system diverge, these moves respond to the same challenge. When dealing with unrequested benefits, any rational system of private law must reconcile the owner's freedom to determine the use of his or her property with the improver's claim that the owner should not be unjustly enriched at the improver's expense. As noted in section 1 of this chapter, this in turn requires attention to two issues. The first issue is whether the improvement is a gift from the improver to the owner; if it is, the improver has no reason to complain that the owner's use of it is unjust. The second issue is whether, even assuming that the improvement was not a gift,

---

[69] Taylor v. Laird [1856] 156 E.R. 1203.

[70] Rashba, above n. 11.

[71] Rabbi Jacob Lorbeerbaum (Poland, 1760–1832), *Netivot HaMishpat* on Shulhan Aruch 375; Karelitz, above n. 62, at 2, 6.

[72] Dirk A. Verse, "Improvements and Enrichment: A Comparative Analysis," (1998) Restitution L. Rev. 85, at 88, 102–3.

acceptance of the improvement can reasonably be imputed to the owner; if it can, there is no injustice in compelling the owner to pay the improver. The first of these issues directs us to consider whether the improver has acted with donative intent; the second directs us to consider the conditions under which an unrequested benefit would nonetheless be consistent with the autonomy of owners with respect to their own property. Taken together, these two issues vindicate the corrective justice conception of private law by insisting that, in the transfer of a benefit from the improver to the owner, both its bestowal and its receipt are the expression of the free will of the parties.

The law's treatment of these two issues, although of course based on the specific events of the transaction in question, is a matter not of fact but of juristic construction. It involves not merely ascertaining what happened but working out the relevant legal categories and ascribing meaning in their light to the conduct of the parties. Different legal systems, while addressing the same issues, can nonetheless reasonably differ in their construction of the legal categories, or in the meaning they ascribe to the parties' conduct, or in their understanding of the relationship between conduct and categories.

The contrasting attitudes toward donative intent in the common law and in Jewish law provide a dramatic illustration of this. Both the common law and Jewish law concern themselves with whether a knowing unsolicited improvement is to be construed as a gift, but they elaborate different answers. Because the common law imputes to the parties the awareness that only the owner can determine the use of what is owned, the common law includes the taking of a risk of being remunerated within its conception of the improver's donative intent, with the result that volunteering or intermeddling becomes a fatal obstacle to the improver's claim. Jewish law does not regard the improver as a risk-taker but looks more single-mindedly at the intent or the presumed intent of the improver, who is therefore assumed not to have acted with donative intent. As a result, the only substantial barrier in Jewish law against liability for unrequested improvements is the second issue of determining the conditions under which acceptance of the improvement can reasonably be imputed to the owner.

It is, accordingly, hardly surprising that the Jewish law, over the eighteen centuries of its recorded discussions of unrequested improvements, has on this issue elaborated the variety of views outlined in this chapter. These discussions direct attention either to the optimal use of the property being improved, or to the necessity for the improvement, or to the genuineness of the owner's reason for not welcoming the increase in the property's value. The common law, in contrast, both because of the relative youth of its law of restitution and because of the filtering effect of the issue of volunteering, is only at the beginning of a similar elaboration of its parallel idea of incontrovertible benefit. However, with the intense interest that the law of restitution is now enjoying in the common law world, we common lawyers can perhaps already sympathize with the observations expressed by the distinguished author of a sixteenth-century responsum about unrequested improvements: "I do not have time to go on at length about these matters, because there are many controversies and the questioner is pressing."[73]

---

[73] Maharashdam (Rabbi Samuel de Medina, Salonika, 16th century), *Responsa of the Maharashdam*, Hoshen Mishpat 227.

8

Poverty and Property in Kant's System of Rights

1. Kant on the public duty to support the poor

In a passage from the *Doctrine of Right* that is particularly enigmatic even by his own high standards, Kant announces the state's right to tax in order to fulfill a public duty to support the poor.[1] The passage raises fundamental issues about the interpretation of Kant's legal philosophy, about the connection between private law and public law, and about the conceptual resources available to a system of rights for dealing with poverty. Kant, however, says almost nothing about the basis of this duty. In his Preface to the *Doctrine of Right* Kant had remarked that he had elaborated the latter sections less thoroughly than the earlier ones, because inferences from the earlier sections could easily be made.[2] The sparseness of his treatment of the duty to support the poor exemplifies this less thorough elaboration, but—as is evident from the perplexity to which the passage has given rise—not the ease of inference.

One might suppose that state taxation to support the poor involves a clash between distributive and corrective justice. Whether the state should satisfy the basic needs of its citizens is, of course, a standard issue of distributive justice. This recourse to distributive justice requires the state to use its taxing powers to take something that would otherwise remain within the private resources of those taxed. In a well-ordered state these resources reflect proprietary rights worked out and protected by private law within a conception of corrective justice.

---

[1] For the text of the passage, see below nn. 7 and 9.
[2] Immanuel Kant, *The Metaphysics of Morals*, tr. Mary Gregor (1996), [6:209].

Thus, the state's support of the poor, one might think, accomplishes distributive justice at the expense of citizens' corrective justice entitlements.

This supposed clash between distributive and corrective justice leads to the temptation to eliminate one form of justice in favor of the other. Contemporary legal and political thinking shows this temptation operating in both directions. Those opposed to the state's distributive operations claim, in effect, that corrective justice is all the justice that there is.[3] On this view, justice is fully satisfied by the private law notions that recognize entitlements to property and personal integrity, allow for the voluntary transfers through contract and gift, and protect rights through the law of contract, torts, and unjust enrichment. These notions themselves are interpreted as embodying a mode of practical reason distinctive to private law in that it works justice between individual parties without reference to any distributive purposes. "Distributive justice" can be regarded merely as a euphemistic term that camouflages the injustice of the state's treating individuals and their entitlements as means to collective ends. This primacy of corrective justice honors private law entitlements while renouncing the existence of a state obligation to satisfy citizens' basic needs.

On the other hand, those who favor the state's distributive role may be tempted to regard the working of distributive justice as normatively fundamental. The doctrines of private law then become nothing more than special operations of distributive justice. On this view, property can then be seen simply as the residue remaining after the state's distributive activity rather than as a locus of independent normative significance.[4] Liability rules also, whether dealing with contracts, torts, or unjust enrichment are regarded as justified to the extent that they embody distributive moves.[5] State support for the poor is then merely one distributive operation among many. Abandoned or explained away is the distinctive significance of the private law concepts as the legal manifestations of corrective justice.

---

[3] The leading representative of this view in recent years was Robert Nozick (though he would not have described his position in the terminology I use in this paragraph); see Robert Nozick, *Anarchy, State, and Utopia* (1974), 149–82.

[4] For a recent example of this, see Liam Murphy and Thomas Nagel, *The Myth of Ownership: Justice and Taxes* (2002), 74–75, 173–77.

[5] Notable examples for contract, torts, and unjust enrichment, respectively, are: Anthony Kronman, "Contract Law and Distributive Justice," (1980) 89 Yale L.J. 472; Gregory Keating, "Reasonableness and Rationality in Negligence Theory," (1996) 48 Stan. L. Rev. 311; Hanoch Dagan, *The Law and Ethics of Restitution* (2004).

Kant's remarks on the state's right to tax in order to fulfill a public duty to the poor indicate that he does not share these one-sided views of justice. As a philosopher working within the tradition of natural right—indeed, as perhaps its greatest expositor—Kant gives a detailed non-distributive account of the principal features of private law, especially of property and contract. Developing corrective justice in terms of his own metaphysics of morals, Kant portrays private law as a system of rights whose most general categories give juridical expression to the coexistence of one person's action with another's freedom under a universal law. Yet despite his affirmation that private law entitlements, understood non-distributively, are the necessary components of a free society, Kant nonetheless holds that there is a public obligation (and not merely a liberty) to support the poor. He thus seems to regard this aspect of distributive justice as compatible with corrective justice, with the state being duty-bound to actualize both. Neither of the temptations that characterize certain contemporary approaches to law attracts him.

However, the question that arises is whether Kant is entitled to the view about the alleviation of poverty that he professes. Kant's view of property is at least as extreme as the most extreme of today's libertarians.[6] How on his view can the state function both as the guarantor of purely non-distributive property rights and as the public authority that levies taxes in order to fulfill a public duty to support the poor? This question is all the more serious because Kant is a systematic philosopher for whom obligation signifies necessity, so that the duty to support the poor that he posits must somehow arise out of, and not merely be consistent with, his non-distributive account of rights. Furthermore, for Kant rights are the juridical vindications of freedom that the state coercively protects against infringement; coercion for the benefit of anyone, including the poor, seems inadmissible within the Kantian framework. Kant offers almost nothing resembling an argument in support of the duty he announces. Nor does he explain how this duty is to be integrated into his austere system of rights.

In the crucial passage, appearing in his section on public right in the *Doctrine of Right*, Kant describes the state's right to tax in order to fulfill its duty to the poor in these terms:

---

[6] Kant, for instance, has nothing like the Lockean proviso that limits property rights for Nozick; see Nozick, above n. 3, at 178–82.

To the supreme commander there belongs *indirectly*, that is, insofar as he has taken over the duty of the people, the right to impose taxes on the people for its own preservation, such as taxes to support organizations providing for the *poor, foundling homes*, and *church organizations*, usually called charitable or pious institutions.[7]

Because for Kant a right is always connected to the authorization to use coercion,[8] Kant goes on to specify that the state's support of the poor should be achieved by coercive public taxation and not merely by voluntary contributions. He explains the basis of the right to tax as follows:

The general will of the people has united itself into a society that is to maintain itself perpetually; and for this end it has submitted itself to the internal authority of the state in order to maintain those members of the society who are unable to maintain themselves. For reasons of state the government is therefore authorized to constrain the wealthy to provide the means of sustenance for those who are unable to provide for even their most necessary natural needs. The wealthy have acquired an obligation to the commonwealth, since they owe their existence to an act of submitting to its protection and care, which they need in order to live; on this obligation the state now bases its right to contribute what is theirs to maintaining their fellow citizens.[9]

No reader of Kant's legal philosophy can fail to be struck by the apparent oddity of these paragraphs. Kant's legal philosophy is an elucidation of the concept of Right—that is, of "the sum of conditions under which the choice of one can be united with the choice of another in accordance with a universal law of freedom."[10] In introducing the concept of Right, Kant notes that "it does not signify the relationship of one's choice to the mere wish (hence also to the mere need) of others, as in actions of beneficence…"[11] The consequence of this abstraction from "mere need" is a complex of proprietary, contractual, and domestic rights which place others under correlative duties of non-interference, "for anyone can be free as long as I do not impair

---

[7] Kant, above n. 2, [6:328].
[8] Ibid., [6:231].
[9] Ibid., [6:326].
[10] Ibid., [6:230].
[11] Ibid.

his freedom by my external action, even though I am quite indifferent to his freedom."[12] Yet when outlining the rights of government in the quoted paragraphs, Kant introduces—seemingly out of the blue—a positive duty, which government takes over from the people, to support those "unable to provide for even their most necessary natural needs." As Jeffrie Murphy remarks, "it is very difficult to see what Kant is up to."[13]

Kant's legal philosophy is so parsimonious and its architecture so austere that little leeway is available in dealing with a perplexity of this sort. Kant's adamantine boundary between right and ethics—the former dealing with externally coercible duties, the latter with uncoercible duties done for their own sake—prevents recourse to appealing ideas found in Kant's writings on ethics. For example, because Kant does not formulate the duty to support the poor as the reflex of any correlative right that the poor have, one might be tempted to regard that duty as somehow connected to the personal duty, postulated by Kant elsewhere,[14] to come to another's aid. However, the duty to aid is an ethical rather than a juridical one; it therefore cannot be associated with the coercive taxation authorized for support of the poor. Kant's own description of the concept of Right, with its contrast between rightful actions and actions of beneficence, confirms that state support of the poor does not fall under the duty to aid.[15]

Some commentators have seen Kant's requirement of support for the poor as an expression not of benevolence but of political prudence.[16] The alleviation of poverty facilitates the state's survival by

---

[12] Ibid., [6:231].

[13] Jeffrie Murphy, Kant: The Philosophy of Right (1970), 145.

[14] Above n. 2, [6:393]; Groundwork of the Metaphysics of Morals, Morals, tr. Mary Gregor (1996), in The Cambridge Edition of the Works of Immanuel Kant: Practical Philosophy, [4:423], [4:430].

[15] For an argument that support of the poor exemplifies a duty of beneficence, see Allen D. Rosen, Kant's Theory of Justice (1993), 173–208. Rosen draws on the duty to aid another that Kant sets out in the Groundwork, above n. 14, to conclude (at 201) that:

> if no one can rationally will the maxim of never helping others *as a law of nature*...then neither can an entire people rationally will *as a law of political society* that the state should allow them to perish rather than supply their basic needs. The *same* reason that makes it impossible rationally to will the maxim of never helping others as a law of nature also makes it impossible rationally to consent to a law of political society that would permit the state to ignore the basic needs of its citizens.

However, it by no means follows from the notion that everyone is obligated to help another that everyone is also obligated to give the state the power to coerce such help.

[16] Mark LeBar, "Kant on Welfare," (1999) 29 Canadian J. Phil. 225; Wolfgang Kersting, "Kant's Concept of the State," in Essays on Kant's Political Philosophy, ed. Howard Williams (1992), 143, 164; Bruce Aune, Kant's Theory of Morals (1979), 157; Mary Gregor, Laws of Freedom (1963), 36.

promoting the state's strength and stability against internal disorder and external attack. Kant elsewhere indeed seems to authorize the state to legislate on this basis for the happiness and prosperity of its citizens.[17] However, the acknowledged instrumentalism of such legislation[18] fits awkwardly into Kant's exposition in the paragraphs quoted above. In these paragraphs the relief of poverty is viewed not as something from which the state might contingently benefit, but as a duty of the people that the state assumes. Like all duties in Kant, this duty presumably reflects a normative necessity rather than a prudential option.[19]

In this chapter I want to develop a different possibility.[20] My contention is that, far from being inconsistent with the internal logic of Kantian right, the state's duty to support the poor is the inexorable outcome of that logic. Kant includes support of the poor as an "effect with regard to rights that follows from the nature of a civil union."[21] The civil union results from the transition to public right from the property regime in the state of nature. Kant's theory of property rights necessitates not only this transition but also—as its consequence—the people's duty to the poor. Just as for Kant the movement from property in the state of nature to the public right of a civil union is obligatory, so the state's support of the poor is an obligatory consequence of that movement. Were the state under no such obligation, the legitimacy of the civil union that replaces the state of nature would itself be impugned. On this reading of Kant, the very idea of private property implies the state's right to tax property owners in order to discharge a public duty to relieve poverty.

---

[17] Kant, "On the Common Saying: That May Be Correct in Theory but Is of No Use in Practice," in *The Cambridge Edition of the Works of Immanuel Kant: Political Philosophy*, tr. Mary Gregor (1996), [8:298].

[18] Ibid.: "If the supreme power gives laws that are directed chiefly to happiness (the prosperity of the citizens, increased population and the like), this is not done as the end for which a civil constitution is established but merely as a means for *securing a rightful condition*, especially against a people's external enemies."

[19] Kant, above n. 2, [6:222] says that duty, "that action to which someone is bound," is "the matter of obligation," and he defines obligation as "the necessity of a free action under a categorical imperative of reason."

[20] For brief suggestions of an approach similar to the one set out here, see Mary Gregor, "Kant on Welfare Legislation," (1985) 6 Logos 49, 55; Leslie Mulholland, *Kant's System of Rights* (1990), 317, 39 (see below n. 81). For a related interpretation see Arthur Ripstein, *Force and Freedom: Kant's Legal and Political Philosophy* (2009), 267–99.

[21] Kant, above n. 2, at [6:318].

Interpreted in this way, Kant's account casts light on two aspects of corrective justice. The first concerns the place of property within a corrective justice theory of private law. It is easy to assume that property is problematic for corrective justice: because private law presupposes an antecedent distribution of property, corrective justice itself seems to rest on a foundation of distributive justice.[22] Kant, however, rejects the assumption that the justification for property lies in an antecedent distribution. For Kant, as the next section of this chapter explains, property arises from the freedom to act in relation to others in accordance with self-chosen purposes. This freedom characterizes the conception of the person—what was termed "personality" in chapter 1—that corrective justice presupposes. Property so conceived completely conforms to corrective justice. In this account property does not arise even notionally through distributive justice—that is, through a determination by a common authority to parcel goods out on the basis of a distributive criterion. To the contrary, common authority itself becomes possible only as a consequence of the rightfulness of property.

The second aspect on which Kant's account casts light concerns the relationship between corrective and distributive justice. As noted above in chapter 1, these two forms of justice connote categorically different structures of justification. Neither of them can integrate the other within it. Given the legitimacy of both forms of justice, what (aside from the sheer positivity of laws within a single jurisdiction) is the nature of the unity of a legal order within which both are present? Clearly, it cannot be the unity of the same justificatory structure applying to all its legal arrangements. Implicit in the Kantian account as interpreted in this chapter is a different answer: it is unity by appropriate sequence.[23] Starting from the underlying conception of personality, Kant traces a series of conceptual steps each of which presupposes but complements the preceding one until the full spectrum of rightful legal arrangements is exhibited. The underlying unity is provided by the idea of what self-determining persons require in order to realize their freedom through law. Under this notion of unity neither corrective justice nor distributive justice trumps the other, nor is either derived from the other. Rather each finds its appropriate

---

[22] Hanoch Dagan, "The Distributive Foundation of Corrective Justice," (1999) 98 Mich. L. Rev. 138.

[23] This phrase is taken from John Rawls, *Political Liberalism* (1993), 259–62.

place in the conceptual sequence that actualizes the reciprocal freedom of all.

In accordance with this conceptual ordering, property generates the distributive justice that consists in the alleviation of poverty through taxation. Far from being a self-sufficient and free-standing institution of justice, property requires redistribution to the poor for its own legitimacy. Thus Kant transcends the categorical difference between corrective and distributive justice while preserving and elucidating the distinct roles that each plays in a free society. In this chapter I attempt to reconstruct the argument, implicit in his theory of law but not articulated by Kant himself, that underlies this remarkable conclusion.

2. Kant's account of property

Kant's account of property in the *Doctrine of Right* features a conceptual progression that starts from the innate right to freedom and culminates in the establishment of property as an institution of positive law.[24] Kant exhibits the phases of this progression as implicit in the relationship of free persons under the conditions of human existence. Because property is consistent with the freedom of all, it is rightly secured and protected by the law's coercive powers.

This progression has three phases, which Kant presents from a variety of standpoints as befits their structural importance. Sometimes he describes these phases in terms of the categories of modality (the possibility, the actuality, and the necessity of possessing objects).[25] Sometimes, he refers to them as divisions of justice (*iustitia tutatrix, iustitia commutativa, iustitia distributiva*).[26] Sometimes he refers to the division

---

[24] A terminological note: The word "property" that I use in this section is not strictly accurate from a Kantian perspective. Kant is dealing with the more general idea of that he calls "having something external as one's own" or "external mine and thine" [6:245]. What we think of as property, namely, things that have an *in rem* legal status, is just part of what Kant is referring to. Kant's "external mine and thine" also includes *in personam* contractual entitlements and entitlements within the status relationships of the household [6:247–48]. Perhaps "ownership" might be a more appropriate English term for capturing Kant's capacious notion of what one has as one's own, although I doubt that English-speakers would differentiate between ownership and property in this way. (Kant himself uses the word "ownership" (*Eigentum*) for what we would call "property" [6:270].) I have simply used the word "property" throughout, despite its inaccuracy.

[25] Kant, above n. 2, [6:306].

[26] Ibid., [6:267], [6:306].

of duties that accompanies the divisions of justice.[27] Sometimes he refers to these phases in terms of form and matter.[28] Sometimes he calls them different variations of right (what is intrinsically right, what is rightful, what is laid down as right)[29] or different kinds of laws of justice (*lex iusti, lex iuridica, lex iustitiae*).[30]

However the phases are referred to, the progression through them exhibits a dialectical structure of argument.[31] In the first phase Kant starts with the universal principle of Right, which mandates the coexistence of one person's action with another's freedom under a universal law, and notes the juridical relationship analytically contained within that principle. This juridical relationship does not include property in external things, but it does encompass certain "authorizations" such as equality and non-dependence,[32] which are normative attributes implicit within the universal principle of Right and therefore ascribable to the parties at this phase. In the second phase he extends this initial argument on the ground that having something external as one's own, although not analytically contained in the universal principle of Right marks a connection to external things that matches the capacity for choice characteristic of self-determining action. This extension, however, is problematic, because although ownership of external things is now permissible, it is not yet put into effect under conditions consonant with the authorizations articulated in the first phase. The second phase, accordingly, is merely provisional. The problems it raises are resolved at the third phase, where the conditions of acquisition take a form that is fully consistent with what was analytically contained in the universal principle of Right. As Kant puts it with unfortunate opacity when he lists the threefold division of duties, the duties of the third phase "involve the derivation of the [duties of the second phase] from the principle of the [duties of the first phase] by subsumption."[33]

Although presented in a sequence, these three phases are conceptual, not temporal. Kant is not offering a philosophical reconstruction of the historical evolution of property. Rather, the three phases represent

---

[27] Ibid., [6:236].
[28] Ibid., [6:306].
[29] Ibid., [6:267], [6:306].
[30] Ibid., [6:236–37], [6:267], [6:306].
[31] Kant, ibid., [6:255] notes that the concept of having something external involves "an antinomy of propositions concerning [its] possibility" that forces reason into "an unavoidable dialectic."
[32] Ibid., [6:237–38].
[33] Ibid., [6:237].

aspects that together are constitutive of property in the juridical relationships of free persons (e.g., that external things can be acquired
through acts of will, that property does not require actual possession,
that property rights are enforceable, and so on), but presented in an
ordering that purports to show property's normative necessity within a
system of rights. The three phases comprise an articulated unity: each
phase proceeds with its distinct mode of argumentation (the first is
analytic, the second is synthetic, the third works by subsumption), but
the account of property stands or falls on the totality of the three
phases taken together. Kant himself presents property as absent at the
first phase and as problematic at the second. If these phases were considered independently, the argument would not get off the ground or
would collapse as soon as it did so. Nor does the third phase stand
alone either; its role is to incorporate what is necessary to reconcile the
second phase to what is analytically contained in the first one. The
result is that the institutions of public law that emerge at the third
phase determine and guarantee the property entitlements that are the
product of the second phase in a way that expresses the normative significance of the principle of right that initiated the first phase.

The first phase features the innate right to freedom. The innate
right to freedom consists in the independence of one's actions from
constraint by the actions of another, insofar as such independence is
consistent with the freedom of everyone else.[34] This right stands in an
analytic relationship with the universal principle of Right, which
requires that one person's action be able to coexist with the freedom
of everyone under a universal law. Formulating freedom as an innate
right adds nothing to what the universal principle already contains; it
merely isolates a constituent element of, and represents what is already
involved in thinking about, that principle.

The innate right is "the only original right belonging to every man
by virtue of his humanity."[35] This right is innate because every person
has it simply by virtue of his or her existence. Similarly, it is original
because it arises independently of any act that would establish it.
Because my innate right is not mine by virtue of some act of acquisition, it is what is internally mine, in contrast to what is externally
mine, which must always be acquired.[36] What is internally mine is my

---

[34] Ibid.
[35] Ibid.
[36] Ibid.

freedom[37]—that is, my capacity to act in the execution of the purposes I form as a self-determining being.

For human beings the paradigmatic manifestation of what is internally mine is the body, the physical organism through which the person expresses his or her freedom as a self-determining being.[38] By mandating actions that can coexist with the freedom of all, the universal principle of Right signals its application to the actions of self-determining agents. In the case of human beings, self-determining activity takes place through the body. Because the body is an "inseparable unity of members in a person,"[39] interference with any part of another's body is a wrong against that person's freedom. This right with respect to one's own body is innate. It arises not through the performance of an act of acquisition (indeed, no such act is conceivable because the body itself is what would have to perform it), but simply by virtue of one's being born. Thus, the body is the primary locus of what Kant calls the "right of humanity in our own person."[40]

The occupation by a person's body of a particular space is an exercise of this right: "All men are originally (i.e., prior to any act of choice that establishes a right) in a possession of land that is in conformity with right, that is, they have a right to be wherever nature or chance (apart from their will) has placed them." [41] Given the finitude of the earth's surface, the occupation of space carries with it the possibility of persons coming into contact with one another.[42] Such contacts are governed by the universal principle of Right. Because no one can interfere with the body of anyone else, a person who occupies a particular space excludes all other persons from that space.

In this phase, where one's only right is the innate right of humanity in one's own person, property as the entitlement to something distinct from the person's body does not exist. Of course, a person may come

---

[37] Ibid., [6:248] ("what is *internally* mine (freedom)"), [6:250] ("what is internally mine (my freedom)").

[38] Kant does not say this explicitly, but it is clear from what he does say about the innate right; see Leslie Mulholland, above n. 20, 214. In addition to the passages Mulholland cites, one can adduce the significance of the right in our own person for legitimate sexual relations (Kant, above n. 2, [6:277], [6:278]) and Kant's reference to "my innate right to security of the person" in his Vorarbeiten, in Immanuel Kant, *Gesammelte Schriften,* XXIII (1910), 287.

[39] Kant, above n. 2, [6:278].

[40] Ibid., [6:236], [6:239]. Other aspects of the innate right that Kant mentions are the infant's right to parental support (ibid., [6:280]), the right to a good reputation (ibid., [6:295]), and the right to one's religious beliefs (ibid., [6:327]).

[41] Ibid., [6:262].

[42] Ibid.

into physical possession of some external object. I might (to use Kant's examples)[43] hold an apple or lie on the earth. But someone who wrested the apple away from me or pushed me off the land on which I was lying would be wronging me with respect to my body, not my property. By disturbing the disposition of my fingers as they grasped the apple or of my physical frame as it rested on the earth, the wrongdoer would be acting inconsistently with my innate right to occupy a particular space, rather than infringing a right that I have in the apple or in the resting place as such. The interference would be with what is internally, not externally, mine.

Property goes beyond innate right by treating the person as entitled to an external thing even when it is not in the person's physical possession. Innate right prohibits another's interference with an external thing only insofar as such interference would simultaneously be an interference with my body as something internally mine. Property, in contrast, entails treating the thing as externally mine, so that the apple I was holding remains mine even when I set it down, and similarly the land upon which I was lying remains mine even when I have moved elsewhere. Under a property regime anyone who interferes with what is mine wrongs me despite the fact that my body is not immediately affected.

The extension of the scope of rights to include what is externally mine is the second phase of Kant's account of property. Kant introduces what he calls "the postulate of practical reason with regard to rights," under which "it is possible to have any external object of my choice as mine."[44] This postulate asserts both the possibility of owning the external objects of a person's will and the existence of a duty of justice to act towards others in recognition of that possibility.[45]

The postulate is based on the notion that external objects of choice have to be conceived in a way that corresponds to the choosing subject. Under the concept of right, what is relevant are not the particular purposes that choosing subjects pursue through their interactions with each other, but rather their purposiveness as choosing subjects whatever their particular purposes. A contract is valid, for instance, because it expresses the purposiveness of both contracting parties, rather than because of the particular purpose that either party has in mind. Thus,

---

[43] Ibid., [6:247].
[44] Ibid., [6:246].
[45] Ibid., [6:252].

from the juridical perspective freedom is a formal concept that refers to the capacity for choice rather than directly to the content of particular choices.[46] It thereby abstracts from the wants and needs that fuel such particular choices. External objects of choice are the objects of choice so conceived. Accordingly, an external object of choice cannot get its juridical status merely from the particular properties that are engaged by particular uses that satisfy particular wants or needs of a particular choosing subject, as when the apple is held in the hand and then consumed. Rather, it must be possible for an object of choice to lie within the choosing subject's capacity for use even when no particular use is being made of it.

Indeed, if an external object of choice could not rightfully be within a choosing subject's power, the latter's freedom would be restricted beyond what the universal principle of Right required. That principle, under which the action of one person must coexist with the freedom of another, makes the freedom of another—the other's innate right of humanity in her own person—the limit of one's action. Accordingly, everything that is distinct from what a person has an innate right to is available as an external object of choice. Nothing intrinsic to such an object of choice can put it beyond the rightful power of the choosing subject to exercise control over it even when not in physical possession of it. In this way the postulate of practical reason with respect to rights makes it possible to have something external as one's own, thus extending the scope of rights beyond the body-bounded regime of innate right.

Yet the rights made possible by the postulate are problematic. Although they are consistent with the regime of innate rights in one respect, they are inconsistent with it in another. They are consistent with it by allowing persons to exercise their freedom by controlling external objects of choice, which are not aspects of innate right, in a way that matches the concept of choice operative within innate right. They are, however, inconsistent with it because their actualization does not treat the parties involved as innately equal. Because in the first phase everyone has an innate right that everyone else is obligated to abstain from coercing, the participants in a regime composed

---

[46] Ibid., [6:230]: "[I]n this reciprocal relation of choice no account at all is taken of the *matter* of choice, that is, of the end that each has in mind with the object he wants; it is not asked, for example, whether someone who buys goods for me for his own commercial use will gain by the transaction or not. All that is in question is the *form* in the relation of choice on the part of both, insofar as choice is regarded merely as *free*..."

exclusively of innate right have innate equality, which Kant defines as "independence from being bound by others to more than one can in turn bind them."[47] This equality does not obtain in the actualization of the external rights allowed by the postulate of practical reason. Unlike the innate right, external rights are acquired through the performance of an act. All such rights presuppose the possibility of original acquisition, when the proprietor comes to own something not owned by anyone. However, the act of original acquisition is the exercise of a unilateral will that puts others under an obligation that they would not otherwise have. Despite the fact that innate right authorizes innate equality, the proprietor, by virtue of his or her unilateral act of acquisition, binds others with respect to the acquired thing without being reciprocally bound to them. This should be beyond the rightful power of one person's unilateral will, for it is inconsistent with innate equality of all that the acquirer should be able to subordinate others to his or her purposes.[48]

This inequality has further consequences. Because an acquired right, like all Kantian rights, carries with it the power to coerce others not to violate it, the unilateral act of acquisition that creates the right also gives the right-holder coercive power. Accordingly, although the universal principle of Right forbids an act that does not coexist with the freedom of another, the coercion occasioned by acquisition is precisely such an act, in that it allows the unilateral will to serve as a coercive law for everyone.[49] Moreover, although others also can create rights through their unilateral will, no one can be sure of how others interpret the extent of their respective rights or of whether they are willing to abide by the rights of others. In the interplay of unilateral wills that results, each person is the judge of his or her own entitlements, doing what seems right and good in his or her own eyes.[50]

Thus, the actualization of the rights made possible by the postulate of practical reason creates a conceptual tension, to be resolved in the subsequent phase, between the unilateralism of the proprietor's conduct and the equality authorized by innate right. The universal principle of Right, in which innate right is analytically contained, forbids one person's coercing the freedom of another. Yet the postulate of practical reason allows one person coercively to restrict another's

---

[47] Kant, above n. 2, [6:237].
[48] Ibid., [6:264]; cf. [6:259].
[49] Ibid., [6:256].
[50] Ibid., [6:312].

freedom through unilateral acts that establish proprietary rights to exclude. Because of this tension, such rights are provisional pending an additional move that brings them back into conformity with the equality of innate right. Accordingly, the postulate of practical reason with respect to rights allows us provisionally to hold the notion of external property in place until the thought of it can be completed in a further phase that establishes the conditions under which external property is conclusively rightful.[51]

This transformation of provisional rights into conclusive ones occurs in the third phase of Kant's account of property. Kant introduces a further postulate, the postulate of public Right, which marks the transition from the state of nature to the civil condition of law-governed society. The postulate declares that "[w]hen you cannot avoid living side by side with all others, you ought to leave the state of nature and proceed with them into a rightful condition."[52] In this rightful condition the state provides duly authorized institutions of adjudication and enforcement. These replace the exercise of private judgment about controversial claims with the authoritative judgments of courts that determine the scope of each person's entitlements according to what is laid down as right.[53] Moreover, the coercion that secures each person's rights is no longer private but emanates from a public lawful regime under which rights are secured by adequate power external to the contending parties.[54]

Entry into the civil condition transforms the significance of original acquisition in two related ways.[55] First, as the assertion of a rightful power to place others under an obligation, acquisition is the prerogative not of any person in particular but of all persons. This means that everyone not only can acquire but is also under an obligation not to interfere with what others have acquired. However, in the absence of reciprocal assurance that others will refrain from interfering with one's own acquisitions, adherence to one's obligations to others runs the risk of subordinating oneself to others' purposes. This would be inconsistent with the equality of innate right. The civil condition provides

---

[51] Ibid., [6:257] (possession "in anticipation of and preparation for the civil condition...is *provisionally rightful* possession"), [6:267] (property arises "before the establishment of a civil condition but with a view to it, that is, *provisionally*").

[52] Ibid.

[53] Ibid., [6:297], [6:313].

[54] Ibid.

[55] Ibid., [6:256–57].

this assurance through state institutions that can compel all to adhere to the obligations that property creates. This assurance reflects not the particular will of any person but a general will of all persons omnilaterally related to one another through the state in which they all participate. All can now both enjoy their property and respect the property of others on terms of equality.

Second (and more fundamentally), the lack of assurance in the state of nature reflects the doubtful basis of any particular obligation to refrain from using what has been originally acquired by another. In the state of nature this obligation is unilaterally imposed by another's act of acquisition, thereby trenching on the freedom of the person obligated. This difficulty applies no matter how many acquisitions take place by how many persons. Each acquisition can be considered only on its own, and therefore each faces the same difficulty, that it unilaterally restricts the freedom of others. The plurality of instances makes no difference to the normative infirmity of every such acquisition. In contrast, the civil condition involves a notional union of all wills that transforms the external acquisition of unowned things from a merely unilateral act on the part of the acquirer to an omnilateral act, to which everyone as possible owners of property implicitly consents and whose rights-creating significance everyone acknowledges. Acquisitions are no longer a series of isolated acts. Instead, all acquisitions are mutually related through a system of property in which all are reciprocally bound and publicly coerced to respect the property rights of others.

This second point can be formulated in terms of the equality of innate right. As already noted, that equality consists in "independence from being bound by others more than one can in turn bind them."[56] In the state of nature, where every act of original acquisition is considered on its own, this equality does not obtain; the acquirer binds others to abstain from the acquired object without being in turn bound by them. Of course, a second person may bind the first acquirer by acquiring a different object, but the difficulty would be replicated, with the first acquirer now in the converse position of being bound without being able to bind. And so on with further acquisitions by others. It is true that across all the acts of original acquisition each acquirer binds with respect to what she acquires and is bound with respect to what others acquire. However, the state of nature

[56] Ibid., [6:237].

supplies no conceptual basis for relating all the acquisitions to one another. They figure in the state of nature simply as a plurality of discrete acquisitions, every one of which is inconsistent with innate equality. The civil condition transforms this plurality into a totality, in which the various acquisitions instantiate a single system of property that applies to all acts of acquisition by all acquirers over time. Within this totality the equality of innate right is satisfied because all the acquisitions taken together form a unity within which different acquirers both bind and are bound.[57]

Kant affirms that leaving the state of nature and entering the civil condition is "objectively necessary, that is, necessary as a duty."[58] This duty follows from the recognition in the second of the three phases that private property is rightful. The postulate of practical reason with respect to rights allows the conclusion that having external things as one's own is an exercise of freedom that, although not analytically contained within the universal principle of Right, is formally consistent with it, and therefore capable of putting others under a duty of non-interference. The duty is only provisional, because in the second phase of Kant's account this formal consistency with the universal principle of Right is not accompanied by conditions that reflect the innate equality entailed by that principle. The absence of these conditions does not negate the validity of the duty. Cancelling the second phase and returning to the first one is therefore not an option. While this regressive move would restore the original innate equality, it would nullify the possibility of external freedom that the postulate of practical reason identified with having something external as one's own, thereby leading to infringements of the duty provisionally established through that possibility. Hence arises the necessity to move forward to the third phase, in which the impediments to the conclusive operation of the duty are eliminated. Just as all are under a duty at the second phase to respect proprietary entitlements, so all are under a duty to create the conditions under which those proprietary entitlements are fully rightful. The establishment of institutions of public right removes—indeed, is the only way to remove—the unilaterality of judgment, coercion, and acquisition that characterizes the state of nature. Accordingly, the duty of non-interference with property that

---

[57] "Thus *allness* or *totality* is just plurality considered as unity." Kant, *Critique of Pure Reason*, tr. Norman Kemp Smith (1929), B111.

[58] Kant, above n.2., [6:264].

makes its appearance in the second phase of Kant's account matures at the transition to the third phase into a duty to leave the state of nature and to enter (and force others to enter) the civil condition.

For Kant, the civil condition is formed through a social contract—what Kant calls the original contract—that unites the will of all under rightful coercive laws.[59] This contract is not a historical event but is rather the idea of reason in terms of which the legitimacy of the state can be conceived. Under this contract every individual gives up the lawless freedom of the state of nature in order to find his or her freedom undiminished under law in the rightful condition formed by the union of all wills. Because the state must live up to the undiminished freedom of the original contract that legitimates the state's formation, the idea of this contract serves as a norm for the internal constitution of any state.[60] Kant regards the public duty to support the poor as a juridical effect of the move from the state of nature through the original contract into the civil condition. As the passage in the first section of this chapter indicated, he does not explain why he posits such an effect or why he regards support of the poor as a public duty.[61] However, he presumably thinks that a state that fails to fulfill this duty would not accord with the idea of the original contract. More specifically, without such a duty the transition to the civil condition would not leave freedom undiminished from its starting point in innate right.

3. Freedom undiminished

Kant's description of the innate right to freedom indicates why this might be so. Kant unequivocally connects innate right to what is needed for self-preservation. Referring to the aspect of innate right that consists in occupying space, Kant writes: "Through the innate possession of land I can exclude everyone from using that which is necessary for sustaining my existence."[62] In accordance with their innate right, possession by humans of the land on which they find themselves "is the supreme condition of the possibility of using this land, as long as this use is absolutely necessary only for purposes of

---

[59] Above n. 2, [6:315–16].
[60] Ibid., [6:313].
[61] Above n. 9.
[62] Vorarbeiten, in Kant, *Gesammelte Schriften*, XXIII, 286.

sustaining their existence."[63] By excluding others from whatever the person is physically connected to, such as the very space that the person occupies, innate right allows the use, unaffected by others, of what is immediately necessary for one's survival. The occupation of space is immediately necessary for one's survival, because, as an embodied creature, a human being cannot exist without being somewhere. Of course, one can physically possess items that do not contribute to one's subsistence, as when I examine the beauty of a flower that I hold between my fingers. But nothing can be used for my subsistence without being physically connected to me.

By linking innate right with the sustaining of one's existence, Kant is not claiming that one has a positive right to the means of existence and that others are under a correlative duty to assist in my continued existence. Such a duty would make their actions subservient to my needs, contrary to our innate equality. If my continued existence depends on my consumption of the only available apple, my neighbor's pulling it off the tree before I do may mean that I die from starvation. However, my neighbor has no duty to abstain from seizing the apple so long as he can do so without physically interfering with me. My starvation would have to be imputed not to his permissible act of seizing the apple or to refusing to give it to me, but to my consequent inability to gain access to the apple without disturbing my neighbor's body.

Kant's argument is rather that the innate right signifies that others have a negative duty not to interfere with the incidents of that right, and that one's existence is therefore immune from deprivation at the hands of others. This is because one's mere existence is not a wrong to anyone (because wrong is imputable only to actions) and accordingly provides no rightful ground for others to interfere with one's body and with whatever one physically possesses. The body, of course, is the organ through which one maintains one's physical existence. Similarly, the objects most immediately implicated in one's continuing survival are things that come into contact with the body (for example, the earth on which one lies, the apple in one's hand). Accordingly, although innate right does not include a positive right to survival, it imposes a duty of non-interference on others.

A regime characterized only by innate right systemically maximizes the mutual non-dependence of all. In such a regime, everything is

---

[63] Ibid., 318.

available for use by everyone, except the space that others occupy and whatever is in their physical possession. Accumulation is impossible because no one has external things as one's own. As long as I occupy a particular space, nobody can push me out of it. But when I move, I can occupy any other space not occupied by someone else, gaining my new space and simultaneously losing the power to prevent others from occupying the old one. Similarly, as long as the apple is in my hand, no one can take it from me. But I cannot store it while gathering others, for as soon as the apple is released from my grasp it becomes available to anyone else who can take it. This general availability of everything except the space that others occupy and the things that they physically possess means that my survival cannot directly be affected by the actions of others. Whatever external things are available to my neighbors are also available to me. So far as my relationship with others is concerned, I am (in the terminology of Kant's authorizations of innate right) my own master,[64] able to act on my own and without dependence on others for my continued existence.

The non-dependence of one's existence on others is the hallmark of juridical relationships restricted to the exercise of innate rights. Innate right protects each person's existence on the basis of the innate equality of all, since everyone was reciprocally bound not to interfere with the bodily integrity of everyone else. Because one's body is the limit of one's rights, everything not immediately connected to the body of someone else is available to everyone. The result is that no one's survival is dependent on anyone else's actions.

In this account, the significance of one's survival is entirely relational. The gross corporeality of the body and its continued existence do not demand attention on the ground that life, taken on its own, forms a basic value in abstraction from one's interaction with others.[65] The standpoint of right is concerned only with the relationship between one person's freedom and another's action. Accordingly, the body has a juridical significance because as the organ through which human beings exercise their freedom, it imposes duties on others whose actions must be capable of coexisting with everyone's freedom. Similarly, when innate right is considered as a regime of equality, the body as the organ of one's freedom cannot rightfully become the

---

[64] Kant, above n. 2, [6:238].

[65] For an example of life treated as a basic value, see John Finnis, *Natural Law and Natural Rights* (1980), 86.

means through which that freedom is compromised through subordination to or dependence on others. Thus, from the standpoint of right, continued existence matters not because of its unilateral importance to the person whose existence it is, but because of its role within a relationship of free, equal, and mutually non-dependent beings.

The inevitable non-dependence that characterizes innate right disappears with the introduction, first provisional and then conclusive, of external property. Because ownership obtains even in the absence of a physical connection between the owner and what is owned, the accumulation of external things is now possible. My range of rightful action is now confined to what might be left over from others' efforts at accumulation. The possibility of amassing land makes it conceivable that, given the finitude of the earth's surface,[66] all the land may be appropriated by others, leaving me literally with no place to exist except by leave of someone else. My continued existence may thus become dependent on the goodwill or sufferance of others, to whom I might then have to subordinate myself, making myself into a means for their ends, perhaps becoming their bondsman or slave.[67] Moreover, my inability otherwise to satisfy my basic needs may make me dependent on the generosity of others—that is, on that to which I have no right. The legitimation of the ownership of external things produces a juridical regime in which the survival of one person may be dependent on how others dispose of what is rightfully theirs.

This transformation of one's position relative to others from assured non-dependence to potential dependence means that in making acquired rights conclusive, a civil condition entrenches the possibility of dependence. Compared to relations characterized solely by innate right, this would, inconsistently with the original contract, diminish freedom in the relations among persons.

It is worth noting that the criteria for determining whether freedom is diminished arise from the conceptual implications of innate right itself, not from a calculus about the effect of property on collective or individual welfare. It may well be, as Locke famously observed, that instituting external property produces an enormous surplus compared to what preceded,[68] and that the judgment of whether this

---

[66] Kant, above n. 2, [6:262], [6:311].
[67] Locke has a similar apprehension: "But we know that God hath not left one man so to the mercy of another, that he may starve him if he please," John Locke, *Two Treatises of Government, First Treatise*, ed. P. Laslett (1965), s. 41.
[68] Ibid., s. 37.

would be an improvement or a worsening of any individual's situation depends on how that individual factors his or her degree of risk aversion into the calculation of the chances of capturing part of the surplus. For Kant, however, the issue is more constrained. Non-dependence with respect to one's continued existence is characteristic of innate right, because such non-dependence is sheltered by the duty not to interfere with another's physical integrity and by the consequent availability of everything to everyone. The standards for judging whether freedom remains undiminished in a civil condition that protects property are provided by the normative ideas authorized by innate right: not probability and welfare, but innate equality and non-dependence. Whether freedom is diminished raises not a quantitative issue ("Will I have less?"), but a relational one ("Will my existence change from not being to possibly being dependent on others' actions?"). In dealing with the undiminished freedom of the original contract, the focus remains where the universal principle of Right put it from the start: on the relationship between the freedom of one person and the action of another.

Thus, the progression from innate right to the state's guarantee of all property holdings seems to reach an impasse. On the one hand, this progression is a normative necessity in which I am obligated to participate. On the other hand, innate right at least has the advantage that no person or aggregate of persons can engross the world's resources, shut me off from access to what is necessary for my existence, and thereby make the exercise of my freedom dependent on the beneficent or exploitative will of another. Entering a civil condition that, by guaranteeing property, also guarantees the circumstances of possible dependence diminishes my freedom inconsistently with the original contract. The civil condition, it seems, is both the fulfilment of my duty as a free person and the diminishing of my freedom.

The public duty to support the poor breaks this impasse. The requirement allows freedom to be undiminished in the civil condition. The sovereign's assumption of the duty to support the poor makes up for the possible inaccessibility of the means of sustenance. The result is that in the civil condition, just as under innate right, no one's subsistence is dependent on the actions of others. Everyone can now participate in the civil condition as one's own master.

Furthermore, the duty is incumbent on the people (and derivatively on the sovereign) rather than on any particular person. The institution of a regime of external property allows for the accumulation of property; no individual commits a compensable wrong simply by engaging in this process. Moreover, the prospect of impoverishment is created by the systemic legitimacy of acquisition, rather than by the appropriative acts of any particular acquirer. The *systemic* difficulty that property poses for innate right is resolved by the *collective* duty imposed on the people to provide subsistence as needed.

To be sure, individuals pay the tax. This, however, is not because they are duty-bound as individuals to support the poor but because the sovereign is authorized to tax them for a necessary state purpose. The obligation of the taxpayers is to the state, not to the poor directly, because the taxpayers whose property is secured by the state are the beneficiaries of the transition to a civil condition. The incidence of this tax is based on a notion of reciprocity that flows from the state's guarantee of property and, with it, of the proprietors' means of survival: because the wealthy "owe their existence to an act of submitting to the [commonwealth's] protection, which they need in order to live,"[69] they are obligated to contribute what is theirs to sustain the existence of those who, because of the property regime, now lack what they need in order to live.

Kant remarks that the sovereign has the right to tax the people "for its own preservation," explaining that "[t]he general will of the people has united itself into a society that is to maintain itself perpetually" and that taxation of the wealthy is therefore authorized "for reasons of state."[70] One might be tempted to think that in these references to the people's preservation, society's self-perpetuation, and reasons of state Kant is pointing to the right of the sovereign to act prudently in order to prevent anarchic social unrest.[71] This is not, however, the most plausible interpretation. Kant presents support for the poor not as a merely permissible exercise of prudence but as a requirement of duty, which the sovereign takes over from the people.

Crucial to the understanding of this passage is the meaning of the assertion that a society (regarded by Kant as the entity made by the civil union)[72] "is to maintain itself perpetually." Perpetuity for Kant does not involve a prediction of the empirical likelihood of social tranquility or upheaval; perpetuity is rather a normative attribute of the constitutional order. Something is "called *perpetual*... if it is bound

---

[69] Above, n. 2, [6:326].
[70] Ibid.
[71] Above n. 16.
[72] Above, n. 2, [6:307].

up with the constitution of the state itself (for a state must be regarded as perpetual)."[73] A form of government is perpetual by virtue of its being institutionally so structured that it can continuously and for the indefinite future function in accordance with the norms that animate it. Perpetuation is thus the temporal dimension of the state as a totality— that is, as a juridical entity that unites a multitude of human beings and of norms into a systematic whole operative over time. A rightful condition strives to be perpetual in this sense. By making freedom its principle, a rightful condition has a constitution "in which *law* itself rules and depends on no particular person."[74] It accordingly has no natural lifespan but rather endures through an unending process of juridical self-animation. Through its institutions, such a state "preserves itself in accordance with the laws of freedom."[75] This, Kant claims, "is the only constitution of a state that lasts."[76]

Society "is to maintain itself perpetually" because the state is under a duty to have a constitution that accords most completely with freedom. As the temporal dimension of the state, perpetuity signifies the continuous process of making the state most fully conform over time to the original contract—that is, to the idea of reason "in terms of which alone we can think of the legitimacy of a state."[77] All institutions of the state are obligated to participate in this process of bringing the state to the fullest possible realization of its own legitimating grounds. In so doing, these institutions act for the state's well-being, which for Kant refers not to the happiness or welfare of the citizens but to the promotion of the state's fullest conformity to the principles of right.[78] Thus, fulfilling the obligation to make the state "suited to the idea of the original contract" leads to the state's having "the only constitution . . . that lasts."[79]

Accordingly, the terms Kant uses in describing the state's duty to support the poor—the preservation of the people, the perpetuation of society, and taxation for reasons of state—fit together as follows. The people requires a state for its own preservation not merely because the state provides protection to its members, but because without a state

---

[73]   Ibid., [6:367].
[74]   Ibid.
[75]   Ibid., [6:318].
[76]   Ibid., [6:367].
[77]   Ibid., [6:315].
[78]   Ibid., [6:318].
[79]   Ibid., [6:340–41].

the people simply does not exist as a distinct collective and juridical entity. The preservation of the people, therefore, entails the perpetuation of the state. Perpetuation in turn involves having the state, through its institutions, live up to its obligation to maintain and perfect its own normative character. In acting to that end, these institutions act for reasons of state, in the sense that they act for the state's well-being as a rightful condition that strives fully to conform itself to the grounds of its own legitimacy. By tying the state's duty to support the poor (and its consequent authorization to tax) to the perpetual maintenance of society, Kant treats that duty as a necessary aspect of the state's obligation to maintain its character as condition that accords with the principles of right. The state's support of the poor is, in other words, a constitutional essential.[80]

This does not mean that, for Kant, the poor have a right to subsistence. Since a right for Kant is always accompanied by the authorization to coerce and the state is the ultimate repository of legitimate coercive power, Kant can recognize no right against the state. The poor are supported not because they hold a right but because they are the beneficiaries of a duty. The sovereign takes over from the people the duty to support the poor that is an incident of the obligation to make the state conform to the original contract.[81]

The operation of this duty re-establishes the non-dependence that marked innate right and was threatened by the introduction of private property. In one's relations with another, everyone continues to have the same right to bodily integrity that they had as a matter of innate right. The availability to everyone of everything that was distinct from

---

[80] On the idea of constitutional essentials, see Rawls, above n. 23, 227–30. Rawls also considers "a social minimum providing for the basic needs of all citizens" to be a constitutional essential; ibid., 228.

[81] Cf. Mulholland, above n. 20, at 317, 395. Mulholland's very brief but instructive treatment of the problem of the needy notes the connection between innate right and Kant's passage about supporting the poor. However, he concludes from this, unnecessarily, that Kant recognizes a right to welfare. For this LeBar, above n. 16, at 247–48, correctly criticizes him, demonstrating that no right to welfare can emerge from innate right. LeBar in turn concludes that the defect in Mulholland's argument means that Kant's remarks can be understood as referring only to political prudence. Mulholland's conclusion is understandable in the sense that in a modern polity the duty could be juridically recognized and enforced only if it was constitutionally expressed through the explicit or implicit positing of a correlative right. For examples of the operation of such a right, see Government of the Republic of South Africa v. Grootboom [2001] (1) SA 46 (Const. Ct. So. Africa); Social Minimum Case, Judgment of the Federal Constitutional Court of Germany, 9 February 2010 (English summary at <http://www.bundesverfassungsgericht.de/en/press/bvg10-005en.html>).

others' bodies has been superseded by the public duty to support the poor. Non-dependence with respect to one's continued existence is as well served by the juridical order of the third phase as it was by the juridical order of the first phase. The danger of being reduced to a means for others, present in the second phase, has been eliminated by the public duty to the poor.

That the requirement of sustaining the poor is a duty of the sovereign rather than a right of the needy against any particular person bears on two possible objections to the interpretation I am proposing. The first objection is that the public duty to support the poor does not, after all, succeed in reconciling property with innate right. Does it not merely replace possible dependency on the actions of others with an equally unsatisfactory dependency on the state? In answer, one may note that Kant's discussion of citizenship expressly differentiates between being dependent on others for one's existence and being dependent on the state.[82] Kant apparently does not consider the relationship of the poor to the state to involve real dependence. In his view, one may surmise, dependence involves a relationship with someone who, without breaching a duty, can withhold a benefit necessary for one's survival. This is the case when someone owes his survival to the choice of another, because in exercising such a choice no one is under a duty of beneficence as a matter of right. The state is different. The poor receive support from the state because it is owed to them as members of the commonwealth. Because the state is under a duty, it has no discretion to withhold the support; and having no private interest of its own,[83] it also has no motivation to withhold support.[84] The receipt of state support thus does not make the needy subservient to the will of others.

The second objection is that the duty of support recognizes need, despite Kant's earlier indication[85] that need is irrelevant to the concept of right. One should, however, consider the context and significance of the earlier reference to the irrelevance of need. In expounding the "concept of Right, insofar as it is related to an obligation corresponding

---

[82] Kant, above n. 2, at [6:314].

[83] Ibid., at [6:324] Kant argues that the state cannot have domains of its own.

[84] In these respects, the duty of the sovereign stands in contrast to voluntary contributions for the support of the poor, which Kant, giving the instance of lotteries, criticizes as exploitative.; ibid., at [6:326]. Conversely, Kant also says that begging "is closely akin to robbery" (ibid., at [6:326]), perhaps because the beggar exercises a kind of emotional coercion on the sympathies of the donor to cause the donor to surrender what the beggar has no right to.

[85] Ibid., at [6:230].

to it," Kant remarks that "it does not signify the relationship of one's choice to the mere wish (hence also to the mere need of the other) as in actions of beneficence or callousness, but only a relation to the other's choice."[86] Kant is affirming that, when the interaction between persons is examined from a juridical viewpoint, one cannot ascribe a right—or a duty corresponding to that right—on the basis of the needs of one of the parties. Kant here is pointing to a conceptual feature of rights and their correlative duties when one person acts upon another.[87] The duty to support the poor, in contrast, deals not with action by one person that is inconsistent with the rights of another, but with the relationship between the individual and the state. To be sure, the state is under a duty defined in terms of the individual's needs; that duty, however, does not arise through its correlativity with the individual's right. The state is under this duty not because the individual has a right to subsistence, but because a rightful property-protecting regime, which there is a duty to create, is legitimate only when the accumulation of property does not render the poor dependent on the actions of others. The public duty to support the poor is, accordingly, not the response of one person to the need of another, but the response of the commonwealth to the possible dependency that is incompatible with the original contract.

4. "Original possession in common"

If, as I have suggested, Kant connected the notion of subsistence under a property regime to the availability of everything to everyone before the emergence of property, he was following a well-marked path. Property theorists in the centuries preceding Kant typically treated the legal issues surrounding subsistence in terms of a notional residue from primordial use rights that had been transformed into property rights. Kant's account of property includes vocabulary and ideas inherited from the older tradition of natural right. Kant, however, reconfigured these to make them consistent with his distinctive philosophy. In this section I want to note the originality of Kant's duty to the poor

---

[86] Ibid.
[87] "The concept of Right...has to do...with the external and indeed practical relationship of one person to another, insofar as their acts, as facts, can have direct or indirect influence on each other"; ibid., [6:230].

by discussing its relationship to the ideas presented by his great predecessors in the natural right tradition, Grotius and Pufendorf. The contrasting views of these two influential figures crystallized the issues that dominated subsequent legal theory. Because Kant was undoubtedly aware of their treatments of property and drew upon them, the comparison also reinforces from a historical perspective the argument that I have so far presented on interpretive grounds.

Like Kant, Grotius posits a connection between a use right in the state of nature and the satisfaction of basic needs in a developed property regime. According to Grotius, humans originally had a common right over things, in consequence of which "each man could at once take whatever he wished for his own needs, and could consume whatever is capable of being consumed.... Whatever each had thus taken up another could not take from him except by an unjust act."[88] Each person's position was similar to that of the theatre-goer, who has a right to the seat in which he is sitting even though the theatre is a public place.[89] With the loss of innocence and the growth of greed and refinement, this primitive ownership in common, as well as the right to immediate use and consumption that it involved, was superseded by a social contract that allowed possession to be replaced by property.[90] One of the implicit terms of this contract was that a person in direst need could, under a claim of necessity, revive the right of the user that was part of the original common ownership.[91]

Kant's account, although differing in its details, is similar in its structure. Kant has the person start off with a right to occupy space with one's body (like Grotius's example of the seat in the theatre) and to satisfy one's needs through a right to use and consume with which others could not justly interfere. This general right to use and consume does not survive the institution of private property. Nonetheless, for both Kant and Grotius, the original ease of access to resources for purposes of survival means that the law that emerges from the social contract must continue to allow for survival. This is the basis both for Grotius's right of necessity and for Kant's duty to support the poor.

Within this shared structure, however, Kant recasts Grotius's argument in two significant ways. The first is that Kant explicitly rejects

---

[88] Hugo Grotius, *De Jure Belli ac Pacis Libri Tres*, 2 vols., tr. Francis W. Kelsey (1925), vol. 2, 186.
[89] Ibid.
[90] Ibid., 188–90.
[91] Ibid., 193.

the notion of a primitive community of common ownership that he assumes underlies Grotius's account.[92] For Kant the challenge is not to derive private ownership from common ownership but to understand the basis of ownership as such. Kant criticizes the notion of a primitive community on the grounds that such a community would itself have arisen from contract and thus, since the possession it yielded would be derived from the antecedent possession of the contracting parties, would cast no light on original acquisition. Moreover, the legitimacy that arises from primitive possession would be merely contingent on the historicity of the contract that instituted it, rather than grounded in principle.[93]

However, although Kant discards Grotius's conception of a primitive community of common property, he signals that he retains the structure of Grotius's argument by replacing it with the "original possession in common."[94] This original possession in common is merely the innate right understood in terms of the space that a person occupies. The possession is in common not because the earth is owned by all, but because the space one occupies can be anywhere and changes with one's change of location. Accordingly the earth on which I now stand and from which, by virtue of my innate right, I cannot be removed becomes part of your innate right when I move away and you take my place.[95] The commonality of this kind of possession thus refers to the access we all have to the earth due to our freedom to be wherever someone else is not. By using the term "original possession in common," Kant reconfigures the inherited notion while retaining the inherited terminology. The rightful response to dire need in the civil condition then emerges from the original common possession as surely as its analogue in Grotius emerges from primitive community.

---

[92] Kant, above n. 2, at [6:251], [6:258]. Grotius in fact posited not a primitive community of common ownership, but merely a right to use. This is made clear in Grotius, *Commentary on the Law of Prize and Booty*, ed. van Itttersum (2006), 315, a work that was not rediscovered until decades after Kant's death. Kant's knowledge of Grotius's view of property was filtered through Pufendorf and Achenwall, who ascribed the notion of common ownership to him. See B. Sharon Byrd and Joachim Hruschka, *Kant's Doctrine of Right: A Commentary* (2010), 123–26.

[93] Kant, above n. 2, at [6:251], [6:258].

[94] Ibid., at [6:262].

[95] "Each person has an innate right to this place or that place on the earth, i.e., each person is in potential but merely disjunctive general possession of all places on the surface of the earth." Above n. 62, at 320.

The second way in which Kant recasts Grotius's argument is by shifting the mechanism for alleviating the dire need that a property regime might occasion. Whereas Grotius focuses on the claim of necessity, Kant posits a public duty of welfare. The claim of necessity would be completely misplaced within Kant's argument about the poor. Necessity relates two individuals through the resource that one seizes from another. However, the need that motivates this seizure is the consequence not of any particular person's owning the resource, but of the system of property ownership as a whole. Hence Kant posits a duty on the state as the guarantor of the entire property regime. Moreover, as Kant's classic discussion of necessity indicates,[96] a claim of necessity involves the existence of a wrong, albeit one that is unpunishable by a court of law. But if the problem presented by innate right was that the non-dependence of free persons must survive into the civil condition, necessity would not be the solution. For it would be inconsistent with freedom to ensure subsistence by the prospect of committing a wrong. The equality of persons under innate right does not give anyone an immunity to commit a wrong against another. Moreover, innate right postulates the blamelessness of a person who commits no wrongful act, not the culpability of someone who is unpunishable because of the wrongful act's necessitous circumstances. In contrast, for purposes of Kant's argument the state's duty to support the poor succeeds where necessity fails, for the duty operates not through the commission of a wrong but as an implication of the original contract.[97]

Grotius was not alone in connecting the satisfaction of basic needs under a regime of private property with the original right to immediate use. The same connection reappears in Pufendorf, despite his extensive criticism of other aspects of Grotius's account.

Pufendorf rejected Grotius's conception of an original community of common ownership. He contrasted what he termed Grotius's "positive community" of common ownership in which all things are owned by everyone, with the "negative community" in which "all things lay open to all men, and belonged no more to one than to another."[98] Pufendorf then traced the development of ownership

---

[96] Kant, above n. 2, [6:235–36].

[97] This is not to say that in the civil condition necessity is unavailable as a response to urgent need, but only that necessity does not deal with the problem that I argue is resolved by the duty to support the poor.

[98] Samuel Pufendorf, *De Jure Naturae et Gentium Libri Octo*, 2 vols., tr. C. H. and W. A. Oldfather (1934), vol. 2, 537.

through a series of social pacts, the first of which was to the effect that "whatever one of these things, which were left open to all, and its fruits, a man had laid his hands upon, with intent to turn it to his uses, could not be taken from him by another."[99]

Kant's conception of the earliest stage in the development of property is more or less identical to Pufendorf's. Both Kant's original possession in common and Pufendorf's negative community of all things imply the same criticism of Grotius, that the task is not to derive private from common ownership but to trace the development of ownership from non-ownership. To this end both Kant and Pufendorf situate persons within a regime of rights and their correlative negative duties. From an early stage—Kant through the innate right and Pufendorf through the initial social pact—both regard interference with another's use as an injustice. Their main difference is that whereas Pufendorf treats the negative community of all things as a historical stage, Kant declares that "[o]riginal possession in common is, rather, a practical rational concept which contains a priori the principle in accordance with which alone men can use a place on the earth in accordance with the principles of Right."[100]

To deal with the problem of subsistence within a fully developed property regime, Pufendorf indicates that the magistrate, as well as other persons of means, has a duty to relieve extreme need.[101] This duty is embedded within Pufendorf's account of necessity. For Pufendorf, assistance to someone in extreme need is an imperfect duty, correlative to the needy person's imperfect right to the assistance. The reason for regarding the duty as imperfect is that, because "it is performed upon a kind of voluntary impulse arising from a man's good nature,"[102] the person who would benefit from the performance of the duty has neither the power to compel him to perform nor the right to be compensated for non-performance.[103] Instances of the breach of imperfect obligations are ingratitude and the failure to give benefactions, as Pufendorf thinks it unjust to neglect occasions for beneficence and not to return the favor for benefactions received.[104]

---

[99] Ibid., 535, see also 537 ("all things should lie open for all, for the promiscuous use of every man").

[100] Kant, above n. 2, [6:362].

[101] Pufendorf, above n. 98, 305.

[102] Ibid., 315.

[103] Samuel Pufendorf, *Elementorum Jurisprudentiae Universalis*, tr. W. A. Oldfather (1931), 66.

[104] Ibid., 60.

In the case of aiding the needy, "[t]he reason why only an imperfect right is allowed, especially to such things as are owed on the grounds of humanity, is that thereby a man finds the opportunity to show that his mind is intent upon voluntarily doing his duty, and at the same time possesses the means to bind others to him by his kindness."[105] But "when necessity does not admit of any other means to secure his safety,"[106] Pufendorf allows the needy person to exercise self-help. "Must some poor fellow die of hunger because he cannot overcome by his prayers the inhumanity of some man of wealth?"[107] The result is that, although aiding the poor is an imperfect obligation, "the urge of supreme necessity makes it possible for such things to be claimed on the same ground as those which are owed by a perfect right."[108] The wealthy person's breach of duty in failing to be beneficent to the needy, when combined with the urgency of the needy person's situation, gives the needy person the right to take for himself what he ought voluntarily to have been given. Necessity, as it were, perfects an otherwise imperfect right.

From Kant's perspective, this account of necessity is rife with confusion. First, the obligation to assist the poor is based on considerations of beneficence, which are ethical rather than juridical. Moreover, the duty imposed on the magistrate is not a public one derived from the political nature of the magistrate's power, but is merely a reflection of the magistrate's opportunity for beneficence. Furthermore, when necessity takes hold, the benefactor's imperfect duty gets matched to a corresponding right that can be treated as perfect, thus destroying the correlativity of duty and right. Finally, necessity is regarded as triggering the operation of a right, rather than excusing the commission of an unpunishable wrong.

For our purposes the basis of the right to subsistence that underlies Pufendorf's account of necessity is of particular interest. For Pufendorf, property emerges from the original availability of everything to everyone through a series of social pacts. These pacts allow for a variety of property arrangements, "provided that they involve no contradiction and do not overturn society."[109] But, Pufendorf notes, all property regimes acknowledge that the necessity of another provides

---

[105] Pufendorf, above n. 98, 305.
[106] Pufendorf, above n. 103, 59.
[107] Pufendorf, above n. 98, 305.
[108] Ibid.
[109] Ibid., 537.

an exception to the proprietor's rights.[110] Pufendorf sees necessity as reviving the right of everyone to everything that characterized the original negative community in which property rights did not exist. This is because Pufendorf is of the opinion that a condition to that effect is implicit in social pacts establishing property: "it is understood that whenever any man in the division of things renounced his right to such things as are assigned others he did so with this reservation: Provided he cannot otherwise secure his own safety."[111] Thus, a person's desperate need does not create a new right in the property of others, but triggers the operation of the condition under which everyone's right to everything was surrendered, that property would not endanger survival. Presumably the reason for Pufendorf's insistence on reading this condition into the social contract is that "individuals would not consent to a system of rights that might require that they starve."[112]

On my suggested reconstruction of Kant's thought, Kant reconfigures the idea that individuals would not contract into the possibility of starvation, by relating that possibility to a dependence on the actions of others. Kant's conception of right eliminates the ethical elements that vitiated Pufendorf's account of necessity and adds a public duty to the poor. The requirement of undiminished freedom in the original contract and the consequent need to reconstruct in the civil condition the lack of dependence on others that was present in innate right enable Kant conceptually to connect the duty to support the poor with each person's innate right. This connection is consistent with the natural right tradition represented by Grotius and Pufendorf, who each in their different ways traced the legal categories for benefiting the poor to the rights that everyone had before the institution of private property. Kant's attention to what he termed "original possession in common" indicates his continuity with this tradition. Kant did not explicitly link innate right in the first phase of his account to subsistence for the poor in the third phase. But it may well be that this connection was so well known from the writings of his predecessors in the natural rights tradition that he regarded it as obvious.

---

[110] Ibid., 538.

[111] Ibid.

[112] Thomas A. Horne, *Property Rights and Poverty: Political Argument in Britain, 1605–1834* (1990), 36. Although Kant lies outside the scope of Horne's treatment, Horne's book in its entirety casts valuable light on the contemporary understanding of the connection between property and the relief of poverty.

Drawing on and arguably perfecting this tradition, Kant purported to show how instituting private property and taxing to support the poor were jointly necessary if society was to be a legitimate union of self-determining agents. His account treats property and taxation to support the poor as distinct but interconnected. On the one hand private property and taxation figure in different kinds of juridical relationship. Property relates one person to another through the correlativity of right and duty; the duty to support the poor relates the taxpayers to the state and the state to the poor. The consequence of this distinction is that considerations of poverty have no effect on the definition and application of property rights. On the other hand, property and the public duty to support the poor are connected through a single sequenced argument that extends the reach of the universal principle of Right while preserving consistency with the ideas of innate equality and non-dependence that this principle implies. For Kant, taxation is not theft, and neither is property. On the contrary, taxation and property are jointly necessary for a civil condition legitimized by the idea of the original contract. On Kant's view as I have reconstructed it, the public duty to support the poor is latent within private property as a rightful institution. Formulating Kant's point in terms of the Aristotelian forms of justice, one may say that the distributive justice of taxing to support the poor is the conceptual concomitant of establishing a legally effective system of corrective justice.

9
Can Law Survive Legal Education?

1. Three activities

Legal education exists at the confluence of three activities: the practice of law, the enterprise of understanding that practice, and the study of law's possible understandings within the context of a university. The first of these, the practice of law, consists of the activities consciously governed by law, including, for example, lawyers giving legal advice, citizens contemplating the legality of prospective actions, legislators creating law within the limits of their jurisdiction, and judges determining the rights and duties of litigants. It thus comprehends the entire field of legal institutions, legal doctrine, and legal interaction. The second activity, the enterprise of understanding law, refers to the elucidation of the character of this practice. This enterprise seeks to determine the extent to which the practice's various characteristics can be grasped as exhibiting, through the coherence of their interrelationships, some generically determinate character. The third activity, university study, requires that the student's reflections about law be appropriate to an institution devoted to caring for the intellectual inheritance—the stock of ideas, images, beliefs, skills, and modes of thinking—that composes the world's civilization.[1]

These three activities exercise a reciprocal effect on one another. On the one hand, the practice of law supplies the materials that are to be understood through university study. On the other hand, that practice is transformed by the very enterprise of articulating understandings of it. Scholars are not merely the passive recipients of the

---

[1] Michael Oakeshott, "The Study of 'Politics' in a University: An Essay in Appropriateness," in *Rationalism in Politics and Other Essays* (1962; new and expanded ed., 1991), 184, 187–94.

law's materials. Rather, their understandings influence the practice by making practitioners conscious of the possibilities that are implicit in it.[2] When these understandings originate in the universities and are thus invested with the authority of prestigious institutions of learning, the practice of law itself can become either (at best) more aware of law's distinct voice in the conversation of civilized humanity or (worse) more prone to succumb to prevailing academic orthodoxies.

The central challenge that has faced legal education since it was wrested from the legal profession and lodged in the universities[3] has been how to integrate the three activities. The relation between the practice and the university study of law has proved particularly problematic. One influential critique of legal education laments the growing disjunction between them:

The schools should be training ethical practitioners and producing scholarship that judges, legislators, and practitioners can use...But many law schools—especially the so-called 'elite' ones—have abandoned their proper place, by emphasizing abstract theory at the expense of practical scholarship and pedagogy...[I]f law schools continue to stray from their principal mission of professional scholarship and training, the disjunction between legal education and the legal profession will grow and society will be the worse for it.[4]

---

[2] The classic statement of this is Friedrich Carl von Savigny's comments on the Roman jurists:

[T]he action of the jurists, appears at first sight a dependent one, receiving its materials from without. However, by their giving to the materials so presented a scientific form which strives to disclose and perfect the unity dwelling in them, there arises a new organic life which shapes and reacts upon the materials themselves, so that from science as such, a new sort of generation of law incessantly proceeds.

Friedrich Carl von Savigny, *System of the Modern Roman Law*, tr. William Holloway (1867), 37–38.

[3] In Canada this happened relatively recently. The decisive event was the defection of three of Canada's leading law professors (Cecil A. Wright, Bora Laskin, and John Willis) from the law school operated by the Law Society of Upper Canada and their establishing the modern Faculty of Law at the University of Toronto in 1949. Within a decade, the Law Society of Upper Canada surrendered control of legal education to the universities by recognizing that graduation from a university faculty of law qualified the graduate to enter the profession without penalty. For a description of this "revolution" in Canadian legal education, see C. Ian Kyer and Jerome E. Bickenbach, *The Fiercest Debate: Cecil A. Wright, the Benchers, and Legal Education in Ontario 1923–1957* (1987). For a recent discussion, see R. C. B. Risk, "My Continuing Legal Education," (2005) 55 U. Toronto L.J. 313.

[4] Harry T. Edwards, "The Growing Disjunction between Legal Education and the Legal Profession," (1992) 91 Mich. L. Rev. 34, 41. Judge Edwards's views are extensively discussed in Symposium, "Legal Education," (1993) 91 Mich. L. Rev. 1921.

Formulated in these terms, the critique forcefully indicates what its author thinks is at stake. The practice of law and its university study as currently constituted are regarded as competitors, such that the university's preoccupation with "theory" operates "at the expense of" practical professional concerns. The proper function of the university study of law, according to this critique, is to produce scholarly work for the professional consumption of those engaged in the practice of law. The diagnosis, in effect, is that the practice of law is effaced through university study, and the remedy suggested is that the latter be recalled to its "principal mission" of being useful to the former.

This criticism has, I think, a truth that should be recognized, though my version of this truth is perhaps not what its author intended. A disjunction between the practice of law and its university study would indeed be disquieting. This is not, however, because the disjunction would be a disservice to the legal profession (though it might be), but rather because it would be a disservice to the university itself.

The university exists as a locus for the study of law not for the sake of the legal profession, but because law is a component of the intellectual inheritance of civilization. The "principal mission" of university study is to care for and develop this inheritance. That the legal profession should benefit from this through the university's graduates and its ideas is all to the good. Moreover, it is both desirable and necessary that those who are most intimately connected with and conscious of the workings of law should support its study within the university—thus manifesting a commitment to the idea that law is integral to civilized modes of thinking and living. But criticism of the university study of law should come from a standpoint internal to university activity itself. Accordingly, the disjunction between legal education and the legal profession is troubling only if it represents a failure on the university's own terms.

The disjunction would be such a failure in the following sense. University study of any kind must have a definite object; it must be the study of something. Law is a phenomenon that exists only through a set of legal doctrines, institutions, and juristic activities. The university study of law can therefore be nothing other than the study of the practice of law. Accordingly, legal education is inevitably concerned with the activity of "judges, legislators, and practitioners," not in order to produce scholarship that they "can use" (though, if they can legitimately use it, so much the better), but in order to reflect upon the meaning and intelligibility of their activity. A disjunction between the practice of law and the university study of law is troubling because it suggests that the university study of law actually has no object, that it is the study of nothing, similar to the zoological study of unicorns. Such study would be a failing from the university's standpoint, quite apart from its uselessness to the legal profession.

But what does it mean to say that the university study of law is disjointed from the practice of law? The answer lies in how these two activities conceptualize the character of law. If the university study of law expressly or implicitly attributes to law a different character than that which is presupposed in the practice of law, then one cannot say that the practice of law is the object of university study. Under those conditions, the practice of law and the university study of law would be activities lacking a common interest; the law that the latter studied would not be the same as the law that the former practiced.

Thus, the difference between the two activities of practice and university study has to be mediated through the third activity, that of understanding the law. For only when that understanding is common to the law as practiced and as studied is there no disjunction between legal education and the practice of law.

So formulated, the issue raised by the supposed disjunction between the legal profession and legal education turns out to be primarily one of legal theory rather than one of straightforward sociological observation. Of course, what is discussed in a university differs from what is discussed in a law office or a judges' conference. What might link the two is a conception of how law is to be understood. Those participating in university life as students, teachers, and scholars regard law as a significant component of civilization's intellectual inheritance and attempt to think through the features implicit in the practice of law that make that practice worthy of academic attention. The process of identifying these features and thinking them through requires reference, implicitly or explicitly, to some understanding of what the practice of law is. This is an exercise in legal theory, because legal theory consists of nothing but a self-conscious examination of the range of possible understandings of law. And so the critic who blames the disjunction on too much "abstract theory" necessarily, if ironically, issues an appeal for further theorizing.

In this chapter, I wish to present more concretely this abstractly formulated notion of disjunction. My focus is on the way that this disjunction arises in the university study of private law. A justification for this focus is that private law, as the enduring bedrock of legal education, is a primary vehicle for the transmission of conceptions of legal understanding. More importantly, the simplicity and the restricted scope of the relationship between the parties allow the disjunction and its implications to be set out with particular clarity. Section 2 of this chapter suggests that prevailing instrumentalist approaches within the legal academy, exemplified by (but not confined to) certain versions of the economic analysis of law, systemically distort legal practice. This distortion effaces the characteristic concepts of private law, ignores the direct relationship between the parties, and assimilates private law into public law. In these respects, economic analysis fails to comprehend private law as the distinctive kind of normative phenomenon that it is.

My purpose in making these observations is not to criticize economic analysis in particular, but to point to a structural problem that accompanies an assumption—that law is to be explained instrumentally—that is widely popular in the academic treatment of law and that yet separates the university study of law from law's practice. Economic analysis thus merely provides the paradigmatic example of an instrumentalism that emerges from a distinctly academic enterprise but that mischaracterizes the legal practice it purports to explain. In section 3, I will sketch a different mode of legal understanding that both respects legal practice and affirms private law as a component of our intellectual inheritance that is worth studying in its own terms. Finally, in section 4, I will trace the implications of this mode of understanding for the interdisciplinary turn that is a conspicuous feature of contemporary legal education.

My goal in this chapter is a modest one. It is easy to read critiques of present legal education as exhortations to exclude, either through curricular change or appointment policy, certain kinds of currently entrenched enquiry.[5] My argument here, however, is not about what to exclude but what to include. By exploring the supposed disjunction between practice and university study, and by suggesting how to overcome that disjunction, I want to point to a conception of the core of legal education, at least for private law, that links the three activities. This in no way denies the insights of other ways of thinking about law. Inasmuch as they are about law, however, those insights

---

[5] This is, for instance, the way Sandy Levinson reads Judge Edwards's critique; Sanford Levinson, "Judge Edwards' Indictment of 'Impractical' Scholars: The Need for a Bill of Particulars," (1993) 91 Mich. L. Rev. 2010.

presuppose—and therefore are ancillary to—an understanding of law that is not disjointed from the practice of law. Thus, my focus is on what legal education should necessarily deal with, whatever else it deals with.

2. Disjunction: the role of instrumentalist analysis

A. The example of economic analysis

To see the sort of disjunction that I have in mind, consider the notion, popular among expositors of the economic analysis of law, that economic efficiency is the key to understanding tort doctrine. The basic assumption of this approach is that a defendant should be liable for failing to guard against an accident only when the cost of precautions is less than the probable cost of the accident. From the economic standpoint, the goal of the liability rules of private law is to provide incentives for cost-justified precautions. Ambitious claims have been made on behalf of this mode of analysis: economic ideas have been said to reveal the inner nature,[6] implicit design,[7] and unifying perspective[8] for tort law.

This approach constitutes a notable attempt to link the university study of law to the practice of law. On the one hand it draws on the insights of economics, the academic discipline that provides a systematic understanding of what Hegel called "the infinitely complex crisscross movements of reciprocal production and exchange."[9] On the other hand, it deploys this discipline to explain leading doctrines in the practice of tort law. The vast academic literature that this attention to economic efficiency has inspired is one of the most impressive achievements of contemporary legal scholarship.

One would have thought that an approach that purports to reveal the inner nature of tort law would be particularly illuminating about the concepts that pertain to tort law. Negligence liability, for instance, involves a conjunction of legal concepts, such as duty, proximate cause, factual cause, and the standard of reasonable care. Such concepts are fundamental to our understanding of tort liability because they structure the thinking of those who participate in the practice. Through

---

[6] Richard A. Posner, *The Problems of Jurisprudence* (1990), 361.
[7] William M. Landes and Richard A. Posner, *The Economic Structure of Tort Law* (1987), vii.
[8] Richard A. Posner, *Tort Law: Cases and Economic Analysis* (1982), 2.
[9] G. W. F. Hegel, *The Philosophy of Right*, tr. T. M. Knox (1952), s. 201.

such concepts, tort law discloses its own normative character, thereby indicating the terms in which it is to be understood. Revealing the inner nature of such concepts would (one would expect) disclose how they function or should function within the reasoning of those engaged in legal practice. Among the issues that would then be addressed are: What are the conditions that call each of these concepts into play? How are they related to each other and do they form a coherent set? What is the relationship between the abstract formulations of these concepts and the institutional processes of adjudication that particularize them for specific cases? And are these concepts suitable vehicles for the normative considerations that justify or can justify the determination of liability? Attention to these issues would involve taking the concepts seriously as objects worth explicating in their own terms, with a view to examining whether they have or could have the significance that tort law ascribes to them when it orients legal practice, as manifested in the reasoning of lawyers and judges, along their lines.

In fact, economic analysis does the opposite. When economic analysis is presented as the key to understanding tort law, the point of the analysis is not to take the fundamental concepts seriously as concepts used in legal practice, but to render them otiose. Economic analysis has its own stock of ideas that operate without reference to the legal concepts. The result is that ideas about economic efficiency replace rather than illuminate the legal concepts. Instead of functioning as vehicles of thought, the legal concepts are at most labels pinned to conclusions once economic analysis has done all the work.

Consider two instances, causation and intention. Causation plays a central role in determinations of liability as a matter of legal practice. For the economic analysis of tort law, however, causation turns out to be an idea "that can largely be dispensed with."[10] Given that the purpose of tort law is thought to be the promotion of efficiency, the defendant will be held liable—and thus deemed to be the cause of an injury—when such liability will promote the efficient allocation of resources to safety. Thus, cause does not mark the law's concern for the transitivity of the relationship between the defendant's conduct and the plaintiff's injury, but functions merely as the label that is attached to the conclusion of a cost–benefit analysis. Because both parties might have taken precautions, the task for economic analysis is

---

[10] Landes and Posner, above n. 7, at 229.

to determine not whether the defendant caused the plaintiff's injury in the conventional legal sense, but which of them could have avoided the accident more cheaply.

Similarly dispensable is the concept of intention.[11] For the economic analyst, intention refers not (as it does in the law itself) to the actor's purpose with reference to a wrongful consequence, but to the connection between the probability of harm and the ease with which the actor could have avoided it. What "establishes a clear-cut economic basis for condemning a distinct form of misconduct" is not the wrongfulness of making another's injury the object of one's conduct but instead the injurer's low cost of avoidance relative to the social benefits of the injurer's activity.[12]

The economic analysis, in other words, produces a disjunction between the significance of tort concepts for legal practice and their significance for academic study. While purporting to offer an account of legal practice—indeed, while claiming to reveal its inner nature—the economic approach instead effaces the very concepts that constitute legal reasoning when determining liability within that practice. In presenting its analysis of concepts like causation and intent, the economic analyst aims not to illuminate those ideas in their own terms, but to make them disappear in the face of the analytic power of economic efficiency. Economic analysis thereby offers a theory that negates rather than explains the concepts supposedly being analyzed. The deficiency of this form of scholarship lies not in its presenting nothing about legal practice that "judges, legislators, and practitioners can use,"[13] but in its presenting nothing about legal practice at all.

There is a second respect in which economic analysis does not reflect legal practice. Through the process of litigation, the practice of law directly links the particular plaintiff to the particular defendant. Liability is thus a relational phenomenon in which the court responds to the wrong or injustice that the defendant has done to the plaintiff. This linkage assumes that the same reasons for liability apply simultaneously to both parties. In contrast, economic analysis does not treat the parties as directly connected. Rather, it views them each as subject to different incentives that somehow happen to be conjoined in a finding of liability. For economic analysis the point of liability is to induce

---

[11] Ibid.
[12] Ibid., at 153.
[13] Edwards, above n. 4, at 34.

the parties to take cost-justified precautions. These incentives, however, apply separately to each of them. Awarding damages against a defendant provides defendants with an incentive to act efficiently, "[b]ut that the damages are paid *to the plaintiff* is, from the economic standpoint, a detail."[14] The plaintiff's receipt of the damage award reflects a different group of incentives (such as the need to induce enforcement of the norm and to prevent prospective victims from pre-empting the precautions incumbent on actors)[15] that do not in themselves entail taking the money from the actual defendant. Both parties are thereby involved in the damage award, but for separate reasons. Efficiency might as easily be served by two different funds, one that receives tort fines from inefficient actors, another that disburses the indicated inducements to victims. Instead of linking each party to the other, economic analysis ascribes the presence of both to a combination of incentives independently applicable to each. Accordingly, liability is the consequence of one-sided considerations that somehow come together, rather than of relational considerations that treat the parties as belonging together because of what the defendant has done to the plaintiff.

This sundering of the parties' relationship leads economic analysis to mischaracterize private law in a third way. The fundamental concepts that express the unity of the parties' relationship make private law a distinctive mode of legal ordering, with its own discourse, its own internal organization, and its own normative presuppositions. Within the legal domain, the distinctiveness of private law allows it to be contrasted to public law. Private law normatively connects the parties directly to each other, not to the state. Although the state is present through the machinery of adjudication, the purpose of this machinery is merely to give authoritative expression to what the relationship between the parties requires. In contrast, public law is concerned with the forms and limits of the state's exercise of power with respect to those who are subject to it. Whereas private law deals with the relationships between participants in the community, public law deals with the relationships between participants and the community as embodied in its official organs.

By denying the significance of fundamental concepts of private law and negating the unity of the defendant–plaintiff relationship, economic analysis divests private law of the possibility of constituting a

---

[14] Richard A. Posner, *Economic Analysis of Law*, 2nd ed. (1977), 143 (emphasis in original).
[15] Richard A. Posner, *Economic Analysis of Law*, 6th ed. (2003), 192.

distinctive mode of legal ordering. From the economic standpoint, private law is to be understood as a judicially created and enforced regime for the taxation and regulation of inefficient activity.[16] Courts act as administrative tribunals that set norms for efficient behavior and exact fines when those norms are breached. The plaintiff's function in initiating a lawsuit is not to secure redress for wrongful injury but to claim a bounty for prosecuting inefficient economic activity. Economic analysis thus submerges the private nature of tort law in a public law of economic regulation.

Thus, the link that economic analysis posits between academic study and the practice of private law is vitiated by its mistaken characterization of that practice. Instead of illuminating private law, economic analysis discards its fundamental concepts, breaks apart its relationships, and subverts its private nature. The economic analysts are not so much concerned with understanding private law as with assessing the degree to which its rules coincide with what efficiency demands. Far from being the focus of their attention, private law is merely the foreign language into which economic discourse has somehow been translated.[17] The result is a profound disjunction between the economic analysis of law as a method of university study and the practice that is being studied.[18]

B. The dynamic of instrumentalism

My point in making these comments is not to criticize economic analysis in particular. Rather, in contemporary legal education, economic analysis is paradigmatic of the instrumentalist structure of academic enquiry. What occasions the disjunction with legal practice is this instrumentalist structure, not economic analysis as such.

---

[16] Richard A. Posner, "A Theory of Negligence," (1972) 1 J. Legal Stud. 29, 48–49, 51.

[17] For law as the translation of economic principle, see Landes and Posner, above n. 7, at 23; Posner, above n. 6, at 361.

[18] Economic analysis may lodge itself within the practice through the influence of economic scholarship on judges, who then apply it in their judgments. Compare the observations of von Savigny, above n. 2. To the extent that this occurs, the disjunction between academic study and legal practice is lessened. However, in its stead a different and ultimately more serious problem arises. Because economic analysis cannot coherently reflect the character of the law, its entry into legal practice sets up irresolvable tensions between the law's fundamental concepts and relational structure, on the one hand, and the economic analysis on the other. Thus, the disjunction between academic study and legal practice is displaced by a disjunction internal to the legal practice, between the economic analysis and the practice's concepts and structure.

Economic analysis is nothing but an instance of a more comprehensive dynamic.

The instrumentalism of economic analysis consists in the interpretation of tort law as forwarding the goal of economic efficiency. As the disjunction just described indicates, the normative attractiveness of this goal—what makes it worthy of being considered a goal that tort law should forward—does not arise out of the law itself, by reflection, for instance on the fundamental concepts of tort law or on the nature of the relationship between the parties. Rather, this goal is thought to be desirable independently of tort law and is then given to tort law from the outside. Tort law is only an instrument in the goal's promotion.

Economic efficiency is merely one of the goals that modern scholarship has proposed. These goals come in many varieties, ranging from the general, such as promoting communal responsibility[19] or basic aspects of the good[20] to the more specific, such as alleviating injury.[21] All such goals base their appeal on some conception of human welfare that is considered desirable independently of the law and that the law should therefore strive to forward.

Regardless of the goal it advances, an instrumentalist analysis of private law mischaracterizes its object in the same way that economic analysis does. An instrumentalist approach makes three errors. First, it imports outside goals for immanent concepts of private law. Second, it ignores the relationship between a plaintiff and a defendant. Third, it wrongly converts all private law into public law.

Instrumentalist approaches substitute for the concepts of private law the outside notions that are appropriate for the promotion of the preferred goal. Instead of working out the meaning of the applicable legal concepts in particular situations, as legal practice requires, the instrumentalist specifies the mechanisms through which the social goal might be forwarded in different circumstances. Because the really important work is done by the apparatus of instrumental reasoning, the law's invocation of the standard legal concepts is regarded as a

[19] Robert A. Baruch Bush, "Between Two Worlds: The Shift from Individual to Group Responsibility in the Law of Causation of Injury," (1986) 33 U.C.L.A. L. Rev. 1473, 1480–502.

[20] John Finnis, *Natural Law and Natural Rights* (1979), 59–75.

[21] Marc A. Franklin, "Replacing the Negligence Lottery: Compensation and Selective Reimbursement," (1967) 53 Va. L. Rev. 774, 785–88.

mere ritual,[22] a veil to be pierced by clear-headed analysis,[23] or even as a salutary obfuscation that itself has instrumental value.[24]

Second, within instrumentalist analysis the plaintiff and defendant are not directly related to each other. The goals are considered elements of the social good, and therefore are concerned with the overall benefit, however construed, to society as a whole, not with the relationship between two particular parties. Instead of linking the plaintiff to the defendant who has done her an injustice, instrumentalist analysis groups each party with those who are, from the standpoint of the goal in question, similarly situated. For example, the alleviation of injury, when considered as a goal of tort law, connects the injured party not to the particular person who has wrongfully caused the injury, but to other injured persons who have a like claim on the distribution of society's resources. Analysis in terms of a goal thus breaks apart the relationship between the parties, in order to apply the appropriate goal to each of them. The result is that reading an independently desirable goal back into private law creates a dissonance between the parties' nexus as a matter of legal practice and the goal's indifference to this nexus within the instrumentalist understanding of law. When university study accepts the instrumentalist understanding and develops it, this dissonance appears as a disjunction between university study and legal practice.

Third, for the instrumentalist, all law is public law. The favored goals must be selected by the state and inscribed into a schedule of collectively approved aims. The various method of elaborating the community's purposes—adjudication, legislation, administrative regulation, and so on—are merely the species of the generically single activity of making the goals a legal reality. The singling out of a particular goal from among all the possible goals, the balancing of one goal against competing goals, and the positing of the means for promoting the chosen goals require legislation by political authority. Norms of private law are therefore considered the product of legislative acts, even when formulated through the adjudicative process.[25] Instrumentalism thereby dissolves the very idea of private law as a distinctive mode of

[22] Jerome Frank, "What Courts Do In Fact," (1931) 26 Ill. L. Rev. 645, 653.

[23] Felix S. Cohen, "Transcendental Nonsense and the Functional Approach," (1935) 35 Colum. L. Rev. 809, 809–12.

[24] Guido Calabresi, "Concerning Cause and the Law of Torts: An Essay for Harry Kalven, Jr.," (1975) 43 U. Chi. L. Rev. 69, 107.

[25] Oliver Wendell Holmes, Jr., "Privilege, Malice and Intent," (1894) 8 Harv. L. Rev. 1, 3.

legal ordering. Private law turns out to be nothing but public law in disguise.[26]

These three features of instrumentalist analysis are intimately connected. The legal concepts (such as causation and intent) are the apparatus that the law has elaborated to treat the relationship between the parties as a single normative unit. The process of determining a defendant's liability by working through these concepts is what stamps private law as a distinctive kind of normative ordering. The concepts, the relational unity, and distinctiveness of its form of legal ordering are thus the mutually entailed aspects of private law as a legal practice. Instrumental analysis distances itself from all of these when it distances itself from any of them.

To the extent that contemporary legal education revolves around instrumental understandings, it inevitably separates itself from private law as a legal practice. Economic analysis is simply exemplary in this respect. Those who, out of skepticism about or antagonism toward economic efficiency as a goal, think that legal education should center on different goals contribute to this disjunction no less than do the economic analysts themselves. The disjunction is the consequence not of one particular goal or set of goals rather than another, but of the very orientation toward goals.

In the face of this disjunction between the instrumentalist understanding and the legal practice, two responses are tempting. Each of these responses leaves the disjunction intact, while submerging one or the other of the disjoined activities.

The first response is embodied in academic work that expressly disconnects the university study of law from legal practice. In private law this work takes the form of "decoupling" the position of the plaintiff from that of the defendant. One suggestion, for example, is that the defendant should pay more and the plaintiff should receive less than the compensatory amount, with the difference going to cover the state's administrative costs.[27] Another example is the suggestion that efficient incentives would be best achieved by arranging that contract damages be awarded to a third party rather than to the victim of the breach.[28] Such decoupling embraces the disjunction by foregoing the

---

[26] Leon Green, "Tort Law: Public Law in Disguise," (1959) 38 Tex. L. Rev. 1.
[27] A. Mitchell Polinsky and Yeon-Koo Che, "Decoupling Liability: Optimal Incentives for Care and Litigation," (1991) 22 RAND J. Econ. 562.
[28] Robert D. Cooter and Ariel Porat, "Anti-Insurance," (2002) 31 J. Legal Stud. 203, 204.

aspiration to see the university study of law as an endeavor to understand the practice of law. In terms of instrumentalist scholarship, proposals of this sort represent an advance over the more traditional project of explaining the law. They are based on the recognition that the relationship between the parties constricts the free play of instrumentalist reasoning. Once one unravels the parties' relationship, the limits of legal scholarship are set not by the law as an object of the enquiry, but by the imagination, ingenuity, and brilliance—all amply present—of the scholars themselves. This allows a more consistent presentation of the kind of instrumentalism favored by the particular scholar. But there is also a parallel disadvantage. Having severed the link to legal practice, these proposals seem to be nothing more than dreamy exercises in instrumentalist utopianism, far removed from the hard-headed contact with the real world that instrumentalists like to profess.

The second response goes in the opposite direction by emphasizing the primacy of legal practice. This response is exemplified in the call, mentioned earlier, for university study to adhere to its "principal mission" of professional training by producing scholarship that can be used by legal practitioners.[29] Offered in the name of overcoming the disjunction between legal practice and university study, the suggestion merely subordinates the latter to the former, raising the question of why this "mission" would require university study at all rather than a more direct system of professional training and apprenticeship. After all, on this conception, what are law professors except legal practitioners with more leisure and lower salaries? By connecting the university study of law with the demands of legal practice rather than with the purposes of the university, the suggestion dismisses the significance of any understanding of law that is not coterminous with legal practice itself. In effect, the university study of law is regarded merely as a parasite on the practice of law.

These two responses are the consequence of viewing law in instrumentalist terms. Instead of attempting to overcome the disjunction between university study and legal practice that instrumentalism creates, the responses cut the Gordian knot by accentuating one element and disregarding the other. The decoupling view has a strong notion of the university study of law, which, however, turns out to be not about law but about the possible artifacts of instrumental reasoning.

---

[29] Edwards, above n. 4, at 41.

In contrast, the parasitic view is attentive to legal practice but, given the open-endedness of instrumentalist analysis, sees little value in university study beyond what can be used by legal practitioners. In their separate ways each responds to the problem of disjunction by giving up on it.

3. Overcoming the disjunction

A. The character of private law

In this section I want to sketch a possible solution to the problem of disjunction. In the previous section I argued that, so far as private law is concerned, the disjunction between the university study of law and the practice of law is a consequence of the instrumentalist framework that dominates contemporary legal studies. The instrumentalist framework subjects private law to analyses that inevitably mischaracterize it. Instrumentalist approaches efface the concepts of private law, fail to connect the parties directly to each other, and assimilate private law to public law. Accordingly, a solution to the problem of disjunction involves rethinking the assumptions that create it.

Two mutually reinforcing moves are involved. Negatively, the instrumentalist framework is to be rejected, since it is the infelicity of this framework that generates the problem to begin with. Positively, the organizing concepts of private law, the direct relationship between the parties and the distinctiveness of private law as a mode of legal ordering must be understood as the indicia of the specific character of private law. The primary task of the university study of private law—what it should do, whatever else it does—is to enquire into this character. By so doing, university study both maintains its continuity with the legal practice, which is its starting point, and yet goes beyond that practice to disclose its implicit structural and normative ideas.

Central to the elucidation of the character of private law is the assumption that private law is (or at least aspires to be) a normatively coherent practice that can accordingly yield a coherent understanding. Under this assumption the organizing concepts of private law are harmoniously connected both to one another and to the institutional structure of private law litigation. This assumption is a necessary starting point for several reasons. First, only on the assumption of the coherence of legal practice can one make sense of the endeavor to regard private law as a systematically intelligible body of knowledge that can be amenable to university study. Otherwise, private law would be assumed to be nothing but a piled aggregate of propositions that together had no specifiable character. Second, coherence is an internal value and aspiration of the private law itself, being integral to its reasoning and discourse. Thus, the assumption of coherence is not only a methodological postulate of university study but also a pervasive premise of legal practice and therefore itself part of the character of the practice. Third, the practice of private law is a normative phenomenon, where the disposition of one person's claim against another has to be justified through the use of public reason. The process of justification presupposes that the private law's entire apparatus of justification is internally coherent, for if elements of that apparatus pulled in different directions, then it could not function to justify anything.

The character of private law provides the general framework for understanding it as a coherent normative phenomenon. Specification of this character arises by a process of scholarly reflection on, and generalization from, the law's particular arrangements (its doctrines, its institutional structure, its ensemble of concepts, its methods of reasoning, and so on). However, the character of private law is not composed simply of the sum total of these arrangements. Some of these arrangements may achieve that character only imperfectly or deficiently, because they may not accord with the practice viewed as a coherent whole. Whether the positive law's treatment of a particular problem bears out the assumption of coherence is a contingent matter. Where it does not, the character of private law then provides the standpoint, internal to private law as a whole, from which to criticize the particular legal arrangement. Character is thus an ideal construct that makes the particulars of the practice of private law intelligible in the light of the practice's most general and pervasive features. Understood in terms of its character, private law is "a unity of particularity and genericity."[30]

The task of specifying the character of private law belongs to the university study of law, but it is rooted in legal practice. Unless university study takes legal practice seriously, the enquiry into its character would, of course, be self-stultifying. No disjunction exists between the character and the practice of private law. Even when some particular arrangement of private law is thought to be deficient in the light of

---

[30] Michael Oakeshott, *On Human Conduct* (1975), 5.

the law's character, the criticism that emerges is consonant with the law's self-critical commitment to "work itself pure,"[31] because it expresses the law's own striving for internal coherence. The character of private law is implicit in its practice, but scholarly reflection brings it into focus, defines and refines it, and presents legal doctrine as its expression. Indeed, any treatment of private law, whether in the classroom or in the academic literature, that focuses on the requirements of coherence helps elucidate the character of private law.

The most ambitious efforts to specify the character of private law are necessarily exercises in "abstract theory."[32] The theorist strives to render what is implicit in the law as explicit as possible. To do this one must have recourse not only to legal material but also to conceptualizations, to the philosophical literature, and to modes of discourse and analysis that, while treating the practice of law seriously in its own terms, are not themselves part of that practice. This exercise in theorizing has to be abstract, in that it abstracts from the brute particularities of legal practice to the more general standpoint inherent in the specification of the law's character. One might even say that the more abstract the better, because the goal is to formulate the most general framework possible. However, throughout this project of specifying the character of private law, continuity with legal practice is always maintained, because otherwise the character specified would not be the character of anything. In this context, abstract theory is the friend of legal practice, not its competitor.

B. The stages of elucidation

The elucidation of the character of private law has three stages: attending to the legal practice, eliciting its inner structure, and enquiring into that structure's normative presuppositions.[33]

The first stage, attending to the legal practice, anchors the elucidation of the law's character in the practice's features. As is evidenced by the operations of those who engage in it with a mastery of its concepts and procedures, the practice of private law is, at least to some extent, an intelligible activity. Disclosure of the character of private

---

[31] Lord Mansfield's famous phrase in Omychund v. Barker [1744] 26 Eng. Rep. 15, 23 (K.B.).

[32] Edwards, above n. 4, at 34.

[33] See Oakeshott, above n. 30, at 1–31 (presenting Oakeshott's suggestive account of the engagement of understanding).

law is intended to render what is incipiently intelligible about private law even more intelligible. This exercise requires that one take notice of the justificatory and institutional apparatus of private law, so that its features are the subject and the starting point for a more general account.

Although the character of private law is an ideal construct, its elucidation does not involve the imagining of a Utopia. The practice of private law is taken as the given object of enquiry, and it is viewed as it views itself: as a specific kind of normative order that governs human interactions according to its own distinctive yet coherent conceptions of fairness and rationality. Subject to confirmation at subsequent stages, the arrangements of private law can provisionally be regarded as the indicia, however indistinct, incomplete, or inadequately articulated, of the kind of normative order that they constitute. The task is not to excogitate a new and perhaps even superior kind of normative order, but to disclose the character of this one.

Of especial significance are the concepts of private law and the institutional linkage of the parties as plaintiff and defendant. Because elucidating the character of private law involves specifying the most general framework for understanding it, particular attention should be paid to aspects of private law that are already general. Every application of private law presupposes a legal institution that directly links a particular plaintiff and a particular defendant. Of course, one can have a normative order in which this linkage is absent, for example where injury is dealt with by payment from a state fund; whatever its merits, such a normative order is not a form of private law. Also general, but having a scope that is more local, are the concepts of private law. These are the ideas through which the law requires us to organize our thinking about issues of liability. In specifying the character of private law, we do not seek, as does the instrumentalist, to show that these concepts are otiose, but to understand their role within a coherent conception of liability. Do these concepts, and other determinants of liability, sustain private law's claim to an internally coherent rationality, or must they be adjusted, abandoned, or supplemented for the sake of that rationality?

To deal with these questions we must move to a second stage in the elucidation of the character of private law. The second stage seeks to bring out the inner structure of the arrangements of private law. Because we are treating private law as a normative phenomenon, our particular interest is in the structure of the considerations that justify liability. The legal concepts and the other determinants of liability are the vehicles for these considerations. The second stage inquires whether these considerations have a uniform general shape. For if they do, that shape would reveal the character of the law in which these considerations are decisive.

Crucial to the disclosure of this structure is the institutional nexus between plaintiff and defendant. Private law works through an adjudicative mechanism by which the plaintiff sues the defendant and, if successful, is given an award of damages or other relief that the defendant must satisfy. As just noted, this direct linkage between plaintiff and defendant is the most pervasive feature of private law. If private law is to be understood as a normatively coherent practice, the justification for liability in any particular case has to reflect the structure of this linkage. The institutional framework for the litigation attests to the fact that the point of liability is to remedy an injustice between the particular parties. Accordingly, the reason for considering the defendant to have done an injustice to the plaintiff can be coherent only if it evinces the same direct link as is present in the institutional framework. Justification within private law is thus the expression of a bipolar normativeness that directly links the particular parties within this institutional framework. The structure of this bipolar normativeness is that of correlativity, in which the same injustice predicates both the doing and the suffering.

As the most general description of the structure of the parties' interaction, correlativity marks the character of private law as a distinctive normative order. No justification that does not participate in this character can find a coherent place within private law. Correlativity accordingly excludes considerations, no matter how appealing, that focus unilaterally on one or the other of the parties (for example, the depth of the defendant's pocket or the plaintiff's insurability against injury). Such one-sidedness was the defect, noted in the previous section, of instrumentalist approaches, which break apart the relationship between the parties by invoking social goals that operate on one or the other of them and on persons who are similarly situated.

To the extent that they form a coherent unity, the legal concepts relevant to any particular basis of liability also partake of this correlativity. Such concepts are the markers of a framework of normative reasoning that operates relationally to connect two particular parties as the doer and the sufferer of an injustice. The role of the concepts is to entrench the correlativity of the parties' situation into the reasoning and discourse of private law. The doing and the suffering of the same injustice is a single normative sequence that preserves its unity while moving from one party to the other. The legal concepts pertaining to each type of injustice are the devices through which legal practice presents and integrates the moments of that sequence.

In negligence law, for instance, the legal inquiry is broken down into a complex yet unified set of concepts (duty, breach, proximate cause, cause in fact). When liability for negligence is being considered, the unreasonableness of risk created by the defendant is seen in terms of the probability and the gravity of its effect on others; the duty not to create the risk is seen in terms of its foreseeable effect on a group that includes the plaintiff; the definition of the risk through proximate cause is seen in terms of the kind of effect that leads us to think of the risk as unreasonable; and the factual causation of injury seen in terms of the materialization of this risk. Thus, the concepts that constitute the negligence enquiry trace the sequence that begins with the defendant's unreasonable exposure of others to risk and is completed by the materialization of that risk in injury to the plaintiff. The two termini of this sequence are linked by the concepts of duty and proximate cause, which keep the plaintiff and the plaintiff's injury, respectively, within the risk by reason of which the defendant's action is negligent, thereby ensuring that the risk that materialized in the plaintiff's injury is the same as the risk that the defendant unreasonably created. Each of the concepts thus refers both to the defendant's wrongful act and to that act's wrongful effects, potential or realized, on the plaintiff. Together the negligence concepts form an integrated ensemble that articulates what it is for the same injustice to be done and suffered when unreasonably created risk matures into injury.[34]

This treatment of legal concepts can be readily contrasted with that of economic analysis. Recall the examples of causation and intention mentioned in section 2. Under the economic approach, factual causation is largely dispensable, to be replaced by a cost–benefit analysis. In contrast, when understood as a feature of tort law's character, factual causation is simply what it purports to be: the concept that deals with the materialization of risk into actual injury. A similar observation can be made about intention. Instead of being twisted (as economic analysis suggests) into a reference to the connection between the high probability of harm and the ease of avoidance, intention is, again, just what it

[34] Above chapter 2.

purports to be: the concept that makes the execution of the defendant's purpose the link between the plaintiff's injury and the defendant's conduct. Both causation and intention are concepts that belong to private law's bipolar normativeness. Each of them has a single normative significance for both parties, and each is an element in an integrated sequence that directly connects what the defendant has wrongly done to what the plaintiff has wrongly suffered. Whereas economic analysis, having pulled the parties apart, is unable to take seriously the legal concepts that normatively link them, the endeavor to specify the law's character allows these concepts to be understood in their own terms and to play a coherent role in the determination of liability.

Understood in terms of the correlativity of the parties' positions, private law is a system of rights and of the duties correlative to them. Such an understanding maintains continuity with the practice of law. Both the understanding and the practice treat rights seriously, not as superfluous proxies for instrumentalist considerations, but as genuinely normative determinants of correlatively structured liability.

But, one might ask, what exactly are these rights, where do they "come from," how are they distinguished from aspects of human well-being, and how is their normative character to be understood? Such questions point to a third stage in the understanding of private law. This stage builds on the other two, the attention to legal practice and the specification of correlativity as the most general structuring idea immanent in that practice. At the third stage one enquires into the normative presuppositions of correlativity and of the notion of rights that emerges from it.

In structuring the interaction between doer and sufferer, correlativity presupposes an abstract conception of the interacting parties. Within this conception the parties are viewed as exercising the capacity for purposive action, whatever might be their particular purposes. In the natural right tradition of legal philosophy, this conception of the capacity for purposiveness without regard to particular purposes is known as personality. Personality is to the actor what correlativity is to the interaction: the most general normative conception immanent in being a party to a private law relationship. Because personality is the presupposition of correlativity, personality and correlativity are complementary conceptions formulated from the perspective of the actor and the interaction, respectively.[35]

---

[35] Above chapter 1.

Personality illuminates the normative standpoint specific to private law, including its mutually entailed conceptions of freedom and equality. In articulating the juridical implications of the parties' purposive capacity, private law treats the parties as endowed with self-determining freedom. The regime of rights and correlative duties is a system of negative freedom, with one's rights demarcating spheres of freedom for the right-holder and limits on freedom for others. Within this regime the parties are formal equals because, when they are conceived as purposive beings without regard to their specific purposes, the sources of substantive inequality, such as differentials in wealth or virtue, become irrelevant. Thus the parties are equal, in that they are both treated as the loci of self-determining freedom; and they are free, in that neither is subordinated to the unilateral purposiveness of the other. Seen in the light of this normative standpoint, the practice of private law involves the continual elaboration and refinement of how personality and its attendant notions of freedom and equality figure in particular determinations of liability.

It might be objected that, given their abstractness and formality, these conceptions of freedom and equality are not very robust or appealing. However, this objection, even if it were true, is irrelevant. The issue is not whether these conceptions are appealing but whether they are immanent in private law. Recall that the three stages outlined here have been presented in order to specify the character of legal practice. The point is not to work out the most attractive conceptions of freedom or equality as if we were constructing a Utopia from the ground up, but to derive the most general framework for understanding private law from the structure and presuppositions of its legal relationships. If the progression from the practice of private law to correlativity and then to personality is sound, then the conceptions of freedom and equality that emerge are those that are presupposed in the practice.

The understanding of private law elucidated through these three stages differs sharply from the instrumentalist conception discussed earlier. The instrumentalist conception starts by specifying goals that are desirable apart from private law and then examines private law in their light. As a consequence, the instrumentalist misconstrues the law's concepts, cuts the direct relationship of the parties, and subsumes private law under public law. Having started outside private law, the instrumentalist does not succeed in re-entering it. The result is a disjunction between instrumentalist scholarship—including the kind of legal education it inspires—and the legal practice that is its subject matter. In the elucidation of the character of private law, no such disjunction appears. The process of elucidation starts from within private law and then considers its legal concepts on their own terms. The direct connection between plaintiff and defendant, far from being the embarrassment that it is for the instrumentalist, is the manifestation of the correlativity that structures the justifications for liability. In this conception, private law is categorically different from public law. Private law can therefore be understood as the juridical realization of a bipolar normativity in which one purposive being is directly related to another through a system of rights and their correlative duties.

When private law is understood in terms of its ideal character, no disjunction exists between two of the three activities with which we began, the practice of law and the enterprise of understanding that practice. The two activities are continuous without being congruent. They are continuous, because the understanding of law is elucidated through reflection on the structure and presuppositions of the practice of private law. They are not congruent, however, because the activity of understanding private law requires a theoretical effort that works out, according to its own methods and idiom, the most general conceptual framework immanent in the practice. The ingredients of that conception—correlativity and personality—deal with legal practice in its own terms, but they are not themselves explicit in that practice. Rather, they are the theoretical constructs that illuminate the character of private law.

C. Legal education

Turning now to the third of our initial three activities, one can see why private law, understood in this way, is suitable for university study. The purpose of university study is to care for the intellectual inheritance of civilized life. Private law is a significant and distinctive part of that inheritance. Private law is the ongoing attempt, actualized through society's legal institutions, to submit the direct interaction of one person with another to a system of reason. It involves an immense collective intellectual effort carried out over centuries and in different jurisdictions, featuring failures as well as successes, mistaken diversions as well as majestic triumphs. Its distinctiveness as a normative ordering lies in its correlative structuring of the parties' relationship, which makes the morality of private law categorically different from that of either personal ethics or political action. Private law is thus the forum for a special mode of thinking, which it is the function of university to impart.

In the enterprise of legal education, the university study and the professional training perform complementary functions, but each has its own focus. Professional training produces familiarity with the present operation of private law, developing skills based on particular legal materials and suitable to particular demands. University study, however, imparts (or should impart) a sense of the intelligibility of private law as a whole. Its interest is not in particular legal materials but in the mode of thinking that has produced them. Or, more accurately, its interest is in particular legal materials not for the information that they convey but for their exemplification of correlatively structured thinking, reasoning, and discourse.

As part of the university study of law, then, legal education is the process by which students of the law are initiated into a world composed of this correlatively structured mode of reasoning. Such reasoning is something students learn by engaging in it—that is, by being exposed to and discussing paradigms of it and by being provided with opportunities to develop their skills at it. This requires serious focus on legal doctrine not merely as a collection of rules or as a checklist for lawyers' dealings with particular situations, but as the crystallization of the distinctive mode of reasoning that directly links the defendant's conduct to the plaintiff's entitlement.

Several facets of this engagement with the law are particularly important. One is attention to the interrelation of the organizing concepts within a given basis of liability, and to the question of whether these concepts, as presented by the positive law, form a coherent set— that is, whether they adequately realize the legal relationship's correlative structure. Another is developing an appreciation of the casuistic reasoning that gives those concepts specific meaning in the rich variety of particular circumstances. A third is the exploration of the relationship between content and process, between the substantive considerations that justify liability, and the adjudicative context in which these considerations are assessed.

In this enterprise the theoretical constructs of correlativity and personality play a background role. They bring to the surface the character of the practice, so one can be aware of the nature of coherent legal discourse. The practice, however, proceeds on its own terms. Just as the practice of law carries on without explicit reference to these constructs, so students must learn to formulate arguments about liability without invoking them. The general conceptual structure of private law cannot serve as a substitute for considering the legal material itself. Correlativity and personality reflect the character of private law reasoning in general, so far as that reasoning is coherent, but it cannot generate a complete legal code to be mechanically applied in particular cases. All that the theoretical constructs can do—and it is enough that they do so—is orient us toward the requirements of justificatory coherence, and thus assist in eliminating considerations that are incompatible with it.[36]

Because the ideas of correlativity and personality are general and abstract, different systems of private law can manifest them in different ways. Although correlativity and personality are the stable theoretical constructs implicit in any regime of private law that values and aspires to its own justificatory coherence, they can have a variable content that is relative to a society's particular tradition of positive law, to the history of its legal responses to given problems, and to the shared social understandings that obtain at a given time and place. Accordingly, the comparative study of law across different jurisdictions and historical periods has a natural place within this conception of legal education.[37]

[36] On orientation as a role of theory, compare the remarks of John Rawls about political philosophy:

> [I]t belongs to reason and reflection (both theoretical and practical) to orient us in the (conceptual) space, say, of all possible ends, individual and associational, political and social. Political philosophy, as a work of reason, does this by specifying principles to identify reasonable and rational ends, and by showing how those ends can cohere within a well-articulated conception of a just and reasonable society.

John Rawls, *Justice as Fairness: A Restatement* (2001), 3. In this vein one might say with respect to private law that legal theory orients us in the conceptual space of all possible justifications for liability. It does this by specifying the constructs of correlativity and personality in order to identify the appropriate kind of justifications and by showing how justifications of that kind can cohere within a well-articulated conception of private law.

[37] The importance of comparative legal studies has long been asserted, as is evident from the following observations of James Bradley Thayer:

> [I]t has been wisely said that if a man would know one thing, he must know more than one. And so our system of law must be compared with others; its characteristics only come out when this is done ... If any one would remind himself of the flood of light that may come from such comparisons, let him recall the brilliant work of Pollock's predecessor at Oxford, Sir Henry Maine, in his great book on Ancient Law. That is the best use of Roman law for us, as a mirror to reflect light upon our own, a tool to unlock its secrets ...
>
> Of the values of such comparative studies, and the immense power to lift different subjects of our law into a clear and animating light, no competent person who has once profited by them can ever doubt.

James Bradley Thayer, "The Teaching of English Law at Universities," (1895) 9 Harv. L. Rev. 169, 178–79.

Because legal education so conceived focuses on legal practice as a culture of justification, comparative study involves the comparison not of differing legal doctrines across systems, but of the justifications offered for differing doctrines, of the conceptual structures into which such justifications fit, and of the adequacy of these conceptual structures to the underlying ideas of correlativity and personality. Such study can create awareness of the possible latitude for actualizing the constructs of correlativity and personality within legal practice, and thus of the particularities and contingencies of one's own legal system. It also allows for an appreciation of the persistence of correlativity and personality in the structure of different legal systems, and thus of the existence of a distinctive mode of normative reasoning that transcends the particularities of different systems of private law and that constitutes the condition for the possibility of productive comparison among them.

Correlativity and personality can also move from the background to the foreground. When this occurs, the focus shifts from legal practice to legal philosophy. Correlativity and personality are then used to connect private law as a normative phenomenon to the corpus of legal and political philosophy. Particularly relevant is the history of reflection about correlativity that begins with Aristotle's treatment of corrective justice[38] and culminates in the accounts of natural right formulated by Kant and Hegel.[39] These texts can then become the vehicle for considering further regressions from personality as a presupposition of correlativity to what is presupposed in the notion of personality itself. They thereby present an opportunity to deepen one's understanding of private law by opening up a further series of questions about its normative foundations, its relationship with other kinds of normative phenomena, and its place within more comprehensive philosophical systems.

What I have suggested in this section with respect to private law is a conception of legal education that remains rooted in the practice of law while focusing on the most general conceptual framework implicit in it. This conception is incompatible with the instrumental approaches to law that now enjoy primacy. It replaces the instrumentalist emphasis on independently justifiable goals with attention to the internal structure of legal relations and to what must be presupposed

---

[38] Aristotle, *Nicomachean Ethics*, V, 1131b25–1132b20.
[39] Hegel, above n. 9; Immanuel Kant, *The Metaphysics of Morals*, tr. Mary Gregor (1996).

if legal relations are to be normatively coherent. Its enquiry is internal in every respect. It is internal to the law in that it purports to make sense of legal thinking in its own terms. In its focus on coherence, it enquires into the internal relationship among the components of an integrated justificatory structure. And in specifying the character of private law, it identifies theoretical constructs that are internally related to one another and to private law. It thereby brings together the three activities of the practice, the understanding, and the university study of private law, so that law can indeed survive legal education.

4. The interdisciplinary turn

In this final section, I explore the implications of this chapter's understanding of private law for interdisciplinary study. The rise of interdisciplinary scholarship has been perhaps the most dramatic development in legal education over the last generation. In place of the previous emphasis on cases and doctrine, a new paradigm of scholarship and teaching has arisen, which brilliantly mobilizes the insights of other disciplines—economics, literature, and philosophy are among the favorites—to the analysis of legal material. Of course, the use of these disciplines can be consistent with the character of private law. In the previous section I suggested that philosophical issues readily emerge from the elucidation of this character, while cautioning that these issues deal with the presuppositions of legal discourse without being explicitly part of it. However, much of the current interdisciplinary interest is not based on such elucidation of the law's character, but is nonetheless rooted in the aspiration to weave the study of law into the intellectual fabric of university life.[40] How does this kind of interdisciplinary work relate to legal education that places the law's ideal character at its core?

The popularity of interdisciplinary scholarship is a natural outgrowth of the instrumentalist approach to private law. As evidenced by its cavalier treatment of the fundamental legal concepts, the instrumentalist approach denies that the content of private law arises indigenously in accordance with the correlative structure of its legal relationships. Rather, the law is merely the passive receptacle of whatever goals are to be imposed on it from the outside. The study of law,

---

[40] See Menachem Mautner, *On Legal Education* (2002) (Hebrew).

accordingly, is not an autonomous body of learning, but an empty shell dependent on non-legal disciplines for the validation of the proposed goals. Hence the proliferation of rich interdisciplinary interests in "Law and...," with the vital element in the pairing being invariably the non-legal one. Law provides only the authoritative form into which the conclusions of non-legal thinking are translated. Law is considered to have no meaning except that which it absorbs from other disciplines and enquiries. Indeed the capacity to funnel insights about law so conceived through alien concepts and terminology is considered the mark of scholarly detachment and sophistication.

The paradoxical consequence of this basis for interdisciplinary scholarship is that the interdisciplinary turn is actually an illusion. For academic work to be truly interdisciplinary, it must engage more than one discipline. Law, however, is regarded not as a discipline in its own right with something of its own to contribute to the interdisciplinary enterprise, but merely as a context for projects from other disciplines. The resulting study is nothing but the application of a particular non-legal discipline to examples drawn from the law. The economic analysis of law, for instance, then turns out to involve not an enlarged study of law but a restricted study of economics. Given that the legal side lacks intellectual resources of its own, what motivates the interdisciplinary scholar is interest in the non-legal discipline. As was once observed about the parallel phenomenon in literary studies:

[a] scholar with a special interest in...economics expresses that interest by the rhetorical device of putting his favorite study into a causal relationship with whatever interests him less. Such a method gives one the illusion of explaining one's subject while studying it, thus wasting no time.[41]

The recognition that private law embodies a distinctive mode of thinking is both a prerequisite of interdisciplinary work about private law and a determinant of that work's nature. It is a prerequisite because without it reference to the insights of another discipline is reductive rather than interdisciplinary; the other discipline is invoked to show that the law, at the most, reflects a deformed version of those insights. It is a determinant of the nature of interdisciplinary work because that work, of whatever kind it is, has to allow private law the independent space entailed by that recognition. Interdisciplinary work can then not

[41] Northrop Frye, *Anatomy of Criticism* (1957), 6.

be conceived as the construction of a repository of homogeneous knowledge, because such homogeneity is inconsistent with the distinctiveness of the legal mode of thinking. Rather, knowledge has to be regarded as pluralistic—that is, as organized into categorically different kinds of enquiry each of which (including the study of law) has its distinct character.

Within the university law school, the point of interdisciplinary study is to present different perspectives for the understanding of the transactions governed by the law. Each of these perspectives has its own validity, rests on its own presuppositions, and operates within its own disciplinary boundaries. A medical misadventure, for example, may raise not only issues of liability, but also issues of economics, of sociology, of political science, of psychology, and so on. Within a law school the legal perspective has of course a certain contextual primacy, because, whatever else it does, a law school must impart to its students a sense of the law's distinctiveness as a mode of normative discourse. This distinctiveness excludes other perspectives, but does not deny their authority within their own spheres. Indeed, exposure to these other perspectives plays an important role for the study of law for several reasons. First, the very contrast between legal and non-legal modes of enquiry casts light on the law's distinctive structure and presuppositions (as the law does on theirs). Second, the contrast reveals the place of law as an intellectual enterprise among other such enterprises, and that civilized life requires the cooperation and mutual respect of all of these. Third, an awareness of the contrast induces an appreciation of the limits of law, and thus a proper sense of humility: although the law governs all of life, the person who is learned in the law is not therefore omniscient.

Accordingly, one can view the interdisciplinary study of law as creating an academic conversation with different disciplinary voices.[42] The object of this conversation is not to have one voice suppress any of the others but to maintain the individuality of each. When every voice contributes the insight that derives from its own distinctive activity, the conversation can enlarge the understanding of its participants.

It is not always easy to maintain the line between respectful attention to a different voice and hearing that voice as a deformed version

---

[42] For the metaphor of a conversation, see Oakeshott, above n. 1, at 195–96; Michael Oakeshott, *The Voice of Liberal Learning* (2001), 109.

of one's own. Consider, for example, the most celebrated and influential piece of interdisciplinary legal scholarship of the twentieth century, Ronald Coase's treatment of social cost.[43] Coase's article deals with what he calls "a technical problem of economic analysis"[44] regarding the harmful effects of one's actions on others. In the exposition of his analysis he uses classic court judgments dealing with the law of private nuisance. It is worth pausing on how he views the relationship between his economic argument and the judicial illustrations.

On the one hand, Coase is admirably sensitive to the difference between economic and legal analysis. The economic problem is how to maximize the value of production.[45] The legal problem is how to determine liability. Coase insists, rightly, that this difference should not confuse economists about the nature of their problem.[46] "The reasoning employed by courts in determining legal rights," he observes, "will often seem strange to an economist because many of the factors on which the decision turns are to an economist irrelevant."[47] In deciding the economic problem, certain legal considerations are "about as relevant as the colour of the judge's eyes."[48] Economists do one thing and judges do another. Therefore, economists should not take their cue from how judges deal with the external effects of the defendant's actions.

On the other hand, Coase does not think that the converse obtains. Although the economists should not be influenced by the judges, he thinks it desirable for judges, because their decisions directly influence economic activity, to take economic analysis into account.[49] His assumption is that although the economist's problem is different from the judge's, the judge's problem is not all that different from the economist's. He takes it for granted that the law of nuisance has no character of its own beyond the influence it exerts on economic activity, and that it therefore should be animated by properly formulated economic considerations. Of course, qua economist Coase has no reason to be alert to (let alone, to explore) the distinctiveness of the legal mode of thinking in matters of private law. However, the consequence of his

---

[43] See Ronald H. Coase, "The Problem of Social Cost," (1960) 3 J.L. & Econ. 1.

[44] Oakeshott, above n. 1, at 1.

[45] Above n. 43, at 15.

[46] Ibid., at 9.

[47] Ibid., at 15.

[48] Ibid.

[49] Ibid., at 19.

justifiable preoccupation with his "technical problem of economic analysis"[50] is that he reads the cases as containing renditions, often inadequate, of the economic argument.

In *Bryant v. Lefever*,[51] for example, the defendants extended upward the wall that ran beside the plaintiff's chimneys, with the result that when the plaintiff lit a fire in any of his rooms, the smoke could not clear but came back into the plaintiff's house. What attracts Coase's attention is not the court's ultimate judgment in favor of the defendants (in the absence, as here, of transactions costs, the parties would bargain toward the efficient result whatever the court decided) but rather the court's misapprehension of the causal relationship between the parties' activities. In dismissing the plaintiff's claim, the court held that, although the defendants erection of the wall materially interfered with the plaintiff's comfort and thus constituted a nuisance, the nuisance was caused not by the defendants act but by the plaintiff's lighting of the fires. Criticizing this crucial element in the court's analysis, Coase observes that it was "fairly clear" that both parties caused the smoke nuisance, because "[g]iven the fires, there would have been no smoke without the wall; given the wall, there would have been no smoke without the fires."[52] Accordingly, "both were responsible and accordingly both should be forced to include the loss of the amenity due to smoke as a cost of deciding whether to continue the activity which gives rise to the smoke"—which in fact is what would happen because of the possibility of costless bargaining. The court made the mistake of assuming that the wall was "the given factor,"[53] thus transforming the parties' joint causation into the self-infliction of harm by the plaintiff.

This criticism ignores the juridical quality of the court's reasoning. The court's task is to determine liability within a system of rights and correlative duties. These rights and duties establish the baseline from which to determine the direction in which causation moves. Causation is, accordingly, not a natural phenomenon that reflects the fact that the smoke was the result of the combination of the defendants wall and the plaintiff's fire lighting. Nor is it an economic conclusion geared to the maximization of the value of production in accordance with what Coase calls "the beauties of a smoothly operating pricing

---

[50] Ibid., at 1.
[51] Bryant v. Lefever [1879] 4 C.P.D. 172 (Eng.).
[52] Coase, above n. 43, at 13.
[53] Ibid.

system."[54] Rather, causation functions here within an argument about the imputation of liability. Liability requires that the defendants' actions have been inconsistent with the rights of the plaintiff and not merely the exercise of one of their own rights. Here by extending the wall upwards, the defendants did nothing but occupy the space that they owned. The legitimacy of occupying space that one owns is inseparable from the right involved in ownership. It therefore does not constitute a wrong that can be imputed to the defendants. Moreover, because the plaintiff's harm was the consequence of the smoke's failure to clear the defendants' building, the plaintiff was wronged only if he had a right to the space over the defendants' property required for clearance. That space, however, belonged to the defendants and was not subject to any right of way in favor of the plaintiff. Of course, the plaintiff was harmed by the defendants' action in the sense that he was worse off than before the wall was built. However, in view of the configuration of rights in this situation, the plaintiff was not wronged.

One can sum up what is problematic about Coase's criticism of the court as follows. For Coase the given factor in the court's analysis was the wall, because the wall made what is properly a cause of the smoke into a condition for ascribing causation only to the plaintiff's lighting of the fire. From the court's perspective, however, it would be more accurate to say that the given factor was not the wall itself, but the right to build it. The court's assumption was simply that within a coherent system of proprietary rights, one has the right to build on one's own property. Instead of viewing the court's decision as exemplifying a properly legal mode of analysis of the relationship between owners of adjoining properties, Coase reads it as a misstatement of the obviously reciprocal causation that should underlie the economist's attitude toward the maximization of the value of production.

Similar observations can be made about Coase's famous treatment of *Sturges v. Bridgman*.[55] The issue in that case was whether activity by the defendant that would otherwise constitute a nuisance escaped liability because it temporally preceded the use by the plaintiff with which it interfered. The defendant was a confectioner who had been using the back section of his property for decades as a kitchen in which he pounded his meats. No problem arose as long as the adjoining property was used as a garden, because the noise did not inconvenience

---

[54] Ibid.
[55] Sturges v. Bridgman [1879] 11 Ch. D. 852 (Eng.).

anyone. The plaintiff, however, was a physician who had recently built a consulting room on the site of the garden, and complained that the noise of the pounding interfered with his practice. The court held the defendant liable.

Coase singles out the court's statement that a different result would "produce a prejudicial effect upon the development of land for residential purposes."[56] He points out that so long as market transactions between the confectioner and the physician were costless, the court's decision could have no effect on the allocation of resources. If one party gained more from the continuation of his activity than the other lost from the cessation of his, the party that stood to gain more would strike a bargain that would allow him to continue even if he lost his case. "The judges' view that they were settling how land was to be used," Coase writes, "would be true only in the case in which the costs of carrying out the necessary market transactions exceeded the gain which might be achieved by any rearrangement of rights...But of this the judges seem to have been unaware."[57]

Here, too, Coase is hearing in the court decision not the distinctive voice of legal discourse but an inferior version of his own economist's voice. Coase treats the court as attempting to achieve a certain economic goal (the development of residential housing) in ignorance of proper economic reasoning. If, however, one reads the judgment as a whole and views the offending sentence in its light, a different picture emerges. The court was concerned not with settling how the land was to be used, but with determining the conditions under which an action by the defendant could diminish a right of the plaintiff. The court's focus was juridical, not economic.

For the court, the problem with the confectioner's position was that it asserted a power unilaterally to restrict another's right. Under the law of nuisance the plaintiff had a right to the use and enjoyment of his property, but this right could not be vindicated in a court of law so long as his use and enjoyment was unaffected. While the property was being used as a garden, the physician (or his predecessor) had no cause of action in nuisance, because the noise from the confectioner's pounding did not inconvenience him. The confectioner's argument once the physician built the consulting room was that the physician had lost the right to complain of the nuisance. But how can one

[56] Ibid., at 866.
[57] Coase, above n. 43, at 10.

person's right be extinguished by the unilateral acts of another? The confectioner might argue that the long history of meat pounding shows that the physician (or his predecessor) implicitly acquiesced in the confectioner's acquisition of an easement. As the court pointed out, however, one can acquiesce only in what one can prevent. Until the physician suffered an inconvenience that allowed him to sue in nuisance, he could not prevent the meat pounding, and therefore cannot be taken to have acquiesced in it.

What, then, is the significance of the court's reference to "the prejudicial effect upon the development of land for residential purposes," around which Coase's treatment of the case revolves?[58] The comment comes after the court considered a hypothetical case, which it rightly regarded as exactly analogical to the case at hand, of "a blacksmith's forge built away from all habitations but to which, in the course of time, habitations approach."[59] The court disqualified two possible treatments of this hypothetical case. On the one hand, it would be unreasonable to extend liability for nuisance to the period before the habitations approached because that would give the adjoining landowners a right to sue for an inconvenience that they have not yet, and may never, suffer. But, the court continued, "it would be on the other hand in an equal degree unjust, and, from a public point of view, inexpedient that the use and value of the adjoining land should, for all time and under all circumstances, be restricted and diminished by reason of the continuance of acts incapable of physical interruption, and which the law gives no power to prevent."[60] This is the sentiment that the subsequent remark about the prejudicial effect on residential development encapsulates. It is not that the court necessarily thinks that the growth of the habitations mentioned in the hypothetical case is itself desirable: the court is not attempting to settle land use for a hypothetical case. What is unjust and inexpedient is that the owners of the land on which habitations might arise should have their rights prejudiced by actions of the blacksmith that they cannot physically interrupt or legally prevent. The "prejudicial effect on the development of land for residential purposes" is not that there will be too few residences, but that right of the hypothetical landowners to develop residences protected by

[58] *Sturges*, above n. 55, at 866.
[59] Ibid., at 865.
[60] Ibid.

the law of nuisance will be abridged by the blacksmith's unilateral activity.

Both *Bryant* and *Sturges* are exemplary displays of the mode of thinking distinctive to private law. Each case treats the alleged injustice as one to which the parties must be correlatively situated as doer and sufferer. The doing and the suffering consist, respectively, in the infringement, and in being the victim of the infringement, of the right to use and enjoy one's property. This right represents a sphere of lawful freedom with which others are obligated not to interfere. The cases enquire into the meaning of this right in the specific circumstances of building up and of pre-existing activity by the defendant. In both cases the court's reasoning provides a sophisticated elaboration in legal terms of the relationship between the plaintiff's right and the defendant's action.

In contrast, Coase assumes that the courts are addressing issues of economic rather than juridical thinking. He reads the reference to causation in *Bryant* not as working out an imputation of liability against the background of the parties' rights, but as overlooking the obvious causal reciprocity that informs a proper economic analysis. Similarly, he reads the reference to the prejudicial effect on residential development in *Sturges* not as underlining the illegitimacy of the defendant's unilaterally restricting the plaintiff's right, but as failing to anticipate the bargaining that would take place when transactions are costless. In each case the court was not making an economic argument in ignorance of the economic consequences that Coase describes; it was making a legal argument about the connection between one person's rights and another person's will that Coase has misapprehended.

This misapprehension, of course, does not mean that Coase's brilliant article has no place in a university program of legal education. To the contrary, it should have a place of great honor as a masterful exhibition of the subtleties of the economic approach to situations that have attracted the law's interest. Both law and economics feature modes of thinking that present systematic and comprehensive understandings of human interaction. In the nuisance context economic thinking, as portrayed by Coase's analysis, is concerned with harms and costs, whereas legal thinking is concerned with rights and remedies. The contrast between these two modes of thinking is not only a matter of genuine intellectual significance in its own right, but also a considerable resource for imparting to students a sense of the character of private law. For we often begin to understand what something is by seeing what it is not.

If the interdisciplinary turn in legal education is to bear fruit, it must be supposed that law has an independent voice that can contribute to the conversation among the university's disciplines. Whatever else it does, legal education is charged with the task of inculcating in students the capacity to speak in this voice and to understand its distinctive character. In the conversation among disciplines this voice is juxtaposed against other voices, so that the significance of each—its presuppositions, its organizing structures, its way of relating to the particulars of the world that all share—can be better appreciated. The idea of a conversation is not that one voice replaces or silences or dominates the others, but that each puts forth the ideas appropriate to it, humble in the awareness of its own limits and respectful of the distinctiveness of others. For in a conversation, "[i]ts integration is not superimposed but springs from the quality of the voices which speak, and its value lies in the relics it leaves behind in the minds of those who participate."[61]

5. Conclusion

The central theme of this chapter—indeed, of this entire book—has been that private law is animated by a distinctive mode of thinking and discourse, marked by the structure of correlativity and informed by the presupposition of personality. Accordingly, with respect to private law, the university study of law, whatever else it does, has the task of engaging the student in this mode of thinking and discourse. The disjunction that critics of legal education have noted between university study and legal practice is the consequence of understanding law in instrumental terms and thereby obscuring the law's distinctive character. One overcomes this disjunction by attending to the role of correlativity and personality in an understanding of private law that is faithful to the law's conception of itself as a normative phenomenon that strives for justificatory coherence in the relationship between plaintiff and defendant.

That law embodies a distinctive mode of thinking and discourse is a venerable idea. One recalls Coke's response to the assertion by James

---

[61] Oakeshott, above n. 42, 110.

I that, because the law was founded upon reason, he as a person endowed with reason was as qualified to sit in judgment as were the judges. Coke replied with a ringing affirmation of the distinctiveness of reason in the legal context:

[T]rue it was that, God had endowed His Majesty with excellent science and great endowments of nature; but His Majesty was not learned in the laws of his realm of England, and causes... are not to be decided by natural reason but by the artificial reason and judgment of the law, which law is an art which requires long study and experience, before that a man can attain to cognizance of it.[62]

In the modern context universities have the responsibility of beginning the process of "long study and experience" that imparts "cognizance" of this "artificial reason and judgment." This is a responsibility in which recognition of the law's distinctive character converges with the university's calling to care for law as one of civilization's pre-eminent achievements.

---

[62] Prohibitions del Roy (1607) 77 Eng. Rep. 1342, 1343 (K.B.).

Conclusion

The preceding chapters have illustrated the significance of corrective justice for various legal contexts: for the grounds of liability, for the relationship between right and remedy, for legal education, for the comparative understanding of private law, and for the compatibility of corrective justice with state support for the poor. The aim has been to show, through the concrete treatment of a variety of issues, how corrective justice illuminates the structure and content of private law. The chapters have thereby set out a broad conception of corrective justice.

The ideas presented here stand in contrast to the rather modest role that others have ascribed to corrective justice. For example, Richard Craswell, writing from the perspective of economic analysis, has asserted that "[w]hile corrective justice theory can give us a way of talking about what to do when the relevant baseline is infringed, it cannot tell us what baseline ought to be selected as relevant."[1] The attraction of this view for proponents of economic analysis is that it allows the baseline to be set by considerations of efficiency, while reducing corrective justice to the task of rectifying violations of those baselines.[2] However, one does not have to be an economic analyst to regard corrective justice as having solely a remedial function. John Gardner, who has evinced little sympathy for economic analysis, has taken the view that corrective justice involves the allocation of something back to the plaintiff; the consequence of this is that corrective justice deals not with the norms that govern a

---

[1] Richard Craswell, "Against Fuller and Perdue," (2000) 67 U. Chi. L. Rev. 99, at 127.
[2] This was the strategy in Richard A. Posner, "The Concept of Corrective Justice in Recent Theories of Tort Law," (1981) 10 J. Legal Stud. 187.

transaction but only with restoring the situation antecedent to the norm's violation.[3]

Common to these views is the limited scope that they postulate for corrective justice. Corrective justice performs a certain operation: correcting the consequences of a transaction that has gone askew. However, the basis on which it performs this operation—what it means for the transaction to go askew—is independent of the operation. In contrast, the argument in this book is that the phenomenon of liability, being correlatively structured, would not coherently correct the injustice between the parties unless the reasons for considering something an injustice were also correlatively structured. The correlativity of the correction presupposes correlativity in the basis for the law's performing this correction. We can term the notion that corrective justice covers both the correction and the basis of liability the "juridical conception," because it exhibits the structure that informs the phenomenon of liability in all its aspects, from how the law conceives of injustice as between the parties to how the law corrects that injustice by awarding a remedy. This is in contrast to what might be termed the "remedial conception," the notion that corrective justice covers only the correction effected through the remedy.

The claim inherent in the juridical conception, that both the operation of the remedy and the normative character of the bases of liability fall under a single conception of justice, is substantive, not terminological. The point of this claim is not to stipulate the proper usage of the words "corrective justice," but to exhibit the complex of ideas that yields a comprehensive and coherent understanding of the private law relationship. To be sure, the juridical conception and the remedial conception each make terminological assumptions about the words "corrective justice." While both regard corrective justice as the form of justice that deals with corrections rather than distributions, they differ in their appreciation of the role of correction within that form. The remedial conception takes corrective justice to be about the operation that corrects and nothing else. The juridical conception takes corrective justice to be about the system of norms within which the operation that corrects makes sense. The task of theory is to determine not which of these conceptions involves a superior terminological

---

[3] John Gardner, "What Is Tort Law For? Part 1: The Place of Corrective Justice," (2011) 30 Law and Philosophy 1. An earlier adumbration of Gardner's views appeared in Gardner, "The Purity and Priority of Private Law," (1996) 46 U. Toronto L.J. 459.

practice (by consulting a lexicon, for example, or surveying linguistic usage) but which of them sheds greater light on the normative character of private law.

Gardner's criticism of the juridical conception illustrates the futility of confusing terminology with argument. Drawing on Nozick's long-ignored terminology, Gardner regards distributive and corrective justice as distinguishing not between different structures of coherent justification but between different subject matters. Norms of distributive justice regulate the allocation of goods among persons, whereas norms of corrective justice regulate the allocation of goods back from one person to another. In his view, norms of either sort of justice are not necessarily just; whether a norm is just depends on soundness of the particular norm, not on its being a norm of justice.[4] Adapting a famous dictum, one might say that Gardner holds that the existence of a norm of justice is one thing, its merit or demerit another.

The result of characterizing corrective justice in this way is that corrective justice has nothing to do with the coherence of the reasons for liability. Presumably, coherence would count toward soundness, but that would be a consideration independent of or additional to corrective justice, not a consideration of corrective justice itself. Even an unsound reason for allocating something back to the plaintiff is for Gardner a reason of corrective justice. Furthermore, corrective justice has nothing to do with matching the reason for the norm breached by the defendant with the correlative structure of liability. The norm can be a distributive one that allocated a certain good to the plaintiff, and yet triggered the allocation of that good back to the plaintiff as a matter of corrective justice. Indeed for Gardner, the tort that leads to the allocation of the good back to the plaintiff is generally not an injustice at all—the tortious act is itself generally neither an allocation nor an allocation back—but is the violation of other sorts of moral norms.[5]

This leads Gardner to make the following criticism of the juridical conception. The juridical conception includes the norms of private law within corrective justice, because the reasons supporting the bases of liability have to be correlatively structured if a correlatively structured finding of liability is to function as a coherent correction of injustice. Gardner objects to this, on the ground that if the norms are

---

[4] Gardner, "What Is Tort Law For?," above n. 3, 12–15.
[5] Ibid., 23.

part of corrective justice, they must be correcting something else, and so on in infinite regress.[6] The norms, in other words, are not corrective because they do not correct anything. Nor does a person correct anything by acting in accordance with them.

To this criticism the reply on behalf of the juridical conception is that the norms indeed do not correct anything, but that is beside the point. Under the juridical conception the norms fall under corrective justice because they belong to the system within which bipolar corrections make sense, not because norms themselves operate to correct. Of course, the reply is circular, but so is Gardner's objection. This is because both the objection and the reply merely rehearse the initial terminological difference between the two conceptions. Gardner thinks that, in pointing to the inconsistency of the juridical conception with what he means by corrective justice, he is making a real criticism. But all that he is doing is drawing out an implication of his own terminology.

Over the more than two millennia that the notion of corrective justice has been in circulation, it has been formulated in many different ways.[7] From the standpoint of the Aristotelian tradition, within which corrective justice originated and was nurtured, Gardner's view, with its consequence that the tortfeasor does not commit an injustice, is eccentric. Of course, Gardner is as entitled to his terminology as others are to theirs. However, the juridical conception cannot be disqualified by terminological fiat. It is no argument against the ideas that the juridical conception brings together under corrective justice that Gardner uses the words "corrective justice" in a different way. In this context as in others, we should think thoughts, not words.

Inherent in the juridical conception is the ambitious claim that a single set of ideas is decisive for understanding the normative character of private law. Whereas the remedial conception confines the remedy to its separate theoretical box, the juridical conception integrates the remedy and the reasons that would justify awarding it. This integration is part of an extensive argument that comprehends all the bases of liability within a single conception that renders the plaintiff–defendant relationship coherent. On this view corrective justice is neither an empty abstraction that cannot account for the content of private law, nor merely a way of referring to the bipolar operation

---

[6] Gardner, "The Purity and Priority of Private Law," above n. 3, 470.
[7] Izhak Englard, *Corrective and Distributive Justice: From Aristotle to Modern Times* (2009).

of the duty to repair, as the remedial conception supposes. Rather, corrective justice is a comprehensive idea based in the self-determining freedom of the interacting parties, extending to the entire range of private law, and operating through the correlativity of right and duty.

This account of the juridical conception of corrective justice weaves together a series of interrelated and mutually dependent ideas.

First and foremost is the idea that correlativity is the organizing structural feature of the relationship between the parties. Corrective justice works out the normative implications of the most general and pervasive characteristic of liability, that the liability of a particular defendant is always a liability to a particular plaintiff. This characteristic is evident in the bipolar process of litigation and in the remedy that obliges the defendant to pay damages or give specific relief to the plaintiff. Because liability corrects an injustice, the structure of liability and the structure of the injustice have to be congruent. Accordingly, the correlativity that provides the structure for the correction presupposes correlativity in the reasons supporting the norm whose breach occasions the correction. For if those reasons are non-correlative, in that their normative force does not link the particular defendant who commits the injustice to the particular plaintiff who suffers it, then the law has no coherent basis for tying the defendant's liability to the plaintiff's entitlement.

Second, because correlativity pervades the phenomenon of liability generally, the juridical conception of corrective justice is pertinent to all the bases of liability in private law, and not merely to particular ones. Corrective justice is, therefore, not to be identified solely with tort law or restricted to specific causes of action. Rather, it displays the structure of legal relationships within a general theory of private law. This book has illustrated this by providing a corrective justice account not only of negligence law, but also of property, contract law, and unjust enrichment.

Third, the correlative structure of the parties' relationship receives its content through a system of rights and their correlative duties. As chapter 1 maintained, the structure and the content are governed by complementary abstractions. Just as the correlativity of the parties' normative positions most abstractly represents the structure of their relationship, so the notion of personality most abstractly represents the content of that relationship. Personality refers to the self-determining freedom of acting for purposes that one sets for oneself in one's relations with another. It gives a conception of the parties in which what counts for their legal relationship is that their actions are the expression of purposiveness, rather than of particular obligatory purposes. Because personality is not the product of a distribution but the conception of agency that underlies the correlatively structured relationships of private law, it is implicit within the juridical conception of corrective justice.

Fourth, the rights and duties of private law reflect this conception of personality. Within a given legal relationship, the rights and duties of the parties articulate a relationship of will to will, in which the actions of each party coexist with the purposiveness of the other, regardless of the independent desirability of any particular purpose. Rights so conceived are not interests that the positive law sanctifies because of their unilateral importance to the plaintiff, but the juridical manifestations of reciprocal freedom in the will-to-will relationship between the parties. This conception of rights and duties accounts (as was noted in chapter 2) for the absence of a tort duty in circumstances of nonfeasance, no matter how important the plaintiff's interest might be. It is also crucial for the corrective justice account of both *in rem* rights and *in personam* rights. Kant's account of property, described in chapter 8, is illustrative of an argument that constructs the institution of property out of the normative implications of freedom in one will's interaction with other wills, without either invoking distributive considerations or mandating particular purposes. Similarly, the discussion of unjust enrichment in chapter 6 suggests that the plaintiff's *in personam* right to the restitution of an unjust enrichment arises out of the law's endeavor to assure that the transfer and retransfer of value accord with the freedom of the will of the two interacting parties.

Fifth, private law achieves coherence within the relationship between the parties by linking them through an integrated ensemble of legal concepts that melds the normative positions of the parties into a single unified normative unit. Accordingly, as set out in chapter 2, negligence law translates into a series of legal concepts, the progression from the defendant's creation of an unreasonable risk to the materialization of that risk in injury to the plaintiff. The termini of this progression are the concepts of breach of the standard of reasonable care and factual causation. However, these two termini do not operate as atomistic elements, one applying to the defendant and the other to the plaintiff, that the law simply adds together. Rather, the law insists that the termini be coherently linked through the concepts of duty and proximate cause. These concepts in turn connect wrong-doing and injury by describing the wrongful risk in terms of the range of the potential victims and consequences through which the risk is to be understood as wrongful. Thus, the risk that materializes into injury to the plaintiff is the same as the risk that the defendant unreasonably created, and the wrong done in its creation is the same as the wrong suffered in its materialization. Through this ensemble of concepts the law treats the defendant's act and its effect on the plaintiff as an integrated sequence.

The treatment of unjust enrichment in chapter 6 presents a more detailed illustration of the same idea. In that context, transfer and unjustness form the two interwoven strands for unjust enrichment. The transfer strand deals with the movement of a gratuitous benefit from defendant to plaintiff. The unjustness strand relates the wills of the two parties through the non-donative making and accepting of the gratuitous transfer, thereby bringing out the normative implications of non-donative transfer for their relationship. Each strand is both correlatively structured and related to the other. Together the four components of liability—the defendant's enrichment, the enrichment's being at the plaintiff's expense, the plaintiff's lack of donative intent, and the defendant's acceptance of the benefit as non-donatively given—form an integrated ensemble that states a coherent basis of liability. Within this ensemble, non-donative intent and acceptance provide a reason, normatively relevant to both parties in their interrelationship, to reverse the transfer of a non-donative benefit.

Sixth, as set out in chapter 3, rights and remedies form a unified sequence. Within the juristic conception of corrective justice, the correlative operation of the remedy implies a matching correlativity in the reasons that justify the award of the remedy. The logic of rights reveals more specifically why the remedy and the ground of liability are so closely aligned. The injustice that the finding of liability corrects is an inconsistency with some right of the plaintiff that is imputable to the defendant. To have a right is to be so connected with the object of the right that another person is under an obligation not to interfere with that object. Because that connection is unaffected by the occurrence of the injustice, the plaintiff's right and its correlative duty survive, though in a different form, and continue to regulate the relationship. The remedy is just that right and its correlative duty at a later stage of their existence.

Seventh, the idea that the remedy is a continuation of the right goes hand in hand with the idea that the plaintiff is not entitled to a remedy that gives more than the right or its equivalent. This accounts for the opposition of corrective justice to punitive damages, which by definition go beyond the plaintiff's rights. The criticism of punitive damages for contractual breach in chapter 5 exemplifies this opposition. The role of the right in limiting and defining the remedy is also at the heart of the analysis of gain-based damages in chapters 4 and 5. The crucial point is that one cannot determine the remedy without ascertaining the precise nature of the right whose infringement is being remedied. Consequently, in many contexts where gain-based damages have been proposed or even awarded—for example for breach of contract in the cases discussed in chapter 5—attention to the nature of the right in question may reveal that such awards are misplaced.

Eighth, corrective justice understands the particularity of specific norms as falling under the abstract and general ideas of correlativity and personality. Bridging the particular and the general are intermediate concepts, including the conceptual ensembles (such as those just mentioned regarding negligence law and unjust enrichment) that integrate the normative positions of the plaintiff and the defendant. This interplay of the general and the particular enables students of comparative law profitably to explore the diversity of the particular norms of different legal systems in the light of the general ideas common to all legal systems insofar as they are coherent. The Jewish law of unjust enrichment, described in chapter 7, provides an example. Although historically unconnected with and uninfluenced by the common law, Jewish law resembles the common law in constructing the parties' relationship by reference to the absence of donative intent by the plaintiff and the acceptance of the benefit by the defendant. However, Jewish law diverges from the common law by specifying donative intent so stringently that it is rarely present and, therefore, can rarely disqualify the plaintiff's claim. As a result, the focus of doctrinal elaboration is on working out what constitutes acceptance, especially what renders benefits incontrovertible. The difference between the two systems reflects their different specification of shared concepts. Corrective justice thus comprises the framework of comparison, within which the observation of difference is embedded in the recognition of similarity.

Ninth, as the actualization of corrective justice, private law is a distinctive normative practice. The complementary abstractions of correlativity and personality allow private law to be understood as having its own relational structure, its own relational set of concepts, and its own relational mode of reasoning. As a field of study, it is a discipline unto itself. As a normative practice, it is categorically different both from personal morality, with its striving for each person's true good, and from politics, with its search for independently desirable social goals. As contended in chapter 9, to understand this disciplinary and practical autonomy and to gain the competence to participate in it is an indispensable object of legal education within the modern university.

To conclude, at the beginning of his great work *The Pure Theory of Law*, Hans Kelsen explains that his theory is pure because it aims "to free the science of law from alien elements."[8] He then laments that the preceding centuries had uncritically adulterated the science of law with elements of psychology, sociology, ethics, and political theory. His pure theory, he continues, undertakes to delimit the cognition of law against these disciplines because their admixture has obliterated the limits imposed on the science of law by the nature of its subject matter. To this end he offers a general theory of positive law.

Kelsen's comments provoke the query: what would a pure theory of law look like if it were not positivist? For Kelsen and other positivists such a theory would be an absurdity. Yet the history of reflection about law contains notable examples. At the end of his Prolegomena to the *De Jure Belli ac Pacis*, for instance, Grotius remarks that he has treated *Jus* in a manner analogous to the mathematician's abstraction from particularity, and that he has refrained from discussing anything that belongs to politics, which has its own special mode of enquiry.[9] Similarly, Kant's legal philosophy, with its austere distinction between the legal and ethical obligation and with its insistence that the positivity of law must itself be justified as an expression of what is rightful, can be viewed as a pure theory of the juridical.

Presumably a non-positivist pure theory would focus not on the validity of law but on the reasons that are properly in play in the determination of legal controversy. How are these reasons suitable to the nexus between the parties? What is the normative nature of that nexus? What does it mean for these reasons to be coherent? Do they

---

[8] Hans Kelsen, *The Pure Theory of Law*, tr. Max Knight (1967), 1.
[9] Hugo Grotius, *De Jure Belli ac Pacis Libri Tres*, 2 vols., tr. Francis W. Kelsey (1925), vol. 2, 29–30.

have a distinctive structure and distinctive presuppositions? What concepts are the appropriate vehicles for this reasoning? Are the considerations that govern liability systemically autonomous from "alien elements" (as Kelsen calls them) taken from other disciplines? In addressing these questions, this book has offered purity without positivism.

Index